CONCEPTS OF PROPERTY IN INTELLECTUAL PROPERTY LAW

Intellectual property law faces the challenge of balancing the interests of rights holders and users in the face of technological change and inequalities in information access. *Concepts of Property in Intellectual Property Law* offers a collection of essays reflecting on the interaction between intellectual property and broader, more traditional notions of property. It explores the way in which differing interpretations of the concept of property can affect the scope of protection in the laws of copyright, patent, trade marks and confidential information. With contributions from leading and emerging scholars from a variety of jurisdictions, the book demonstrates how concepts of property can assist in shaping a conceptually coherent and balanced response to the challenges faced by intellectual property law.

HELENA R. HOWE is a Lecturer in Law at the University of Sussex.

JONATHAN GRIFFITHS is a Reader in Intellectual Property Law at Queen Mary, University of London.

CAMBRIDGE INTELLECTUAL PROPERTY AND INFORMATION LAW

As its economic potential has rapidly expanded, intellectual property has become a subject of front-rank legal importance. *Cambridge Intellectual Property and Information Law* is a series of monograph studies of major current issues in intellectual property. Each volume contains a mix of international, European, comparative and national law, making this a highly significant series for practitioners, judges and academic researchers in many countries.

A list of books in the series can be found at the end of this volume.

CONCEPTS OF PROPERTY IN INTELLECTUAL PROPERTY LAW

Edited by

HELENA R. HOWE

AND

JONATHAN GRIFFITHS

CAMBRIDGE
UNIVERSITY PRESS

CAMBRIDGE
UNIVERSITY PRESS

University Printing House, Cambridge CB2 8BS, United Kingdom

Cambridge University Press is part of the University of Cambridge.

It furthers the University's mission by disseminating knowledge in the pursuit of education, learning and research at the highest international levels of excellence.

www.cambridge.org
Information on this title: www.cambridge.org/9781107041820

First published 2013

A catalogue record for this publication is available from the British Library

Library of Congress Cataloguing in Publication data
Concepts of property in intellectual property law / Edited by Helena R. Howe & Jonathan Griffiths.
pages cm
Includes bibliographical references and index.
ISBN 978-1-107-04182-0 (hardback) – ISBN 978-1-107-66897-3 (pbk.)
1. Intellectual property. 2. Property. I. Howe, Helena R., 1976– editor of compilation. II. Griffiths, Jonathan, 1965– editor of compilation.
K1401.C667 2013
346.04′8–dc23
2013012185

ISBN 978-1-107-04182-0 Hardback

CONTENTS

TABLES

CONTRIBUTORS

SHYAMKRISHNA BALGANESH is Assistant Professor of Law at the University of Pennsylvania Law School.

LIONEL BENTLY is Herchel Smith Professor of Intellectual Property Law and Director of the Centre for Intellectual Property and Information Law (CIPIL) at the University of Cambridge.

HUGH BREAKEY is a Postdoctoral Fellow at Griffith University, Australia.

ROBERT BURRELL is Winthrop Professor of Law at the University of Western Australia.

MICHAEL A. CARRIER is Professor of Law at Rutgers, State University of New Jersey.

THOMAS DREIER is Professor of Law and the Director of the Institute for Information and Economic Law at the Karlsruhe Institute of Technology (KIT), Germany and Honorary Professor at the Law Faculty of the University of Freiburg.

SÉVERINE DUSOLLIER is Professor of Law at the University of Namur (Belgium), and the Head of the Research Centre in Information, Law and Society (CRIDS).

DEV S. GANGJEE is Senior Lecturer in Law at the London School of Economics.

JONATHAN GRIFFITHS is a Reader in Intellectual Property Law at Queen Mary, University of London.

HELENA R. HOWE is a Lecturer in Law at the University of Sussex.

ALASTAIR HUDSON is Professor of Equity and Finance Law at the University of Southampton and a National Teaching Fellow.

EMILY HUDSON is a Career Development Fellow in Intellectual Property Law at the University of Oxford and is an Academic Member of the Oxford Intellectual Property Research Centre.

DAVID LAMETTI is Associate Professor of Law at McGill University and a member of the Institute of Comparative Law, and of the Centre for Intellectual Property Policy (CIPP).

ALAIN POTTAGE is Professor of Law at the London School of Economics.

BRAD SHERMAN is Professor of Law at Griffith University, Australia.

ACKNOWLEDGEMENTS

We would like to thank Bea Myers, Ph.D. candidate at Sussex University, for her editorial assistance. We would also like to thank Kim Hughes and all at Cambridge University Press for their help in the production of the book. Thanks also go to Helena's academic and administrative colleagues at Sussex. Particular thanks are due to Amanda Sims and Lynn Gibbs for their help in organising the workshop for the contributors to the collection held at the university in August 2011. Finally, thank you to Ilanah Simon Fhima, Senior Lecturer in Law at UCL, for first providing the idea for the collection.

Introduction

HELENA R. HOWE AND JONATHAN GRIFFITHS

This book comprises a collection of essays that reflect on one of the most fascinating aspects of intellectual property law, namely the interaction between intellectual property and broader notions of property in law. As a primary mechanism for organising the allocation of valuable resources, 'property' matters. From its ideological basis to the content of the rules governing the existence and exercise of proprietary rights, the choices we make about property play a huge role in shaping social and individual welfare. Interpretations of 'property' in the context of intellectual property are similarly critical. Whilst not perhaps of the same order as land and water for instance, the subject matter of intellectual property law – creative works, inventions, commercially significant signs and trade secrets – is nonetheless essential for social and economic development. The meanings ascribed to property in this context will help determine the contours of the rights in a range of intangible assets of substantial cultural, scientific and economic value. The need for sustained enquiry into the relationship between intellectual property and broader, or more traditional, concepts of property, might seem obvious. However, it is only relatively recently that real interest in this relationship has grown, as intellectual property has increasingly been treated as 'property' by right-holders, legislators, courts and commentators.

For the last couple of decades intellectual property law has faced the challenge of balancing the interests of right-holder and user in a world of rapidly changing technology and inequalities of development and access to information resources. At the same time, intellectual property has become a huge source of wealth for some economies and corporations, in many instances overshadowing tangible proprietary assets in significance. This rise in economic importance, coupled with uncertainty over the justifiable scope of intellectual property rights in the light of technological change and various global crises relating to health, environmental protection and so forth, has given rise to a resurgence of 'property' talk in intellectual property. It is unsurprising that, in seeking to legitimate intellectual property and to stabilise the notion of rights in intangibles, reference has been made to the well-established category of property in 'things'. Nor is this a new phenomenon. The 'battle of the booksellers' in eighteenth-century England saw attempts to gain support for perpetual copyright protection through the presentation of literary property as analogous to real property.[1] The advocates of such protection presented the author's interest as 'an absolute right of property, a freehold, grounded in labour and invention'[2] and sought to benefit from the association with real property because, as Blackstone (counsel in *Tonson* v. *Collins*[3]) would famously observe, there is 'nothing which so generally strikes the imagination and engages the affections of mankind, as the right to property'.[4] Recent years have again seen attempts by those in favour of strong intellectual property rights to present intellectual property as analogous to the home or the castle of the landowner, and thus to present the copyright or patent owner as the legitimate recipient of far-reaching rights to control the use of their property.[5] Moreover, the rhetoric appears to have been successful as, in many respects, intellectual property has increasingly come to exhibit features of the tangible property to which it has been compared.

However, such analogies are problematic and the relationship between intellectual property and tangible property concepts is far more complex than it may, at first sight, appear to be. Many commentators have challenged the use of traditional property rhetoric, highlighting the conceptual and normative ambivalence of the 'property' label and questioning its application to intellectual property.[6] Notions of property that are suitable for land or chattels may be wholly inappropriate for the non-

[1] For example, *Tonson* v. *Collins* 96 Eng. Rep. 169 (KB) (1761).

[2] Mark Rose, *Authors and Owners: The Invention of Copyright* (Cambridge, Massachusetts: Harvard University Press, 1993).

[3] 96 Eng. Rep. 169 (KB) (1761).

[4] William Blackstone, *Commentaries on the Laws Of England* (first published 1765), (Chicago and London: University of Chicago Press, 1979), vol. II, p. 2.

[5] See, for example, the many examples given in the context of copyright by Michael Carrier in his chapter 'Limiting Copyright Through Property' in this collection.

[6] See, for example, L. Ray Patterson, 'Free Speech, Copyright and Fair Use' (1987) 40 *Vanderbilt Law Review* 1; Margaret J. Radin, 'Property Evolving in Cyberspace' (1996) 15 *Journal of Law & Commerce* 509; Mark A. Lemley, 'Romantic Authorship and the Rhetoric of Property' (1997) 75 *Texas Law Review* 873; James Boyle, *Shamans, Software and Spleens: Law and the Construction of the Information Society* (Cambridge, Massachusetts: Harvard University Press, 1996); Jessica Litman, 'Information Privacy/Information Property' (2000) 52 *Stanford Law Review* 1283; Robert Burrell and Allison Coleman, *Copyright Exceptions: The Digital Impact* (Cambridge University Press, 2005); Lionel Bently

rivalrous subject matter of intellectual property law. In fact, as many have pointed out, property rights constructed on such a basis have the potential to undermine one of intellectual property's chief functions by stifling future creation and innovation.[7] The relationship between intellectual property and property is extremely complex and a substantial body of literature has emerged, considering the issue from a range of perspectives. For some, a 'full value model' of intellectual property,[8] closer to the traditional model of property in land, may often be appropriate for intellectual property law.[9] Others have continued to focus on the fundamental question of whether 'property' paradigms developed for tangible resources can ever be appropriate for the intangible assets governed by intellectual property law.[10] For some, the relevant concern has been

and Brad Sherman, *Intellectual Property* (Oxford University Press, 2009); Ronan Deazley, *Rethinking Copyright History, Theory, Language* (Cheltenham and Northampton, MA: Edward Elgar, 2006); Neil W. Netanel, *Copyright's Paradox* (Oxford University Press, 2008); Shyamkrishna Balganesh, 'Debunking Blackstonian Copyright' (2009) 118 *Yale Law Journal* 1126.

[7] Dan Hunter, 'Cyberspace as Place and the Tragedy of the Digital Anti-Commons' (2003) 91 *California Law Review* 439; Michael A. Heller, 'The Tragedy of the Anti-Commons: Property in Transition from Marx to Markets' (1998) 111 *Harvard Law Review* 621; Michael A. Heller and Rebecca S. Eisenberg, 'Can Patents Deter Innovation? The Anti-Commons in Biomedical Research' (1998) 280 *Science* 698; Boyle, *Shamans, Software and Spleens: Law & the Construction of the Information Society* (Harvard University Press, 1996); Mark A. Lemley, 'Property, Intellectual Property and Free Riding' (2005) 83 *Texas Law Review* 1031; Lawrence Lessig, *The Future of Ideas: The Fate of the Commons in a Connected World* (New York: Vintage Books, 2001).

[8] To use Lemley's term. See Lemley, 'Property, Intellectual Property and Free Riding'.

[9] Including Frank H. Easterbrook, 'Intellectual Property is Still Property' (1990) 13 *Harvard Journal of Law & Public Policy* 108; William Landes and Robert Posner, 'An Economic Analysis of Copyright Law' (1989) 18 *Journal of Legal Studies* 325; Robert P. Merges, 'A Transactional View of Property Rights' (2005) 20 *Berkeley Journal of Law and Technology* 1477; David Friedman, 'In Defense of Private Orderings: Comments on Julie Cohen's "Copyright and the Jurisprudence of Self- Help"' (1998) 13 *Berkeley Technology Law Journal* 1151.

[10] In addition to the literature already noted see, for example, Henry E. Smith, 'Intellectual Property as Property: Delineating Entitlements in Information' (2007) 116 *Yale Law Journal* 1742; Stewart E. Sterk, 'Intellectualizing Property: The Tenuous Connection between Land and Copyright' (2005) 83 *Washington University Law Quarterly* 417; Brett M. Frischmann and Mark A. Lemley, 'Spillovers' (2007) 107 *Columbia Law Review* 257; Peter S. Menell, 'The Property Rights Movement's Embrace of Intellectual Property: True Love or Doomed Relationship?' (2007) 34 *Ecology Law Quarterly* 713; Séverine Dusollier, 'Tipping the Scale in Favour of the Right Holders: The European Anti-Circumvention Provisions' in Eberhard Becker *et al.* (eds.), *Digital Rights Management. Technological, Economic, Legal and Political Aspects* (Berlin: Springer-Verlag, 2003); Thomas Dreier, 'Balancing Proprietary and Public Domain Interests: Inside or Outside of Proprietary Rights?' in Rochelle C. Dreyfuss, Diane L. Zimmerman and Harry First (eds.), *Expanding*

the role of different property traditions in the protection of traditional knowledge and culture,[11] others have explored property analogies in historical perspective[12] or (re)considered the philosophical justifications for property and their application to intellectual property.[13] Yet others have assessed the impact on intellectual property of protecting property as a fundamental human right.[14] Whilst many have seen the attempts to align intellectual property with more traditional notions of property as being problematic in terms of clarity and the desire to restrain the expansion of intellectual property rights, others have at least recognised that 'property' need not always entail extensive private rights to exclude[15] and some

the Boundaries of Intellectual Property Innovation Policy for the Knowledge Society (Oxford University Press, 2001); Hugh Breakey, 'Two Concepts of Property: Property in Things and Ownership of Activities' (2011) 42 *The Philosphical Forum* 239; Andreas Rahmatian, *Copyright and Creativity: The Making of Property Rights in Creative Works* (Cheltenham: Edward Elgar, 2011).

[11] Including Kristen Carpenter, Sonia Katyal and Angela Riley, 'In Defense of Property' (2009) 118 *Yale Law Journal* 1022.

[12] Including Jennifer Davis, 'European Trade Mark Law and the Enclosure of the Commons' [2002] *Intellectual Property Quarterly* 342; James Boyle, 'The Second Enclosure Movement and the Construction of the Public Domain' (2003) 66 *Law and Contemporary Problems* 33; Yochi Benkler, 'Free as the Air to Common Use: First Amendment Constraints on Enclosure of the Public Domain' (1999) 74 *New York University Law Review* 345; Brett Frischmann and Katherine J. Strandberg, 'Constructing Commons in the Cultural Environment' (2010) 95 *Cornell Law Review* 657.

[13] Including Wendy Gordon, 'A Property Right in Self-Expression: Equality and Individualism in the Natural Law of Intellectual Property' (1993) 102 *Yale Law Journal* 1533; Peter Drahos, *A Philosophy of Intellectual Property* (Aldershot: Dartmouth Publishing, 1996); Alfred Yen, 'Restoring the Natural Law: Copyright as Labour and Possession' (1990) 51 *Ohio State Law Journal* 517; Benjamin G. Damstedt, 'Limiting Locke: A Natural Law Justification for the Fair Use Doctrine' (2003) 112 *Yale Law Journal* 1179; Carys J. Craig, 'Locke, Labour and Limiting the Author's Right: A Warning Against the Lockean Approach to Copyright' (2002) 28 *Queens Law Journal* 1; David Lametti, 'How Virtue Ethics Might Help Erase C-32's Conceptual Incoherence' in Michael Geist (ed.), *From "Radical Extremism" to "Balanced Copyright": Canadian Copyright and the Digital Agenda* (Toronto: Irwin Law, 2010); Hugh Breakey, 'Natural Intellectual Property Rights and the Public Domain' (2010) 73 *Modern Law Review* 208.

[14] Laurence R. Helfer, 'The New Innovation Frontier? Intellectual Property and the European Court of Human Rights' (2008) 49 *Harvard International Law Journal* 1; Jonathan Griffiths and Luke McDonagh, 'Fundamental rights and European IP law' in Christophe Geiger (ed.), *Constructing European Intellectual Property* (Cheltenham: Edward Elgar, 2012).

[15] Including Elinor Ostrom and Charlotte Hess, 'Ideas, Facilities, and Artifacts: Information as a Common-Pool Resource' (2003) 66 *Law and Contemporary Problems* 111; Carol Rose, 'The Comedy of the Commons: Custom, Commerce and Inherently Public Property' (1986) 53 *University of Chicago Law Review* 711; Carol M. Rose, 'The Several Futures of Property: Of Cyberspace, Folk Tales, Emission Trades and Eco Systems' (1998) 83 *Minnesota Law Review* 129; James Boyle, *The Public Domain: Enclosing the Commons of*

have seen the potential for re-balancing intellectual property in that very 'propertisation'.[16]

The main aim of this collection is to provide new insights into the relationship between intellectual property and property. The intention, in particular, is to further our understanding of the ways in which concepts of property can inform the development of intellectual property laws that are both conceptually coherent and serve the public interest. Two main themes run through the chapters in this collection. The first theme, explored in Part I, is the extent to which intellectual property can be seen as 'property' and the implications of this analysis for the scope of intellectual property rights. The chapters within this theme consider the nature of the property in various aspects of intellectual property. They ask, for instance, whether intellectual property is property at all and whether the rights granted can, and should, be seen as analogous to those in the ownership bundle of more traditional forms of property. Other chapters in this Part explore the challenges of formulating identifiable subject matter in intellectual property and analyse the methods by which the boundaries of the subject matter and the rights in respect of it are drawn by courts and policy-makers. The second theme of the collection, explored in Part II, is whether concepts developed in the sphere of tangible property – whether theoretical or substantive – can be employed to support the reformulation or reinterpretation of intellectual property laws in order to ensure an appropriate balance between the interests of right-holders and potential

the Mind (New Haven: Yale University Press, 2008); James Boyle, 'A Politics of Intellectual Property: Environmentalism for the Net?' (1997) 47 *Duke Law Journal* 87; Maureen Ryan, 'Cyberspace as Public Space: A Public Trust Paradigm for Copyright in the Digital World' (2000) 79 *Oregon Law Review* 647; Molly S. Van Houweling, 'Cultivating Open Information Platforms: A Land Trust Model (2002) 1 *Journal of Telecommunications & High Technology Law* 309; Christine D. Galbraith, 'A Panoptic Approach to Information Policy: Utilizing a More Balanced Theory of Property in Order to Ensure the Existence of a Prodigious Public Domain' (2007) 15 *Journal of Intellectual Property Law* 1; Geertrui Van Overwalle (ed.), *Gene Patents and Collaborative Licensing Models. Patent Pools, Clearinghouses, Open Source Models and Liability Regimes* (Cambridge University Press, 2009); Lior Zemer, 'Moral Rights: Limited Edition' (2011) 91 *Boston University Law Review* 1519; Helena R. Howe, 'Copyright Limitations and the Stewardship Model of Property' (2011) *Intellectual Property Quarterly* 183.

16 Including Michael A. Carrier, 'Cabining Intellectual Property through a Property Paradigm' (2004) 54 *Duke Law Journal* 1; Jacqueline Lipton, 'Information Property: Rights and Responsibilities' (2004) 56 *Florida Law Review* 135; Constance E. Bagley and Gavin Clarkson, 'Adverse Possession for Intellectual Property: Adapting an Ancient Concept to Resolve Conflicts Between Antitrust and Intellectual Property in the Information Age' (2003) 16 *Harvard Journal of Law and Technology* 327.

users of intellectual property. These broad themes reflect the central concerns of much of the developing literature and formed the framework for a workshop where many of the chapters were discussed in the summer of 2011.

Alain Pottage and Brad Sherman begin Part I of the collection by exploring the tensions inherent in constituting the 'invention' as the subject matter of property comprising both intangible and tangible aspects. These are tensions that, they suggest, go to the heart of the conception of the patent as a form of property and that illustrate the surprisingly materialist nature of patent law. This is followed in Chapter 2 by Dev Gangjee's analysis of the strategies used by courts and administrative officials to determine the boundaries of the property in brands and to reify the fluctuating 'conversation' between manufacturer and consumer. With the aim of contributing to the debate about the extent to which property in brands is desirable, Gangjee challenges the approach of the Court of Justice of the European Union, arguing that it does not take account of relevant interdisciplinary scholarship suggesting an alternative approach. In Chapter 3 Lionel Bently pushes this theme to its boundary, exploring the question of whether trade secrets are to be considered as property at all and the implications for intellectual property law more generally of confidential information being treated as 'intellectual property' but not 'property'. This is followed by Alastair Hudson's chapter, in which he draws attention to the way in which property is understood very differently by specialists in different fields, specifically by reference to the very different conceptual understandings of breach of confidence in equity and in intellectual property law. In particular, he argues that equity uses conscience-based proprietary rights to achieve desirable outcomes in individual cases, especially in relation to constructive trusts and confidential information, by contrast to the comparatively formalistic conceptions of property rights in intellectual property law.

In Chapter 5 Thomas Dreier presents a valuable civil law perspective on the extent to which intellectual property – and copyright in particular – can be regarded as property. The focus here is on Germany, which, as is suggested, provides a paradigm example of the difficulties in satisfactorily describing the property in intangibles by reference to the incidents of traditional, tangible property. In the following chapter, Hugh Breakey provides a sustained theoretical consideration of the application of the right to exclude in copyright law. Beginning with a Hohfeldian framework and drawing on the works of Penner, Waldron and Singer, amongst others, Breakey analyses the extent to which different notions of exclusion fit with copyright law. Whilst Breakey's focus is on the right to exclude, the chapter by Shyamkrishna Balganesh provides an in-depth analysis of the significance of the right to alienate as an incident of property in the context of US copyright law. Like Breakey, he provides insights into the copyright–property relationship that have structural and normative consequences in terms of the scope of the entitlement and its limitations.

The chapters in Part II explore the extent to which concepts of property associated with tangible property might enable intellectual property to achieve a balance between the interests of the right-holder and user. To this end, in Chapter 8, Michael Carrier presents a very clear challenge to the notion that the 'propertisation' of intellectual property necessarily entails expansion. Whilst providing a range of illustrations of the recent tendency for copyright to be presented as analogous to real or moveable property, he claims that, in reality, such property rights are limited and argues for analogous limits in copyright law. Abandonment of property is the focus of Chapter 9, in which Robert Burrell and Emily Hudson advocate the adoption of a rule that would enable an owner to abandon copyright in the European Union, in the same way as one can abandon other forms of property. In so doing, they demonstrate that the Court of Justice's harmonisation agenda may have potentially far-reaching consequences for any attempts to use broader property concepts to restrain intellectual property rights. In Chapter 10, David Lametti challenges the value of the anticommons concept as applied to intellectual property and suggests that the notion of an anticommons is unnecessary, lacks clarity and contributes to the perpetuation of false notions regarding the scope of proprietary rights.

The final two contributions in Part II explore the idea that the liberal concept of private property, characterised by extensive rights to exclude, is by no means the only available model of property. One alternative is provided by forms of common-property regime and, in Chapter 11, Séverine Dusollier presents an analysis of the development and features of different types of commons in intellectual property law, including the 'copyleft' licence. Her examination includes assessment of the relationship between these different forms of commons and property and she argues for a greater role for 'inclusivity' in intellectual property rights. In the final chapter, Helena Howe recognises the importance of patent law reform if patent law is to make an effective contribution to the promotion of sustainability goals and the mitigation of climate change in particular.

However, she suggests that proposals to bolster patent exceptions are undermined by the model of property dominating patent law and that an alternative 'stewardship' model of property, increasingly recognised in the context of property in land, would be more compatible with the sustainability agenda.

PART I

Intellectual property as property?

1

On the prehistory of intellectual property

ALAIN POTTAGE AND BRAD SHERMAN

Hohfeld's analysis of fundamental legal conceptions takes as one of its starting points Justice Holmes' observation that '[i]t is one of the misfortunes of law that ideas become encysted in phrases and thereafter for a long time cease to provoke further analysis'.[1] We focus in this chapter on one such 'encysted' idea – namely, the compound assumption that intellectual property rights relate to 'ideas', that ideas are intangible things and that the architecture and operation of intellectual property rights is shaped by a real difference between tangible and intangible things. From this premise, intellectual property lawyers derive a set of conclusions that are famously expressed in Thomas Jefferson's letter on the patentability of Oliver Evans' automatic mill:

> If nature has made any one thing less susceptible than all others of exclusive property, it is the action of the thinking power called an idea, which an individual may exclusively possess as long as he keeps it to himself; but the moment it is divulged, it forces itself into the possession of every one, and the receiver cannot dispossess himself of it. Its peculiar character, too, is that no one possesses the less, because every other possesses the whole of it. He who receives an idea from me, receives instruction himself without lessening mine; as he who lights his taper at mine, receives light without darkening me.[2]

[1] Wesley Newcomb Hohfeld, 'Fundamental Legal Conceptions as Applied in Judicial Reasoning' (1916–1917) 26 *Yale Law Journal* 710–70 at 711, note 4.

[2] Thomas Jefferson, Letter to Isaac McPherson, 13 August 1813, available at: http://press-pubs.uchicago.edu/founders/documents/a1_8_8s12.html (last accessed 4 April 2013).Jefferson misunderstood the true nature of Evans' invention. The real innovation was not in the specific improvements that Evans made to the familiar mechanical elements of the milling process, nor even in the aggregate effect of these discrete improvements; it lay instead in the conception of the milling process as an automated production line: 'Thomas Jefferson's opinion of Oliver Evans' devices was low. He saw only the details, not the thing as a whole ... If Evans' invention be split into its simple components, Jefferson is of course right. The chain of pots was used throughout the Ancient World for raising water, and the endless Archimedean screw, the screw conveyor, is found in almost every

In the language of modern intellectual property scholarship, ideas are said to be by their nature non-excludable and non-rivalrous;[3] no person can be prevented from accessing and possessing an idea that has been publicly disclosed, and no person's use restricts or diminishes the use of another. So, for example, modern writers suggest that intellectual property rights are monopoly rights rather than property rights,[4] that the institutions of intellectual property analogize ideas to material things by creating 'artificial scarcity',[5] or that intellectual property is especially 'costly to protect'.[6] For some purposes, theoretical questions about the distinction between material and immaterial things are beside the point. Anyone who wants to intervene in the politics of intellectual property probably has to work with the old theory that intellectual property is just 'a temporary state-created monopoly given to encourage further innovation'.[7] But our interest is in the historical or sociological 'reality' of intellectual property rights, and patents in particular. In an earlier work we explored the fabrication of the invention as an intangible thing.[8] Our hypothesis was that intangibility was a 'figment'; there is no dimension of reality in which inventions might subsist independently of the artefacts, texts or drawings from which they are elicited. Intangibility is an effect of representation, interpretation and argumentation. We started from the premise, first, that 'the difference between idea and embodiment is an effect of interpretation, and interpretations are artefacts of representational and communicative practices',

late Renaissance book dealing with machinery … [B]ut for Oliver Evans, hoisting and transportation have another meaning. They are but links within the continuous production process: from raw material to finished goods, the human hand shall be replaced by the machine. At a stroke, and without forerunner, Oliver Evans achieved what was to become the pivot of later mechanization' (Siegfried Giedion, *Mechanization Takes Command: A Contribution to Anonymous History* (Oxford University Press, 1948), p. 23).

3 In economic terms, ideas are 'public goods'; on the capture of the justificatory language of intellectual property by (neoliberal) economic theory see Philip Mirowski, *Science Mart. The Privatization of American Science* (Cambridge, MA: Harvard University Press, 2011).

4 James E. Penner, *The Idea of Property in Law* (Oxford University Press, 1997), pp. 119–20.

5 James W. Harris, *Property and Justice* (Oxford University Press, 1996), p. 44: 'The law takes an intangible thing and builds around it a property structure modelled on the structure which social and legal systems have always applied to some tangible things.'

6 William M. Landes and Richard A. Posner, *The Economic Structure of Intellectual Property Law* (Cambridge, MA: Belknap, 2003), p. 18.

7 James Boyle, *The Public Domain. Enclosing the Commons of the Mind* (Yale University Press, 2008), p. 21. On the question whether this premise is truly 'Jeffersonian', see Adam Mossoff, 'Who Cares What Thomas Jefferson Thought About Patents? Re-evaluating the Patent "Privilege" in Historical Context' (2007) 92 *Cornell Law Review* 953–1012.

8 Alain Pottage and Brad Sherman, *Figures of Invention. A History of Modern Patent Law* (Oxford University Press, 2010).

and, second, that 'to explain how the invention is produced and held steady, we [need] a material theory of how the invention is distinguished from its embodiment and how that specific distinction is recorded, communicated, and sustained'.[9]

In this chapter, we develop that line of argument by turning our attention to the other side of the distinction – the legal figure of the tangible thing. We do so by way of what might be called the prehistory of intellectual property rights; more precisely, the history of a period in which literary and artistic productions were construed as material things rather than as the embodiments of intangible works. We draw on Marta Madero's history of the medieval legal rubric of *tabula picta*,[10] which suggests that in the course of analysing property rights medieval lawyers generated a 'material' reality that was relatively autonomous from reality as it was conventionally understood. Borrowing a phrase from the art historian Michael Baxandall, Madero suggests that the language of the glossators was 'a conspiracy against experience in the sense of being a collective attempt to simplify and arrange experience into manageable categories'.[11] Materiality in property law was not materiality as it was commonly experienced.

[9] Pottage and Sherman, *Figures of Invention*, pp. 9 and 14, respectively.

[10] Marta Madero, *Tabula Picta. Painting and Writing in Medieval Law* (Philadelphia: University of Pennsylvania Press, 2009).

[11] Madero, *Tabula Picta*, p. 3, citing Michael Baxandall, *Giotto and the Orators. Humanist Observers of Painting in Italy and the Discovery of Pictorial Composition* (Oxford: Clarendon Press, 1971), p. 44. It is not clear how closely this resonates with Baxandall's own approach. Although Baxandall treated the humanist discourse on art as a language that configured the way things were seen – 'observation was linguistically enforced' (Baxandall, *Giotto and the Orators*, p. 9) – he promptly restored this same discourse to the milieu of artists, patrons and viewers. Expanding on the Wittgensteinian proposition that 'meaning is use', Baxandall observed that 'in classical Latin much of the meaning of words lay in an institution of relationship with other words, a system of cross-references, distinctions, contraries, and metaphorical habits' (Baxandall, *Giotto and the Orators*, p. 14). See also Christopher Wood, 'When Attitudes Became Form' (2009) *Artforum* 43–4, at 43: 'In Baxandall's Florence, "art" was the medium of a social relation among artists, patrons, and other beholders, sustained by a common repertoire of skills, mental and affective habits, and bodily disciplines. This was a world in which art was still woven tightly into the tissue of daily experience, and of civic life, and yet was already recognizable *as* art – that is, as a refined and beautiful supplement to practical life.' Madero has in mind a more restricted horizon of use. Although *Tabula Picta* is characterized as a contribution to 'legal anthropology', this is not the kind of anthropology that seeks to flesh out the social practices in which legal texts or semantics are implicated. Madero's concern is not with the 'judicial processes or sociological dynamics through which conflicts are resolved in a given society', but with 'the technical processes specific to a modal understanding of experiences and practices which, together, subjects them to the logical

This sense of 'things' as contingent artefacts is not especially novel. The terms of Madero's analysis were foreshadowed in Yan Thomas' classic analysis of the Roman legal form of the thing (*res*). In Roman law, *res* was actually a name for the trial process, and for the legal issue that the parties were disputing through that procedure: '*res* meant first and foremost the trial, or the issue in dispute.'[12] Things took the form of a *res de qua agitur*, or 'thing in question'. Of course lawyers recognized that legal arguments had to do with things in the world, but the 'real' or 'material' existence of these things was eclipsed by the existence that they came to have within the discursive or rhetorical frame of legal debate: 'The objectivity of a *res* was simply that which was conferred upon it by a *causa* [a legal name or definition]: this kind of objectivity resulted from the dialogue in which the partners in the controversy were engaged.'[13] The form of the *res* has inspired theoretical reflection on the composition of things. Thomas' account of the Roman lawyers' sense of the thing as *res de qua agitur* is taken up in Bruno Latour's construction of the 'matter of concern', or that which 'brings people together *because* it divides them'.[14] Again, material things are effects of representational and communicative practices.

We draw on Madero's history of *tabula picta* to make a simple point: intellectual property rights are not peripheral, exceptional, fictional or tenuously analogous forms of true property rights. In the context of adjudication, as in other specialized theatres, things, whether they are imagined as tangible or intangible, are the products of discursive schematization; they are 'semantic artefacts'. In the case of even the most material of things, the lawyer's apprehension of the object will be framed and conditioned by layer upon layer of (documentary) representation.[15] For example, land is

articulation of legal categories and gives them a reality removed from the evidence of the senses' (Madero, *Tabula Picta*, p. 2). The proposition that legal technicalities construct a reality 'removed' from the world is the basic premise of Madero's analysis, but this 'remove' is affirmed rather than explained.

12 Yan Thomas, 'Res, Chose et Patrimoine (Note sur le Rapport Sujet-Objet en Droit Romain)' (1980) 24 *Archives de la Philosophie du Droit* 413–26 at 415. In fact, the relation between *res* and *causa* was just one strand in a metonymic knot of *res–lis–causa*, which bound together the sense of *res* (the thing that was at stake in the trial), *causa* (the case in the sense of legal issue or question) and *lis* (the procedural frame of the trial, action or litigation). This triad represented 'the different perspectives from which one could consider the 'legal value' attached to a given set of circumstances' (*Ibid.*, 416).

13 Thomas, 'Res, Chose et Patrimoine', 421.

14 Bruno Latour, 'From Realpolitik to Dingpolitik' in *Making Things Public* (Cambridge, MA: MIT Press, 2004), p. 13.

15 See Bruno Latour, *The Making of Law. An Ethnography of the Conseil d'Etat* (Cambridge: Polity, 2010), Chapter 2.

materialized in cadastral plans, geological or environmental surveys, evidence of occupation and use, records of transactions, and so on. Each of these layers of representation is a considerable technical, administrative or organizational achievement, and only if we forget this, as first-order participants are bound to do, can we overlook the role of communicative techniques in translating materiality into and across the courtroom. And similar processes of translation are involved in the other theatres in which the shape of the invention is negotiated: the lawyer's office, the process of patent examination, the valuation of a patent or patent portfolios, and so on. Ultimately, our suggestion is that far from being the poor relation of 'true' property rights, the making of intellectual property rights exemplifies what is involved in the emergence and maintenance of property rights in even the most material of things.

1 Utility

Before turning to intellectual property's prehistory, we briefly take in the 'patent controversy' in late nineteenth-century Europe. For a brief moment it seemed that a number of European nations were about to abolish their patent regimes. The strength of the movement for abolition was such that *The Economist*, one of the most influential voices in the argument against patent rights, declared in 1869 that '[i]t is probable enough that the patent system will be abolished ere long'.[16] Although the terms of the debate were shaped by particular political and legal traditions, arguments for the abolition of patents were based on the common premise that patent rights did not stimulate and diffuse innovation but actually obstructed free trade. Not all economists were opposed to the maintenance of patent regimes,[17] but all were agreed that the justification of patent regimes turned on the criterion of social utility. Because the new 'patent republics' of the late eighteenth century defined themselves in opposition to the old regimes of privilege and monopoly,[18] it was difficult to find a normative idiom for the justification of rights based on social utility. Nowhere was this clearer than in France, where the tension between natural right and utility was especially acute. Augustin-Charles Renouard, writing in 1836, observed

[16] Cited in Fritz Machlup and Edith Penrose, 'The Patent Controversy in the Nineteenth Century' (1950) 10 *Journal of Economic History* 1–29 at 1.

[17] For a survey of positions in the debate see generally Machlup and Penrose, 'The Patent Controversy in the Nineteenth Century'.

[18] See Mario Biagioli, 'Patent Republic: Representing Inventions, Constructing Rights and Authors' (2006) 73 *Social Research* 1129–72.

that the most fundamental question to be addressed in relation to literary property was 'whether property is based on a necessary and natural right, or whether it is just a creation of civil law, born of a convention established by positive laws, with a view to increasing social utility'.[19] The problem was that limited rights granted by governments were apt to be seen as lapses back into the privileges of the *ancien régime*, but the effect of treating intellectual property rights as founded in natural right would be almost as bad; it would, as Renouard put it, re-establish a kind of aristocracy, and would grant 'privileges and favours that our social order rejects'.[20]

The first republican patent statute of 1793 affirmed in its first article that an invention was the property of the inventor, but then went on to require the same inventor to make a full disclosure of the invention and to deposit documents, models or specimens, and, crucially, limited the term of a patent to five, ten or fifteen years, depending on the fee paid by the patentee, after which period the invention would fall into the public domain. Writing in 1852, the economist Charles Coquelin pointed out the absurdity of this formulation; having declared that the invention belonged to the inventor by natural right, how could one then limit the duration of the right to a maximum of fifteen years and then make a gift of it to the public?[21] It may be that the promoters of the legislation were entirely alive to the contradiction. Machlup and Penrose suggest that the promoters of the legislation adopted the idiom of natural right in 'deliberate insincerity', in an attempt to make acceptable a measure that would have been less acceptable under the name of a privilege.[22]

Coquelin's entry for 'Brevets d'Invention' in the *Dictionnaire de l'Economie Politique* (1852), which he edited with Gilbert Guillaumin, took on the argument that inventors acquired a true property right in their invention by virtue of 'first occupation'. Coquelin proposed to consider the nature of patent rights from the two conventional perspectives of utility and right [*de l'utilité et du droit*]'.[23] He agreed that all inventions were discoveries, if only because 'the forces set to work by an inventor existed in nature prior to their discovery, and someone else might just

[19] Augustin-Charles Renouard, 'Théorie du Droit des Auteurs sur les Productions de Leur Intelligence' (1836–37) 5 *Revue de Legislation et de Jurisprudence* 241–74 at 244.

[20] Renouard, 'Théorie du Droit des Auteurs sur les Productions de Leur Intelligence', 253.

[21] Charles Coquelin, 'Brevets d'Invention' in Charles Coquelin and Gilbert Guillaumin (eds.) *Dictionnaire de l'Economie Politique* (Paris: Librairie de Guillaumin, 1852), vol. I, pp. 209–23 at p. 214.

[22] Machlup and Penrose, 'The Patent Controversy in the Nineteenth Century', 16.

[23] Coquelin, 'Brevets d'Invention', p. 216.

as well have discovered them'.[24] But the 'discovery' of an invention was peculiar because 'ideas' were carved out of a process that was thoroughly social. What the inventor might mistake for the product of an individual mind was in fact generated by a social process. In 1850 *The Economist* said of inventors that 'their minds and their inventions are, in fact, parts of the great mental whole of society'.[25] Coquelin's point was similar; each invention was an effect of 'circumstances, location, and period [*les circonstances, la situation et l'époque*]'. And, if this was so, it followed that 'in any invention there is always a good part that already belongs to the public'.[26]

However inventions originated, they could not be occupied or possessed in the same manner as material things. Some of Coquelin's examples might now seem eccentric, but they were commonplace topics in the nineteenth-century debate. Take, for example, the analogy between Christopher Columbus' discovery of America and Vasco da Gama's discovery of the passage to India around the Cape of Good Hope.[27] Coquelin observes – at some length – that although Columbus had actually been in search of a passage to the Indies, the unanimous view in Europe was that title to the lands that he had so fortuitously discovered belonged to Spain, whereas in the case of da Gama no one had ever imagined that the passage could become the exclusive dominion of Portugal: 'The passage to the Indies was not one of those bounded material objects which necessarily have to be possessed [*exploités*] by one nation alone, but rather one of those which, of their very nature, are accessible to the whole world and are necessarily the common property of humanity.'[28]

In terms that resonate very closely with Jefferson's formulations, Coquelin went on to observe that 'by its very nature' an invention 'escapes true appropriation'.[29] Invoking the same metaphor of fire, 'which is communicated and spreads without diminishing at its hearth or source',[30] he pointed out that 'twenty, thirty, or a hundred individuals can use the invention in as many different places, and the exploitation by one in no way affects the exploitation of another'.[31] So one could have a natural right to land, but not an invention:

[24] *Ibid.*, p. 217.

[25] Cited in Machlup and Penrose, 'The Patent Controversy in the Nineteenth Century', 15.

[26] Coquelin, 'Brevets d'Invention', p. 222.

[27] *Ibid.*, pp. 217–18. [28] *Ibid.*, p. 218.

[29] *Ibid.*, p. 214. [30] *Ibid.*, p. 214, citing Renouard.

[31] *Ibid.*, p. 219. In the case of an invention one could say that ideas could be circumscribed: 'They can be specified, delimited, and clearly fixed on paper by means of descriptions and

> In granting to one person or another the exclusive possession of an estate in land, the law does no more than respect the nature of things, which prevents this estate from being enjoyed by many people; it merely decides between competing claimants. In securing to one man the benefit of an industrial invention the law goes against the nature of things, which is such that this invention should be exploited by many people; it creates a monopoly where none existed before.[32]

It is not possible here to embark on a proper analysis of the implications of the nineteenth-century debate as to natural right and utility, but we draw three points from the line of argument in Coquelin's discussion. First, the distinction between material and immaterial things echoes or derives from a broader distinction between those things that are capable of 'true' appropriation and those that are not. Second, these distinctions were settled in the course of the nineteenth century through a debate about the relation between property founded in natural right and property founded in utility. Third, the effect of making this distinction was to settle a division of labour between the legal theory of property and an economic theory of property, and to do so very much in favour of the latter.

2 Before intellectual property

Madero's history excerpts the Roman texts and medieval glosses and commentaries that were collected under the heading of *tabula picta*. Under this heading, the glossators worked out the legal principles that should govern cases concerning the ownership of books and paintings. A *tabula picta* was a panel painting, a wooden board onto which the painter would layer a ground of glue and gesso before applying the pigments that were used to compose the finished painting. By extension, *tabula picta* came to include texts and commentaries related to the question of the ownership of manuscript books (*chartae*). For medieval lawyers, paintings and books were species of the same genus because 'painting and writing happened when someone applied colour or ink to a surface, to a *tabula* in the case of paintings, to a *charta* or *membrana* in the case of texts'.[33] Because they understood books and paintings as composites of different kinds of material – in essence, the wooden or parchment substrate and the pigment or ink applied to it – lawyers treated them as tangible objects rather than

drawings, and they can even be given tangible form in the model made by the hands of the inventor.'

[32] *Ibid.*, p. 219.

[33] Madero, *Tabula Picta*, pp. 4–5, translation modified.

as embodiments of a literary or artistic work. Perhaps this was a residue of the Roman lawyer's tendency to apprehend fabricated things as 'sets of composite parts'.[34] In any case, the terms themselves, *tabula* (board)[35] and *charta* (parchment) should be taken literally, as references to the material surfaces upon which characters or motifs were drawn, rather than as shorthand terms for works of authorship.

The doctrinal texts compiled under the rubric of *tabula picta* worked with a basic *casus* – a dispute between the owner of the substrate (parchment or panel) and the owner of the inks or pigments applied to that substrate as to the ownership of a finished manuscript or painting. According to the basic logic of *dominium*, a right over a thing survived, and could be transmitted from one *dominus* to the next, so long as the material thing in which the right was inscribed remained identifiable. If the thing in question ceased to exist, or ceased to have the identity originally ascribed to it, then *dominium* was extinguished. The difficulty of the question of *tabula picta* was precisely the difficulty of specifying this relation between property rights and the material things in which they were inscribed. Did the property right of the owner of the raw parchment or *tabula* persist through to the finished book or painting on the basis that the innate 'power of attraction'[36] of *dominium* caused it to absorb the added inks or pigments, or did the addition of these materials extinguish the original *dominium* by creating a new thing? How closely did the legal identity of a thing depend on the continuity of its material substance? The material substance of things is continually being eroded, fractured, accreted to, dissolved, transformed, mixed, compounded or dispersed, if only in the most marginal or imperceptible of ways.[37] When these processes

[34] See Yan Thomas, 'L'Institution Civile de la Cité' (1993) 74 *Le Débat* 23–44 at 30.

[35] Madero emphasizes that *tabula* always meant 'a painting' (*Tabula Picta*, p. 27), rather than the kind of wax tablet that was used in various kinds of social transaction in Rome (on this latter sense of *tabula* see Elizabeth A. Meyer, *Legitimacy and Law in the Roman World. Tabulae in Roman Belief and Practice* (Cambridge University Press, 2004).

[36] On this power of attraction see Madero, *Tabula Picta*, Chapter 7.

[37] The human body provided a ready and universal frame for this experience of change and continuity: '[L]et us imagine that, when its parts change, a body becomes another: following that reasoning, we ourselves would not be who we were a year earlier, because, according to the philosophers, we are made of minuscule particles, some of which leave our body every day, while others come from the outside to replace them. This is why, when the species of a body remains the same, we consider that the body also remains the same' (*D.* 5.1.76). Some early Christians were concerned to know how, if they were to die a martyr's death after being thrown to the lions in the arena, they could then be resurrected in the Kingdom of God, given that their material substance would inevitably be dispersed by the process of dismemberment and digestion. See further Caroline

are noticed, one can either hold the nominal identity of the thing steady, saying that material changes do not go to the essence of that identity, or one can decide that material transformations warrant the ascription of a new identity. According to Madero, the conceptual action in the rubric of *tabula picta* was driven by this tension 'between *materia* and *species*'.[38]

One approach to the question of whether the ownership of the board or parchment prevailed over the ownership of pigments or inks was through the basic categories of *accessio* and *specificatio*. The textbook examples of *accessio* were cases such as the gradual augmentation of the *dominium* of a riparian landowner by means of alluvial deposits, or the extension of the *dominium* of the owner of a female slave to a child born to that slave. The first example was sometimes characterized as *accessio continua* because the thing that was the subject of *dominium* was enlarged by the addition of material substance to material substance, while the second was called *accessio discreta* because a new species or individual was born into the *dominium* of the owner. The classic examples of *specificatio* were cases in which a raw material had been transformed into an artefact (grapes made into wine), where two different materials were mixed to make a new species (gold and silver to make *electrum*), or where one material was affixed to another to form a new and indivisible object. The general principle was that the new *species* belonged to the person who made it (subject to a duty of compensation) unless the original material could be recovered and restored to the *dominus* (say, by melting a statue down into a mass of metal). Paintings and manuscripts did not fit very easily into these categories. Even if the broad trend, from the Roman period onwards, was for lawyers to recognize that a *tabula picta* belonged to the painter, and for the later medieval glosses and commentaries to recognize that a manuscript belonged to the scribe, the arguments that generated these conclusions were far from straightforward.[39]

Walker Bynum, *The Resurrection of the Body in Western Christianity, 200–1336* (New York: Columbia University Press, 1995).

[38] Madero, *Tabula Picta*, p. 7.

[39] Yan Thomas observes, with a reference to Madero's study, that although the analyses of the materiality 'borrowed eclectically from various philosophical currents, they were always specific because beyond the identity of the *res*, what was sought was the imputability of a right: to whom should the changeable and transformed thing remain or become imputed? (Yan Thomas, 'L'Extrême et l'Ordinaire. Remarques sur le Cas Médiévale de la Communauté Disparue' in Jean-Claude Passeron and Jacques Revel (eds.), *Penser par cas* (Paris: École des Hautes Etudes en Sciences Sociales, 2005), pp. 45–73 at p. 56). To borrow Geertz's borrowing of terms first used by the anthropologist Alexander Goldenweiser, one might say that the inventiveness of the glossators was just a mode of 'involution' – 'virtuosity within monotony'. Clifford Geertz, *Agricultural Involution. The*

The late twelfth-century commentaries of Placentinus adapted the logic of *specificatio* to a novel theory of the 'dignity' of paintings. According to Placentinus, a *tabula picta* would qualify as a new *species* if the painter had created a work that had the 'dignity' proper to an *icona* or *imago*.[40] The dignity of a work was a function not of value but of the subject matter of the painting and of the pigments used in its execution; a work of appropriate dignity would depict 'a man rather than a bear or a lion', and would employ 'a range of man-made colours'.[41] The resulting species would belong to the *specificator* – that is, the painter – rather than the owner of the unprepared *tabula*. Madero suggests that the insistence on man-made pigments signifies an appreciation of the 'technical competence'[42] involved in their use; the shapes and textures of the finished motifs had already to be anticipated by the painter in the process of mixing and preparing the substances of which pigments were made. Indeed, even the process of preparing the *tabula* – priming its surface with glue and sawdust, applying to it successive layers of mashed parchment, various qualities of plaster and more glue, then outlining the subject in ink – might have seemed to turn the wooden support into a new *species*, even before the picture was actually painted.[43] For Placentinus, the form of an *icona* or *imago* did not emerge from the mixing of materials: 'the conditions for the creation of a new species were the dignity of the subject represented, the use of proper pigments that were carefully prepared, and a respect for painterly techniques – not the logic of the transformation of substances.'[44]

The glossator Azo, writing in the early thirteenth century, when the trade in manuscript book production had become established, mocked Placentinus' 'fabulations' about the dignity of painting and proposed a criterion of value (*pretiositas*) that was based not on dignity but on cost and aesthetic value. On that basis a painting attached its *tabula*, and, because 'the scribes of our times have become painters',[45] so too did a text attach its parchment support. For the post-glossator Odofredo, the skill achieved by contemporary scribes was such as to elevate writing above painting; as a rule, writing carried its parchment support with it, precisely because of the artistry expressed in textual inscriptions, whereas

Processes of Ecological Change in Indonesia (Berkeley: University of California Press, 1963), p. 81.

[40] Madero, *Tabula Picta*, pp. 38–43, 62.

[41] *Ibid.*, pp. 38–40. [42] *Ibid.*, p. 41.

[43] *Ibid.*, p. 66. [44] *Ibid.*, p. 45.

[45] Cited in Madero, *Tabula Picta*, p. 79. See also p. 33: 'the writing was more precious than the *charta*.'

a painting would carry its support with it only in certain cases. Bartolus proposed yet another criterion of value (*pretiositas*), which started from the premise that liquid things were more precious than dry things. In the case of a *tabula picta*, the pigments covered the surface of a *tabula* so entirely that the liquid prevailed over the dry and the paints attached the board; in the case of *chartae*, the inscriptions accrued to the substrate. By contrast with Placentinus' theory, this medieval theory of *pretium* might well have been that, rather than forming a new *species*, a *tabula* and the pigments applied to it subsisted as two distinct but inseparable material layers, and the pigments carried the board with them by an effect of prevalence. Or, as in the case of Placentinus, the theory may have been that although pigments and board were unalike in raw substance, according to the principle of *ferruminatio* they nonetheless formed a single thing that was continuous in 'spirit'.

3 A legal physics

The materialism of medieval glossators was a legacy of Roman law, which treated both rights and objects as 'things'. Rights were incorporeal things (*res incorporales*) and the objects to which they referred were corporeal things (*res corporales*). Roman lawyers imagined rights as external or incidental attributes of their corporeal referents. Rights were attached to corporeal things rather than compounded into them. The exception was property: a property right was treated as a 'real right' (*ius reale*) because the right was so tightly implicated in its material object that the one merged into the other. Right and thing formed a single *corporale*. To transfer the object was to transfer the right, and the modalities of the right were directly conditioned by the material properties of the thing. This gave rise to the medieval sense of land as 'real' property. The rights that persons might have in relation to land were supposed to be inscribed or rooted in the land itself –hence Heinrich Brunner's characterization of the relation as one of 'racination [*Radizierung*]'.[46] Inspired by this general premise, doctrinal arguments about the ownership of books and paintings paid very close attention to the nuances of material fabrication, to the way that *tabulae* were prepared for painting, to the composition and texture of pigments and inks, and to the relative weight, extension or proportion of material ingredients. Yet the effect of the lawyers' 'conspiracy against experience' was that materiality in the ordinary sense was

[46] See Jean Clam, *Trajectoires de l'Immateriel* (Paris: CNRS, 2006).

translated into a set of categories and processes that owed their existence to the dynamics of legal argument rather than any 'natural' properties or propensities. Figuratively, one might say that law ascribed its own 'physics' to material things.

The construction of this legal 'physics' can be illustrated by reference to the categories of *ferruminatio* and *adplumbatio*, which were mobilized in the analysis of *tabula picta* because they addressed compositions of worked (*factae*) as distinct from unworked (*infectae*) materials.[47] Both categories took their names from real material processes. *Ferruminatio* described the process by which, for example, the parts of an iron statue were welded together with iron, or in which silver was used to fuse silver to silver. In such cases the principle was that continuity of material substance produced 'a substantial coherence which gathered originally distinct objects into a single body imbued with an internal force, contained *uno spiritu*, or, as the gloss had it, *una elementatione*'.[48] The legal effect was that *dominium* in the originally distinct parts was extinguished by the process of soldering. By contrast, *adplumbatio* described configurations in which parts made of one material were soldered together by another – where lead (the generic soldering medium) was used to fuse iron to iron, or silver to silver. Here, the principle was that the original parts remained recoverable, so that the *dominium* of their owner(s) persisted into the composite artefact.

The theory of *ferruminatio* was interesting to Placentinus because it met an objection to the argument that the technique of the painter and the dignity of the subject transformed the board into a new *species*. The objection was as follows: if a painted *tabula* could be scraped back to its original condition and restored to its original *dominus*, then, according to the basic principles of *specificatio*, *dominium* in the original *tabula* was not extinguished. Placentinus countered that such an operation could not be performed 'without damage', and that the pigments were fused to the *tabula* by something akin to a process of *ferruminatio*. Although the finished *tabula* was made of diverse material substances, Placentinus

[47] Cases concerning mixtures of things such as grains or fluids were treated as instances of *confusio* or *commixtio*; see Madero, *Tabula Picta*, p. 60: 'Essentially, while *ferruminatio* and *adplumbatio* weld two things that retain a definite form, *confusio* and *commixtio* mix liquid or solid things of unstable or fluid form.' The distinction between *factae* and *infectae* was not exactly the difference between raw materials and products of workmanship; artefacts were treated as *infectae* if, like inks and pigments, they did not have a determinate form (see *ibid.*, pp. 102–3).

[48] *Ibid.*, p. 88 (translation modified).

invoked the example of seeds and trees[49] to argue that things that were not of the same substance could nonetheless form a compound with the quality of coherence or unity that characterized the products of *ferruminatio* (as distinct from *adplumbatio*). In the process of taking root, a tree or seed effectively became 'one' with the soil; and although this mode of oneness was conceptually distinct from the coherence achieved by a process of *ferruminatio*, it had the same legal effects.[50] This two-stage analogy – between things that were truly *ferruminatae* and plants, and then between plants and paintings – suggested a more general legal category of things that were indissoluble, whether they were made of the same or different substances.

The physics of medieval property law was forged through analogies of this sort. The analogy between welded statues, plants and paintings suggested that these different kinds of material composition had something in common. Each process generated a material form that could be considered to be indissoluble. But this quality of 'coherence' or 'indissolubility' was not a matter of fact; it was generated by introducing legal criteria or schemata into 'real' material textures or propensities. One could equally well say – against Placentinus' theory – that a painting was analogous to something joined by *adplumbatio*. Indeed, the fourteenth-century commentator Alberico de Rosate construed paintings in precisely these terms; the form of the painting was a kind of body that was soldered to the substance of the *tabula* by the intermediate substance of pigments.[51] Placentinus and Alberico de Rosate construed the same material composition, the same set of material textures, in radically different ways, and they did so because the logic of medieval property law was such that normative effects had to be drawn out of the material composition of things. Lawyers scrutinized the texture and behaviour of material things in search of features to which they might ascribe legal significance, and which might, more precisely, be taken as a basis on which to qualify, refine or redefine the legal categories that were brought to bear in questions of property. The more intense the lawyers' scrutiny of material reality, the more readily that reality dissolved into a plastic resource for analogical arguments.

49 The Digest assimilated things joined by *ferruminatio* to 'things that are planted, bodies that are nourished by food found in nature, and things resulting from specification' (*ibid.*, p. 54).

50 For Placentinus, 'painting was *ferruminata* only in its appearance' (*ibid.*, p. 62), but it yielded the same procedural consequences.

51 *Ibid.*, pp. 64–6.

4 The materiality of the intangible

Property lawyers no longer spend much time scrutinizing the materiality of things. Ownership transactions are made by means of paper documents or digitized forms, and it is rarely necessary to retrace the 'chains of reference'[52] that connect these two-dimensional representations to real things.[53] Speculatively, one might say that the Roman and medieval doctrines of *specificatio* and *accessio* are now largely obsolete[54] because craft techniques such as welding, soldering, mixing and embellishing have been eclipsed by the technologies of the industrial production line. In a culture in which both products and the wrappings in which they are packaged are mass produced, the question whether one person's grain has been confused with another's, or whether the work of the artisan should prevail over the rights of an owner of raw materials, is rather less likely to arise. The prime mover in the making of a series of manufactured artefacts is either the design – the patented invention – from which they are produced or the production line itself as a complex artefact of organizational knowledge. Intellectual property doctrine emphasizes the former at the expense of the latter. In so doing, it overlooks the sense in which the 'ground' of invention is constituted by the organizational logic of the production line.[55] But the point is that the property law that pertains to 'things' in the age of manufacturing is intellectual property law. The laws of tangible property have given way to the laws of the intangible, but this has not been accompanied by a radical change in the way that lawyers apprehend 'things'. In the context of the infringement action, the appreciation of intangible 'ideas' involves the close scrutiny of the materiality of things.

Although adjudication is now a very different process, if only because its social ecology is so different, it is difficult not to see the similarity between

[52] For this notion, see Bruno Latour, *Pandora's Hope* (Cambridge, MA: Harvard University Press, 1999).

[53] A rare modern example is *Borden (UK)* v. *Scottish Timber Products* (1981) Ch. 25. For a classic analysis of *accessio* and *specificatio* in English law see Anthony G. Guest, 'Accession and Confusion in the Law of Hire-Purchase' (1964) 27 *Modern Law Review* 505–20 at 506.

[54] The question of 'how property behaves in mixtures' has been revived by the law of restitution, but most exercises in tracing property rights have to do with funds rather than grains or liquids, and so with accounting procedures rather than some material 'physics'. See Peter Birks, 'Mixing and Tracing Property and Restitution' (2001) 54 *Current Legal Problems* 69–98.

[55] See James Beniger, *The Control Revolution* (Cambridge, MA: Harvard University Press, 1986), pp. 241–2 where the paradigmatic nineteenth-century invention, the

the scrutiny of brush-strokes or other material textures in a copyright infringement action,[56] or the comparison of two mechanical artefacts in a patent infringement action, and the medieval lawyers' decomposition of the material form of a painting or manuscript. Although the conceptual schemata are very different – modern intellectual property lawyers decipher material form and texture as the traces of an intangible work or invention rather than as manifestations of qualities such as unity or dignity – in both cases the effect is to generate a factitious physics, which in one case is called 'tangible' and the other 'intangible'.

In the case of patent law, the best example of this effect is the role of patent models in patent litigation in the United States in the nineteenth century. We have already explored various aspects of the use of models in patent litigation,[57] but we return to the example here to make a simple point about the distinction between tangible and intangible things. For patent lawyers, the art of demonstrating a patent model was to decompose the material form of the model to reveal the shape of the intangible invention. As we have suggested, the assumption in classic patent law was that the invention was immanent in its material embodiment. According to this understanding, the invention was 'manifested only in the material shape, configuration and operation of a material artefact or process. It [was] the material embodiment seen under a particular aspect.'[58] A patent model could be set on a table, pointed at from any aspect, picked up, rotated or upended so as to display a point of interest to the audience and, if need be, brought to the bench or the jury so as to facilitate closer inspection. The object was not to evidence the shape of the machine, but to reveal the outline of the intangible invention, which nineteenth-century patent

sewing machine, was used to explain the importance of coordination: 'Sewing machine manufacturers, for example, had to control a major flow of metals from the foundry through tumbling, annealing, japanning (enamelling and laquering), drilling, turning, milling, grinding, polishing, ornamenting, varnishing, adjusting, and testing. Meanwhile, these processes had to be coordinated with parallel work lines producing metal attachments, needles, and tools, while woodworking and cabinet-making operations – among the most complicated in the mass production of furniture in the nineteenth century – kept pace in still other departments. Output from these various production lines had to be coordinated in a final line that completed the tasks of assembly, gauging, inspection, final testing, and preparation for shipment.'

[56] See Jose Bellido, 'Looking Right: The Art of Visual Literacy in British Copyright Litigation' (2012) *Law, Culture & the Humanities*.

[57] Pottage and Sherman, *Figures of Invention*, Chapter 5; Alain Pottage, 'Law Machines. Scale Models, Forensic Materiality and the Making of Modern Patent Law' (2011) 41 *Social Studies of Science* 621–43; Pottage, 'Forensic Machinery' (2011) 43 *Cabinet* 75–80.

[58] See generally Pottage and Sherman, *Figures of Invention*, pp. 12–13.

doctrine called the principle of a machine. Our hypothesis is that there is a close resonance between the way that patent lawyers in the classical age saw through the form of the model to the outline of the invention and the way that medieval lawyers saw through the composites of substrate and pigment to the spiritual essence of materials – their dignity, *pretiositas*, or unity of spirit.

One might say that things are very different in the contemporary age, which is characterized by the emergence of truly immaterial intangibles, notably software inventions that (at least as far as lawyers are concerned) have neither material form nor material effect. But even here there is a kind of materiality in play, namely the materiality of text. As we have suggested elsewhere, the patent claim now functions as a kind of textual machine:

> The elements of the patent claim represent the mechanical components of a machine or artifact but they do so by means of elements that are defined and articulated not by physical or chemical forces or complementarities, but by the 'physics' of syntax, convention, and discursive action ... The patent claim is an abstract machine, and claim drafting and interpretation are themselves mechanical arts, practised in the medium of semantics, rather than physics.[59]

For some purposes – particularly in relation to information-based inventions – textual materiality might seem to be an inadequate substitute for physical materiality. Hence the suggestion that it might now be time to reinstitute the old requirement that inventors submit a patent model with their applications, less for the purposes of litigation than in the interests of more effective patent examination.[60] No matter how ephemeral the subject matter might be, texts or documents are the media in which even the most intangible of things becomes real and tractable in the courtroom

[59] See generally Pottage and Sherman, *Figures of Invention*, Chapter 7.

[60] See Brendan Koerner, 'Make an Old Idea New to Fix the Patent Backlog' (30 August 2011) *Wired*: 'The USPTO could instantly slash the number of applications by compelling inventors to submit working models whenever feasible. The most abstract inventions would be exempt, of course, but these constitute a small minority of applications; business models, for example, made up about 2 percent of the patents issued last year, and drug compositions were roughly 3 percent. The bulk of inventors would have to come up with three-dimensional examples of how their creations would look and function. Have a great idea for a longer-lasting semiconductor? A sturdier toxic-waste container? A safer lawn dart? Don't just submit a diagram; make a model the examiner can touch. Perhaps that requirement would have been draconian in decades past, when creating models from complex designs was prohibitively expensive. But rapid-prototyping tools now make it possible for anyone to produce a high-quality mock-up, typically by hiring a service that specializes in such technology.'

or fora in which they are judged. In the context of adjudication, as in other specialized theatres, things, whether they are imagined as tangible or intangible, are the products of discursive schematization; they are 'semantic artefacts'. This is because there is no dimension of reality in which inventions, signs or designs might subsist independently of the artefacts, texts or drawings from which they are elicited. Intangibility is an effect of representation, interpretation and argumentation.

The upshot is that intellectual property rights are not peripheral, exceptional, or tenuously analogous forms of property. Indeed, the discourse of intellectual property is now more materialist than almost any other language of property law. Intellectual property lawyers probably spend more time scrutinizing the material compositions and textures of things than do other species of property lawyer; and, in so doing, they carry on the old art of eliciting a properly legal physics from things. If tangibility and intangibility are just two alternative names for this spectral physics, then intellectual property law may be the true heritor of the old European tradition of 'real' property. Hence our suggestion that, for from being the poor relation of 'true' property law, intellectual property actually exemplifies what is involved in the making of property rights in even the most material of things.

2

Property in brands

The commodification of conversation

DEV S. GANGJEE

Introduction

This chapter traces the emergence of a new *res* or object of protection within European trade mark law. Proprietary rights in trade marks have conventionally been premised upon the mark's ability to communicate useful information, namely the commercial source of goods or services.[1] Granting exclusive rights to a mark preserves its ability to reliably signal origin. This ability reduces consumer search costs and protects producer goodwill.[2] Contemporary EU trade mark law goes further and protects the more expansive brand dimension associated with a successful trade mark. The Court of Justice of the European Union (CJEU) has enabled this by recognising not only the origin indication function of marks, but also their advertising, investment and communication functions as well. Viewed comparatively, it is the most generous trade mark regime in this regard[3] and therefore of considerable interest. The brand is a remarkably elusive and protean, yet undeniably valuable intangible. So what are the doctrinal tools and

[1] This source or commercial origin indicating function is referred to as the essential function in the EU. See Ilanah Simon Fhima, 'How Does "Essential Function" Drive European Trade Mark Law?' (2005) 36 *International Review of Intellectual Property and Competition Law* 401.

[2] See for example Case C-10/89 *SA Cnl-Sucal NV* v. *Hag GF AG* (1990) 3 CMLR 571 at 582–583 (AG Francis Jacobs) ('[T]rade marks reward the manufacturer who consistently produces high-quality goods and they thus stimulate economic progress ... they [also] act as a guarantee, to the consumer, that all goods bearing a particular mark have been produced by, or under the control of, the same manufacturer and are therefore likely to be of similar quality').

[3] *L'Oreal* v. *Bellure* [2010] EWCA Civ 535 at [20] (Jacob, LJ) (observing that as a result of the increasing recognition of brand value, 'the EU has a more "protective" approach to trade mark law than other major trading areas or blocs').

techniques available to courts, registrars and litigants, enabling them to work with such elusive subject matter? What are the assumptions about brand creation and sustenance that reinforce these techniques? And can they be reconciled with recent conceptualisations of branding emerging from within marketing and consumer studies scholarship? These are the questions motivating this chapter.

In pursuing these questions, this chapter has two interrelated agendas. The first is conceptual in orientation, where the aim is to investigate the brand as 'thing' within EU law. All intellectual property (IP) shares a foundational difficulty, which is to identify and delimit the object to which property rights are attached. As Drahos observes, IP law 'deals with abstract objects [which] are not like physical objects. They do not, for instance, have obvious boundaries.'[4] For registration-based regimes, the setting of boundaries involves acts of representation within the limits set by bureaucratic rules and procedures. While the registration process for real property is similarly preoccupied with representation and abstraction, intellectual property lacks an equivalent material referent and its physical characteristics which otherwise provide a point of reference.[5] Legal techniques for identifying these intangibles therefore have particular significance. For instance, although the intangible invention is only partially captured in the patent specification document, this nevertheless allows registrars and courts to work with it.[6] Similarly copyright, which lacks an accompanying registration apparatus, invokes the concept of the 'work' as shorthand for authorial output. The work exists in relation to the material form of the underlying object (such as a book); yet copyright protection of the work is not limited to the surface of this object (the literal text of the book) and extends to a certain depth below it.[7] When it comes to the delimitation of trade marks, the issue of representation was considered less problematic. Trade marks conventionally consisted of words and images, which were relatively straightforward to represent

[4] Peter Drahos, *A Philosophy of Intellectual Property* (Vermont: Ashgate Dartmouth 1996), p. xi.

[5] For an overview of the abstract, dematerialised *res* and the constitutive functions of property law, even in the case of tangible property, see Andreas Rahmatian, *Copyright and Creativity: The Making of Property Rights in Creative Works* (Cheltenham: Edward Elgar, 2011), pp. 10–12.

[6] For a history of the constitutive roles of material media, including working models, used to represent the intangible invention, see Alain Pottage and Brad Sherman, *Figures of Invention: A History of Modern Patent Law* (Oxford University Press, 2010).

[7] Brad Sherman, 'What is a Copyright Work?' (2011) 12 *Theoretical Inquiries in Law* 99.

graphically on trade mark registers with a high degree of fidelity.[8] The mark, as registered, formed the core of the object of protection and was the starting point for any subsequent infringement analysis. The introduction of the brand complicates this story, however. Semiotic analysis suggests that trade marks can be understood 'as a three-legged stool, consisting of a signifier (the perceptible form of the mark), a signified (the semantic content of the mark, such as the goodwill or effect to which the signifier refers), and a referent (the product or service to which the mark refers)'.[9] It is the signified that is commodious enough to incorporate the brand dimension. Yet while both signifier and referent are relatively easy to depict on registration forms, how does one represent the signified? Since looking to the register is not an option, its content only crystallises in the context of a specific dispute. The process of filling in this content can in principle draw on direct evidence of consumer perceptions but increasingly relies on indirect proxies. Retracing this juridical reification of the brand, the first section of this chapter argues that the brand is presently conceived of within a 'broadcast' or one-way information transmission model, where the trade mark owner projects a defined brand identity that is received unmodified by a passive audience. This faithfully reproduced image subsequently triggers predictable affective and cognitive effects in consumers. For this model, consumption is situated within a rational choice paradigm with a corresponding focus on purchasing behaviour and it is not considered to be an interactive, meaning-based activity. This model is best understood as an extension of the trade source information transmission logic that generally underpins trade mark doctrine. However, the assumption of a one-way flow of content is unsustainable in the branding context.

As the title to this chapter suggests, a dialogic or conversational model has greater explanatory potential instead. The second section investigates the co-creation of brands and the agency of consumers in their formation. It subsequently considers the implications of these ontological insights for normative debates, which is the other agenda pursued by this chapter. The manner in which the brand is conceived has implications for justifying

[8] By contrast, the interest in non-conventional mark registrations – shapes, colours, sounds, scents, tastes, texture and so on – has foregrounded the importance of representation techniques. See Robert Burrell and Michael Handler, 'Making Sense of Trade Mark Law' (2003) 4 *Intellectual Property Quarterly* 388; WIPO, 'Methods of Representation and Description of New Types of Marks' 29 March 2007 (SCT/17/2).

[9] Barton Beebe, 'The Semiotic Analysis of Trade Mark Law' (2004) 51 *UCLA Law Review* 621 at 625.

proprietary interests in it. Stated briefly, the broadcast model attributes image creation solely to the mark owner. Creation, including the components of effort and investment, is subsequently the basis for ownership. Yet the judicial recognition of brands is a controversial development. The scope of trade mark protection has steadily expanded in recent years and this expansion has been causally connected to the recognition of brand value. Concerns about a resultant imbalance are frequently articulated, when the interests of trade mark proprietors are privileged over those of competitors and consumers.[10] This leads to the following question: while brands have palpable social and economic value, why should this be recognised by granting additional proprietary rights to trade mark owners?[11] If the creation model is the proposed answer, is it up to the task?

These questions are worth pursuing, since there are compelling arguments ranged against expansive brand protection. Approaching this debate from the perspective of overall social welfare, some scholars suggest that the persuasive effects of brands grate against the core informational efficiency logic of trade mark law. They hinder rational purchasing decisions and distort competition.[12] Drawing on Pierre Bourdieu, Beebe has forcefully argued that enhanced brand protection is a form of sumptuary law, which seeks to reinforce processes of consumption-based social distinction by suppressing the revolutionary social and cultural

[10] Jennifer Davis, 'Between a Sign and a Brand: Mapping the Boundaries of a Registered Trade Mark in European Union Trade Mark Law' in Lionel Bently, Jane Ginsburg and Jennifer Davis (eds.), *Trade Marks and Brands: An Interdisciplinary Critique* (Cambridge University Press, 2008), p. 65 (describing pressures on the trade mark registration system to accommodate brand dimensions at the time of registration, which favours mark owners at the cost of competitor and consumer interests); Martin Senftleben, 'Trade Mark Protection: A Black Hole in the Intellectual Property Galaxy?' (2011) 42 *International Review of Intellectual Property Law* 383 at 384 ('The question, then, is whether the creation of a brand image should be rewarded with enhanced protection even though this is a selfish endeavour'); Mark P. McKenna, 'The Normative Foundations of Trade Mark Law' (2007) 82 *Notre Dame Law Review* 1839 at 1843 ('Modern [US] law … sees a mark itself as a repository for value and meaning, which may be deployed across a wide range of products and services. [It] amounts to little more than industrial policy intended to increase brand value').

[11] For criticisms of the 'if value, then right' proposition, which entails a normative commitment to the internalisation of all externalities arising from the use of an intangible, see Mark A. Lemley, 'Property, Intellectual Property, and Free Riding' (2005) 83 *Texas Law Review* 1031; Anne Barron, 'Copyright Infringement, "Free-Riding" and the Lifeworld' in Lionel Bently, Jennifer Davis and Jane C. Ginsburg (eds.), *Copyright and Piracy: An Interdisciplinary Critique* (Cambridge University Press, 2011), p. 93.

[12] Katya Assaf, 'Brand Fetishism' (2010) 43 *Connecticut Law Review* 83; Jeremy Sheff, 'Biasing Brands' (2010) 32 *Cardozo Law Review* 1245.

implications of increasingly powerful mimetic technology.[13] Meanwhile Katyal suggests that the ambit of cultural conversations is being constricted, since 'public spaces have become converted into vehicles for corporate advertising [and] the law has generously offered near-sovereign protection to such symbolism'. The time is ripe for semiotic disobedience, which requires the interruption, appropriation and substitution of branding messages through artistic practices.[14]

An emerging corpus of trade mark scholarship therefore attempts to reconcile the acceptance of brand value within trade mark doctrine with concerns about the ever expanding sphere of protection. This body of work recognises that brands are meaningful for consumers and valued by them. Yet it challenges the assumption of a passive consumer, instead valorising the interpretative agency and creative contributions of individual consumers as well as brand communities. Acknowledging trade marks in their brand incarnation need not commit us to a one-way ratchet of ever expanding protection and could instead result in improved doctrinal coherence as well as greater leeway for unauthorised referential activity by consumers or the general public.[15] However, this scholarship may not go far enough. Instead of favouring a carve-out for consumers, the argument in this chapter is directed further upstream. Since EU law has embraced the brand more fully than other legal regimes, are proprietary claims based on creation defensible in the first place? Drawing on recent work situating approaches to branding within the historical emergence of informational capital, the concluding part of the chapter outlines the processes by which the 'immaterial labour' of consumers involved in brand creation is recognised, yet co-opted. Acknowledging the extent to which consumers participate in the creation of both brand content and value allows us to fundamentally question the epistemic logic of the creation argument. The final section concludes.

[13] Barton Beebe, 'Intellectual Property Law and the Sumptuary Code' (2010) 123 *Harvard Law Review* 809.

[14] Sonia Katyal, 'Semiotic Disobedience' (2006) 84 *Washington University Law Review* 489.

[15] Deborah R. Gerhardt, 'Consumer Investment in Trade Marks' (2010) 88 *North Carolina Law Review* 427; Laura A. Heymann, 'The Law of Reputation and the Interest of the Audience' (2011) 52 *Boston College Law Review* 1341; Deven Desai, 'From Trade Marks to Brands' (2012) 64 *Florida Law Review* 981; Irina D. Manta, 'Hedonic Trade Marks', (2013) 74 *Ohio State Law Journal* 241. For an earlier and influential study advocating the public authorship of marks by drawing on literary criticism scholarship and the agency of readers, see Steven Wilf, 'Who Authors Trade Marks?' (1999) 17 *Cardozo Arts & Entertainment Law Journal* 1.

1 Branding and the CJEU: a managerial approach

1.1 Conventional perspectives on branding

A trade mark is a legally constituted sign, whose defining feature is that it is 'capable of distinguishing the goods or services of one undertaking from those of other undertakings'.[16] By contrast, a brand is notoriously difficult to define, since the attributes emphasised vary depending upon the perspective adopted. The mainstream marketing literature depicts it as an intangible asset and source of sustained competitive advantage. Kapferer settles for 'a name with power to influence buyers',[17] while Keller's definition circulates widely: 'a brand is a set of mental associations, held by the consumer, which add to the perceived value of a product or service.'[18] These associations should be unique to the brand as far as possible, have saliency or strength and be positive or desirable. Building brand equity – the capacity of a brand to generate value – is therefore 'about fostering a number of possible attachments around the brand, be these experiences, emotions, attitudes, lifestyles or, most importantly perhaps, loyalty. From a managerial perspective brand value represents the monetary value of what a brand can mean to consumers.'[19] Brands are valuable because they produce real world effects in the consumer decision-making process. Researchers have concluded that they 'have a positive influence on consumer choice, preferences and intention of purchase, their willingness to pay a price premium for the brand, accept brand extensions and recommend the brand to others'.[20] The processes generating these effects include both cognitive (mental associations) and affective (emotional associations) components. As regards the former, each brand is envisaged as the central node of an associative network constituted by consumers' learned connections between the brand and a variety of cues, benefits and symbolic meanings. This information can be absorbed into

[16] TRIPS Agreement (Agreement on Trade-Related Aspects of Intellectual Property Rights), Art. 15(1).

[17] Jean-Noel Kapferer, *The New Strategic Brand Management: Creating and Sustaining Brand Equity Long Term*, 4th edn (London: Kogan Page, 2008), p.11.

[18] Kevin L. Keller, *Strategic Brand Management: Building, Measuring, and Managing Brand Equity* (Upper Saddle River, NJ: Pearson Prentice Hall, 2008), cited by Kapferer, *The New Strategic Brand Management*, p. 10.

[19] Adam Arvidsson, 'Brands: A Critical Perspective' (2005) 5 *Journal of Consumer Culture* 235 at 238–9.

[20] Ana Belén del Río, Rodolfo Vázquez and Victor Iglesias, 'The Effects of Brand Associations on Consumer Response' (2001) 18 *Journal of Consumer Marketing* 410 at 413.

a cognitive schema, which in turn influences consumer attitudes and behaviour. Recalling the trade mark also invites the associated schema along for the ride.[21] Affect has a complementary role, since brands engage consumers at an emotional level and the subconscious or involuntary influence of emotions on consumer decision-making has important consequences, such as strengthening loyalty to the brand and building long-term relationships.[22]

This potential to influence conduct is reflected in the behavioural concept of the brand image. Situated within the associative network hypothesis, a brand image 'refers to the set of associations linked to the brand that consumers hold in memory'.[23] Once desirable product attributes or functions are removed from the equation, the brand image explains why individual purchases are made or ongoing relationships established with manufacturers. Alongside benefits and attitudes, brand attributes are an important category of brand associations that make up the image, consisting of the descriptive features that characterise a brand.[24] Typical examples would be ruggedness, youthful energy, sophistication or luxury. Different approaches exist to measure the impact of brand image (considering brands in isolation; or relative to competitors; or in relation to consumer self-image) as well as to fill in its content (ranging from quantitative methods to free verbalisations of associations through interviews).[25] Brand image may also provide the resources for individual and collective identity projects. Since consumers fabricate their identities within a market context, brands also signal social identity or status – compare those who drive reliable Toyotas with flashy Ferraris.[26] Brand

[21] Stijn M. J. van Osselaer and Joseph W. Alba, 'Consumer Learning and Brand Equity' (2000) 27 *Journal of Consumer Research* 1. For judicial recognition of this network of associations hypothesis, see *Cadbury Schweppes Pty. Ltd.* v. *Darrell Lea Chocolate Shops* [2007] FCAFC 70 at paras. 24–25. For a sustained critical engagement with this hypothesis within the trade mark law context, see Rebecca Tushnet, 'Gone in Sixty MilliSeconds: Trade Mark Law and Cognitive Science' (2008) 86 *Texas Law Review* 507.

[22] Laura R. Bradford, 'Emotion, Dilution and the Trade Mark Consumer' (2008) 23 *Berkeley Technology Law Journal* 1227.

[23] Kevin L. Keller, 'Conceptualizing, Measuring, and Managing Customer-Based Brand Equity' (1993) 57 *Journal of Marketing* 1 at 2.

[24] Belén del Río *et al.*, 'The Effects of Brand Associations', 411.

[25] See Dawn Dobni and George M. Zinkhan, 'In Search of Brand Image: A Foundation Analysis' in Marvin E. Goldberg, Gerald Gorn and R. W. Pollay (eds.), *Advances in Consumer Research – Volume 17* (Provo, UT: Association for Consumer Research, 1990), p. 110.

[26] Douglas Holt, *How Brands Become Icons* (Cambridge, MA: Harvard University Press, 2004) (for the general argument that brands become cultural icons only when they resonate with the identity projects of large groups of consumers).

image is considered to have additional traction where there is congruence with a consumer's own self-image.[27] However, 'the debate is ongoing as to whether an image is something that is conveyed or something that is received.'[28] Within the literature, this has led to the conceptual separation between (1) brand identity, as crafted and projected by corporate brand managers and (2) brand image, the subjective and perceptual impression that is formed through a process of interpretation in the minds of consumers. The possibility of identity and image being imperfectly aligned is a source of concern. 'According to the basic communications model, the company (source) encodes and sends a message to the consumer (receiver), who decodes the message based on his or her frame of reference ... A communication gap can exist if there is a discrepancy between the encoding and decoding processes.'[29] Even this potential gap can be dynamically managed or corrected, which reinforces the fundamental managerial assumption that sustains much of this marketing scholarship – brand managers, through a combination of experience, insight and strategic choices, can control the message.[30] Within this tradition: 'it is often assumed that the brand owner exerts considerable control over the brand. From this perspective, successful brand management becomes a matter of finding the brand's true and timeless essence and carrying out brand-building activities that will translate the identity into a corresponding brand image.'[31] Such thinking tracks the dominant approach to marketing in economics, which held sway until the late 1980s:

> Modern marketing logic, as derived from economics, advanced a view of the firm and the customer as separate and discrete; the customer is exogenous to the firm and is the passive recipient of the firm's active value creation efforts, and value is created in the factory.[32]

[27] Brian T. Parker, 'A Comparison of Brand Personality and Brand User-Imagery Congruence' (2009) 26 *Journal of Consumer Marketing* 175.

[28] Dobni and Zinkhan, 'In Search of Brand Image', p. 116.

[29] Shiva Nandan, 'An Exploration of the Brand Identity–Brand Image Linkage: A Communications Perspective' (2005) 12 *Journal of Brand Management* 264 at 265. See also Rajendra K. Srivastava and Gregory M. Thomas, 'Managing Brand Performance: Aligning Positioning Execution and Experience' (2010) 17 *Journal of Brand Management* 465.

[30] See generally, David Aaker and Erich Joachimsthaler, *Brand Leadership* (New York: Knopf, 2000).

[31] Anders Bengtsson and Jacob Ostberg, 'Researching the Cultures of Brands' in Russell W. Belk (ed.), *Handbook of Qualitative Research Methods in Marketing* (Cheltenham: Edward Elgar, 2006), pp. 83, 85.

[32] H. Jensen Schau, Albert M. Muñiz Jr. and Eric J. Arnould, 'How Brand Community Practices Create Value' (2009) 73 *Journal of Marketing* 30 at 30.

This approach has been challenged by an efflorescence of recent scholarship from within marketing itself, as well as consumer studies research incorporating sociological and anthropological approaches to consumption. A central insight reiterated by this body of work is that meaning as well as value creation for brands is located in consumer perceptions and practices.[33] Deven Desai characterises this as a split into 'two major dimensions. One, the corporate dimension, sees the brand as owned and controlled by the corporation and shaped by the marketer. The other, the noncorporate dimension, accepts that brands are social constructs driven by individuals at a personal level and communities at a social level.'[34] While we return to notions of consumer co-creation in section 3, the remainder of this section will demonstrate that European trade mark law adheres closely to the corporate or managerial approach to brands, by articulating the advertising, investment and communication functions of trade marks almost completely in terms of the agency of the trade mark proprietor. It has taken a further and decisive step towards recognising brand value by prohibiting free-riding on a brand image per se. The section concludes with an analysis of the presumptions and techniques relied upon by courts to work with this managerial concept of brands, within a broadcast or one-way information transmission model.

1.2 *The functional approach to brands within EU trade mark law*

The CJEU has approached the recognition of brand value tangentially and incrementally. After hinting for several years that trade marks perform other unspecified functions, the CJEU finally declared in *L'Oréal*:

> These functions include not only the essential function of the trade mark, which is to guarantee to consumers the origin of the goods or services, but also its other functions, in particular that of guaranteeing the quality of the goods or services in question and those of communication, investment or advertising.[35]

[33] *Ibid.* See also: Douglas B. Holt, 'How Consumers Consume: A Typology of Consumption Practices' (1995) 22 *Journal of Consumer Research* 1; Stephen L. Vargo and Robert S. Lusch, 'Evolving to a New Dominant Logic for Marketing' (2004) 68 *Journal of Marketing* 1; Leyland F. Pitt, Richard T. Watson, Pierre Berthon, Donald Wynn and George Zinkhan, 'The Penguin's Window: Corporate Brands from an Open-Source Perspective' (2006) 34 *Journal of Academy of Marketing Science* 115.

[34] Desai, 'From Trade Marks to Brands', 992.

[35] Case C-487/07 *L'Oréal SA* v. *Bellure NV* [2009] ETMR 55 at para. 58. The analysis has been confirmed on several occasions, including: Cases C-236/08, C-237/08 and C-238/08 *Google* v. *Louis Vuitton Malletier et al.* [2010] ETMR 30 (Grand Chamber)

The use of 'in particular' in the above quote suggests that this is not a closed list and new functions may be identified in the future.[36] On the one hand, *L'Oréal* can be seen as moving with the times and as a development that was overdue.[37] It seems artificial to restrict the legal understanding of trade mark functions to commercial source and consistent quality, when brands like Apple® form the basis for consumer communities, inspire tribal loyalties and are framed in the language of relationships rather than transactions.[38] On the other hand, there is some uncertainty as to the interactions and overlaps between these newly identified functions, as well as their content. Advocate General Jääskinen notes that there is 'no terminological or substantial consensus as to how the "functions" of the trade mark should be understood. The same goes for the conceptual relationships that exist between the various functions, especially whether some (or all) of the functions can actually be seen as included in the essential function that is to guarantee to consumers the origin of the goods or services.'[39] He concludes that the communication function operates as a

at para. 77; Case C-278/08 *Die BergSpechte Outdoor Reisen und Alpinschule Edi Koblmüller GmbH* v. *Günter Guni, trekking.at Reisen GmbH* [2010] ETMR 33 at para. 31; Case C-558/08 *Portakabin Ltd and Portakabin BV* v. *Primakabin BV* [2010] ETMR 52 at para. 30.

[36] Potential candidates are considered by Advocate General Trstenjak in Case C-482/09 *Budějovický Budvar* [2012] ETMR 2 at para. 63, n. 26 (AG) ('They include, according to legal writing on trade mark law, inter alia the coding, guarantee, origin, identification and individualisation, information and communication, monopolising, naming, quality, distinction, confidence, distribution and advertising functions, without the individual functions always having legal relevance').

[37] *Arsenal Football Club Plc* v. *Reed* [2002] ETMR 82 (AGO) at para. 46 (AG Colomer) ('It seems to me to be simplistic reductionism to limit the function of the trade mark to an indication of trade origin … The trade mark acquires a life of its own, making a statement, as I have suggested, about quality, reputation and even, in certain cases, a way of seeing life'); Jerre B. Swann 'An Interdisciplinary Approach to Brand Strength' (2006) *Trade Mark Reporter* 943 at 972 ('Just as trade marks have evolved, we have moved legally from source as king to the salience of quality; we should now move to brand imagery as an object of trade mark concern').

[38] See Albert M. Muñiz, Jr. and Thomas C. O'Guinn, 'Brand Community' (2001) 27 *Journal of Consumer Research* 412 (describing the Apple Macintosh 'community' using the markers of shared consciousness, rituals and traditions, and a sense of moral responsibility). In response, it is worth restating a question posed by Graeme Dinwoodie in 'Trade Marks and Territory: Detaching Trademark Law from the Nation-State' (2004) 41 *Houston Law Review* 885 at 889–90 (should 'trade mark law be structured *reactively* to protect whatever consumer understandings or producer goodwill develops, or should it *proactively* seek to shape the ways in which consumers shop and producers sell or seek to acquire rights, thus shaping how the economy functions?').

[39] Case C-324/09 *L'Oréal SA* v. *eBay* [2011] ETMR 52 at n. 20.

prerequisite and is therefore integrated into the other functions, such that it does not require separate consideration.[40]

In the face of this uncertainty, courts have begun the process of establishing the contours of these newer functions. The following paragraphs demonstrate that since they are perceived to stack cumulatively upon the essential function of indicating origin and this function was situated within a broadcast model, the same assumptions of one-way communication apply to them as well. Commencing with the essential or origin function, its identification preceded the enactment of the EU Trade Marks Directive.[41] It is the ability:

> [To] guarantee the identity of origin of the marked goods or services to the consumer or end user by enabling him, without any possibility of confusion, to distinguish the goods or services from others which have another origin. For the trade mark to be able to fulfil its essential role in the system of undistorted competition which the Treaty seeks to establish and maintain, it must offer a guarantee that all the goods or services bearing it have been manufactured or supplied under the control of a single undertaking which is responsible for their quality.[42]

The essential function was initially identified in the context of furthering the goals of a competitive common market. In *HAG-II*[43] the CJEU revisited the issue of whether national trade mark rights could operate as obstacles to the free movement of goods, leading to the artificial partitioning of markets. Here trade marks were justified as 'an essential element of the system of undistorted competition which the Treaty aims to establish and maintain. In such a system enterprises must be able to gain customers by the quality of their products or services, which can be done only by virtue of the existence of distinctive signs permitting identification of those products and services.'[44] Such marks would allow producers to signal reliable quality and consumers could depend upon these signs, since third parties would be prohibited from making unauthorised use of them. With the mark viewed as an information carrier, transmitted by producers and received by consumers, the origin function thus

[40] *Ibid.* at n. 58.

[41] First Council Directive 89/104/EEC of 21 December 1988 to Approximate the Laws of the Member States relating to Trade Marks, [1989] OJ L40/1. The substantive provisions under consideration remain unmodified in its successor, Directive 2008/95/EEC of 22 October 2008, [2008] OJ L299/25.

[42] *Arsenal* v. *Reed* [2003] ETMR 19 at para. 48 (CJEU).

[43] *Cnl-Sucal NV SA* v. *Hag GF AG* (C-10/89) [1990] ECR I-3711; [1990] 3 CMLR 571.

[44] *Ibid.* at para. 13.

facilitated a process of identification and choice.[45] As Advocate General Colomer described it: 'The *manufacturer gives the consumer information* in order to make him aware of the goods, and sometimes persuades him as well.'[46] It did not matter that consumers were unaware of the production location so long as they knew that an identifiable undertaking stood behind the product. Legal protection to preserve this broadly construed origin function would ensure that an uncluttered signal would reach the market, which accounts for the core infringement test being historically designed to prevent the likelihood of confusion.[47] Conceived in the context of market signalling and sustained by informational efficiency logic, the essential or origin function therefore clearly presumes a one-way flow of information from producers to consumers.

The 'guarantee of quality' function follows closely from the essential function and they are seen as two sides of the same coin. The 'mark is a sign to the customer both that the goods are the goods of a particular source (whether he knows or cares what that source is) and that the proprietor of the mark holds himself out as responsible for those goods and their quality. This representation of responsibility for quality is inseparable from the mark's function as an indication of source.'[48] While this is a signal of consistent, as opposed to minimum, quality, in theory it encourages producers to invest in maintaining or improving the quality of the underlying products.[49] Once we move beyond origin and quality, brand dimensions become more apparent. In *L'Oréal* itself, Advocate General Mengozzi addressed the communication function. Marks were 'a vehicle for providing consumers with various kinds of information on the goods identified by them', which included '"accumulated" information on the mark as a result of promotion and advertising carried out by the proprietor – for example, advertisements relating to non physical

45 *Memorandum on the Creation of an EEC Trade Mark* SEC (76) 2462 (6 July 1976) reprinted in (1976) 7 *International Review of Intellectual Property and Competition Law* 367 at paras. 12–14.

46 Case C-273/00 *Sieckmann* v. *Deutsches Patent- und Markenamt* [2005] CMLR 40 at para. AG19 (emphasis added).

47 The resultant increase of informational efficiency and the reduction of transaction (search) costs form the theoretical basis for law and economics justifications of trade mark protection. See William M. Landes and Richard A. Posner, 'Trade Mark Law: An Economic Perspective' (1987) 30 *Journal of Law and Economics* 265.

48 *Glaxo Group* v. *Dowelhurst* [2000] ETMR 415 at 425–26 (Ch) (Laddie J). See also *Parfums Christian Dior* v. *Evora* [1998] 1 CMLR 737 at para. AG41 (AG Jacobs).

49 Spyros M. Maniatis and Anselm Kamperman Sanders, 'A Consumer Trade Mark: Protection based on Origin and Quality' (1993) 11 *European Intellectual Property Review* 406.

characteristics which the image of the product or the company may generally be associated with (for example, quality, trustworthiness, reliability, etc.) or particular attributes (for example, a certain style, luxury, strength)'.[50] Thus construed, the communication function recognises that marks are semantically roomy enough to carry a range of promotional messages and this seems indistinguishable from a mere combination of the investment and advertising functions. Turning from the content to the nature of communication, the one-way model, which resonates closely with the managerial approach to branding, is evident in the reasoning of Advocate General Colomer:

> A trade mark is in reality communication ... Communication means one person imparting something that he knows to another. Consequently, every act of communication requires a sender, a message, a medium or channel for its transmission, and a recipient who can decipher or decode it. The code in which it can be expressed depends on the type of decoder the recipient uses to receive, comprehend and assimilate it. Homo sapiens is thus a recipient with a wide variety of decoders.[51]

As opposed to the ever implicit and arguably unnecessary communication function, the advertising function is relatively well established in EU doctrine. It has emerged across a series of cases that acknowledged that the positive reputation associated with a well-known mark deserved protection independently of whether the origin function was threatened; that is, even where consumers would not be confused by the defendant's use.[52] More recent decisions have overtly resorted to the language of brand image.[53] Thus, highly reputed marks 'frequently perform functions [beyond origin indication]. They present a powerful image of quality, exclusivity, youth, fun, luxury, adventure, glamour or other reputedly desirable lifestyle attributes, not necessarily associated with specific

[50] Case C-487/07 *L'Oréal SA* v. *Bellure NV* [2009] ETMR 55 at para. 54.

[51] Case C-273/00 *Sieckmann* v. *Deutsches Patent- und Markenamt* [2005] CMLR 40 at paras. AG19–AG20 (footnotes omitted).

[52] Reviewed in Ilanah Simon Fhima 'The Court of Justice's Protection of the Advertising Function of Trade Marks: an (Almost) Sceptical Analysis' (2011) 6 *Journal of Intellectual Property Law and Practice* 325.

[53] See for example *L'Oréal SA* v. *Bellure NV* [2007] ETMR 1 (Ch) at para. 99 (Lewison J) ('The proprietor of a trade mark has a legitimate interest in protecting the image that the registered mark represents'); *Datacard Corporation* v. *Eagle Technologies* [2011] EWHC 244 (Pat) [272] (Arnold J) ('[It] seems to me that the key point is that the advertising function of a trade mark is its function of conveying a particular image to the average consumer of the goods or services in question').

products but capable of presenting a strong marketing message in itself.'[54] This ability to convey 'images and feelings' gives reputed marks 'an inherent economic value which is independent of and separate from that of the goods or services for which it is registered ... [and] which deserves protection'.[55] The Grand Chamber of the CJEU observes that a trade mark proprietor may have the objective 'of using its mark for advertising purposes designed to inform and persuade consumers ... as a factor in sales promotion or as an instrument of commercial strategy'.[56] This is considered to be a legitimate objective that is granted legal protection.

Finally, this representation of positive qualities and the successful assemblage of a brand image is an expensive proposition, which is the cue for the investment function. Encouraging the investment required to develop a reputation is considered important because greater visibility serves as the engine for other functions.[57] The CJEU describes this as the investment 'to acquire or preserve a reputation capable of attracting consumers and retaining their loyalty'.[58] While it 'may overlap with the advertising function, it is nonetheless distinct from the latter', since not just advertising but also various 'commercial techniques' may be used to create and sustain this reputation.[59] Considered cumulatively, these newly acknowledged functions reflect the judicial recognition of trade marks as brands. Accordingly, these 'other functions are relevant in contemporary business life where trade marks *often acquire independent economic value as brands* that are used to communicate wider messages than the simple origin of goods or services'.[60]

Throughout this process, consumers are depicted as remarkably inert, functioning as little more than a living screen for image projection, while the process of creating associations is unambiguously unidirectional and linear. As presently conceived, these functions conveniently map onto a formalistic approach to 'three distinct stages of trade mark development:

[54] Case C-252/07 *Intel Corporation* v. *CPM United Kingdom Ltd* [2009] ETMR 13 at para. 8 (AG Sharpston).

[55] Case T-93/06 *Mülhens* v. *OHIM – Spa Monopole* [2008] ETMR 69 at para. 26.

[56] Cases C-236/08, C-237/08 and C-238/08 *Google* v. *Louis Vuitton Malletier et al.* [2010] ETMR 30 (Grand Chamber) at paras. 91–92.

[57] *Parfums Christian Dior* v. *Evora* [1998] 1 CMLR 737 at para. AG42 (AG Jacobs) ('Those functions are said to arise from the fact that the investment in the promotion of a product is built around the mark').

[58] Case C-323/09 *Interflora* v. *Marks and Spencer* [2012] ETMR 1 at para. 60.

[59] *Ibid.* at para. 61.

[60] Case C-324/09 *L'Oréal SA* v. *eBay* [2011] ETMR 52 at para. 46 (AG Jääskinen) (emphasis added).

the initial reservation of a sign with the help of trade mark law ("sign reservation"), the programming of the sign through advertising and quality control ("sign programming") and, finally, the creation of a potentially precious brand image that is the outcome of time and money spent on the two previous steps ("brand image creation")'.[61]

The immediate consequence of recognising the communication, advertising and investment functions is an expanding field of trade mark protection. Although these additional functions are perceived to rest upon the origin function,[62] it has now been established that they can be protected independently, even where the origin function is unaffected.[63] The CJEU has indicated that harm to these extended functions will be actionable in the context of a number of provisions of the Trade Marks Directive:

- Art. 7 – which stipulates the exhaustion of the proprietor's rights upon first sale of the goods, except where a legitimate interest (such as harm to functions) is threatened;[64]
- Art. 8(2) – licensors retaining rights to proceed against licensees in certain circumstances involving detriment to functions;[65]
- Art. 5(1)(a) – where the defendant is using an identical mark on identical goods or services and this interferes with the functions of the proprietor's mark;[66] and
- Art. 5(2) – trade mark dilution as a form of infringement, which consists of prohibitions on blurring, tarnishment and free-riding, all involving non-confusing yet allusive uses of marks and which recognises the full range of functions.[67]

[61] Martin Senftleben, 'The Trade Mark Tower of Babel – Dilution Concepts in International, US and EC Trade Mark Law' (2009) 40 *International Review of Intellectual Property and Competition Law* 45 at 46.

[62] *Memorandum on the Creation of an EEC Trade Mark* SEC (76) 2462 (6 July 1976) reprinted in (1976) 7 *International Review of Intellectual Property and Competition Law* 367 at para. 68; *Parfums Christian Dior* v. *Evora* [1998] 1 CMLR 737 at para. AG42.

[63] Max Planck Institute, *Study on the Overall Functioning of the European Trade Mark System* (2011) [hereinafter Max Planck Study] at para. 2.179.

[64] Case C-427/93 *Bristol-Myers Squibb* v. *Paranova* – [1996] ECR I-3457; *Parfums Christian Dior* v. *Evora* [1998] 1 CMLR 737.

[65] Case C-59/08 *Copad SA* v. *Christian Dior Couture SA* [2009] ECR I-3421.

[66] Case C-487/07 *L'Oréal SA* v. *Bellure NV* [2009] ETMR 55; Cases C-236/08, C-237/08 and C-238/08 *Google* v. *Louis Vuitton Malletier et al.* [2010] ETMR 30 (Grand Chamber).

[67] Case C-252/07 *Intel Corporation* v. *CPM United Kingdom Ltd* [2009] ETMR 13; Case C-487/07 *L'Oréal SA* v. *Bellure NV* [2009] ETMR 55; Case C-323/09 *Interflora* v. *Marks and Spencer* [2012] ETMR 1 at para. 50 (AG Jääskinen) (describing dilution as a 'property-based approach [that] also protects the communication, advertising and investment

Given their role in delimiting the scope of liability, there is concern that these brand-inspired functions have not been adequately theorised or delimited.[68] If doubts persist about the content of the advertising or investment functions, how should we determine when they are harmed? Ill-defined functions tend to lead to overbroad protection, uncertainty and a chilling effect on third party activities in practice.[69]

These developments have incrementally reoriented European trade mark law over the past two decades, moving it closer to full-fledged brand protection, and the decision in *L'Oréal* may be seen as the culmination of that process. L'Oréal had objected when a manufacturer of low-price smell-alike or replica perfumes resorted to look-alike packaging and the use of comparison lists to indicate olfactory equivalence with some of L'Oréal's leading brands for fine fragrances. No consumers were confused by this and the imitator was otherwise free to produce the perfumes, since they were not protected by other intellectual property rights. It was also established that alternative forms of detriment to L'Oréal's mark, such as detriment to distinctiveness (blurring) or detriment to repute (tarnishment) were not in issue. L'Oréal claimed this amounted to the taking of unfair advantage under Art. 5(2) of the Directive[70] and the CJEU was asked to interpret this provision.[71] A specific issue was whether any advantage-taking was deemed to be unfair, or did 'unfair' have independ-

functions of trade marks with a view of [*sic*] creating a brand with a positive image and independent economic value (brand equity or good will)').

[68] It has recently been recommended to the Commission that these additional functions be identified and clarified in the Preamble to the Directive. See Max Planck Study at para. 2.187. See also *Interflora* v. *Marks and Spencer* [2010] EWHC 925 (Ch) at para. 18 (referring to concerns by the Commission that the precise scope of the exclusive rights afforded by Art. 5(1)(a) are ambiguous, because the underlying functions it seeks to protect are unclear).

[69] Max Planck Study at [2.187]; A. Horton, 'The Implications of *L'Oréal v Bellure* – a Retrospective and a Looking Forward: The Essential Functions of a Trade Mark and When is an Advantage Unfair?' [2011] *EIPR* 550 (asking what 'is meant by the communication, investment and advertising functions of a mark? These are unclear and undefined concepts which offer no certainty to businesses').

[70] In the relevant part, it provides 'the proprietor shall be entitled to prevent all third parties not having his consent from using in the course of trade any sign which is identical with, or similar to, the trade mark in relation to goods or services ... where the latter has a reputation in the Member State and where use of that sign without due cause takes unfair advantage of, or is detrimental to, the distinctive character or the repute of the trade mark'.

[71] For an in-depth discussion of the case, see Dev Gangjee and Robert Burrell, 'Because You're Worth It: *L'Oréal* and the Prohibition on Free Riding' (2010) 73 *Modern Law Review* 282.

ent substantive content and require (say) that there was some detriment accompanying the free-riding? The CJEU responded as follows:

> [Where] a third party attempts, through the use of a sign similar to a mark with a reputation, to ride on the coat-tails of that mark in order to benefit from its power of attraction, its reputation and its prestige, and to exploit, without paying any financial compensation and without being required to make efforts of his own in that regard, *the marketing effort expended by the proprietor of that mark in order to create and maintain the image of that mark*, the advantage resulting from such use must be considered to be an advantage that has been unfairly taken of the distinctive character or the repute of that mark.[72]

By prohibiting conduct that allows the defendant to benefit from someone else's brand image and reputation, regardless of any harm to the image, the court has in effect recognised the brand as an independent object of proprietary rights. It is the equivalent of a 'keep off the grass' sign for a patch of semiotic space and allows the proprietor of a reputed mark to prevent third parties from using the same or a similar sign where such use is likely to take advantage of positive brand associations. While the brand is the object of property rights, the creation and maintenance of this attractive image, through investment and marketing effort, is the apparent basis for such legal recognition. The creation argument is otherwise generally underdeveloped in trade mark law scholarship, since this area has historically evolved from deception prevention foundations and subsequently transitioned into utilitarian logic. Formerly descriptive terms (BRITISH AIRWAYS) or family names (HARRODS) – that is not very innovative or creative subject matter[73] – may nevertheless work well as source indicators. The few scholars who do consider creation-based rationales situate them within a specific epistemic tradition (for example Lockean labour) usually derived from the real property context,[74] but the ECJ has provided us with scant guidance as to the source of its inspiration.

[72] Case C-487/07 *L'Oréal SA* v. *Bellure NV* [2009] ETMR 55 at para. 49 (emphasis added).

[73] Case 40/70 *Sirena Srl* v. *Eda Srl* [1971] ECR 69, [1971] CMLR 260 (AG de Lamothe), 264–265 (whilst acknowledging the investment in advertising, the Advocate General observed: 'If it is considered from the point of view of humanity, certainly the debt that society owes to the "inventor" of the name "Prep Good Morning" [a brand of shaving cream] is not of the same nature (this is the least that may be said) as that which humanity has contracted with the "inventor" of penicillin').

[74] See for example Spyros Maniatis, 'Trade Mark Rights – A Justification Based on Property' (2002) 2 *IPQ* 123; Mohammad Naser, 'Rethinking the Foundations of Trade Marks' (2007) 5 *Buffalo Intellectual Property Law Journal* 1.

1.3 *The doctrinal mechanics of brand image*

While image creation has been attributed solely to the efforts of the trade mark proprietor, the brand image is portrayed as something bounded and stable enough to be appropriated. The paradigm case of unfair advantage – also referred to as free-riding or parasitism – is identified by the Court in the following terms:

> It covers, in particular, cases where, by reason of a transfer of the image of the mark or of the characteristics which it projects to the goods identified by the [defendant's use of an] identical or similar sign, there is clear exploitation on the coat-tails of the mark with a reputation.[75]

The image transference therefore constitutes the advantage. Much of the subsequent analysis of *L'Oréal* has been concerned with the lack of any content for the 'unfair' component,[76] described as the appropriation of a benefit without any independent effort by the defendant or recompense to the brand owner. The stated approach adopts an atomistic, arguably neoliberal worldview characterised by unaided individual effort, when social existence and even marketplace activity inevitably involves give and take.[77] For the purposes of this chapter, it is the relatively unexplored mechanics of the 'advantage' dimension that is of interest, because it is here that the brand – as closed and transferrable object – should be most visible.

When applying the test, the legal analysis proceeds in two stages. First, courts must establish whether a link, in the form of a mental association or bringing to mind, is likely to be triggered due to the similarity between the two signs in dispute.[78] Second, an open-ended multifactor test is applied to determine whether the transfer is likely as a result of this link. The CJEU requires that 'national courts will have to undertake a global assessment based on factors including the degree of distinctiveness and

[75] Case C-487/07 *L'Oréal SA* v. *Bellure NV* [2009] ETMR 55 at para. 41.

[76] For criticism, see for example *L'Oréal SA* v. *Bellure NV* [2010] EWCA Civ 535 at paras. 49–50; Gangjee and Burrell, 'Because You're Worth It'. For attempts to give substance to this requirement, considering factors such as the defendant's intention to imitate, or the defendant's own reputation as a counterweight, see Ilanah Simon Fhima, *Trade Mark Dilution in the European Union and the United States* (Oxford University Press, 2010) at paras. 6.43–6.57; Horton, 'The Implications of *L'Oréal v Bellure*'.

[77] For a law and economics based critique of this worldview, see Mark Lemley and Mark McKenna, 'Owning Mark(et)s' (2010) 109 *Michigan Law Review* 137.

[78] The factors to establish this link were identified in Case C-252/07 *Intel Corporation* v. *CPM United Kingdom Ltd* [2009] ETMR 13 at paras. 41–61.

reputational strength of the claimant's mark, the similarity between the marks and proximity between the goods, as well as the immediacy of the mental linkage between the claimant and defendant's signs'.[79] In effect, the test resorts to categories of circumstantial evidence, leading to conjecture as to whether an image transfer is likely. Early indications suggest that the factors driving outcomes are the strength of the link between the two marks, the extent to which there is an overlap between the claimant's and defendant's customers and the existence of a nexus between both sets of goods.[80] In many of these cases, an intentional allusion to the reputed mark is evident and one mark may very well call another to mind. Whether the image transfer occurs with mechanical predictability is less certain and an alternative explanation may have more to do with the moral disapprobation directed towards those copying another's mark.[81] Consider the following two illustrations, where the image transfer theory was applied.

A trade mark registration for ROYAL SHAKESPEARE, used for non-alcoholic as well as alcoholic drinks and bar or restaurant services, was successfully invalidated by the Royal Shakespeare Company (RSC), based on its ROYAL SHAKESPEARE COMPANY mark.[82] The junior user claimed that the perceived reference for the mark would be the immortal bard, as opposed to the RSC. It also asked, quite reasonably, how a reputation and image associated with high quality theatre productions could transfer across to bar and restaurant services, when consumers were clear that the disputants were unrelated commercial undertakings.[83] In response, the General Court emphasised the RSC's exceptional reputation, the fact that the relevant publics would overlap, the existence of a strong mental association between the two marks and concluded that despite the apparent dissimilarity between the products and services offered, a viable nexus existed since it 'is common practice, in theatres, for bar and catering services to be offered either side of and in the interval of a performance'.[84] Since the circumstantial factors favoured the RSC,

[79] Case C-487/07 *L'Oréal SA* v. *Bellure NV* [2009] ETMR 55 at para. 45.

[80] Ilanah Simon Fhima and Robin Jacob 'Unfair Advantage Law in the European Union' in D. Bereskin (ed.), *International Trade Mark Dilution* (Thomson Reuters, 2013), p. 243.

[81] An issue considered in Mark Bartholomew, 'Trade Mark Morality' (2013) *William & Mary Law Review* [forthcoming]. Available at: http://ssrn.com/abstract=2227106 (last accessed 5 April 2013).

[82] Case T-60/10 *Jackson International Trading Co. Kurt D. Brühl GmbH & Co. KG* v. *OHIM – ROYAL SHAKESPEARE* [2012] ECR II-0000.

[83] *Ibid.* at para. 52. [84] *Ibid.* at paras. 57–60.

an image transfer was deemed likely. A more speculative application of the *L'Oréal* test is found in *You-Q BV*.[85] The senior mark was the name of the famous band, the Beatles, registered for various goods. The junior mark was BEATLE, applied for use with mobility scooters, wheelchairs and related equipment. The senior mark's image was 'even after fifty years of existence, still synonymous with youth and a certain counter-culture of the 1960s, an image which is still positive and could still benefit the [applicant's] goods'.[86] This could be of benefit in relation to mobility equipment 'since the relevant public, on account specifically of the handicap in question, would be particularly attracted by the very positive image of freedom, youth and mobility associated with the earlier marks'.[87] The conclusion is worth restating, to emphasise its incongruity: it is likely that a mobility scooter manufacturer is successfully misappropriating the Beatles' image.[88] The test seems designed to encourage a finding of unfair advantage based on the suspicion that where one mark brings another to mind, some form of brand pilferage is taking place. This in turn presumes that brand image, as an object, is stable enough to be pilfered. A speculative approach is further encouraged by the relatively low threshold requirement, since the test can accommodate the likelihood of unfair advantage, as opposed to looking for empirically grounded evidence of an actual image transfer. The CJEU has recently confirmed that the claimant needs to adduce prima facie evidence of a future risk that is not hypothetical, and this can be established 'on the basis of logical deductions made from an analysis of the probabilities and by taking account of the normal practice in the commercial sector as well as all the other circumstances of the case'.[89] No claimant need ever submit actual proof of brand image transference.

Apart from these circumstantial evidence factors, there is no further guidance on how the content of brand image is to be divined. When it

[85] Case (T-369/10) *You-Q BV* v. *OHIM* – BEATLE [2012] E.C.R. II-0000. The General Court's decision has been appealed to the ECJ.

[86] *Ibid.* at para. 71. [87] *Ibid.* at para. 72.

[88] This vast oversimplification is at odds with the extensive scholarship on the Beatles, the processes contributing to their image and their cultural significance. See K. Womack and T. F. Davis (eds.), *Reading the Beatles: Cultural Studies, Literary Criticism, and the Fab Four* (Albany: SUNY Press, 2006), p. 1 ('The reasons behind the phenomenon of the Beatles and their sustained success are as multifarious and as eminently complex as Western culture itself').

[89] Case C-100/11 *Helena Rubinstein SNC and L'Oréal SA* v. *OHIM* [2012] ETMR 40 at para.96.

comes to detailing this content, it is helpful to unpack the notion of reputation a little further. It has two dimensions in trade mark litigation – quantitative and qualitative. Satisfying the former is a threshold condition for unfair advantage claims and requires quantitative evidence of the visibility and consumer awareness of a mark (how many people are familiar with it). There is judicial guidance for this aspect.[90] However, there is a lack of corresponding guidance for determining the qualitative dimension of reputation, which relates to brand image. In practice, this evidence is usually provided by the trade mark owner, often in the form of witness statements from employees responsible for marketing. Thus before the trial judge in *L'Oréal*, the image of one of the high-end fragrances was established by the trade mark owner in the following terms:

> Trésor's image in the United Kingdom is that of a beautiful traditional fragrance with a classic elegant scent. It is particularly popular among customers aged more than 35 (whom Lancôme classify as 'older' customers).[91]

By contrast, for the Miracle perfume it was accepted that the 'brand concept focuses on positive values and is underlined by the name and advertising of the product with modern and fresh imagery. It is popular among younger customers.'[92] Another illustration is found in a dispute over the use of comparative advertising between providers of prescription glasses, where the mark owner's marketing director gave evidence that 'included Specsavers' marketing spend and the messages that Specsavers sought to communicate by it – value, style and professionalism/quality'.[93] As a result, the imagery is presumed to be solely the brand owner's creation. The assumption that brand identity, as fashioned by mark owners, translates into brand image, as received by consumers, has been successfully transplanted from the conventional marketing literature into the legal domain. The approach is unabashedly Fordist, since an allusive reference is presumed to generate behavioural effects in consumers and result in increased sales for the defendant. Throughout this analysis, the relevant public is a legal construct and a conveniently passive one at that.

[90] Case C-375/97 *General Motors Corp.* v. *Yplon SA* [1999] ECR I-5421, [2000] RPC 572; Case C-301/07 *Pago* v. *Tirolmilch* [2009] ECR I-9429, [2010] ETMR 5.

[91] *L'Oréal SA* v. *Bellure NV* [2007] ETMR 1 (Ch) (Lewison J) at para. 17.

[92] *Ibid.* at para. 19.

[93] *Specsavers* v. *Asda* [2010] EWHC 2035 (Ch) at para. 12.

2 Brands and consumers: co-creation or immaterial labour?

2.1 Co-creation and the celebration of consumer agency

As matters presently stand, an authorial relationship with brand image is the basis for proprietary claims over its associative content and economic value. The broadcast model, building upon informational efficiency foundations, attributes this authorship to the trade mark owner. Yet to what extent are these interlinked claims valid? There is much to be learned from recent scholarship on branding, which provides both empirical evidence and alternative theoretical perspectives as to the respective roles of trade mark owners, consumers and others involved in the process of branding. The fault lines are evident at an early stage. To begin with, the process itself is viewed as dialectical and iterative, as opposed to a one-way broadcast. The point of departure is that since the brand is generated in the minds of consumers, corporate control over its content has always been brittle. Its content is negotiated, context-sensitive and constantly reproduced.[94] As the symbolic, social and cultural aspects of consumption have come to be better understood,[95] the consumer's investment of time, creativity and effort into this process of negotiation is better appreciated. Today 'co-creation of value is emerging as the new frontier and leading edge in marketing thought. It is quickly gaining currency as one of the most provocative, paradigm shifting, and practical ideas in the field.'[96] This transition in marketing is traced to influential work on co-creation by C. K. Prahalad and Venkataram Ramaswamy,[97] as well as to the related notion of 'service-dominant logic' adopted by Stephen Vargo and Robert Lusch.[98] As Prahalad and Ramaswamy describe it:

> The meaning of value and the process of value creation are rapidly shifting from a product- and firm-centric view to personalized consumer experiences. Informed, networked, empowered, and active consumers

[94] Pierre Berthon, Leyland F. Pitt and Colin Campbell, 'Does Brand Meaning Exist in Similarity or Singularity?' (2009) 62 *Journal of Business Research* 356.

[95] Research addressing these aspects is often associated with the label of Consumer Culture Theory. See Eric J. Arnould and Craig J. Thompson, 'Consumer Culture Theory (CCT): Twenty Years of Research' (2005) 31 *Journal of Consumer Research* 868.

[96] Dan Fisher and Scott Smith, 'Cocreation is Chaotic: What it Means for Marketing when No One Has Control' (2011) 11 *Marketing Theory* 325 at 326.

[97] C. K. Prahalad and Venkatram Ramaswamy, 'Co-opting Customer Competence' (2000) 78 *Harvard Business Review* 79; C. K. Prahalad, 'The Co-creation of Value' (2004) 68 *Journal of Marketing* 23.

[98] Vargo and Lusch, 'Evolving to a New Dominant Logic for Marketing'.

> are increasingly cocreating value with the firm. The interaction between the firm and the consumer is becoming the locus of value creation and value extraction.[99]

According to a recent survey, the 'roots of collaborative marketing approaches reside in innovation and design studies that view users as a company's potential collaborators – in line with the concept of lead users … They also derive from service marketing studies … which view the co-production of services as the basis for servuction systems (i.e. production of services).'[100] In the remainder of this chapter I will briefly introduce collaborative marketing research that has begun to address the following two questions in an empirically rich and theoretically nuanced manner: (1) Who creates brands? (2) How is value added by the consumer, increasingly referred to as a participant or stakeholder?[101] However, the chapter concludes by moving beyond this literature, since the practitioner-driven practices of collaborative marketing ultimately seek to manage or co-opt consumers as a form of governmentality. A much needed critical edge is provided by perspectives characterising such brand value creation as unpaid, 'immaterial labour'. Acknowledging consumption as meaningfully productive, within the context of a broader critique of informational capital, provides us with the resources to contest creation-based claims resting on sole authorship of brand image, which otherwise seek to appropriate its full exchange value.

In response to the first question, the assertion that corporations are the sole authors of successful brands is relatively easy to destabilise. Despite the best efforts of marketers, the majority of new brand propositions fail, with the disastrous attempts to introduce 'New Coke' in the USA in the 1980s being a favoured cautionary tale. When Coca Cola changed the formula to an alternative based on corn syrup as opposed to cane sugar that tasted better in blind taste tests, there was a consumer rebellion since it was not perceived as 'the real thing'. The company recanted.[102] Qualitative research indicates that brands have multiple authors and identifying these

99 C. K. Prahalad and Venkatram Ramaswamy, 'Co-Creation Experiences: The Next Practice in Value Creation' (2004) 18 *Journal of Interactive Marketing* 5 at 5.

100 Bernard Cova and Veronique Cova 'On the Road to Prosumption: Marketing Discourse and the Development of Consumer Competencies' (2012) 15 *Consumption Markets & Culture* 149 at 154 (citing to the work on lead users and open innovation by Eric von Hippel in this context).

101 See for example Anne Gregory, 'Involving Stakeholders in Developing Corporate Brands: The Communication Dimension' (2007) 23 *Journal of Marketing Management* 59.

102 Gerhardt, 'Consumer Investment in Trade Marks', 450–3; Desai, 'From Trade Marks to Brands', 983.

co-authors, within a field of asymmetric power relations, is an ongoing project. According to Douglas Holt, one of the leading proponents of a contextual approach to branding, strong or iconic brands – those doctrinally recognised as being most deserving of enhanced trade mark protection – are collaboratively authored by four categories of agents. They are: (i) companies, who are trade mark proprietors, (ii) the culture industries, (iii) intermediaries, such as critics and salespeople, and (iv) customers as individuals, but more significantly as communities.[103] As opposed to the perceptions of individual consumers that are prioritised in the information transmission model, for a cultural perspective locating brands within the context of social processes is of fundamental importance. It is only when the brand image is collectively shared that it becomes accepted as an everyday truth, which requires that the public must invest the brand with meaning before it gains in cultural salience. Holt follows up on this categorisation with a more detailed study on the contributions of culture industries in subsequent research on JACK DANIEL'S Tennessee whiskey. Image-rich, iconic brands achieve this status 'when they are woven into the most potent ideological currents in society. The power of Jack Daniel's symbolism came from its articulation to the gunfighter myth.'[104] This myth in turn facilitated its adoption by the military as the whiskey of choice; by celebrity male drinkers such as movie stars renowned for their 'masculinity'; and by journalists emphasising its rugged, frontier-facing image. He concludes:

> Cultural products other than brands – including films, television programs, politicians, sports teams, and novels – do the ideological heavy lifting in modern culture, reconstructing myths to pioneer emerging ideals, creating ... myth markets. Brand marketing laps up what these other media produce ... In sum, iconic brands are *ideological parasites*. Brands succeed in becoming powerful cultural symbols when they tag along on emerging myth markets led by far more potent cultural forms (films, books, sports, politics and so forth).[105]

Depicting brands as free-riders in this way is an apt riposte to the logic of *L'Oréal*, which implausibly champions the possibility of hermetically contained and self-sufficient brand creation. Another empirical study of a Finnish footwear brand identifies eight different roles for the multiple

[103] Holt, *How Brands Become Icons*, p. 3.

[104] Douglas B. Holt, 'Jack Daniel's America: Iconic Brands as Ideological Parasites and Proselytizers' (2006) *Journal of Consumer Culture* 355 at 373.

[105] *Ibid.* at 374 (emphasis added).

parties involved in the co-construction of the brand: *messenger* (including word-of-mouth promotion by consumers), *entertainer* (such as songwriters or artistes who reinterpret and integrate the brand within cultural practices), *watchdog*, *authoriser*, *storyteller*, *champion* (prominent persons who adopt the brand, including entertainers and in this case war veterans), *connector* and *director*.[106] As opposed to the CJEU's endorsement of the corporate projection of sharply defined brand image, marketing researchers propose that the range of authors and diversity of meaning-making practices makes it preferable to work with the notion of a brand gestalt consisting of multiple brand meanings or brand images associated with the same trade mark.[107] While 'the work of describing how brands are co-created with their stakeholders has barely begun',[108] the awareness that brands are co-authored is now well established.

Turning from the identity of the participants to the question of value addition, the 'social science literature indicates that many variables contribute to trade mark value'.[109] From the perspective of consumer or user authorship, social communication adds value to brands and recent technological developments have greatly facilitated such interaction. This communication is particularly pronounced in brand communities, which have the important function of circulating information about brands,[110] and in some cases facilitating innovation by drawing upon an expert knowledge base.[111] In terms of what consumers actually do, Närvänen observes that they not only 'co-create the brand meaning, but also branding activities themselves. The activities can range from communication to product and service development, creating unique brand experiences and even engaging in public relations management.'[112] The authors of an in-depth study across nine brand communities conclude that there are twelve common practices across brand communities, through which consumers

[106] Elina Närvänen, 'The Brand as a Cultural Network Hub: Acknowledging Multiple Parties in Branding' in *Proceedings of the 21st Nordic Conference on Business Studies: NFF 2011 A Practice About Practice* (Stockholm University School of Business, 2011), p. 1.

[107] Nina Diamond, John F. Sherry, Albert M. Muñiz Jr, MaryAnn McGrath, Robert V. Kozinets and Stefania Borghini, 'American Girl and the Brand Gestalt: Closing the Loop on Sociocultural Branding Research' (2009) 73 *Journal of Marketing* 118.

[108] Mary Jo Hatch and Majken Schulz, 'Toward a Theory of Brand Co-Creation with Implications for Brand Governance' (2010) 17 *Journal of Brand Management* 590 at 591.

[109] Gerhardt, 'Consumer Investment in Trade Marks', 449.

[110] Muñiz and O'Guinn, 'Brand Community'.

[111] Johann Fuller, Kurt Matzler and Melanie Hoppe, 'Brand Community Members as a Source of Innovation' (2008) 25 *Journal of Product Innovation Management* 608.

[112] Närvänen, 'The Brand as a Cultural Network Hub', p. 6.

realise value beyond that which the firm creates or anticipates. They also find that practices interact with one another, function like apprenticeships, endow participants with cultural capital, produce a repertoire for insider-sharing, generate consumption opportunities, evince brand community vitality and create value.[113] Thus within the broader analytical category of impression management, it was observed that consumers 'justify' or develop rationales for devoting time and effort to the brand aimed at outsiders or marginal brand community members. Within this category, they also 'evangelise' or preach from the mountain top to gain new converts. They also observe practices of 'customising' within the category of brand use, such as efforts to modify the factory specifications of a product in order to enhance performance or personalise it. While technology – and web-based technologies in particular – have facilitated brand community formation, consumers also influence brands by sharing information more generally:

> In the participatory world of Web2.0 ... millions of common people have started publishing their own brand-related content. As evidenced by YouTube videos, Facebook groups, Twitter messages, Wikipedia articles, Amazon book reviews and other social media activities, such amateur pieces may achieve significant reach.[114]

A related body of scholarship that analyses consumer investment is concerned with brands as the symbolic raw material of individual and group identity formation.[115] Much of this research is situated with the broader agendas of Consumer Culture Theory.[116] Consumer culture theory scholarship is interested in the active reworking and transformation of the messages encoded in advertisements, brands and retail settings by consumers to further their identity projects and lifestyle goals, even if these goals are sometimes tacit and internally contradictory.[117] Even this brief outline suggests that significant aspects of brand image content formation and value creation occur outside of the direct control of the brand owner. En

[113] Schau *et al.*, 'How Brand Community Practices Create Value'.

[114] Editorial, 'A Call for "User-Generated Branding"' (2010) 18 *Journal of Brand Management* 1 at 1 (internal citations omitted).

[115] An influential work is Richard Elliot and Kritsadarat Wattanasuwan, 'Brands as Symbolic Resources for the Construction of Identity' (1998) 17 *International Journal of Advertising* 131.

[116] For a useful literature review, see Arnould and Thompson, 'Consumer Culture Theory', 871–3.

[117] See generally, A. F. Firat and N. Dholakia, *Consuming People: From Political Economy to Theaters of Consumption* (London: Routledge, 1998).

route to displacing the single author brand creation model, this research also undermines any attempts to develop an incentive-based rationale for the grant of property rights in brands. Brand development is driven by a range of motivations and practices, associated with a number of different actors, many of whom are unconcerned by the absence of a formal property framework and nevertheless create significant value.

2.2 *Informational capitalism and immaterial labour: everyday life and economic value*

While the tone for much of this co-creation scholarship is upbeat and appears to celebrate the agency, capacity and independence of consumers, it has also been subjected to thoughtful critiques. If co-creation makes descriptive claims about the extent of consumer value addition and the limits of corporate authorship, the critique has a more overtly normative dimension. This chapter is not the appropriate canvas for a detailed account of this critique and I can only present the flavour of the arguments, as well as highlight their significance for trade mark law. An excellent entry point is provided by Adam Arvidsson:

> [Brands] should be understood as the institutional embodiment of a new form of informational capital – much like the factory embodied the logic of industrial capital. Brand management is a matter of putting to work the capacity of consumers (and increasingly other kinds of actors to produce a common social world through autonomous processes of communication and interaction … Like informational capital in general brands extract value by putting to work the very basic human capacity to create a common social world.[118]

Viewed through the lens of a Marxist and Neo-Marxist perspective, contemporary branding practices transform everyday life into economic value. This critique of brands is situated within the broader interrogation of 'informational' or 'digital' capitalism, which is concerned with immaterial, informational production rather than industrial production. The current iteration of capitalism blurs the distinctions between production and consumption, such that the production process now relies on and appropriates sources of value from a series of activities that used to be regarded as consumption and are considered externalities. Social knowledge is exploited with increasing frequency and this knowledge may

[118] See the Preface to Adam Arvidsson, *Brands: Meaning and Value in Media Culture* (New York and London: Routledge, 2006).

consist of 'different forms, contacts and "social capital", fads, fashions or style and image "capital"'.[119]

This critique also addresses the putting to work of communication, whereupon the concept of 'immaterial labour' becomes relevant. It has been described as the labour that produces the informational and cultural content of the commodity,[120] as well as labour that 'creates immaterial products, such as knowledge, information, communication, a relationship, or an emotional response'.[121] This kind of labour produces important immaterial or symbolic qualities of goods and in many instances it is free, both in the sense of not being paid for and being unsupervised. The 'productivity of immaterial labour builds on the ability of human communication to produce a surplus sociality' such as a shared meaning that was not there before.[122] In the case of consumers, 'consumption produces a common in the form of a community, a shared identity or even a short lived "experience" that adds dimensions of use-value to the [brand]'.[123] To bring this invisible labour to light, a new terminology is being developed, including labels such as the 'working consumer'. Ignoring these consumer-driven social processes runs the risk of further entrenching unequal relations. 'Producers receive the revenue derived from the market, while consumers do not. Besides, although they do not produce in the traditional sense, consumers do work. They are active in the value creation process through immaterial labour and primary (direct) social relationships.'[124]

According to its critics, the co-creation agenda is problematic since it is ultimately restricted to being a strategic response to the active consumer, in the form of subtler and less directive mechanisms of control. Drawing on Foucault's notion of government, it has been suggested that:

> co-creation represents a political form of power aimed at generating particular forms of consumer life at once free and controllable, creative and docile. [It] stands for a notion of modern corporate power that is no longer aimed at disciplining consumers and shaping actions according to a given

119 *Ibid.*, p. 9.

120 Maurizio Lazzarato, 'Immaterial Labor' in Paulo Virno and Michael Hardt (eds.), *Radical Thought in Italy: A Potential Politics* (Minneapolis: University of Minnesota Press, 1996), p. 133.

121 Michael Hardt and Antonio Negri, *Multitude: War and Democracy in the Age of Empire* (New York: Penguin 2004), p. 108.

122 Arvidsson, *Brands: Meaning and Value*, p. 10.

123 Arvidsson 'Brands: A Critical Perspective', at 242.

124 Bernard Cova and Daniele Dalli, 'Working Consumers: the Next Step in Marketing Theory?' (2009) 9 *Marketing Theory* 315 at 315.

> norm, but at working with and through the freedom of the consumer. In short, administering consumption in ways that allow for the continuous emergence and exploitation of creative and valuable forms of consumer labor.[125]

There is genuine concern that co-creation's programmatic agenda is directed towards 'establishing ambiences that program consumer freedom to evolve in ways that permit the harnessing of consumers' newly liberated, productive capabilities'.[126]

By formalistically attributing sole authorship to trade mark proprietors and propertising the brand dimensions of trade marks, EU trade mark law legitimates this collapsing of social communication into production, of use value into exchange value. The CJEU's juridical transformation of trade marks into brands reinforces the process by which the immaterial labour of consumers is rationalised, measured and commodified. Its doctrinal approach reinforces the exploitation of consumers and others involved in brand creation by editing them out of the narrative and it is therefore normatively unattractive. It is also premised on assumptions relating to brand authorship that are being reconsidered and rejected within the marketing profession. A property model based on the unaided efforts of the individual mark owner in shaping and sustaining brand image looks increasingly unconvincing. Before concluding, there is one further insight that this critique may suggest to an IP audience. Both the co-creation scholarship and its critique find common ground in the appreciation of brands as open-ended constructs, renewed by social communication processes. This suggests that we may be reaching for the wrong metaphors when characterising brands in legal discourse. It is instead possible to reconceive of brands as a commons or elements of the public domain,[127] but this is a possibility to be pursued in future research.

3 Conclusion

The judicial recognition of the brand as *res* in trade mark doctrine serves as a reminder that intangible objects give rise to property description

[125] Detlev Zwick, Samuel K. Bonsu and Aron Darmody, 'Putting Consumers to Work: "Co-creation" and New Marketing Govern-mentality' (2008) 8 *Journal of Consumer Culture* 163 at 163.

[126] *Ibid.* at 166.

[127] On the generative significance of the public domain for Intellectual Property regimes, see James Boyle, *The Public Domain: Enclosing the Commons of the Mind* (London and New York: Yale University Press, 2008).

issues that are distinct from the law of real property. Foregrounding the underlying doctrinal assumptions and legal techniques for working with such intangibles is therefore illuminating for both conceptual and normative reasons. For those who favour a balanced trade mark regime, where the interests of mark owners are accommodated alongside those of competitors, consumers and the general public, the CJEU's uncritical embrace of the brand dimension of reputed marks is a cause for concern. In approaching the brand dimension through trade mark functions, which cumulatively rest upon the origin function, the Court has – perhaps inadvertently – aligned itself with a managerial approach to branding based on a Fordist paradigm of production, where the consumer is merely the passive recipient of the firm's active value creation efforts. The origin function was quite reasonably situated within an information efficiency paradigm, to facilitate consumer choice in a competitive marketplace by signalling reliability. A one-way communication or broadcast analogy made sense in this context. However, by merely bolting on the advertising and investment functions, the Court has committed itself to erroneous assumptions about image creation and processes of meaning-making. While brands undeniably have cultural significance and economic value, assuming that a single corporate author is responsible for this is questionable, to say the least. This approach has culminated in *L'Oréal*, where the brand is acknowledged as the object of property rights. The 'unaided' effort and investment by the trade mark owner to create the brand is recognised as the basis for preventing the unauthorised misappropriation of brand image. Yet the doctrinal mechanics of an unfair advantage claim reveal that image transfer can only be presumed on the basis of indirect or circumstantial evidence, while the consumer remains a passive legal construct. The formalism of the CJEU's approach to brand creation can be contrasted with the paradigm shift within marketing scholarship. Current research views consumers and other intermediaries as active partners or co-creators of brand significance. It suggests that brand formation is dialogic and iterative, as opposed to being the result of a one-way broadcast. Since brands are generated in the minds of consumers, they are negotiated, context-sensitive and constantly reproduced by a range of actors. Value is created in the interaction between firm and consumer. Building further on these insights, a more critical school of sociological research argues that in this new dialogic avatar, brands transform everyday life into economic value. Drawing on a more broad-based interrogation of informational capitalism, critics recast consumer involvement as immaterial labour, which produces important symbolic qualities of goods by building on the surplus sociality arising from human communication. The CJEU's approach to brand propertisation is therefore not only inaccurate in presuming single author brand creation, but also deeply troubling since it marginalises consumer agency and reinforces the exploitation of their immaterial labour through the instrumentality of trade mark law.

3

Trade secrets

'Intellectual property' but not 'property'?

LIONEL BENTLY

It has become commonplace in contemporary scholarship to attribute the expansion of protection of patents, copyright, trade marks and related rights to the power of the designation 'property'.[1] This position is perhaps most clearly put by Harvard Law Professor Yochai Benkler:

This chapter draws on work undertaken in the co-authoring of Tanya Aplin, Lionel Bently, Philip Johnson and Simon Malynicz (eds.), *Gurry on Breach of Confidence: The Protection of Confidential Information* 2nd edn (Oxford University Press, 2012). I am grateful to my co-authors and to Oxford University Press for permission to do so, as well as to my friends and colleagues at the workshop on Concepts of Property in Intellectual Property Law, Sussex, August 2011, and to Professor Robert Burrell and Professor Tanya Aplin for their comments on a draft of the chapter.

[1] Glynn Lunney, 'Trademark Monopolies', (1999) 48 *Emory Law Journal* 367 ('property mania' has induced 'a radical and ongoing expansion of trademark protection, both in terms of what can be owned as a trademark and in terms of what trademark ownership entails'); Mark Lemley, 'The Modern Lanham Act and the Death of Common Sense' 108 *Yale Law Journal* 1687 at 1697 ('Courts seem to be replacing the traditional rationale for trademark law with a conception of trademarks as property rights, in which trade-mark "owners" are given strong rights over the marks without much regard for the social costs of such rights'); Robert Burrell and Alison Coleman, *Copyright Exceptions: The Digital Impact* (Cambridge University Press), pp. 180–7, 200, 225–6, 239; Neil W. Netanel, 'Why Has Copyright Expanded? Analysis and Critique' in Fiona MacMillan (ed.), *New Directions in Copyright Law* (Cheltenham: Edward Elgar, 2008), pp. 1, 11–15; Siva Vaidhyanathan, *Copyrights and Copywrongs: The Rise of Intellectual Property and How It Threatens Creativity* (New York University Press, 2001), p. 12. But the concern is by no means new. Over a century ago, the international lawyer Thomas Baty referred to the 'misleading and absurdly sentimental analogy' between copyright and 'property': 'Once style a composition "property", and the whole train of ideas involved in property law follows. Copying is "theft", innocent infringement is visited with the consequences of conversion, a man thinks at his peril. A composition is utterly unlike a physical thing, and those simple rights over physical things which are termed property.' See 'VI. –Copyright', (1909–10) 35 *Law Magazine and Quartely Rev Juris* (5th Ser) 59.

> In the seven decades since [the Supreme Court decision in *INS*], we have seen a shift in prevailing assumptions about copyrights, patents, and related laws. Increasingly, they have come under the umbrella of 'intellectual property'. That semantic umbrella has infused these laws with the conceptual attitudes we have toward property in physical things. We expect things to be owned and exclusively controlled by someone. We think that protecting private property is good policy, good political theory, and just.[2]

Stanford University Professor Mark Lemley makes a similar claim. Lemley argues that an 'absolute protection or full value view ... draws significant intellectual support from the idea that intellectual property is simply a species of real property rather than a unique form of legal protection designed to deal with the public goods problem'.[3] For Professor Lemley, 'treating intellectual property as "just like" real property is a mistake as a practical matter'.[4] One driver of this mentality, he claims, is the use of the term 'intellectual property' itself.[5] In short, Lemley's analysis is that 'intellectual property = property = expansionism'. Consequently, one way to curb expansionism would be to delete both 'intellectual property' and 'property' from legal discourse in this field. To that end, he suggests that 'intellectual property' be reframed as 'IP',[6] and talk of property be replaced with talk of 'subsidy'.[7]

Needless to say, the 'property = expansion' thesis has been challenged by a number of scholars. Some have questioned the analysis itself, doubting whether conceptualisation of copyright and trade marks as 'property' has historically had the effects attributed by Lemley and others.[8] The implication of this work is that 'property talk' is not necessarily

[2] Yochai Benkler, 'Free As The Air To Common Use: First Amendment Constraints on Enclosure of the Public Domain' (1999) 74 *New York University Law Review* 354.

[3] Mark Lemley, 'Property, Intellectual Property, and Free Riding' (2004–05) 83 *Texas Law Review* 1031 at 1031–2.

[4] Lemley, 'Property, Intellectual Property, and Free Riding', 1032.

[5] Lemley, 'Property, Intellectual Property, and Free Riding', 1033 ('the term "intellectual property" may well be a driver in this shift').

[6] Lemley, 'Property, Intellectual Property, and Free Riding', 1075. Hence, perhaps, the title of Lemley's article 'The Surprising Virtues of Treating Trade Secrets as IP Rights, (2008) 61 *Stanford Law Review* 311.

[7] Lemley, 'Property, Intellectual Property, and Free Riding', 1032, 1072–3.

[8] Justin Hughes, 'Copyright and Incomplete Historiographies: Of Piracy, Propertization and Thomas Jefferson' (2006) 79 *Southern California Law Review* 993; Lionel Bently, 'From Communication to Thing: Historical Aspects of the Conceptualisation of Trade Marks as Property' in Graeme Dinwoodie and Mark Janis, *Trademark Law and Theory: A Handbook of Contemporary Research* (Cheltenham: Edward Elgar, 2008).

expansionist. Others have refined the claim. Some, seemingly assenting to the analysis, have proposed a different response: to take seriously analogies with 'property' in a manner that highlights how property concepts provide tools for the limitation of rights as well as for their extension.[9]

In this chapter, I want to highlight a different problem with the 'intellectual property = property = expansionism' analysis, namely the assumption that designation of a right as 'intellectual property' inevitably leads to it being understood in proprietary terms (the 'intellectual property = property' part of the argument). The chapter adopts a historical approach, albeit with a relatively recent focus, describing developments over the last half-century in the classification of confidential information.[10] The 1960s and 1970s witnessed an extended debate amongst scholars and jurists about how the action for breach of confidence should be understood in jurisdictional and conceptual terms. Much of the debate was inconclusive, but the single point on which virtually all interventions agreed was that confidential information should not be classed as 'property'. Nevertheless, from the 1980s onwards, confidential information began to be treated as part of 'intellectual property', and from the mid 1990s it became widely accepted as such. This chapter suggests that the designation of confidential information as 'intellectual property' has not had any significant effect on the debate over whether confidential information should be described as 'property': the view that confidential information is not 'property' remains as strong as ever. The implication, then, is that despite the taxonomical assumption that 'intellectual property' must be a sub-set of 'property', confidential information can be, and frequently is, classed as 'intellectual property' but not 'property'.[11] The chapter considers how such a taxonomical oddity has occurred, before concluding with a few reflections on what this implies for the broader arguments about the conceptual and linguistic basis for expansion of rights in this field.

[9] Robert Burrell and Emily Hudson, 'Property concepts in European copyright law: the case of abandonment' and the other chapters contained in Part II of this collection.

[10] Lest it be thought that this is an unfair example to choose, it is notable that Lemley himself includes trade secrets when discussing the relationship between intellectual property and expansionism: Lemley, 'Property, Intellectual Property, and Free Riding', 1035. See also, Mark Lemley, 'What's Different About Intellectual Property?' (2004–05) 83 *Texas Law Review* 1097 at 1101.

[11] As Lord Neuberger MR put it, 'while the prevailing view is that confidential information is not strictly property, it is not inappropriate to include it as an aspect of intellectual property.' *Coogan* v. *News Group Newspapers Ltd and Mulcaire* [2012] EWCA Civ 48, para. 39.

1 The debate over the status of confidential information as property

The post-Second World War period witnessed a proliferation of reported cases concerning confidential information, sparking a growing academic interest in the field. From the 1960s onwards, this interest focussed on the 'jurisdictional nature' of the action for breach of confidence, in particular over whether the action was to be seen as a tort, an equitable action or as based in property. In some respects the debate sought to locate a categorical home for the growing body of law, but it was also recognised that the process of categorisation could have a normative dimension. By categorising the action for breach of confidence in a particular way, practitioners and courts would be able to draw on the general principles applicable to the relevant category of law in order to develop the action itself. In a fast-developing field of law that was filled with uncertainties, such a 'model' could offer a framework that had stood the test of time, and assist judicial development without requiring legislative intervention.

The scholars who entered the debate were some of the most powerful legal intellects of their era working in the British Commonwealth: Sir Peter North;[12] Professor Gareth Hywel Jones;[13] Professor Bill Cornish;[14] Professor Sam Ricketson;[15] Justice (once Professor) Grant Hammond;[16] Justice and Professor Paul Finn;[17] and Francis Gurry.[18] This stellar cast of intellects all recognised the confusion over the jurisdictional basis of the action, in particular whether it was based on contract, equity, property, tort or good faith.[19] They then debated the appropriate characterisation

[12] P. M. North, 'Breach of Confidence: Is There a New Tort?' (1972–73) 12 *Journal of the Society of Public Teachers of Law* 149.

[13] Gareth Jones, 'Restitution of Benefits Obtained in Breach of Confidence' (1970) 86 *Law Quarterly Review* 463.

[14] William R. Cornish 'Protection of Confidential Information in English Law' (1975) 6 *International Review of Intellectual Property and Competition Law* 43.

[15] S. Ricketson, 'Confidential Information – A New Proprietary Interest?' (1977–78) 11 *Melbourne University Law Review* 223 (Part I), 289 (Part II); 'Public Interest and Breach of Confidence' (1979–80) 12 *Melbourne University Law Review* 176.

[16] G. Hammond, 'The Origins of the Equitable Duty of Confidence', (1979) 8 *Anglo-Am L R* 71; 'Developments in the Equitable Doctrine of Breach of Confidence' (1976) *New Zealand Law Journal* 278.

[17] Paul D. Finn, *Fiduciary Obligations* (Sydney: Law Book Co, 1977), p. 131 ('Perhaps the most sterile of the debates which have arisen around the subject of information received in confidence is whether or not such information should be classified as property').

[18] Francis Gurry, *Breach of Confidence* (Oxford: Clarendon, 1984).

[19] Jones, 'Restitution of Benefits' 463 ('great conceptual confusion'); Hammond, 'The Origins of the Equitable Duty of Confidence' 71 ('conceptual confusion abounds in

of the law of confidence with a view to clarifying its future development. The debate over the nature of rights in confidential information was conducted with a variety of techniques. One type of argument involved an appeal to history and to the claim that the action 'originated' in the courts of Chancery, and hence the best understanding is that it is equitable in nature.[20] Another looked for a legal concept that could explain all, or the majority of cases, seeing the academic task as locating suitable concepts that would fit the established case law.[21] Some appealed to 'realism' and 'logic', to support the view that information as a valuable commercial asset should be treated as 'property',[22] while others saw the key as offering the judiciary a flexible tool that they could adapt to a rapidly changing technological environment.[23]

the reported Commonwealth cases as to the basis of the jurisdiction'); Ricketson, 'Confidential Information' (suggesting four alternatives: contract, property, equity based on good faith and equitable property); Gurry, *Breach of Confidence*, p. 25 ('a source of lingering uncertainty and controversy'). Others shared the same view: *Breach of Confidence* (Law Com. No. 110), Cmnd 8388, para. 5.2.

[20] Hammond, 'The Origins of the Equitable Duty of Confidence' 72 ('the good faith doctrine was ... espoused by the early Chancellors before that doctrine was mistakenly departed from by common law Judges in an (ultimately) unfruitful alliance with contract and property'); 73–4 (noting the potential limits, as well as benefits of taking a historical approach); 84 ('If the early history of this branch of the law is taken as a guide, it suggests that breach of confidence may properly be rationalized in a principle restraining unauthorized use in breach of good faith, rather than in a somewhat disjointed attempt to make the cases fit conventional notions of contract or property'); Ricketson, 'Confidential Information' 235 (claiming that 'common law copyright cases', which were in fact Chancery injunction cases, 'provide some basis for arguing that equitable intervention today in respect of written confidences has a proprietary basis. It is a logical extension to argue from this that a similar principle applies to unwritten confidences'); 305 (arguing it would be 'odd' if the action were regarded as a tort because '[e]ver since the old cases on common law rights of property in unpublished works it has been a creature of the courts of equity and thus its origins owe nothing to common law principles').

[21] Ricketson, 'Confidential Information' 232, (regarding contractual explanation as inadequate on the basis that it fails to account for cases imposing liability in non-contractual situations or in relation to third party recipients who have not deliberately induced a breach of contract); 239–43 (rejecting Jones' theory of 'good faith' as inadequate to explain many of the non-fiduciary cases); Jones, 'Restitution of Benefits' 464–5, 478 (dismissing analysis in terms of 'property' and 'contract' as either not sufficiently determinative or failing to encompass most cases, and instead arguing in favour of a broad equitable principle of good faith').

[22] North, 'Breach of Confidence' 164.

[23] Hammond, 'The Origins of the Equitable Duty of Confidence' 73 ('Flexible concepts, capable of judicial application to a wide variety of situations are more than ever necessary in a technological world').

A number of areas of uncertainty were understood as capable of resolution through the process of classification (though certainly they did not all agree that there could only be one way to classify the action).[24] Although the areas of concern were not limited in this way, two examples of the styles of thinking will suffice to illustrate what was (or was thought to be) at stake – the circumstances in which third party recipients would be treated as owing duties of confidence and the remedies available to a holder of confidential information who discovered information had been used in breach of a duty of confidence.

The first area of concern related to who was to be regarded as subject to legal obligations of confidentiality: did obligations of confidence 'bind the world', or only parties with notice of an initial obligation of confidence, or indeed only parties to such an obligation? If confidential information was 'property', then according to some commentators, conclusions could be drawn to the effect that all recipients, and even independent, innocent, third parties who acquired information, were to be regarded as bound.[25] If, instead, the action for breach of confidence merely vindicated an equitable proprietary interest (or some sort of equitable right), it seemed that only third parties with notice would come under an obligation. If, however, the obligation were personal, only those who were party to the obligation or who induced its breach would be liable.

The second area of concern related to remedies for breach of confidence. Could a claimant obtain damages, as if the wrong was tortious,[26] or only disgorgement (as might be conventional in relation to equitable wrongs)?[27] Were exemplary or aggravated damages a possibility (as with some torts)? Would deliberate misappropriation of confidential information count as 'theft' and give rise to criminal sanctions? Once again, the answers to these questions were thought to flow from prior characterisation of the

[24] North, for example, seems to have envisaged both tortious and equitable actions operating side-by-side. See 'Breach of Confidence', especially at 161.

[25] North, 'Breach of Confidence' 163 ('It may well be that where an interest in confidential information can be defined in terms of a property interest, then interference with that interest, albeit innocently, should sound in damages at common law'); Norman Palmer, 'Information as Property' in Linda Clarke (ed.), *Confidentiality and the Law* (London: Lloyds of London Press, 1990), pp. 85–6; Roger Toulson and Charles Phipps, *Confidentiality* (London: Sweet and Maxwell, 2006), p. 38, paras. 2-061–2-066. But cf. Jones, 'Restitution of Benefits' 465 ('No property theory can satisfactorily determine, even with the aid of equity, the question of the liability of the person who innocently exploits a trade secret').

[26] North, 'Breach of Confidence' 149 ('The incidence of the award of damages is some pointer towards judicial acceptance of a tortious liability for breach of confidence').

[27] Toulson and Phipps, *Confidentiality*, pp. 39–45, paras. 2-067–2-089.

nature of the information (was it 'property'?) or the obligation of confidence (for example as embodying the principle of good faith).[28]

Looking back at the debate, three peculiar features stand out. First, the rather surprising legal formalist premises on which many of these leading academic lights were building their claims.[29] Second, the debate over the character of the action for breach of confidence has, in fact, never been formally resolved. Some courts adopted the Gurry thesis that the action is *sui generis*,[30] having been developed by the courts through mixing and matching the existing legal doctrines that were most readily to hand.[31] This is the position of the Canadian Supreme Court.[32] Other courts came to the conclusion, or acted on the assumption, that the action was equitable.[33] The tort thesis was not widely adopted (despite the US precedent),[34]

[28] Jones, 'Restitution of Benefits' 466, 483; Gurry, *Breach of Confidence*, p. 27; Palmer, 'Information as Property' 84 (principal area where analogy with property might help judicial reasoning is remedies); Toulson and Phipps, *Confidentiality*, p. 29, para. 2-030.

[29] Two notable exceptions were Finn and Cornish. Finn, *Fiduciary Obligations*, Chapter 19. Cornish explained that he preferred the arguments that the action was based on good faith because then 'the issue is not hedged behind conceptual dogma which all too readily states legal results without properly considering their justification': W. R. Cornish, *Intellectual Property: Patents, Copyright Trade Marks and Allied Rights* (London: Sweet & Maxwell, 1981), p. 268. This statement has survived for virtually three decades: William Cornish, David Llewelyn and Tanya Aplin, *Intellectual Property: Patents, Copyright, Trade Marks and Allied Rights* 7th edn (London: Sweet & Maxwell, 2010), p. 334, para. 9-07.

[30] Although it has become widely associated with him, whether this thesis really originated with Gurry is doubtful: Law Commission, Working Paper No. 58 (1974), para. 16 ('it would seem more realistic to regard the modern action as being sui generis').

[31] Gurry, *Breach of Confidence*, p. 26 ('The courts' attitude to jurisdictional sources has thus been a pragmatic one. Their principal concern has been, not to classify the breach of confidence action into an existing conceptual category, but to use existing categories to enforce the more fundamental notion of confidence ... The action should properly be regarded, therefore, as sui generis, and attempts to confine it exclusively within one conventional category should be resisted.')

[32] *Lac Minerals Ltd* v. *International Corona Resources Ltd* [1989] 2 SCR 574 at para. 171, per Sopinka J ('The foundation of action for breach of confidence does not rest solely on one of the traditional jurisdictional bases for action of contract, equity or property. The action is sui generis relying on all three to enforce the policy of the law that confidences be respected'); *Cadbury Schweppes Inc* v. *FBI Foods Ltd* [1999] 1 SCR 142 at paras. 26–28 per Binnie J; *Apotex Fermentation Inc* v. *Novopharm* (1998) 162 DLR (4th) 110 at 144. See also the endorsement of the *sui generis* theory by the New Zealand Court of Appeal in *Hunt* v. *A* [2008] 1 NZLR 368 at para. 64 ('The doctrine is a sui generis cause of action').

[33] *OBG* v. *Allan* [2008] 1 AC 1 at 276 per Lord Walker ('Where there is no contractual tie the cause of action is the equitable jurisdiction to restrain (or if it cannot be restrained, to award compensation or an account of profits for) breach of confidence'); *Deta Nominees Pty Ltd* v. *Viscount Plastic Products Pty Ltd* [1979] VR 167; *Aquaculture Corporation* v. *New Zealand Green Mussel Co Ltd* (1985) IPR 353, 385.

[34] Restatement of Torts §§ 757–58 (1939).

though it has gained some impetus since 2000 with the growing use of breach of confidence to protect Article 8 rights,[35] and Lord Nicholls' suggestion that '[t]he essence of the tort is better encapsulated now as misuse of private information'.[36]

Third, if there was one matter of consensus, it was almost certainly the view that 'confidential information' was not property. At a judicial level, this was regarded as established by the House of Lords in *Boardman* v. *Phipps*.[37] In that case Boardman was the solicitor to a trust, and in that capacity had learned information about the value and performance of a company, Lester and Harris, a manufacturer of textiles, in which the trust held shares. Boardman, with the knowledge of two of the three trustees,[38] used the information to launch a personal take-over bid for the company, which would redound both to his own benefit and to the benefit of the trust (because the firm was underperforming).[39] Once in charge of the company, Boardman reorganised its assets, making various sales and paying out substantial dividends on the shares, including those held by the trust. Nevertheless, a beneficiary claimed the profits Boardman had made for himself, asserting that the information that Boardman had used was trust property, and/or that Boardman was liable as a fiduciary to account for any profits made by putting himself in a position where his duty to the trust and personal interest were in conflict. The House

[35] Tort lawyers have long been interested in the potential of the common law to develop a new tort of privacy, and have thus quickly moved to include within the covers of their textbooks the case law that utilises the law of confidence to protect informational privacy: see J. F. Clerk, M. A. Jones and W. H. B. Lindsell, *Clerk and Lindsell on Torts* 20th edn (London: Thomson Reuters, 2010), Chapter 27 (by Hazel Carty); Simon Deakin, Angus Johnston and Basil Markesinis, *Markesinis and Deakin's Tort Law* 7th edn (Oxford: Clarendon, 2012), Chapter 22; Mark Lunney and Ken Oliphant, *Tort Law: Texts and Materials* 4th edn (Oxford University Press, 2010), Chapter 14; John Murphy, Christian A. Witting and James Goudkamp, *Street on Torts* 13th edn (Oxford University Press, 2012), Chapter 22 ('Misuse of Private Information' and treating *Campbell* as having created a new tort). There are persuasive arguments for treating the breach of non-contractual obligations of confidence as tortious for the purposes of private international law: T. M. Yeo, *Choice of Law for Equitable Doctrines* (Oxford University Press, 2004), p. 296, para. 77.

[36] *Campbell* v. *Mirror Group Newspapers Ltd* [2004] 2 AC 457, para. 14. In a previous passage Lord Nicholls recognised that historically protection of breach of confidence had been granted by the courts of equity. In *Coogan* v. *News Group Newspapers Ltd* [2012] EWCA Civ 48 at para. 48, Lord Neuberger MR observed that 'it is probably fair to say that the extent to which privacy is to be accommodated within the law of confidence as opposed to the law of tort is still in the process of being worked out'.

[37] [1967] 2 AC 46.

[38] [1967] 2 AC 46 at 81G-82A, 95B-C, 113D-E.

[39] [1967] 2 AC 46 at 76F-G, 80A-B (Viscount Dilhorne).

of Lords divided, the majority finding for the Plaintiff on a mixture of grounds,[40] but three of their Lordships expressed the view that information is not 'property'.[41] Perhaps most famously, Lord Upjohn stated that information is 'not property at all' and while the courts may prevent use or disclosure of confidential information, 'the real truth is that it is not property in any normal sense'.[42] Viscount Dilhorne, while admitting that 'some information can properly be regarded as property' and 'information is not infrequently described as property', indicated he did not think that the information obtained by Boardman about the assets of Lester and Harris could be so considered, as it was not 'of any value to the trust' because the trust could not buy the shares in the company.[43] Lord Cohen, too, agreed that information was not 'property in the strict sense of the word',[44] so it did not follow that 'because an agent acquired information ... while acting in a fiduciary capacity he is accountable to his principals for any profit that comes his way as the result of the use he makes of that information'.[45]

[40] The majority comprised Lords Cohen, Hodson and Guest, the primary basis for liability being that Boardman had acted in a fiduciary capacity and had made a profit in that capacity. The minority, Lord Upjohn and Viscount Dilhorne, appeared to take the view that the 'no profit' rule was inapplicable because there was no potential conflict between Boardman's duty and interest.

[41] Lord Hodson disagreed, saying he dissented from 'the view that information is of its nature something which is not properly to be described as property': [1967] 2 AC 46 at 107C (Lord Hodson). He added, 'we are aware that what is called "know-how" in the commercial sense is property which may be very valuable as an asset.' On the facts of the case before him, he said he thought that the confidential information acquired by Boardman could 'be properly regarded as the property of the trust'. Lord Guest, [1967] 2 AC 46 at 115E-F, likewise asserted that 'all the information he obtained ... became trust property. The weapon which he used to obtain this information was the trust holding. And I see no reason why information and knowledge cannot be trust property.' Although the reasoning is not completely clear, neither Lord Hodson's nor Lord Guest's views on the status of information as property appeared to play a critical part in their reasoning that Boardman was liable. Moreover, their reputations – one a probate lawyer, the other a valuation specialist from the Scottish bar – were not comparable to the esteem of the Chancery specialist, Lord Upjohn. Lord Upjohn's remarks have been widely preferred: Toulson and Phipps, *Confidentiality*, p. 33, para. 2-041; Paul Stanley, *The Law of Confidentiality: A Restatement* (Oxford: Hart, 2008), p. 149 n. 1 (where Lord Hodson's analysis is described as a 'confusion', and Lord Upjohn's remarks cited as a lucid restatement); *Coogan* v. *News Group Newspapers Ltd* [2012] EWCA Civ 48 at para. 34 (Lord Neuberger MR).

[42] [1967] 2 AC 46 at 127F-128A.

[43] [1967] 2 AC 46 at 89G-90B; 91F; 91G (Viscount Dilhorne).

[44] [1967] 2 AC 46 at 102G (Lord Cohen).

[45] [1967] 2 AC 46 at 102G-103A (Lord Cohen).

Most commentators agreed with the view that confidential information was not property. Early in the debate Gareth Jones observed that:

> Information is not like other choses in action, such as debt or copyright, which lend themselves more easily to a classical analysis in terms of property.[46]

Jennifer Stuckey, writing in 1981, stated that property analysis of breach of confidence was 'juristically misguided and unhelpful'.[47] Even Francis Gurry, who was sympathetic to recognition of property as a further basis for the '*sui generis*' action, acknowledged that most of the references in the case law to confidential information as property were 'metaphorical',[48] and the exceptions where property was referred to as the basis of jurisdiction had only 'a very tenuous foothold on authority'.[49] After a lengthy review of the arguments and authorities in 1990, Robert Dean concluded that:

> a close analysis of the courts' treatment of trade secrets reveals that it is doubtful that the courts have taken the step to include property as a basis for protecting confidential information ... It is concluded therefore, that the burden of proof is on those maintaining property in trade secrets; and that this burden has not yet been discharged.[50]

Several reasons were offered for the determination that confidential information was not property. Not surprisingly, many emphasised the absence of legal precedent, noting that references to 'property' in the nineteenth-century case law were in the context of common law property rights in unpublished works (cases which after 1912 came to be understood as precursors of modern copyright).[51] Some emphasised the difficulties inherent in conceiving of 'information' as an object of property.[52] Others pointed to the undesirable consequences that might flow from inflexible application of property rules to confidential information. More commonly, however, scholars highlighted the lack of analytical value that derives from referring to confidential information as property,[53] referring to Oliver

[46] Jones, 'Restitution of Benefits' 464. See also Cornish, *Intellectual Property* (1981), 290.

[47] Jennifer Stuckey, 'The Equitable Action for Breach of Confidence: Is Information Ever Property?' (1981) 9 *Sydney Law Review* 402 at 404.

[48] Gurry, *Breach of Cofidence*, pp. 47–8.

[49] Gurry, *Breach of Confidence*, p. 54 (although the author argued, at p. 55, that it was desirable 'that its existence be confirmed').

[50] Robert L. Dean, *The Law of Trade Secrets* (Sydney: Law Book Co, 1990), pp. 83, 84.

[51] Finn, *Fiduciary Obligations*, pp. 131–2, para. 294; Stuckey, 'The Equitable Action for Breach of Confidence' 406.

[52] Jones, 'Restitution of Benefits' 464.

[53] Stuckey, 'The Equitable Action for Breach of Confidence' 405ff.

Wendell Holmes' statement about the use of the term 'property' in *EI du Pont de Nemours Co* v. *Masland*, as an 'unanalysed expression of certain secondary consequences of the primary fact that the law makes some rudimentary requirements of good faith'.[54] Indeed, it was by reference to the analysis of Holmes that Paul Finn described the debate over whether confidential information could be described as property as probably 'the most sterile' of all the debates in the field.[55] Only a very few scholars were sympathetic to proprietary analysis.[56]

2 Confidential information as 'intellectual property'

In contrast with the intensity of the debate over whether confidential information is 'property', fewer people have questioned the appropriateness of categorising confidential information as intellectual property. In fact, the idea that confidential information is intellectual property seems to have slipped into the deep structure of legal thinking without even the raising of academic eyebrows. All the UK textbooks on 'intellectual property' include chapters on breach of confidence,[57] while books

[54] 244 US 100, 102 (1917). The case is cited by Jones, 'Restitution of Benefits' 465; Gurry, *Breach of Cofidence*, p. 47; Dean, *The Law of Trade Secrets*, p. 5.

[55] Finn, *Fiduciary Obligations*, p. 131, para. 293.

[56] Gurry apart, only Norman Palmer was prepared to suggest that, when handled in a nuanced fashion, proprietary analysis was not 'without its resources': Palmer, 'Information as Property', p. 107. See also Paul Kohler and Norman Palmer, 'Information as Property' in Norman Palmer and Ewan McKendrick, *Interests in Goods* (London: LLP, 1998), p. 23.

[57] Tanya Aplin and Jennifer Davis, *Intellectual Property: Cases and Materials* (Oxford University Press, 2009), Chapter 8; David Bainbridge, *Intellectual Property* 9th edn (Harlow: Pearson, 2012), Chapter 10 ('Law of Breach of Confidence'); Lionel Bently and Brad Sherman, *Intellectual Property Law* (Oxford University Press, 2009), Chapters 44–46; Catherine Colston, *Principles of Intellectual Property Law* (London: Cavendish, 1999), Chapter 6 ('Breach of Confidence'); Catherine Colston and Kirsty Middleton, *Modern Intellectual Property Law* 2nd edn (London: Cavendish, 2005), Chapter 7 ('Breach of Confidence'); Cornish *et al.*, *Intellectual Property*, Chapter 8; Jennifer Davis, *Intellectual Property Core Text* 4th edn (Oxford University Press, 2012), Chapter 3; Hector MacQueen, Charlotte Waelde, Graeme Laurie and Abbe Brown, *Contemporary Intellectual Property Law and Policy* 2nd edn (Oxford University Press, 2010), Chapter 18 ('Breach of Confidence'); Paul Torremans, *Holyoak and Torremans Intellectual Property Law* 6th edn (Oxford University Press, 2010), Chapter 29 (entitled 'Confidentiality and Trade Secrets' but positioned in the part on 'Issues in Intellectual Property'). One of the more reflective treatments is Michael Spence, *Intellectual Property* (Oxford: Clarendon, 2007), p. 313 (action for breach of confidence 'comes close to, but never quite, constitutes a common law intellectual property right').

on particular aspects of intellectual property often include sections on confidentiality.[58]

There are numerous examples of situations where intellectual property – now a well-established part of the legal furniture – has been treated as encompassing confidential information. Perhaps the most prominent is the inclusion of confidential information in the TRIPS (Agreement on Trade-Related Aspects of Intellectual Property Rights) Annex to the World Trade Organization (WTO) Agreement, binding on the 157 member countries of the WTO, Article 39 of which recognises obligations to protect 'undisclosed information'. Article 39 reads as follows:

> Article 39
>
> 1. In the course of ensuring effective protection against unfair competition as provided in Article 10bis of the Paris Convention (1967), Members shall protect undisclosed information in accordance with paragraph 2 ...
> 2. Natural and legal persons shall have the possibility of preventing information lawfully within their control from being disclosed to, acquired by, or used by others without their consent in a manner contrary to honest commercial practices[59] so long as such information:
>   (a) is secret in the sense that it is not, as a body or in the precise configuration and assembly of its components, generally known among or readily accessible to persons within the circles that normally deal with the kind of information in question;
>   (b) has commercial value because it is secret; and
>   (c) has been subject to reasonable steps under the circumstances, by the person lawfully in control of the information, to keep it secret.

[58] Lionel Bently, 'Patents and Trade Secrets' in Neil Wilkof and Shamnad Basheer (eds.), *Overlapping Intellectual Property Rights* (Oxford University Press, 2012), Chapter 3; Thorsten Kaseberg, *Intellectual Property, Antitrust and Cumulative Innovation in the EU and US* (Oxford: Hart, 2012) (covering patents, copyright and trade secrets); Graham Dutfield and Uma Suthersanen, *Global Intellectual Property Law* (Cheltenham: Edward Elgar, 2008), Chapter 5 ('Patents and Trade Secrets'); Andrew Burrows (ed.), *English Private Law* 2nd edn (Oxford University Press, 2004), pp. 513–16 (by William R. Cornish); Christopher May and Susan Sell, *Intellectual Property Rights: A Critical History* (Boulder, CO: Lynne Rienner, 2006), p. 11 ('it is sometimes also useful to think of trade secrets as intellectual property'. But cf. James Edelman, *Gain-Based Damages: Contract, Tort, Equity and Intellectual Property* (Oxford: Hart, 2002) (which includes breach of confidence in Chapter 6 on equitable wrongs rather than Chapter 7 on intellectual property wrongs).

[59] A note explains: 'For the purpose of this provision, "a manner contrary to honest commercial practices" shall mean at least practices such as breach of contract, breach of confidence and inducement to breach, and includes the acquisition of undisclosed

The TRIPS Agreement defines 'intellectual property' by reference to the subjects covered by the Agreement. Article 1(2) states that the 'term "intellectual property" refers to all categories of intellectual property that are the subject of Sections 1 through 7 of Part II [of the Agreement]', thus including copyright, related rights, trade marks, geographical indications, patents, plant breeders' rights and rights in undisclosed information. This definition is reiterated in the now notorious 2011 Anti-Counterfeiting Trade Agreement,[60] which repeats the definition of 'intellectual property' in the TRIPS Agreement.[61] Similarly, the EU–Korea Free Trade Agreement (2011) defines intellectual property rights as 'embodying', in addition to copyright, related rights, patents, trade marks, service marks, designs, plant varieties and geographical indication, 'the protection of undisclosed information';[62] while the Euro-Mediterranean Agreement between the EC, its Member States and Egypt (2004) defines 'intellectual property' as including the 'protection of undisclosed information on [*sic*] know-how'.[63] A further example is provided by the Agreement between the European Union and the Government of the United States of America on the Security of Classified Information (2007), which is designed to ensure that the two entities willingly share security information by undertaking to restrict its circulation, and which states that:

information by third parties who knew, or were grossly negligent in failing to know, that such practices were involved in the acquisition.'

[60] The Anti-Counterfeiting Trade Agreement, a multilateral agreement, was negotiated in secret between selected countries in the period between 2008 and 2011, but became notorious when as a result of widespread public protest, particularly relating to obligations with respect to infringement of copyright on the Internet, a number of countries including the EU indicated that they would not ratify the agreement. To date, Japan is the only country to have done so.

[61] Anti-Counterfeiting Trade Agreement, Art. 5(h). The Free Trade Agreements entered into by the United States with countries such as Australia, Singapore, Columbia and South Korea do not define 'intellectual property rights', nor do they include specific provisions on 'undisclosed information' (other than data disclosed in seeking marketing approval). It is not clear, therefore, whether the general obligations contained in these agreements apply to trade secrets.

[62] Free Trade Agreement between the European Union and its Member States, of the one part, and the Republic of Korea, of the other part, OJ L 127/6, Art. 10.2(2). See also, Economic Partnership, Political Coordination and Cooperation Agreement between the EC and Its Member States and the United Mexican States (2000), (2000) OJ L 276/45, Art. 12; Partnership and Cooperation Agreement between the EC and Its Member States and the Republic of Iraq (2011), Art. 60, note 1 (see Council Doc 5784/11, at http://trade.ec.europa.eu/doclib/docs/2012/november/tradoc_150084.pdf).

[63] Euro-Mediterranean Agreement Between the European Community and Its Member States and Egypt, 2004, Art. 37 and Joint Declaration on Article 37 and Annex VI: see http://trade.ec.europa.eu/doclib/docs/2004/june/tradoc_117680.pdf.

> The recipient Party shall ensure that the rights of the originator of classified information provided or exchanged under this Agreement, as well as intellectual property rights such as patents, copyrights *or trade secrets*, are adequately protected.[64]

Similar examples of 'intellectual property' being defined as including the protection of confidential information can be seen in EU law. Undoubtedly the most important example is the European Union's Intellectual Property Rights Enforcement Directive (often referred to as IPRED).[65] That instrument requires Member States to provide certain remedies in relation to infringements of intellectual property rights. This begs the question: what precisely are intellectual property rights, and, more specifically, do they include rights in confidential information? The European Commission issued a Communication on the definition of intellectual property, but it contains a non-exhaustive list and so has not provided an answer.[66] Nevertheless, the English courts have taken the view that confidential information is a subject of an intellectual property right for the purpose of the Directive. In *Vestergaard* v. *Bestnet*,[67] the Court of Appeal considered whether the judge at first instance ought to have granted an injunction against a defendant who had manufactured anti-mosquito nets using confidential information derived from the claimant's database. The Judge had granted an injunction in relation to the immediate product (NetProtect) that relied most heavily on the confidential data, but declined to award injunctions in relation to two derivative products (called Whopes I and Whopes II) that were developed a considerable period after the confidential information had been taken and with the benefit of substantial efforts by the defendants. The Judge decided that in relation to the two Whopes products, the award of an injunction would be disproportionate.[68] The Court of Appeal declined to overturn these decisions. Giving the judgment, Jacob

[64] 30 April 2007, OJ L 115/30, Art. 4(6) (emphasis added).

[65] Enforcement Directive, 2004/48/EC.

[66] The Commission issued a statement to the effect that 'at least the following intellectual property rights are covered by the scope of the Directive: copyright, rights related to copyright, sui generis right of a database maker, rights of the creator of the topographies of a semiconductor product, trademark rights, design rights, patent rights, including rights derived from supplementary protection certificates, geographical indications, utility model rights, plant variety rights, trade names, in so far as these are protected as exclusive property in the national law concerned.' No mention is made of business secrets or confidentiality.

[67] *Vestergaard Frandsen S/A and Ors* v. *Bestnet Europe Ltd* [2011] EWCA Civ 424, para. 56 (CA).

[68] *Vestergaard Frandsen S/A and Ors* v. *Bestnet Europe Ltd* [2009] EWHC 1456 (Ch) at para. 110; [2009] EWHC 1623 (Pat) (Arnold J).

LJ acknowledged that while conventional principles of English law relating to the grant of injunctive relief did not refer to the fashionable concept of 'proportionality', the condition was made explicit in relation to 'intellectual property' by Article 3 of the EC Enforcement Directive. Whether or not proportionality would have been a relevant consideration under the traditional rules, it was 'accepted that a claim for misuse of technical trade secrets ... is a claim to enforce an intellectual property right', so that the Directive was assumed applicable, and the judge 'was right to consider proportionality'.[69]

Another European example is provided by Article 15 of the Dangerous Preparations Directive.[70] This requires Member States to implement certain requirements in the labelling of dangerous substances, and allows a manufacturer to decline to label products with their chemical names where to do so 'will put at risk the confidential nature of his intellectual property'. To similar effect is the Flavouring Substances Regulation of 1996,[71] which created an EU procedure for the evaluation and authorisation of use of such substances in food, and which also provides for the protection of information disclosed to the regulatory authority as to the ingredients of the flavouring substances. The Regulation states that 'it is necessary to protect intellectual property linked to the development and production of flavouring substances' and, in turn, the Commission's Communication states that '[i]ntellectual property can be protected through the confidentiality of the technical data concerning the flavouring substances in question'.[72] This suggests that the Commission sees the protection of confidential information as a part of 'intellectual property'.

[69] *Vestergaard Frandsen S/A and Ors* v. *Bestnet Europe Ltd* [2011] EWCA Civ 424 at para. 56 (CA). But see Tanya Aplin, Lionel Bently, Philip Johnson and Simon Malynicz (eds.), *Gurry on Breach of Confidence: The Protection of Confidential Information* 2nd edn (Oxford University Press, 2012), p. 720, para. 7.05 (in a passage written by Phillip Johnson, pointing out that the matter was not contested and arguing that Member States have a discretion as to whether to apply the Directive to trade secrets and that the UK government, when implementing it, had elected not to do so).

[70] Directive 1999/45/EC of 31 May 1999 concerning the approximation of the laws, regulations and administrative provisions of the Member States relating to the classification, packaging and labelling of dangerous preparations.

[71] Regulation (EC) No 2232/96 of the European Parliament and of the Council of 28 October 1996 laying down a Community procedure for flavouring substances used or intended for use in or on foodstuffs, OJ L 299/1 recital 14, Art. 3(2).

[72] Commission Communication on the ways in which the Commission is to protect the intellectual property in connection with the development and manufacture of flavouring substances covered by Regulation (EC) No 2232/96 of the European Parliament and of the Council, OJ 98/C 131/03; Commission Recommendation of 21 April 1998 on the ways in which the Member States and the signatory states of the Agreement on the European

The treatment of confidential information as intellectual property is also evident in UK statute law. Section 72 of the Senior Courts Act and section 15 of the Law Reform (Miscellaneous Provisions) (Scotland) Act 1985 provide that a person is not excused from answering questions put in proceedings or complying with an order on the basis that this would tend to expose that person to proceedings for a related offence if proceedings are civil proceedings 'for infringement of rights pertaining to any intellectual property or passing off'. Subsection 5 defines 'intellectual property' as 'any patent, trade mark, copyright, design right, registered design, *technical or commercial information* or other intellectual property' (emphasis added). We will return to consider precisely what this has been found to encompass later in this chapter, but for now it suffices to note that intellectual property is treated as including technical or commercial information. The Atomic Energy Authority Act 1986, which conferred various powers on the Atomic Energy Authority including the power to exploit commercially the results of research, including dealing in 'intellectual property', defined this as including 'patents, trademarks (*sic*), copyrights, design rights, registered designs and *other scientific or technical information of commercial value*' (emphasis added). The Building Societies Act 1986 (as amended in 1997), which regulates the circumstances in which building societies can acquire other businesses in part by reference to the cost of 'intellectual property' required to run the prospective business, defines 'intellectual property' as 'any patent, *know how*, trade mark, service mark, registered design, copyright or design right' (emphasis added).[73] Another example is the Corporation Tax Act 2009, section 712(3) of which defines 'intellectual property' as including 'any information or technique … having industrial, commercial or other economic value'. A less well-known example is The Personal Accounts Delivery Authority Winding Up Order 2010,[74] which winds up and dissolves the Personal Accounts Delivery Authority (PADA) that was set up to bring independent pensions expertise into the process of the formulation of pension schemes for small firms. The PADA was wound up when the National Employment Savings Trust (NEST) was established as a mechanism for a low-cost workplace saving scheme, and the Order transferred PADA's property, rights and liabilities

Economic area should protect intellectual property in connection with the development and manufacture of flavouring substances referred to in Regulation (EC) No 2232/96 of the European Parliament and of the Council, 98/282/EC, OJ 98 L 127/32.

[73] Building Societies Act 1986, s. 92A(9).

[74] SI 2010/911.

to the NEST Corporation. For that purpose, the Order defined 'intellectual property' as:

> copyright, rights related to or affording protection similar to copyright and rights in databases, patents, inventions, trade marks, internet domain names, website addresses, trade names, designs, *know-how, trade secrets and confidential information* [emphasis added].

The idea that 'intellectual property' encompasses – or at least can encompass – confidential information thus seems to have become increasingly prevalent.

3 If confidential information is intellectual property, is it therefore property?

Does it matter that confidential information is often treated as 'intellectual property'? If Lemley and Benkler are right, one would have expected it to have resolved the debate over whether confidential information is 'property'. If confidential information is 'intellectual property', it is likely that as it is assumed that 'intellectual property' is itself 'property',[75] so confidential information will be treated as 'property'. Thus, through a combination of historical development and taxonomic logic, the status of confidential information would transform from non-property to property.

Perhaps the strongest evidence that such a shift might have occurred is provided by the Court of Appeal decision in *Veolia ES Nottinghamshire Ltd and Nottinghamshire County Council* v. *Dowen*.[76] The Council had entered into an agreement with Veolia for waste management services. Dowen was keen to discover the terms of the arrangement, and applied to the Council under the Audit Commission Act 1998. Section 15 of that Act provides that 'any person interested' may inspect 'the accounts to be audited and all books, deeds, contracts, bills, vouchers and receipts relating thereto'. Dowen claimed that the contract with Veolia related to Council accounts, so he was entitled to see it. Cranston J agreed, interpreting the right of access conferred by section 15 literally, even though the effect was to require the Council to reveal confidential information.[77] The Court of Appeal reversed. Rix LJ, giving the lead judgment,

[75] Burrows, *English Private Law*, Part III ('The Law of Property', including Chapter 6 'Intellectual Property').

[76] [2010] EWCA Civ 1214 (29 Oct ober 2010).

[77] [2009] EWHC 2382 (Admin) at paras. 79–81 (Cranston J).

took the view that Veolia's right to its confidential information fell either within Article 8 or constituted a possession protected under Article 1 of the First Protocol to the European Convention on Human Rights.[78] Consequently, the statutory power should be read down so as to accommodate rather than override that right.[79] However, as human rights need to be balanced against other freedoms, Rix LJ acknowledged that this was not an absolute exemption from disclosure: rather it required the local authority to examine the facts closely and determine whether any public interest in disclosure of the information would outweigh the fundamental rights of Veolia to keep the terms of the contract secret. On the facts before it, the Court concluded that it would be inappropriate to set aside the Council's earlier decision to disclose a section of the contract, but that it had no power to disclose further confidential information of Veolia to Dowen under the 1998 Act.

Although *Veolia* might be thought to indicate a shift towards treating confidential information as property (or at least as a possession), in truth no such shift in the status of confidential information from non-property to property has occurred. For one thing, the reasoning in *Veolia* has been trenchantly criticised, most notably in the new edition of *Gurry on Breach of Confidence*.[80] Moreover, even if *Veolia* is rightly decided, the case is very much an outlier: elsewhere English courts and commentators have continued to deny that confidential information is property. The continued denial that confidential information is property can be seen most clearly in the Court of Appeal and House of Lords decisions in *Douglas* v. *Hello!*[81] In this case, Michael Douglas and Catherine Zeta Jones agreed with *OK!* magazine that it would have exclusive coverage of their wedding. Despite making considerable effort to ensure that no unauthorised photographs were taken, an unauthorised photographer called Thorpe managed to gain access to the hotel where it was being held, and sold the unauthorised photos to *OK!*'s competitor *Hello!*, enabling the latter to publish a spoiler.

[78] [2010] EWCA Civ 1214 at para. 122 (Rix LJ). See also para. 141.

[79] In so doing, Rix LJ followed the approach of Lord Hoffmann in *Regina (Morgan Grenfell & Co Ltd)* v. *Special Commissioner of Income Tax* [2002] UKHL 21, [2003] AC 563 to the effect that the Taxes Management Act 1970 did not override a person's right to claim legal professional privilege.

[80] Aplin *et al.*, *Gurry on Breach of Confidence*, p. 129, para. 4.93 (the lead author of this section was Professor Aplin). See also *Force India Formula One Team* v. *1 Malaysian Racing Team* [2012] EWHC 616 (Ch), para. 376 (Arnold J, pointing out the failure of the Court to cite any of the many authorities).

[81] *Douglas* v. *Hello! (No 3)* [2006] QB 125 (CA).

OK! brought an action claiming breach of confidence, and succeeded at trial,[82] Lindsay J holding that the benefit of an obligation of confidence could be 'shared between and be enforceable by co-owners or by a successor in title'.[83] The Court of Appeal allowed *Hello!*'s appeal,[84] explaining that Lindsay J had erroneously 'treated the information about the wedding as if it were property'.[85] While the House of Lords restored Lindsay J's judgment,[86] Lord Hoffmann noting that there was no reason why *OK!* should not be treated as beneficiary of an obligation of confidence, nothing therein cast doubt on the views of Lord Phillips MR that confidential information is not property. Indeed, Lord Walker (dissenting) reiterated that 'information, even if it is confidential cannot properly be regarded as a form of property'.[87] Although confidential information is 'often referred to, loosely or metaphorically' as property, the jurisdiction to prevent disclosures of confidential information was not dependent on treating information as property.[88]

Other, more recent case law confirms this view. In *Fairstar Heavy Transport NV* v. *Adkins*,[89] the High Court (Technology and Construction Court) was asked to decide whether the Claimant firm had proprietary rights in emails created by its former CEO, such that the award of relief prohibiting their deletion was justified.[90] The issue arose in the context of a dispute over what the former CEO had known about the claimant's liabilities in relation to the purchase of two ships. The emails had been forwarded to Adkins from Fairstar and deleted from its system. Edwards-Stuart J reviewed the authorities and concluded that there was no proprietary claim available to Fairstar. He said it was clear that 'the preponderance of authority points strongly against there being any proprietary right in the content of information',[91] and, having mooted various

82 Damages of £1,033,156 were awarded to *OK!*: *Douglas* v. *Hello!* [2004] EMLR 2 (Ch D) at para. 55.

83 *Douglas* (Ch D) at para. 187.

84 *Douglas* v. *Hello! (No 3)* [2006] QB 125 (CA).

85 *Ibid.* at para. 128. See *OBG Ltd* v. *Allan* [2007] UKHL 21; [2008] 1 AC 1, 80 at para. 282 (Lord Walker, leaving open whether the Court of Appeal was correct in this criticism of Lindsay J).

86 *OBG Ltd* v. *Allan* [2007] UKHL 21; [2008] 1 AC 1.

87 *Ibid.* at 76 at para. 275.

88 *Ibid.* at 77 at para. 276. Counsel for *OK!* had not, however, relied on such a claim: para. 277.

89 [2012] EWHC 2952 (TCC).

90 A proprietary basis was asserted because Adkins was not in direct contractual relations with Fairstar, having contracted through an intermediary.

91 [2012] EWHC 2952 (TCC) at para. 58.

possible arrangements (ownership by the generator of the email/ownership by recipient/co-ownership by both), he concluded that there was 'no practical basis for holding that there should be property in the content of an e-mail, even if I thought that it was otherwise open to me to do so'.[92]

Furthermore, in *Dais Studio Pty Ltd* v. *Bullet Creative Pty Ltd*,[93] an Australian case in which an action was brought by the claimant, a firm specialising in website design against an ex-employee web developer who was alleged to have utilised certain aspects of the claimant's confidential content management system, the court considered the scope of the reference to 'proprietary information' in the employment contract. Rejecting the view that confidential information in relation to which there was no obligation was 'proprietary', Jessup J reaffirmed the widely held view that the property concept is only applicable *metaphorically* to confidential information:

> Information as such, of course, is not property ... When information is secret or truly confidential in fact, there is a sense in which the person by whom the information is known might be said to own the information. At times, the concept of property has been used metaphorically as I appreciate it to describe the position existing when information cannot be used or revealed without breach of the equitable obligation of confidence.[94]

Moreover, commentators continue to deny that confidential information is property, if anything with more determination than in the period before 1990.[95] Robert Dean, in the 2002 edition of *The Law of Trade Secrets and Personal Secrets*, restates that 'the courts do not regard secret information as property', arguing that such an analysis is 'an unnecessary complication' and would endanger 'legislative regimes based on sound policy'.[96] Because 'Australian, English and North American authorities have made it clear that the property analysis, while academically interesting, is not a judicial reality', Dean offers a 'much briefer' analysis than was regarded as necessary in the first edition from 1990.[97] Similarly, Roger Toulson and Charles Phipps, in the 2006 edition of their work, review the authorities and arguments and conclude that:

92 [2012] EWHC 2952 (TCC) at para. 69.
93 [2007] FCA 2054. 94 [2007] FCA 2054 at para. 96.
95 Clerk *et al.*, *Clerk and Lindsell on Torts*, p. 1839, para. 27–04 (by Hazel Carty).
96 Dean, *The Law of Trade Secrets*, p. 4, para. 1.20 (citing *Du Pont* v. *Masland*), p. 37, para. 2.49.
97 Dean, *The Law of Trade Secrets*, pp. 49–57, paras. 2.115–2.150.

> there are formidable difficulties in the way of any treatment of the action for breach of confidence as an action in tort based on infringement of a proprietary interest. The objections may be grouped under the headings of precedent, conceptual analysis and legal consequence.[98]

As to precedent, they find little that supports a property analysis, and much that contradicts it. In relation to conceptual analysis the authors reiterate Gareth Jones' objections (first articulated in 1970). Moreover, when considering its desirability, they conclude that adopting a property analysis would create more problems than it would solve.[99] Two years later, Paul Stanley declared that 'it is now clear that, in English law, information is not property'.[100] Most recently, the new edition of Gurry (of which I was a co-author, but the relevant chapter of which was written by Professor Aplin) also reiterates Gurry's original conclusions that confidential information is not property, but with added force. Whereas the 1984 edition observed that 'the status of the property basis must, therefore, be regarded as uncertain', the 2012 edition says that status is 'highly uncertain' and whereas the 1984 edition suggests that proprietary analysis might be helpfully developed by the courts, the 2012 edition sets itself categorically against this: the desirability of its existence should be 'seriously questioned'.[101] Precedent apart, four arguments are made against the suitability of confidential information as the subject of property: that information is not easily demarcated or defined, that confidentiality does not confer exclusivity, that confidential information can be easily disseminated and that it is frequently shared in ways that are difficult to describe in terms of ownership.[102]

The status of confidential information as 'intellectual property' has thus not been perceived as resolving the old debates as to the nature of confidential information. Quite the contrary: the view that confidential information is not property seems to be more trenchantly expressed

[98] Toulson and Phipps, *Confidentiality*, p. 30, para. 2–033.

[99] Toulson and Phipps, *Confidentiality*, p. 307, para. 2–059.

[100] Stanley, *The Law of Confidentiality*, p. 149.

[101] Aplin *et al.*, *Gurry on Breach of Confidence*, p. 137, para. 4.108; cross-referring to para. 8.03. Cited by Edwards-Stuart J in *Fairstar Heavy Transport NV* v. *Adkins*. See also, Cornish *et al.*, *Intellectual Property*, pp. 363–6.

[102] Aplin *et al.*, *Gurry on Breach of Confidence*, p. 312, para. 8.03 (also by Professor Aplin). The approach seems to have been influenced by the arguments of Professor Samuelson against moves in the USA to treat information as property: Pamela Samuelson, 'Information as Property: Do Ruckelshaus and Carpenter Signal a Changing Direction in Intellectual Property Law?' (1988–89) 38 *Catholic University Law Review* 365 at 368–71.

today than twenty years ago. The dominant view seems to be that confidential information might often be regarded as intellectual property, but that does not make it property. To understand how this can be so, we need thus to think about the changing nature of the legal system and with it the changing assumptions that can be made about legal taxonomy.

4 Why the status of confidential information as 'intellectual property' tells us nothing about whether it is 'property'

If confidential information is 'intellectual property', but the courts and commentators remain resistant to treating confidential information as 'property', some sort of explanation is required. This section considers two points: first that the concept of 'intellectual property', a relatively new term in the legal glossary, lacks the sort of conceptual potency assumed by Lemley and Benkler; second, and related, that the legal system has become fractured in such a way that the influence that might formerly have been assumed to exist between concepts employed in one field (intellectual property), and those in another (private law relating to confidential information), no longer exists.

4.1 The 'impotence of intellectual property'

One possibility is that the attribution of a right as 'intellectual property' itself has little, if any, significance in terms of the characterisation of the nature of confidential information and the rights and obligations attached thereto. Such an explanation seems plausible, given the Supreme Court's recent description of intellectual property as a concept that was 'impotent'. But before we get to *Phillips* v. *Maguire*, it is worth reflecting for a few moments on the evolution of the concept of 'intellectual property'.

Although it is possible to trace the origins of the term 'intellectual property' back to the mid nineteenth century,[103] it only gained widespread use in the latter third of the twentieth century. Indeed, as Justin Hughes and others have shown, it was only after international bureaucrats recast the name of the joint international Bureaux relating to the Paris and Berne Conventions as 'BIRPI' (so that the 'PI' referred to intellectual property)

[103] Brad Sherman and Lionel Bently, *The Making of Modern Intellectual Property Law: The British Experience, 1760–1911* (Cambridge University Press, 1999), p. 95 (citing J. Thomson's, *A Letter to the Right Honourable Sir Robert Peel* (London: Smith, Elder & Co, 1840) and T. Turner, *On Copyright in Design in Arts and Manufactures* (London: Elsworth, 1849)).

that the term 'IP' started to be widely deployed as a category of laws.[104] In 1981, when Professor Cornish authored the first edition of his pioneering textbook on intellectual property, he spent a little time explaining that 'intellectual property' was a category of distinct laws (copyright, patents, trade marks, designs and so on) that had developed somewhat by analogy with the general legal rules of property in tangible movables.[105] In this context, the gathering together of these fields was as much for educational convenience as anything else: certainly, there was little sense that the various regimes shared a single coherent framework. As Cornish argued, '[t]he various aspects of the subject differ in purpose and in detailed rule. Nonetheless there is good sense in studying them together.'[106]

However, as should now be clear, there has been a dramatic, though largely unnoticed, shift in the function of the concept of intellectual property over the last forty or so years: 'intellectual property' has rapidly moved from being a category *of laws* developed for the convenient presentation of distinct legal regimes into a legal concept – a category *in law*. The concept of intellectual property is now ritually used by lawmakers at international, regional and national levels: as already noted the WTO-TRIPS Agreement requires Contracting Parties to provide various remedies for infringement of 'intellectual property rights'; the EU's Enforcement Directive (2004/48) likewise requires Member States to offer certain procedures and remedies in relation to 'intellectual property rights'; the Access to Documents Regulation (1049/2001), which entitles citizens to examine documents held by EU institutions, provides an exemption from disclosure where it would undermine the protection of 'commercial interests of a natural or legal person, including intellectual property'; and Article 17(2) of the EU's Charter of Fundamental Rights even declares that '[i]ntellectual property shall be protected'. Today, whether something constitutes intellectual property can have significant legal implications.

But what is 'intellectual property'? Although intellectual property is often defined as including confidential information, there are many

[104] When the term 'intellectual property' was used in the period between 1850 and 1950 it operated as a synonym for 'literary and artistic property', 'authors' rights' or 'copyright'. See Justin Hughes, 'A Short History of Intellectual Property in Relation to Copyright' (2012) 33 *Cardozo Law Review* 1293.

[105] Cornish, *Intellectual Property* (1981), pp. ix, 3–4.

[106] See more recently, William R. Cornish, *Intellectual Property: Omnipresent, Distracting, Irrelevant?* (Oxford University Press, 2004), pp. 2–5 (arguing that while 'IP' may now be a 'convenient genus ... its various species remain distinct').

circumstances in which intellectual property is defined so as not to include confidential information. Indeed, the WIPO Treaty, establishing obligations on the World Intellectual Property Organization to promote the protection of intellectual property throughout the world,[107] defines 'intellectual property' as encompassing patents, copyright and trade marks, as well as the 'protection of unfair competition and all other rights resulting from intellectual activity in the industrial, scientific, literary or artistic fields', but makes no specific reference to confidentiality.[108] Moreover, a joint declaration attached to the free trade agreement between the EU and Serbia of 2010 categorises undisclosed information as 'commercial property', in contrast to 'industrial and intellectual property' (which includes patents, trade marks and copyright), though the agreement seems to require similar levels of protection to be afforded to commercial property as to intellectual property.[109] The Aarhus Convention on rights of access to environmental information also distinguishes between 'confidential information' and 'intellectual property'. Article 4 of the Convention identifies a number of grounds on which an exemption from an obligation to disclose information might be based with separate grounds relating to 'the confidentiality of commercial and industrial information, where such confidentiality is protected by law in order to protect a legitimate economic interest', 'intellectual property rights' and 'the confidentiality of personal data'.[110] This clearly presupposes confidentiality and intellectual property are distinct categories. The same is true at UK level – there are many statutory definitions of 'intellectual property' that refer only to

[107] Convention Establishing the World Intellectual Property Organization, Stockholm, 14 July 1967 (as amended, 28 September 1979), Art. 3.

[108] WIPO Convention, Art. 2(viii).

[109] Interim Agreement on trade and trade-related matters between the European Community and the Republic of Serbia, [2010] OJ L/28/2, Art. 40 and Joint Declaration on Article 40 of this Agreement. See, to similar effect, Council and Commission Decision of 29 March 2010 on the conclusion of the Stabilisation and Association Agreement between the European Communities and their Member States, of the one part, and the Republic of Montenegro, [2010] OJ L 108/1, Art. 75 and Joint Declaration on Article 40 of this Agreement. These can be contrasted with the Euro-Mediterranean Agreement Between the EC and the People's Democratic Republic of Algeria (2005), (2005) OJ L 265/2, which also deploys the phrase 'intellectual, industrial and commercial property' in Article 44, a term which is defined as a totality in a Joint Declaration to include, in addition to patents, copyright etc., undisclosed information and 'confidential information concerning 'know-how'.

[110] Convention on Access to Information, Participation in Decision-making and Access to Justice in Environmental Matters 1998, Aarhus, 25 July 1998, in force 30 October 2001, 2161 UNTS 447.

statutory rights and thus do not include the protection of confidential information,[111] and some that distinguish between 'confidential information' and 'intellectual property'.[112]

Although, as we have seen, 'intellectual property' is frequently defined so as to include protection of confidential or undisclosed information, in many important areas of EU and UK law the question of whether confidential information is 'intellectual property' remains a matter of speculation. Is confidential information protected for purposes of the Charter, which states that intellectual property shall be protected? Is it within the scope of Article 118 of the consolidated TFEU (Treaty on the Functioning of the European Union), which empowers the EU to legislate using the ordinary legislative procedure for 'European intellectual property rights'? Is it within the concept of 'intellectual property' or that of 'unfair competition' for the purposes of the Rome Convention on applicable law?[113]

[111] Forestry Act 1967 (as amended in 2006), s. 8 ('any patent, trademark [*sic*], copyright, design right, registered design or plant breeders' right'); National Heritage Act 1983 (as amended in 2002), s. 33B ('any patent, trade mark, registered design, copyright, design right, right in performance or plant breeders' right'); Finance Act 2000, s. 129 ('(a) any patent, trade mark, registered design, copyright or design right, (b) any plant breeders' right or rights under section 7 of the Plant Varieties Act 1997, (c) any licence or other right in respect of anything within paragraph (a) or (b) and (d) any rights under the law of a country or territory outside the United Kingdom that correspond to or are similar to those within paragraph (a), (b) or (c)'); Finance Act 2000, Sch. 15, para. 29; Company Act 2006, s. 861(4) ('any patent, trade mark, registered design, copyright or design right'); Income Tax Act 2007, s. 95(6) ('any patent, trade mark, registered design, copyright or design right, plant breeders' right'); Scientific Research Organisations Regulations 2007/3426, reg. 2 Corporation Tax Act 2009, s. 712 ('any patent, trade mark, registered design, copyright or design right, plant breeders' right or rights under section 7 of the Plant Varieties Act 1997').

[112] The Employment Tribunals Extension of Jurisdiction (England and Wales) Order 1994, SI 1994/1623, Ord. 5 (exempting from tribunal's jurisdiction in relation to contractual claims by an employer against a former employee any claim for breach of a contractual term 'relating to intellectual property' or 'imposing an obligation of confidence', with 'intellectual property' defined as including 'copyright, rights in performances, moral rights, design right, registered designs, patents and trade marks').

[113] Regulation (EC) No 864/2007 of the European Parliament and of the Council of 11 July 2007 on the law applicable to non-contractual obligations (Rome II) (2007) OJ L 199/40. The relevant rule for determining the applicable law in relation to misuse of confidential information depends on interpretation of Articles 2(g), 4, 6, and 8 as well as recital 26. Article 4 contains a rule on tort, Article 6 a rule on unfair competition (except where the act of unfair competition affects exclusively the interests of a specific competitor, in which case Article 4 applies) and Article 8 a rule on intellectual property. Recital 26 states that 'the term "intellectual property rights" should be interpreted as meaning, for instance, copyright, related rights, the sui generis right for the protection of databases and industrial property rights', leaving unclear whether they might encompass

Recently in the United Kingdom the question of whether confidential information is 'intellectual property' was the subject of litigation that went right up to the Supreme Court. In *Phillips* v. *Mulcaire*,[114] Nicola Phillips alleged that her phone had been hacked and confidential information obtained by Mulcaire on behalf of News International, and sought disclosure of documents held by Mulcaire to support her case.[115] Mulcaire argued that disclosure would be likely to incriminate him. As already noted, section 72 of the Senior Courts Act provides that a person is not excused from complying with an order in civil proceedings on the basis that this would tend to expose him to proceedings for a related offence where the civil proceedings are 'for infringement of rights pertaining to any intellectual property or passing off'. Subsection 5 defines 'intellectual property' as 'any patent, trade mark, copyright, design right, registered design, technical or commercial information or other intellectual property'. The phone messages that it was said Mulcaire had accessed were from clients of Phillips, and contained both their private information and information about their 'finances, commercial business transactions, professional relationships and future career plans'.[116] The questions facing the Supreme Court were whether the subject matter of these messages constituted 'technical or commercial information' or, if not, whether the information was 'other intellectual property'.

The Supreme Court held that the information constituted 'technical or commercial information' and so must be disclosed by Mulcaire. The Court rejected Mulcaire's argument that 'technical or commercial information' must be interpreted narrowly as covering only such information as could properly be referred to as 'intellectual property'. Lord Walker, giving the only speech, explained that the term 'intellectual property' lacked 'potency' – there were some matters (copyright, patent, trade marks) that everyone agreed fell within its remit, but there was no agreement as to its

commercial secrets. Article 2(g) excludes from the scope of the Regulation 'non-contractual obligations arising out of violations of privacy and rights relating to personality, including defamation', seemingly therefore offering no harmonisation in relation to personal confidences.

114 [2012] UKSC 28 (4 July 2012). For earlier proceedings, see [2010] EWHC 2952 (Ch) (Mann J) and [2012] EWCA Civ 48 (where the Phillips case was joined with an appeal by Stephen Coogan in a parallel action against News Group: [2011] EWHC 349 (Ch) (Vos J). The following text draws on Lionel Bently, 'What Is Intellectual Property?' (2012) 71 *Cambridge Law Journal* 501.

115 The action was initially brought against News Group Newspapers, but Mulcaire was joined.

116 [2012] UKSC 28 at para. 6.

outer boundaries.[117] 'Intellectual property' would include some statutory rights not listed, such as database rights or plant breeders' rights, but the notion was not of assistance in interpreting the phrase 'technical or commercial information'.[118] That said, Lord Walker recognised that there were difficulties with defining 'technical or commercial information', though it clearly included as part of its core content 'trade secrets', that is not only 'products and processes' but also 'a wide range of financial information about the management and performance of a business, and plans for its future'.[119] He appeared to approve of Lord Neuberger MR's holding in the Court of Appeal that whether information was 'commercial' was a matter of character rather than value. As the claimant's pleadings alleged that the messages that had been accessed contained commercial as well as personal information, the House of Lords was satisfied that the statutory exemption to the privilege against self-incrimination was applicable.

This meant the Court did not need to address Phillips' argument that personal information that was covered by the obligation of confidence amounted to 'other intellectual property'. Nevertheless, recognising that the point was an important one and could be determinative of other claims, Lord Walker proceeded to consider it. Significantly, the Supreme Court did not agree with the Court of Appeal that such information could be regarded as falling within the designation 'intellectual property',[120] in part because the statutory definition had explicitly referred to technical and commercial information, but also because section 72 had been enacted in response to 'commercial piracy' and thus was intended to 'fortify remedies against unlawful trading practices'.[121] Consequently, personal information was in general not to be regarded as intellectual property (even if confidential). The Court left open whether in situations where celebrities treated their own personal information as material

[117] [2012] UKSC 28 at para. 20. The idea of potency was discussed before Vos J in *Gray and Coogan* v. *News Group Newspapers Ltd* [2011] EWHC 349 (Ch) at para. 74, by reference to Francis Bennion's text on statutory interpretation: Francis A. R. Bennion, *Bennion on Statutory Interpretation* 5th edn (London: LexisNexis, 2008). Bennion gives section 72(5) as an example of a situation where the approach taken is 'to specify the main ingredients, and rely for any others on the potency of the term defined'. This is cited by Lord Walker at para. 19, though clearly he differs from Bennion's view that 'intellectual property' has any such potency.

[118] Lord Walker at para. 21 stated that had the meaning of 'technical and commercial information' been so limited, 'in practice it would be almost nullified'.

[119] [2012] UKSC 28 at para. 22.

[120] [2012] EWCA Civ 48, [2012] 2 WLR 848, sub. nom. *Coogan* v. *News Group Newspapers*.

[121] [2012] UKSC 28 at paras. 28–29.

for commercial exploitation, that information could properly be called 'commercial information'.[122]

Although *Phillips* v. *Mulcaire* is important in that it highlights that confidential information is not necessarily 'intellectual property' (so the strongest one could put the proposition is that confidential information is often regarded as intellectual property), the reference to the 'impotence' of the concept of intellectual property may also explain why, even where confidential information is intellectual property, that categorisation has little relevance for the question of whether confidential information is property. The designation of something as intellectual property provides assistance in a variety of matters, but not the intrinsic characterisation of the right (or jurisdictional basis of the action to protect confidential information within the common law). Indeed, there are plenty of matters that are designated 'intellectual property' that are not normally characterised as 'property': the former term embraces moral rights of authors (which are not treated as 'property' because they are non-assignable), the rights of those entitled to use geographical indications (which are not regarded as 'property' because of their non-exclusive character), as well as rights to prevent 'unfair competition' (which tend to be treated as tortious or delictual, in large part because a prohibitive remedial response is not automatic).[123] The designation 'intellectual property' is thus 'impotent' not just in the way that Lord Walker understood that term, as offering no determinative indication as to the content included, but also as a description of the very nature and character of the rights.

4.2 Global legal pluralism

A second way to understand the proposition that confidential information is 'intellectual property but not property' is in terms of the changing nature of the English legal system. While once the English legal system was identified with the common law, and understood – aspirationally if not realistically – as a coherent body of principles, concepts and rules,[124]

[122] [2012] UKSC 28 at para. 31.

[123] In addition, it is worth noting that there are some who deny that the core rights of intellectual property, such as patents and copyright, are properly described as 'property'. See e.g. James Penner, *The Idea of Property in Law* (Oxford: Clarendon, 1997), pp. 109, 118–20.

[124] Jan M. Smits, 'The Complexity of Transnational Law: Coherence and Fragmentation of Private Law', University of Helsinki, Legal Studies Research Paper Series, Paper No. 1; (2011) 1 *Isaidat Law Review* 1 at 3 ('For most scholars, the traditional picture is one in which private law is a coherent, unitary and national system … In that picture …

today the English legal system is recognised as fragmented, the product of multiple sources of law,[125] and comprising concepts and rules that are not necessarily consistent in meaning or even coherent. This multiplicity of sources is difficult to integrate into national law. This new legal fragmentation, common to all countries, has been widely dubbed 'legal pluralism'.[126] Inevitably, such pluralism has come at the expense of coherence: the terminology and conceptual structures employed in laws forged in an array of different fora, for different purposes and frequently as compromises between different legal traditions, cannot and should not be assumed to have the same meaning and content.[127] As a consequence, legal texts and decisions need to be understood in their specific context, in the light of their origins and purpose, and cannot be assumed to form part of a coherent system formulated by a single legislature or judiciary. Formal laws are not the commands of 'a sovereign', but the result of multiple voices.

cases, rules, standards and concepts are all part of a consistent whole without any contradictions within the system itself'). Whether English law ever was a coherent system of principles, concepts and rules, must be regarded as rather doubtful. Indeed, the debate in the 1970s and 1980s over the status of confidential information was itself a response to the plurality of sources of protection for confidential information (contract, tort, equity, property, good faith). However, as we have seen, the idea that the system should be coherent underpinned the instinctive reaction amongst academics and commentators to seek to select one such jurisdictional foundation in order to simplify the law and make it more coherent. Jurists pledged allegiance to particular historically informed strands of thinking, with a view to silencing, or harmonising, the legal cacophony that had emerged. Standing out from that tendency was Gurry's view that breach of confidence was *sui generis*, and that the various sources of law offered flexibility – opportunities to develop the most suitable legal response to the circumstances of the case. In some ways, Gurry's thesis was a precursor of those commentators who see legal pluralism and fragmentation today as an opportunity.

125 Most obviously not just the common law, but also legislation, subordinate legislation, European legislation, case law of the Court of Justice of the European Union, the European Convention on Human Rights, the case law of the Strasbourg Court, as well as international law developed in a number of fora (WIPO, the WTO, multilateral trade agreements, bilateral trade agreements, etc.) and treaty interpretation under the WTO Dispute Resolution system.

126 Paul Schiff Berman, 'Global Legal Pluralism' (2007) 80 *Southern California Law Review* 1155; Daniel Halberstam, 'Pluralism in Marbury and Van Gend' in Miguel Poiares Maduro and Loic Azoulai, *The Past and Future of EU Law* (Oxford: Hart, 2010), p. 26; Gregory Shaffer and Mark Pollack, 'Hard vs Soft Law: Alternatives, Complements, and Antagonists in International Governance' (2010) *Minnesota Law Review* 706 at 737–41.

127 As Smits puts it, '[p]rivate law has become a building ground where there are several architects'. Smits, 'The Complexity of Transnational Law' 119.

The debate over whether confidential information is 'property' was conducted within the former paradigm; the designation of confidential information as 'intellectual property' is a reflection of, and indeed an example of, the new 'kaleidoscopic reality' of disaggregation,[128] or legal pluralism: the forging of terms, rules and categories outside the courts of England, in various international and regional fora, or within the legislature, with little or no concern for ensuring consistency with common law concepts such as 'property'.

For the most part, the debate over the nature of confidential information (as 'equity', 'tort' or 'property') was a debate by academics about judicial conceptualisation. It was a debate by jurists of the common law, in the context of the common law. The debate had a traditional tone and purpose: the concern of the academics was to make sense of the decisions and reasoning of the courts, to build a systematic account of those cases, and particularly of the underlying principles, that could guide further development. In so doing the jurists typically disregarded legislative developments involving statutory obligations of confidence (despite the fact that these seemed to have almost as lengthy a pedigree as the case law was understood to possess), and other matters that might have disrupted their attempts to organise the array of individual legal decisions into coherent and 'principled' systems of concepts and rules. It was in this rather aseptic, if fantasised, context that the conclusion that confidential information was not property took shape.

In contrast, the treatment of confidential information as 'intellectual property' has emerged in the informal regime of academic textbook writing (driven by pedagogical goals rather than a desire for coherent system-building), in the international law-making of the TRIPS Agreement and subsequent free trade agreements, as well as in European legislative initiatives (such as the regulation of foodstuffs), where the term 'intellectual property' seems to be selected as a shorthand useful to describe particular sets of rights for functional purposes (either of inclusion or exclusion). Confidential information thus may be 'intellectual property' within certain norm-setting mechanisms, but that description can be said to have no necessary or immediate impact on the debates over the character of the rights recognised at common law, or indeed the jurisdictional underpinnings of those common law rights and obligations. Confidential

[128] The phrase 'kaleidoscopic reality' is borrowed from Martti Koskenniemi and Paivi Leino, 'Fragmentation of International Law? Postmodern Anxieties' (2002) 15 *Leiden Journal of International Law* 553 at 559.

information may be 'intellectual property' for the purpose of TRIPS or even the EU Enforcement Directive, but in a pluralist legal environment that can leave intact and unaffected the characterisation of such confidential information for the purposes of the domestic legal action.

Fragmentation frequently produces its effects because courts and commentators operate in particular legal bunkers. As a result, they are simply unaware of developments in other bunkers: for example, the employment law, information law and media law specialists dealing with confidential information often act in blissful ignorance of the tendency amongst intellectual property practitioners to categorise confidential information as 'intellectual property'. Thus two of the leading English commentaries on the law of confidential information, Toulson and Phipps and Stanley, do not refer to 'intellectual property' or TRIPS at all.[129] The authors, all barristers and judges, operate outside the world of intellectual property: Charles Phipps is a barrister specialising in professional negligence, as was his co-author, (now Lord Justice) Roger Toulson, before he took judicial office. Paul Stanley advises on insurance-related arbitrations. None are significantly involved with intellectual property. Likewise, Baroness Hale (by training a specialist in family law) seems to have displayed this bunker mentality when she observed in *Douglas* v. *Hello!* that she could not understand how it could be said that their Lordships were creating some kind of unorthodox intellectual property right.[130]

The absence of impact of international legal conceptions on domestic characterisation of rights can also be a matter of design. It might be said that, at least in the context of TRIPS, the formulation of the obligation to protect undisclosed information was specifically designed to leave open the possibility for its protection at a national level through non-proprietary means. Indeed, the final text of Article 39 of TRIPS, which nested the obligation within Article 10bis of the Paris Convention,

[129] Toulson does cite Cornish's textbook: Toulson and Phipps, *Confidentiality*, p. 30, para. 2.033 n. 26; p. 35, para. 2-049; while Stanley, *The Law of Confidentiality*, p. 113, refers to two intellectual property cases when discussing accessorial liability. Interestingly, in his preface Stanley refers to confidentiality as an area of law on which 'so many specialists bring their particular concerns and characteristic techniques to bear' and warns that 'intellectual property lawyers … may be too swift to treat all rights as if they were intellectual *property* rights' (emphasis in original).

[130] *OBG Ltd* v. *Allan* [2007] UKHL 21; [2008] 1 AC 1, 87, para. 307 ('I confess to having some difficulty understanding what this has to do with the law of intellectual property'). She seems to identify two distinctions: one based on purpose (intellectual property rights reward their creators rather than keep information quiet); and another based on form (intellectual property rights are statutory, whereas the law of confidentiality is judge-made).

appears carefully to have avoided the use of proprietary language, referring not to 'owners' but to persons having information 'lawfully within their control', and conferring not 'rights' but merely 'the possibility of preventing' that information from being disclosed to, acquired by or used by others. In some ways, TRIPS seems to have deliberately preserved the very possibility that confidential information might be 'intellectual property but not property'. The same point might be true of European legal initiatives, in so far as they are embodied in Directives that are intended to be prescriptive only as to the effect to be achieved, leaving to Member States the method of implementation: the Enforcement Directive thus might require certain remedies to be available for misuse of confidential information, but it does not purport thereby to delimit the conceptual structure deployed by a particular Member State to determine how that effect is to be achieved. More significantly still, perhaps, the Treaty leaves as the exclusive preserve of Member States the formulation of rules on ownership of property.

Confidential information, it seems, can be (and often is) 'intellectual property' but not 'property'. The two explanations for this – the impotence of the concept of intellectual property and the growth of global legal pluralism – are, of course, interrelated: the fact that the concept of 'intellectual property' is deployed in different environments and for disparate purposes in addition to its relatively novel status, means that it lacks a particular, standardised or well-understood meaning – it lacks potency.[131] The term must be read in context both to understand what is referred to and what consequences should flow from any given reference to 'intellectual property'.[132]

[131] These observations should not be understood as denying the possibility that the concept of 'intellectual property' could ever come to be understood as having a particular content when used in a range of legislative, judicial, national, regional and international contexts; just that we are a long way from that situation right now.

[132] Although this particular example of incoherence is hardly likely to undermine the credibility of the rule of law, when viewed in the broader context of legal pluralism, we might well ask whether it does not have not serious implications for the idea of the accessibility of the law. After all, the complexity and incoherence associated with fragmentation threatens the very comprehensibility of legal norms. Informed legal actors such as judges may understand the importance of contextual interpretation, but the public at large may be misled by the use of similar terms and concepts to convey different, and often unarticulated, meanings. One strategy to reduce levels of complexity is referred to as 'universalism', to reduce fragmentation through the surrender of national legal autonomy (its associated concepts and traditions) to regional and international arrangements. This might be attempted unilaterally by a particular legal system, but more plausibly through further cooperation and intensification of harmonised norms.

5 Conclusion

This taxonomic surprise (that confidential information may be 'intellectual property' but not 'property') must, at the very least, raise questions about the claim of Lemley, Benkler and others that the very designation 'intellectual property' leads to thinking about the specific regimes (copyright, trade marks and so on) in proprietary terms, and in turn to expansion of rights.[133] Indeed, subsequent work by Lemley himself suggests he has acknowledged the problem. In an article written in 2008,[134] he described the US courts' references to trade secrets as 'property' as references to such rights being intellectual property, and suggested that there were 'surprising virtues' to such treatment (as opposed to one which treated trade secrets as a subject of tort or unfair competition). For Lemley, treating trade secrets as 'IP' had the virtues of providing a justification (in terms of incentives to create and disclose), and limiting the circumstances in which protection might arise. Implicit in this claim is the supposition that calling confidential information 'intellectual property' might not lead to it being thought of as (real) property and might restrict, rather than expand protection.

Whatever Lemley's revised position might now be, one plausible response to the observations I have made is that the effects of designating certain rights as 'intellectual property' will take longer to have an impact in relation to those rights, such as confidential information, that are at the 'periphery' and that are sometimes treated as 'intellectual property' and sometimes not. But, it might be countered, Benkler's claim is that the use of the terminology is already having its effects, and that it is precisely at the margins that one would expect to witness the impact of the 'conceptual attitudes' associated with what Benkler describes as the 'semantic umbrella'. After all, patents, copyright and trade marks – the 'core' rights within the umbrella – have been regarded as some type of property for over a century, and indeed are statutorily defined as 'property'. So the

[133] This is not to suggest that the adoption of 'intellectual property' as a rubric, and now a category in law, is, or will be, wholly neutral in its effects. Richard Stallman has a distinct objection to the use of the term, arguing that it leads to an assumption that all intellectual products should be protected, and thus to tendencies to fill the gaps in the coverage of patents, copyright and trade marks by new rights. Certainly, there has been a proliferation of such rights, but whether a causal connection can be shown to use of the term 'intellectual property' would require a sustained analysis.

[134] Lemley, 'Surprising Virtues'.

effects of the 'intellectual property' designation on attitudes towards patents, copyright and trade marks are likely to be limited (and much more difficult to discern).[135]

At the very least, the critique of the use of 'intellectual property' as a category of laws (and *a fortiori* as a category in law) needs to be refined to account for the case of confidential information. It may well be that, as with the argument that property talk leads to expansionist visions for trade marks and copyright, such a refinement would differentiate between the many contexts in which the concept of 'intellectual property' is deployed. Neil Netanel has argued that while high-level judges are unlikely to draw conclusions formalistically from the use of particular terminology, lower-court judges might well do so.[136] In the United Kingdom, 'property talk' seems to have been more consistently and successfully used as a rhetorical tool by lobbyists seeking to influence Parliamentarians to expand copyright than when used in attempts to influence judges or civil servants.[137] So it might be that the increasing prevalence of the treatment of confidential information as 'intellectual property' would yield some expansionist effects were that field to be the subject of legislative action.[138] In this respect it is notable that, in December 2012, the European Commission began a process of consultation of stakeholders with a view to harmonising the law of trade secrets in Europe.[139]

135 Another possibility is that academic warnings by Lemley and Benkler have had the desired effect: alert to the dangers of misinterpreting the designation 'intellectual property' as implying anything about the content of particular rights, scholars and courts have carefully defined the characteristics of confidential information by resort to policy-reasoning. Although Lemley's 2004 article is referred to in Aplin *et al.*, *Gurry on Breach of Confidence*, p. 137, n. 342, the question of the treatment of confidential information as 'intellectual property' and its effects is, for the most part, simply ignored or assumed to be of marginal importance.

136 Netanel, 'Why Has Copyright Expanded?', p. 13.

137 Lionel Bently, 'R v Author: From the Death Penalty to Community Service' (2008–09) 32 *Columbia Journal of Law and the Arts* 1 at 41–5, 90.

138 But this, of course, is not what Lemley was arguing. Indeed, he singled out 'courts and scholars' as those already imprisoned by the terminology of 'intellectual property'. Lemley, 'Property, Intellectual Property, and Free Riding' 1035.

139 European Commission, *Public Consultation on the Protection of Business and Research Know-How* (Brussels, 2012).

4

Equity, confidentiality and the nature of property

ALASTAIR HUDSON

The argument

This chapter is an exercise in differentiation in that it identifies the ways in which intellectual property law specialists and equity specialists think differently about obligations of confidence and about property rights, and considers why this might be so. Two principal observations are made.

The first observation is that intellectual property lawyers in particular, and common lawyers in general, do not connect with the language of equity, and in consequence they have a tendency to overlook its doctrinal core. An illustration of this tendency is presented below in an analysis of the way in which the *Spycatcher* litigation[1] has been understood differently in relation to its treatment of liability for breach of confidence by lawyers schooled in different traditions. Nine different judges gave judgments in that litigation, and yet the common law commentators have tended to telescope their focus down to half a paragraph in the judgment of Lord Goff because it appeals to their methodological culture. This is in spite of the fact that it was the authoritative discussion of the 'obligation of conscience' at the heart of the equitable action for breach of confidence, set out in the judgment of Scott J, which summarised the law at the time, and which was accepted as a correct statement of the law by all of the other judges who expressed a view. Nevertheless, that latter judgment is entirely unremarked upon in the common law literature.

Second, the way in which equity uses proprietary rights is very different from the way in which intellectual property law models property rights. In doctrines such as proprietary estoppel and constructive trust, equity deploys proprietary rights on some occasions and personal rights on other occasions so as to reach the most equitable outcome in any given circumstances. Equity revolves around a central notion of 'conscience'. In

[1] *Attorney-General* v. *Guardian Newspapers* [1990] 1 AC 109: hereafter '*Spycatcher*'.

this sense, equity is built on case law that fleshes out high-level, deontological principles in individual circumstances, albeit that many of these doctrines have become set in stone in practice by means of the doctrine of precedent.[2] This contrasts starkly with the approach taken in intellectual property law, which is to commodify property rights so that they can be exploited commercially in accordance with detailed statutory codes. Whereas equity uses property rights both flexibly in doctrines such as proprietary estoppel and more formalistically in relation to doctrines such as express trusts, intellectual property law is concerned with a rigid and predictable model of property right that is used to protect innovation as well as controlling the dissemination of (and access to) those innovations.[3] An illustration of this distinction between the different uses of property in equity and intellectual property law is presented below in an analysis of the leading trusts law case of *Boardman* v. *Phipps*,[4] which related to the equitable doctrines of constructive trust and account concerning a misuse of confidential information by a fiduciary. This serves as an illustration of the way in which equity conceives of proprietary rights as arising in many circumstances where 'good conscience' requires it: in that instance so as to prevent the possibility of a fiduciary taking a benefit from a conflict of interest. This contrasts markedly with the concept of the property right as used in intellectual property law.

1 The action for breach of confidence

1.1 Introduction

It is accepted in the equity literature that there has been an action for breach of confidence in equity since the sixteenth century at the very least.[5] Much of the common law scholarship in this area has tended to treat that doctrine as though it is lost in the mists of time, even though there continue to be decisions based on it in the twenty-first century.[6]

[2] 'Deontological' thinking is a way of establishing an objective set of moral duties and then using those high-level, central principles to decide individual cases. Equity has formal rules as to the way in which those central principles are developed, particularly in the form of the doctrine of precedent. Moreover, the individual cases contribute (consequentially one might think) to the evolution of those central principles.

[3] See, for example, the chapters by Helena R. Howe and Michael A. Carrier in this collection.

[4] *Boardman* v. *Phipps* [1967] 2 AC 46.

[5] *Coco* v. *AN Clark (Engineers) Ltd* [1969] RPC 41; where Megarry J cited the dicta of Lord Chancellor More from the 16th century, see n. 23.

[6] *Imerman* v. *Tchenguiz* [2011] 2 WLR 592.

What is particularly interesting is that the common law commentators rarely give a detailed account of the equitable nature of the doctrine. For an equity specialist, however, it is clear that this doctrine is based on an 'obligation in conscience', which means that a court will prevent misuse of confidential information or other matters arising in confidence by use of the equitable remedies of injunction or equitable damages where that court considers that the defendant has acted unconscionably. What is meant by acting 'unconscionably' in the equitable context is something that has been explored in centuries of precedent. The point that is made here is that this way of thinking from general principles that are then applied to individual circumstances is anathema to common lawyers. Indeed, this way of thinking is so alien that when judges use this language of conscience, common lawyers tend to fail to notice that it is there and highlight other aspects of those judgments instead.

1.2 The essence of the equitable action for breach of confidence

It was treated as settled law in *Attorney-General* v. *Guardian Newspapers (No. 2)*,[7] referred to throughout in this chapter as '*Spycatcher*', that the equitable principle governing the action for breach of confidence was an 'obligation in conscience' not to misuse confidential information.[8] However, the very full analysis of the law set out in this context by Scott J at first instance in *Spycatcher* (analysed below) is not mentioned in any of the significant common law accounts of breach of confidence. It is suggested that the reason for this oversight is twofold. First, the idea of 'conscience' is not a concept that has any traction in common law scholarship and therefore its highly nuanced meaning in equity scholarship simply fails to connect with common lawyers. Second, Lord Goff usefully (from the perspective of a common lawyer) suggested a narrowing of the action for breach of confidence from a focus on confidential relationships to a focus on information that in itself is clearly confidential. These relational concepts set out by Lord Goff are the meat and drink of the common law: the idea that liability is based on specific forms of relationship is central both to tort and to contract law. Therefore, it was Lord Goff's ideas that have appealed to the common law community. Ironically, as is explored below, Lord Goff himself was at great pains to explain that he was not

[7] [1990] 1 AC 109.

[8] *Spycatcher* [1990] AC 109 at 281, per Lord Goff and at 255, per Lord Keith.

intending to analyse (let alone restate) the law on breach of confidence in full, and that he accepted the account of the law that had been set out in the universally praised judgment of Scott J at first instance. Nevertheless, the common law commentary on this case focused on Lord Goff having purportedly signalled a departure in the law and makes no mention of the judgment of Scott J.

It is worth noting, of course, that the *Spycatcher* litigation was treated in turn by public lawyers as presenting an entirely new dimension in national security law: not least in the 'enlarged D-notice' proposal suggested by Lord Donaldson MR, which offered entirely new possibilities for our law that were not envisaged in even the most disturbing writings of Franz Kafka.[9] For public lawyers, the private law concept of breach of confidence was of little or no interest compared to the pre-Human Rights Act impact on freedom of expression and the expansion of covert state activity. Refinements to the private law concept of breach of confidence simply did not sound in the register in which they worked.[10] This reinforces the central point of this chapter. It is another example of lawyers from different specialities deriving very different messages from the same case law. The talk of an 'obligation in conscience' mattered as little to public lawyers as it did to common lawyers, even though it is central to equity.

1.3 The treatment of the equitable basis for breach of confidence by common lawyers

It is a habit of common lawyers to treat the equitable roots of the action for breach of confidence as being lost in time or as being in some way unknowable. It seems to be treated as a sort of 'known unknown': that is, a concept that they encounter in reading the judgments but that is considered to be unknowable due to its seeming vagueness. What is interesting is that none of the commentators who have addressed this equitable root to the breach of confidence action (including Aplin and Bently,[11] Stanley[12] and others, considered below) have identified what the equitable doctrine actually *is*. That it is based on 'conscience' and that it is predicated on a long line of precedent is never mentioned. That is not to suggest for one

[9] [1990] 1 AC 109 at 200.

[10] Keith Ewing and Conor Gearty, *Freedom under Thatcher* (Oxford: Clarendon Press, 1990), pp. 152–69.

[11] Tanya Aplin, Lionel Bently, Phillip Johnson and Simon Malynicz, *Gurry's Law of Confidence* 2nd edn (Oxford University Press, 2012).

[12] Paul Stanley, *The Law of Confidentiality* (Oxford: Hart, 2008).

moment that common lawyers are ignorant of equity or trusts law; simply that they prefer a move positivist way of dealing with law than the uncertainties which are commonly thought to infect equity.

Let us begin with the field-leading *Gurry on Confidence*. It would be impossible to question the scholarship in this work, and that is why it is so useful as an example of one way of approaching this subject. Professor Bently begins his account[13] with the idea that the roots of the action are 'obscure'. It is said that 'Claims to the "Equitable" essence of the action are overstated, even if Courts of Equity did make important contributions to the development of protection'.[14] This dismissal of equity overlooks the continued use of injunctions – the principal equitable remedy – throughout the history of this doctrine, even in relation to the tort of misuse of private information today.[15] It also overlooks the ubiquitous description of breach of confidence as being based on an 'obligation in conscience' in equity in cases such as *Spycatcher* and *Douglas* v. *Hello! Ltd. (No 3)*,[16] as is considered immediately below. Indeed, Professor Bently, in a masterly analysis of the common law principles attendant on the use and misuse of confidential information, does not need to mention the word 'conscience' at all, even though it is used frequently in the cases in England and in Australia. What this indicates, it is suggested, is that 'conscience' is simply not a concept that connects with an intellectual property lawyer, albeit that it is of central importance to an equity specialist. Specialists from those two legal fields simply talk in different registers, using different concepts and different modes of thought. That is not to suggest that one way of thinking is better than another; it is simply to observe that they are different. It is simply a continuation of a debate which has carried on for centuries as to whether the common law or equity has the better approach; one which was conducted between Lord Coke and Lord Ellesmere around the *Earl of Oxford's Case* in 1615 and by countless judges and scholars ever since.

Instead, Professor Bently begins his analysis with *Prince Albert* v. *Strange*[17] and associates it with the concept of 'common law

[13] Aplin *et al.*, *Gurry's Law of Confidence*, p. 12.

[14] *Ibid.*, p. 13.

[15] See Alastair Hudson, *Equity & Trusts* 7th edn (Oxford: Routledge, 2012), 27.7 and 27.8 for an alternative, equitable account.

[16] [2008] 1 AC 1.

[17] (1849) 2 De G & Sm, 64 ER 293, which is considered in detail below. Professor Cornish considers that the 'modern law began to be settled around 1850' with the decision in *Prince Albert* v. *Strange*: W. Cornish and D. Llewelyn, *Intellectual Property* 6th edn (London: Sweet & Maxwell, 2007), p. 311. What is interesting about *Prince Albert* v.

copyright',[18] as opposed to equity; whereas an equity specialist might have stressed that the action began in the Vice Chancellor's equity court and resolved around an action for the equitable remedy of injunction. There is talk of 'the modern law of confidence' and of the *Spycatcher* litigation as having 'marked a new beginning' for the law on confidence, whereas the only judgments that explicitly considered the law on confidence in *Spycatcher* dwelt exclusively on the equitable roots of that action, as considered below. As such, by overlooking the equitable doctrine, it is said that the 'modern action of confidence is of surprisingly recent vintage'.[19]

Professor Aplin treats the equitable roots of the doctrine in a similar way, preferring to place its origin in 1948 with the judgment in *Saltman Engineering Co Ltd* v. *Campbell Engineering Co Ltd*[20] (on the basis that it was not 'until [that time] that its existence was firmly established').[21] Perhaps it is that reference to the doctrine needing to be 'firmly established' that is most revealing. For formidable common lawyers like Professors Aplin and Bently, law must be contained in solid concepts that arise predictably, just like the statutory models of copyright, patent and so forth in intellectual property law. It is part of their project precisely to establish the law on a more predictable body of rules. Consequently, a concept that is based on a high-level principle of 'conscience' simply does not appear to have a useful role to play.[22] It is as though there was nothing deserving of the label 'law' before it was solidified and concretised in the mid twentieth century.

However, this is to overlook the presence as early as the sixteenth century of the principle in the equitable canon stated by Lord Chancellor Thomas More whereby three things were 'apt to be helpt in Conscience: Fraud, Accident and things of Confidence', as Megarry J made clear in *Coco* v. *AN Clark (Engineers) Ltd*[23] in demonstrating the antiquity of the

Strange is that it is generally taken as authority for the proposition that equity enjoins any 'breach of trust, confidence or contract', even though that phrase appears in a single sentence in a judgment by Lord Cottenham that otherwise proceeds almost entirely (and erroneously) on the basis of the claimant's alleged property rights in etchings that the defendant had intended to exhibit and to describe in a catalogue.

18 Aplin *et al.*, *Gurry's Law of Confidence*, p. 13.

19 *Ibid.* 20 (1948) 65 RPC 203.

21 Aplin *et al.*, *Gurry's Law of Confidence*, p. 107.

22 Ironically, the case could be made that it is the modern law that has introduced confusion by not sticking simply to the traditional equitable doctrines and instead by seeking to erect the law on a variety of different bases: see Law Commission, *Breach of Confidence*, Working Paper 58 (1974), p. 10.

23 [1969] RPC 41 at 47.

concept. The reason for this treatment of an ancient equitable principle is in the common lawyer's attitude that a high-level principle like that set out by Thomas More is not really 'law' in any meaningful sense. It is this fluidity in equity that is so alien to the common law mind. It is no accident that common lawyers borrow the three-stage, categorical rule from equity (as in *Strange* and in *Coco*) because they appear to establish clear-cut 'tests' that set out the elements that must be proved by a claimant so as to establish a right, as opposed to seemingly vague, high-level principles such as 'good conscience' that only have content if one is conversant with the detailed manner in which they are expounded in the authorities in equity.

Again, my point here is not to criticise the approach of the common lawyers. It is simply to recognise a methodological difference between us. The historical account given in *Gurry* is scholarly and precise. There is no doubting that. However, as is well known, the telling of history changes our understanding of what that history was. History is something that we use to present ideas about ourselves that are useful at the time we tell those stories.[24] A history quite literally comprises a 'story' and like all stories it will evolve over time, with different factors or details seeming to acquire more or less significance. The importance that the treatment of confidential information has acquired in the modern age (and the challenges offered to it by the Internet, by Wikileaks and by a schizophrenic culture in which we both 'tell all' and enjoin all from repeating those revelations) has meant that we have come to understand the law on confidence differently from the way we used to understand it. The purposes to which we want to put that doctrine in the modern world are different from their traditional uses. And, in consequence, we have begun to tell this story differently through common law and human rights law, as opposed to equity.

What is interesting for an equity specialist is to see two such prominent intellectual property lawyers as Professor Bently and Professor Aplin take such pains in their several contributions to *Gurry's Law of Confidence* to separate the law off from its equitable roots, to trace a development in the law away from equity and to treat equity as being somehow 'other'. To make that observation is neither to doubt this drift in the law (from equity towards human rights and tort law) nor to criticise the viewpoint of Professors Bently and Aplin; rather, it is simply to observe a difference in our conceptual worldviews. In identifying that drift, however,

[24] See, for example, Edward Hallett Carr, *What is History?* (Harmondsworth: Penguin, 1961).

we should bear in mind that actions for breach of confidence still rely on the equitable remedy of injunction as their principal remedy, and therefore the equity continues in existence. Moreover, the equitable doctrine of confidence remains in rude health beyond the world of celebrities seeking to protect their private lives from public scrutiny by means of the new tort of misuse of private information, as demonstrated most recently by the decision of the Court of Appeal in *Imerman* v. *Tchenguiz*,[25] which was based entirely on the equitable doctrine of confidence.

Nevertheless, the common lawyers are in the ascendant, and the thought processes of the intellectual property lawyers in particular are informing our modern understanding of the law on confidence, particularly in relation to the new tort. Therefore, the way in which *the telling* of this story about the development of the law on privacy and confidence begins is with that one paragraph in the judgment of Lord Goff in *Spycatcher.* The equitable doctrine is therefore marginalised because the story that it tells is out of keeping with the prevailing, celebrity-led modern sensibility. In the next section we drill down a little more deeply into this equitable principle.

1.4 *The 'obligation in conscience' underpinning breach of confidence in* Spycatcher

1.4.1 The traditional equitable principle

The judgment of Scott J in *Spycatcher*[26] is the most complete account of the equitable doctrine of breach of confidence in the modern law. The central principle that was accepted by Scott J and by the entirety of the Court of Appeal, and that was not objected to by the House of Lords, was that the doctrine of confidence in equity is predicated on the defendant having an 'obligation in conscience' in relation to confidential information. And yet that concept, which drew on a wealth of earlier authorities in England and Australia, is invisible in the common law discussions of the law in this area.

The earlier authorities, as relied upon by judges in all three courts (including Lord Goff in the House of Lords), were unanimous in identifying the principle as being equitable. By way of example, it was held

[25] [2011] 2 WLR 592. Indeed, it should be remembered that damages were available in equity from the time of Lord Cairns' Act in confidence actions.

[26] [1990] 1 AC 109. Another account on very similar grounds was set out at first instance in *Douglas* v. *Hello! (No. 3)* [2003] 3 All ER 996 by Lindsay J.

by Mason J in *Commonwealth of Australia* v. *John Fairfax & Sons Ltd*[27] and by Deane J in *Moorgate Tobacco Ltd* v. *Philip Morris Ltd*[28] that there is a 'general equitable jurisdiction' to grant relief in relation to breaches of confidence, and that '[l]ike most heads of exclusively equitable jurisdiction, its rational basis does not lie in proprietary right. It lies in the notion of an obligation of conscience arising from the circumstances in or through which the information was communicated or obtained.'[29]

This statement of the principle – specifically that the equitable doctrine of breach of confidence is predicated on 'an obligation of conscience' – was adopted by Scott J[30] and by Bingham LJ in the Court of Appeal.[31] In relation to the discussion below about the nature of property rights in equity, it is useful to note that this equitable right of confidence is not based on a property right but rather on the general moral requirement of good conscience. Their Lordships adopted the dicta of Mason J in *Commonwealth of Australia* v. *John Fairfax & Sons Ltd*[32] to the effect that the 'equitable principle has been fashioned to protect the personal, private and proprietary interests of the citizen' as opposed to the interests of the state.[33] Similarly, in the New South Wales Court of Appeal, Street CJ had held that while the doctrines of equity often operate through proprietary interests, the appropriate form of remedy is in the largest sense an '*in personam*' remedy, which is a reference to the underlying principle of equity[34] where a court looks to the conscience of the individual in deciding which remedy or doctrine, if any, is appropriate.[35] This is a very different usage of legal doctrines, which may have an effect on property rights, from intellectual property law. In equity, the concretised identification of a pre-existing property right is not as significant as it is in intellectual property law, where the purpose of the right is to safeguard commercial exploitation of copyrights, patents, trade marks and particular types of commercially sensitive, confidential information.

That the equitable doctrine stands aside from contract law, tort law and property law was made plain in *Fraser* v. *Evans*[36] by Lord Denning MR on the basis that the duty of confidence 'is based not so much on property

[27] (1980) 147 CLR 39. [28] (1984) 156 CLR 414. [29] *Ibid.* at 437.
[30] *Spycatcher* [1990] 1 AC 109 at 147. [31] *Ibid.* at 216.
[32] (1980) 147 CLR 39.
[33] *Ibid.* at 50. Again, therefore, the doctrine is not dependent on a property right, although it might arise in relation to a property right in some circumstances.
[34] Hudson, *Equity & Trusts*, p. 23.
[35] [1990] 1 AC 109 at 152, quoting from the judgment of that court in *Spycatcher.*
[36] [1969] 1 QB 349 at 361.

or on contract as on the duty to be of good faith'. Similarly, in *Seager* v. *Copydex*,[37] Lord Denning MR had based the duty of confidence on 'the broad principle of equity that he who has received information in confidence shall not take unfair advantage of it'. To an equity specialist, these ideas of unfairness and good faith are at one with the central idea of 'good conscience'. The Court of Appeal, in turn, quoted these statements with approval in *Spycatcher*.[38] Equally, more recently, the judgement of Lord Neuberger MR in *Imerman* v. *Tchenguiz*[39] has re-emphasised the distinction between equity and the common law in cases of confidence. These conceptualisations of the principles are in the grand tradition of equity and are signifiers of well-understood lines of precedent within equity.

1.4.2 The limits of Lord Goff's judgment

By contrast, common law commentators have cited Lord Goff's judgment in *Spycatcher* as being the *fons origio* for a modern law of confidence.[40] Significantly, however, Lord Goff made clear in the first sentence of his judgment that he was not attempting a restatement of the law on breach of confidence.[41] Nevertheless, the following dicta have informed every common law account of the law in this area in spite of its author's reluctance to have his judgment taken as a definitive statement of the law:

> a duty of confidence arises when confidential information comes to the knowledge of a person in circumstances where he has notice, or is held to have agreed, that the information is confidential, with the effect that it would be just in all the circumstances that he should be precluded from disclosing the information to others.[42]

Lord Goff emphasised at the beginning of that same sentence that 'I do not intend [this] in any way to be definitive'.[43] In any event, the reliance on the justice of the situation in those dicta, together with the statement in the following paragraph of his Lordship's judgment that a duty of confidence arises in equity and that there is an obligation of conscience, support the equitable model of this doctrine, even though they are habitually used by estimable common lawyers such as Aplin and Bently to justify the

[37] [1967] 1 WLR 923 at 931.
[38] [1990] 1 AC 109 at 215, per Bingham LJ.
[39] [2011] 2 WLR 592.
[40] E.g. Aplin *et al.*, *Gurry's Law of Confidence*, pp. 13, 107.
[41] *Spycatcher* [1990] 1 AC 109 at 280.
[42] *Ibid.* at 281. [43] *Ibid.*

new tort of misuse of private information and the creation of a 'modern law of confidence'.

1.5 The roots of the equitable doctrine of breach of confidence

1.5.1 The nature of equitable doctrines

Questions of confidence have long been a concern of equity. As Lord Chancellor Sir Thomas More said in the sixteenth century: 'Three things are apt to be helpt in Conscience: Fraud, Accident and things of confidence.'[44] The reference to the capitalised 'Conscience' is a reference to the courts of Chancery, which were avowedly less concerned with common law rules than with 'things in conscience'.[45] Textbooks on 'Equity' often begin with the identification of equity in Aristotle's Ethics as being 'superior' to formal justice,[46] or with the *Earl of Oxford's Case* in 1615 and the idea that the role of equity is both to 'correct men's consciences for frauds, breach of trusts, wrongs and oppressions … and to soften and mollify the extremity of the [common] law'.[47] These sorts of statements of the high-level principles abound in early equity cases. They are central to the way in which equity specialists think. In philosophical terms, this is deontological thinking where one begins with a core moral statement and then works outwards from there by applying that central moral precept to individual cases. Equity, however, operates on the basis of the doctrine of precedent whereby that central moral statement can be adapted and informed by its use in the case law.

In this way, the equitable doctrine of breach of confidence is said to operate on the basis of a principle of conscience. A straight line can be drawn from those cases to the 'obligation of conscience' in *Spycatcher*.[48] It can also be seen in the identification of the remedy as being a form of 'equitable relief' that is predicated on the ancient equitable 'clean hands' doctrine by Ungoed-Thomas J in *Duchess of Argyll* v. *Duke of Argyll*.[49] The 'clean hands' doctrine is one of the longest standing equitable principles, identified as being one of the key equitable maxims by Edward Snell in

[44] Quoted by Megarry J in *Coco* v. *AN Clark (Engineers) Ltd* [1969] RPC 41 at 46.

[45] Fortescue CJ declared in 1452 that 'We are to argue conscience here, not the law': Mitch 31 Hen VI, Fitz Abr, *Subpena*, pl 23.

[46] Hudson, *Equity & Trusts*, p. 11.

[47] (1615) 1 Ch Rep 1. Similar sentiments appear in *Lord Dudley* v. *Lady Dudley* (1705) Prec Ch 241 at 244, per Lord Cowper LC and Sir Nathan Wright LK.

[48] *Spycatcher* [1990] 1 AC 109 at 147, per Scott J.

[49] [1967] Ch 302.

1868.[50] The doctrine was identified by Sir George Turner VC in *Morison* v. *Moat*[51] as being based on conscience. Lord Neuberger held similarly in *Imerman* v. *Tchenguiz*[52] that 'Equity fashions the appropriate relief to fit the rights of the parties' in the traditional way. Nevertheless, to common lawyers this intellectual heritage is all but invisible. It is not how common lawyers think.

As to the precise equitable remedy of injunction in this area, the award of an injunction arises 'on the simple ground that equity gives relief against all the world, including the innocent, save only a bona fide purchaser for value without notice'.[53] Lord Nicholls held in *Mercedes Benz AG* v. *Leiduck*[54] that the courts' inherent, equitable jurisdiction is 'unfettered by statute, [and] should not be rigidly confined to exclusive categories by judicial decision. The court may grant an injunction against a party properly before it where this is required to avoid injustice.' Therefore, the courts have a very broad, inherent power to grant injunctions in the interests of avoiding injustice. This focus on 'avoiding injustice' has been part of the conceptualisation of equity since Aristotle,[55] for all that it may seem at first blush like empty rhetoric. In consequence, the equitable action will lie against third parties who come into possession of the confidential information provided that there is something about the circumstances that raises 'an obligation of conscience'[56] or if there is something about those circumstances that means that that person's use of the confidential information is 'precluded in conscience'.[57] The most obvious examples of confidence in equity in the early cases would be in relation to fiduciary duties such as trusteeship, although the doctrine of confidence is not limited to fiduciary duties.[58]

[50] Edmund H. T. Snell, *The Principles of Equity* (London: Stevens and Haynes, 1868), p. 34; referencing *Overton* v. *Banister* (1844) 3 Hare 503. See also *Jones* v. *Lenthal* (1669) 1 Ch Cas 154, 22 ER 739.

[51] (1851) 9 Hare 241 at 255.

[52] [2011] 2 WLR 592 at para. 74.

[53] *Attorney-General* v. *Observer Ltd*, The Times, 26 July 1986, CA; approved in *Spycatcher* [1990] 1 AC 109 at 155.

[54] [1996] AC 284 at 308.

[55] See Aristotle, *The Nicomachean Ethics*, J. A. K. Thomson (trans.) (Harmondsworth: Penguin, 1955), p. 198. Aristotle considered that 'equity is superior to justice' in that it rectifies shortcomings in formal statutory law by ensuring that just conclusions are reached on the facts of individual cases.

[56] *Spycatcher* [1990] 1 AC 109 at 156 and at 177, per Scott J.

[57] *Ibid*. at 216, per Dillon LJ.

[58] John Glover, 'Is Breach of Confidence a Fiduciary Wrong? Preserving the Reach of Judge Made Law' (2001) 21 *Legal Studies* 594.

1.5.2 The persistence of equity

It is important to remember that the injunction remains the principal remedy in cases of breach of confidence: where the claimant prefers initially to *prevent* misuse of the information by means of an injunction, with the result that an award of damages after the event is second best. There is a stream in common law thought that tends to think of the remedy as necessarily attaching to the right, just as damages in contract attach to a breach of contract.[59] However, in equity the remedy does not necessarily follow unless the general principles of equity can be made out (for example, that the claimant has come with clean hands, that there has been no delay and so forth). Indeed, there will often be a choice of remedies available in equity. Therefore, the equitable remedy of injunction does not necessarily attach to a successful claim for breach of confidence as surely as night follows day. Rather, the equitable grounds for the grant of an injunction (such as the need to avoid injustice) must also be made out.

It has been suggested by Richardson, Bryan, Vranken and Barnett[60] that the equitable doctrine had been 'virtually extinguished' by the first half of the twentieth century on the basis, it is to be assumed, that there were few reported cases on the topic. However, Judge Story, in his excellent *Equity Jurisprudence* published in the nineteenth century, only ever gave over one paragraph to injunctions that are used to 'restrain the party from making a disclosure of secrets communicated to him in the course of a confidential employment'.[61] That does not mean that it formed no part of the law. Similarly, Snell in his *Principles of Equity*[62] and Ashburner in his *Principles of Equity*[63] did not consider that this doctrine required more than six or seven pages within their general discussions of injunctions. None of that, however, means that the doctrine was extinguished; just that the law was settled and that interlocutory injunctions were obtained in the ordinary way without being reported. Within the scope of equity more generally, this area of law still commands little more than a few pages among all the many, teeming doctrines that make up modern equity. Similarly, the approach of the 'British courts' [*sic*] is treated by Richardson *et al.* as being

[59] Peter Birks, 'Rights, Wrongs and Remedies' (2000) 20 *Oxford Journal of Legal Studies* 1.

[60] Megan Richardson, Michael Bryan, Martin Vranken and Katy Barnett, *Breach of Confidence – Social Origins and Modern Developments* (Cheltenham: Edward Elgar, 2012).

[61] Joseph Story, *Equity Jurisprudence*, William Ebenezer Grigsby (ed.) (London: Stevens and Haynes, 1884), p. 621.

[62] Snell, *The Principles of Equity*, pp. 468ff.

[63] Walter Ashburner, *Principles of Equity* (London: Butterworth & Co, 1903), p. 372.

based on 'restitution and unjust enrichment', which is a modern fallacy with no basis on the authorities.[64] The case of *Moses* v. *Macferlan*[65] is cited as authority for the root of this unjust enrichment thinking but, when one actually reads that case, one finds Lord Mansfield held that the action was an equitable action to recover money 'when the defendant ought not in justice to keep the money'[66] and that 'the gist of this kind of action is, that the defendant, upon the circumstances of the case, is obliged by the ties of natural justice and equity to refund the money'.[67]

This puts this area of law squarely within equity at the time, where the early law on breach of confidence was also to be found. Lord Mansfield clearly referred to this as being an equitable action, concerned with justice, natural justice and equity. In dismissing equity, Richardson *et al.* describe it as having 'deliberately vague parameters'.[68] Of course, the word 'deliberately' gives the lie to the argument: that equity acts 'deliberately' in this fashion merely demonstrates that its practitioners are consciously engaged in a different methodological project from taxonomic common law projects. They choose to have flexible parameters. Richardson *et al.* also quote the same half-paragraph from Lord Goff's judgment in *Spycatcher* and so overlook the sophistication of the equitable principles that had been in existence, according to Megarry J in *Coco*,[69] since the sixteenth century.

1.5.3 Understanding the conscience in equity

Much of the criticism of equity is predicated on the common lawyer's preference for schemes of rigid rules that resemble a biologist's taxonomy of plants. There is also a presumption that the idea of 'conscience' is an entirely random and entirely subjective phenomenon that is unique to each individual mind. As I have argued elsewhere,[70] the conscience is best understood in line with the psychological literature as being something that is privately situated but objectively constituted.[71] That is, the contents of any person's conscience are formed by interaction with the

[64] Richardson *et al.*, *Breach of Confidence*, p. 115.
[65] (1760) 2 Burr 1005, 97 ER 676.
[66] *Ibid.* at 679.
[67] *Ibid.* at 681.
[68] Richardson *et al.*, *Breach of Confidence*, p. 120.
[69] [1969] RPC 41. [70] Hudson, *Equity & Trusts*, p. 10.
[71] See e.g. Sigmund Freud, *Beyond The Pleasure Principle* (Harmondsworth: Penguin, 1923), and Carl Gustav Jung, 'Structure of the Psyche' (1927) in Anthony Storr (ed.), *Essential Jung* (London: Fontana, 1998).

outside world, and therefore its deficiencies are open to criticism and to a court's judgment on the basis of what the law considers that a person's conscience *ought to have* contained. Thus, equity is engaged on a deontological, moral project, which it does by reference to the doctrine of precedent and centuries of careful worrying at its core concepts.

The equitable concept of an 'obligation of conscience' is not a hollow, rhetorical vessel. For example, the fundamentals of the law of trusts can only be understood by reference to it. The core of the express trust is well understood as being predicated on the conscience of the legal owner of the property being affected.[72] Even though the vast majority of express trusts are created in writing by lawyers in practice, equity accepts that express trusts may be created informally and unconsciously by people who intend to benefit another person and where the dictates of conscience would prevent the legal owner of that property from denying the existence of the trust.[73] The conscience of the legal owner of property is said to be affected so as to give rise to a constructive trust, inter alia, by knowledge of a mistake;[74] by acquiring property further to murder,[75] theft[76] or bribery;[77] by taking an unauthorised profit as a fiduciary under a conflict of interest;[78] by creating a specifically enforceable contract for the sale of land[79] or other property;[80] by denying the rights of another person in a property development.[81] In these ways, the concept of 'conscience' is well understood in the case law.

Consequently, the idea of an 'obligation in conscience' in relation to confidential information is simply another example of this idea of conscience at work in the case law. Furthermore, the equitable doctrine would deny an injunction to a person whose information had been used without their permission if they had themselves committed a wrong, or permitted too much time to pass before bringing their action, or if the balance of

[72] *Westdeutsche Landesbank* v. *Islington* [1996] AC 669.

[73] *Re Kayford Ltd* [1975] 1 WLR 279; *Re Lehman Brothers International (Europe)* v. *CRC Credit Fund Ltd* [2012] UKSC 6.

[74] *Westdeutsche Landesbank* v. *Islington* [1996] AC 669.

[75] *In the Estate of Crippen* [1911] P 108.

[76] *Westdeutsche Landesbank* v. *Islington* [1996] AC 669.

[77] *Attorney-General for Hong Kong* v. *Reid* [1994] AC 324; *Daraydan Holdings Ltd* v. *Solland International* [2005] Ch 1; Cf. *Sinclair Investments (UK) Ltd* v. *Versailles Trade Finance Group plc* [2011] EWCA Civ 347.

[78] *Bray* v. *Ford* [1896] AC 44; *Boardman* v. *Phipps* [1967] 2 AC 46.

[79] *Lysaght* v. *Edwards* (1876) 2 Ch D 499. Cf. *Jerome* v. *Kelly* [2004] 2 All ER 835.

[80] *Neville* v. *Wilson* [1997] Ch 144.

[81] *Banner Homes Group plc* v. *Luff Development Ltd.* [2000] Ch 372.

justice and injustice of the case militated against such an award. In equity, the remedy does not follow on automatically from the assertion of the substantive claim in all cases.

2 The distinction between understandings of property rights in intellectual property law and in equity

2.1 Equity's methodology in relation to proprietary rights

Two things should be understood about the way in which equity uses the concept of proprietary rights. First, while there are doctrines such as the express trust that do use rules (reminiscent of the common law in some senses) to create predictable models of property rights,[82] there are many equitable doctrines that create proprietary rights as a *response* to circumstances. So, where one of the trigger categories of unconscionable behaviour is identified (as outlined immediately above), then equity will recognise the existence of a property right as a result of that behaviour. These features of the equitable use of proprietary rights distinguish them from the use of property rights in intellectual property law. Intellectual property law requires predictable and stable models of property rights to protect the commercial value of innovations and works such as copyrights, patents and trade marks.

Second, the metaphors that are used in a lot of property law cling to ideas of property as being tangible, when in truth much of our modern world involves rights in intangible property.[83] Consequently, there is a 'thingness' to a large amount of property law, which is concerned with a conception of property as being a thing that is physical and that is capable of being owned by virtue both of its separability from other items of property and its transferability.[84] In the English case law on trusts this tendency reached its zenith (or is that nadir?) in *Westdeutsche Landesbank*

[82] See, for example, the 'three certainties' required for the establishment of an express trust: *Knight* v. *Knight* (1840) 3 Beav 148.

[83] Alastair Hudson, 'The Unbearable Lightness of Property' in Alastair S. Hudson (ed.), *New Perspectives on Property Law, Obligations and Restitution* (London: Cavendish, 2004), p. 1.

[84] In *Fisher* v. *Brooker* [2009] UKHL 41, [8] Lord Hope referred to property as being concerned with 'rights in things' that overlooked the entirety of the law on intellectual property (which was ironic given the subject matter of that case) and much of English property law, which is concerned with competing rights and obligations (such as equitable interests under trusts) as items of property in themselves.

v. *Islington*[85] when Lord Browne-Wilkinson referred to the availability of a proprietary right further to payments having been made under a void interest rate swap as being analogous to ownership of a 'stolen bag of coins'. Consequently, the most sophisticated 'financial product'[86] of its time was to be conceived of not as an amalgam of mathematical principles and predictions about future movements in market rates that compelled both sides to make or receive electronic payments one to another,[87] but instead as though the transaction was for the transfer of possession of a physical bag of coins that were made of a precious metal and so intrinsically worth their face value. It is a metaphor taken from the world of cutpurses and coin-clippers. And yet, apparently, it remains at the heart of our commercial property law today.

2.2 *The problematic confidential information in* Boardman *v.* Phipps

With those observations in mind, we turn to the equitable treatment of confidential information. The decision of the House of Lords in *Boardman* v. *Phipps*[88] illustrates equity's comparatively relaxed attitude to questions of property rights, which are nevertheless central to intellectual property law. In that case a proprietary constructive trust was imposed over profits without any property being clearly identified. What emerges is that intellectual property law and equity are instrumentally different.

Mr Boardman was the entrepreneurial and energetic solicitor to the Phipps family trust. He was a fiduciary, not least because the trustees allowed him to conduct trust business on their behalf and also because he was solicitor to the trust. One of the trust's principal investments was in a private company that had factory premises in England and in Australia. The Phipps family trust held the largest single shareholding in the company, but did not have a majority shareholding. By virtue of his position in relation to the company's largest shareholder, over a period of about eighteen months, Boardman was given access to large amounts of commercial

[85] [1996] AC 669.

[86] The use of the word 'product' by bankers to describe their creations is another form of tangible property usage: in truth, participants in the banking 'industry' on their trading 'floors' are constantly spinning their artificial creations with reassuringly industrial metaphors.

[87] On which see Alastair Hudson, *The Law on Financial Derivatives* 5th edn (London: Sweet & Maxwell, 2012), paras. 1–96.

[88] [1967] 2 AC 46.

information relating to the company's business that was not in the public domain, including detailed accounts as to the turnover of the company's various factories. This information was treated as being confidential in correspondence between directors of the company and Boardman. Later, Boardman procured a proxy from the trustees so that he could attend a general meeting of this private company. Armed with all of this information, and the access that he had to the management of the company, Boardman hit upon the idea of asset-stripping the Australian business so as to increase the value of all of the shares in the company.

To do this, Boardman and the trust together acquired a majority shareholding in the company, sold its Australian assets and consequently made a very large profit. Ultimately, the House of Lords held by a majority that Boardman should be required to account to the beneficiaries of the Phipps family trust for the personal profits that he had made from this transaction in which he had been acting both in his personal capacity and as a fiduciary. In so doing the court relied on the old principle in *Keech* v. *Sandford*,[89] which had been confirmed by the House of Lords in *Bray* v. *Ford*,[90] to the effect that not even the possibility of a conflict of interest can be permitted for a fiduciary. In such a circumstance, the fiduciary would be required to account for any personal profits taken. This meant that Boardman was required to hold his profits on constructive trust for the Phipps family trust.[91] This proprietary constructive trust was therefore a response to the conflict of interest and not a defence of a pre-existing property right.

2.3 *Whether the confidential information was property in* Boardman *v.* Phipps, *and whether or not it matters*

It was argued on behalf of the appellant that the appeal in *Boardman* v. *Phipps* could have been decided on the basis that the confidential information was trust property that was used by Mr Boardman while acting as a fiduciary so as to procure personal profits for himself. On that basis, the profits could have been explained as belonging in equity to the beneficiaries of the trust more straightforwardly than using the traditional equitable

[89] (1726) Sel Cas Ch 61. [90] [1896] AC 44.

[91] If the profits or their traceable proceeds can be identified, then they are held on constructive trust; but if they cannot be identified, then the obligation to account for the profits is a personal obligation to made good the amount of those profits: *CMS Dolphin Ltd* v. *Simonet* [2001] 2 BCLC 704; *Sinclair Investment Holdings SA* v. *Versailles Trade Finance Ltd (No. 3)* [2007] EWHC 915.

principle of preventing conflicts of interest. This would have required that the confidential information was accepted as being property, and that it was accepted as being property belonging in equity to the beneficiaries of the Phipps family trust. The case law in equity as to whether confidential information will be property is somewhat conflicted. In his judgment in *Douglas* v. *Hello! (No 3)*,[92] Lord Walker held that there is no property right in confidential information. The breadth of that finding seems unlikely in the context of intellectual property law. In the context of constructive trusts, this unqualified remark did not consider the various judgments in *Boardman* v. *Phipps* in any great detail (mentioning only Lord Upjohn).

In *Boardman* v. *Phipps*, Lord Upjohn rejected the idea that confidential information could be property, but his Lordship did so as part of an inquiry into the circumstances in which 'courts of equity will restrain the recipient from communicating [such information] to another': that is, his Lordship could be understood as simply reiterating the idea that the doctrine of confidence is not predicated on a pre-existing property right but rather on a more general obligation in conscience.[93] The result of that principle is that a court of equity may restrain use of confidential information wherever it is considered to be appropriate, whether there is misuse of a property right or not. Lord Hodson expressly found that confidential information *may* be considered to be property, giving the example of 'knowhow'.[94] Similarly, Viscount Dilhorne accepted that in some circumstances information can be understood to be property, although on these facts (without much explanation) his Lordship concluded that it was not.[95] Lord Cohen considered that confidential information is 'not property in the strict sense of that word',[96] but because Boardman had acquired the opportunity to make this profit while acting as agent (and thus fiduciary) for the trust, then he was required to account for those profits due to 'the rigour of equity' when dealing with such conflicts of interest.[97]

What flows from all of this judicial analysis is that confidential information may or may not be property in any given circumstance in equity, although in the preponderance of cases it will not be. More significantly, what also flows from this judicial analysis is that liability to account for profits flowing from the use of confidential information may

[92] [2008] 1 AC 1 at paras. 125–126.

[93] [1967] 2 AC 46 at 127.

[94] *Ibid.* at 107. [95] *Ibid.* at 89–90. [96] *Ibid.* at 102.

[97] It is interesting to note that Lord Cohen referred to the information being 'acquired' and Lord Guest to the information being 'obtained' (*ibid.* at 117): both words suggest the ownership or possession of an item of property.

arise in any event, without the need for a pre-existing property right, on the basis that a fiduciary's obligations in conscience to the beneficiaries of a trust preclude him from permitting even the possibility of a conflict of interest.[98] Therefore, the obligation in conscience entitles the claimant to a remedy irrespective of any right in property.

By contrast, in intellectual property law there is a need to know whether or not confidential information is property; or, alternatively, to know in which situations confidential information will and will not be property. In consequence, the three-stage test identified by Megarry J in *Coco* has served as the bedrock of the common law in this area because it identified three attributes of confidential information that can be considered to be property. While Megarry J was himself a great equity specialist, and while his judgment made repeated reference to equitable concepts, the common lawyers have mined it for a rigid, tri-cameral rule that can identify confidential-information-as-property in future cases, and the case law has proceeded from there. For the purposes of equity, the dispute in *Boardman* v. *Phipps* was resolved by reference to a general principle of equity as to conflicts of interest that had been in existence since at least 1726. Intellectual property law, with its hard-nosed commercial application, requires greater formal certainty than this.

Interestingly, in *Boardman* v. *Phipps*, their Lordships seemed to conflate the question of whether or not confidential information could be property in general terms with the narrower question as to whether or not this particular information could have been the property of the Phipps family trust. If the House of Lords had made that distinction, then a number of interesting difficulties would have presented themselves that call into question whether or not this information should have been considered to be property in the sense that it could have been owned by anyone other than Boardman.

Three issues arise. First, it is not clear to whom the confidential information would have belonged. The company would have been the owner of the information and therefore the beneficiaries of the Phipps family trust as shareholders would have had no ownership of it under the *Salomon* principle in company law.[99] Boardman owed no fiduciary duties to the company and therefore no constructive trust would have arisen. Second, it is not clear that this confidential information was entirely responsible

[98] *Boardman* v. *Phipps* [1967] 2 AC 46 at 103, per Lord Cohen; at 125–7, per Lord Upjohn; predicated on *Bray* v. *Ford* [1896] AC 44 at 51, per Lord Herschell.
[99] *Salomon* v. *A Salomon & Co* [1897] AC 22.

for the profitable scheme that Boardman hatched for the trust. The information was confidential in the sense that it had not been released to the public; but Boardman formulated his investment strategy based on his own analysis of the information because it was not present on the face of that information itself. Consequently, the information was only profit-bearing because of the analysis that Boardman placed on it. Without that analysis, it was inert. Third, there is a clear difference between raw financial data of the volume that was provided to Boardman, which does not tell any one, single story without close analysis, and, for example, a secret formula that has not yet been patented, or as yet unpublished news about a putative takeover. The latter types of information are clearly confidential and their exploitation would lead to profit directly, but the former category is more difficult to identify as being property.

In truth, *Boardman* v. *Phipps* in this context is concerned with a broader equitable principle of holding fiduciaries to the highest standards of behaviour in good conscience, which includes an obligation to avoid any conflict of interest. In that sense, equity was maintaining the 'trust and confidence' that should exist between a fiduciary and the beneficiaries of the trust.[100] The property rights that flow from the use of this confidential information are an equitable response to the unconscionability of a fiduciary using his or her position to obtain personal profits through a conflict of interest. Equity is not concerned with commercial exploitation directly per se; it would only become concerned with it once there were some conflict of interest or breach of an equitable duty. Rather, in *Boardman* v. *Phipps*, equity was using the idea of confidential information as a salve for applying its own, necessarily strict principles about fiduciary duties. In this sense, equity's property law principles are instrumentally very different from those in intellectual property law.

3 Conclusion

Marking the boundary of my property at home is a tall, very full hedge. At one end of that hedge is a particularly handsome fir that has retained a very healthy pear shape. At least, that is the view from my front door. Some years ago, a relative of my next-door neighbour took it upon himself, in flagrant breach of the law governing conservation areas, to shave the foliage off that fir on his side so as to give the impression to potential purchasers that the garden was three or four feet wider. His successor in

[100] *Bristol and West Building Society* v. *Mothew* [1998] Ch 1.

title always comments, whenever he finds himself in my driveway: 'That tree looks completely different from this side.' I remind him that that is because it was savaged on his side some years before, whereas on my side it has been allowed to grow as nature intended. It is all a matter of perspective: the same fir can look entirely different depending on one's viewpoint.

Much the same is true of the doctrine of breach of confidence. Seen from the perspective of an intellectual property lawyer, the tendency is to begin with the dicta of Lord Goff in *Spycatcher* and to praise its orderly modernity. By contrast, an equity specialist sees a different beauty in the complex ethics underpinning equity that have crystallised into their current form over the centuries. As Lord Jessel explained in *Re Hallett's Estate*,[101] it is possible to identify the judges who gave birth to particular doctrines in equity, whereas the common law has generally maintained the fiction that its doctrines have been part of the law since time immemorial.[102] For equity lawyers, who have been immersed in that culture and literature, equity's high-level principles are nuanced and meaningful. However, a common lawyer either finds them messy and vague, or simply fails to notice that they are there. Hence the differing treatment of *Spycatcher* by different schools of legal specialist, and their differing approaches to the law on confidences. The specialists in each camp interpret those judgments in accordance with the register in which they ordinarily communicate with one another. Their view of those judgments will be shaped by the way in which they expound the principles with which they ordinarily deal. They will see these judgments through their own spectacles[103] and filter them through their own conceptual worldview. After all, nothing is either good or bad, but rather thinking makes it so.

[101] (1880) 13 Ch D 696.

[102] Roger B. M. Cotterrell, *The Politics of Jurisprudence: A Critical Introduction to Legal Philosophy* 2nd edn (London: LexisNexis Butterworths, 2003), p. 24.

[103] Mason J observed in *Commonwealth of Australia* v. *John Fairfax & Sons Ltd* (1980) 147 CLR 39, at 51, that equity looked at the private interest and the public interest in confidential information through 'different spectacles'. Of course, if one looks through *different* spectacles then, by definition, you will not see properly through either.

5

How much 'property' is there in intellectual property?

The German civil law perspective

THOMAS DREIER

Introduction

Before discussing the question, 'How much "property" is there in intellectual property?' by way of a comparative analysis, a caveat seems to be called for. Although 'propriété intellectuelle', 'propriedad intellectual' and 'geistiges Eigentum' are all literal translations of 'intellectual property', they rather seem to be 'false friends' in that the precise meaning of these notions in the national legal systems to which they respectively belong may vary to a considerable extent. For this, two main reasons can be given.

Firstly, by choosing the notion of 'property', differences in the general construction of 'property' as a legal concept applied to tangible goods are transported into the construction of the special legal regime governing intangible goods. In particular, whereas the Anglo-American legal system has come to understand 'property' generally as a bundle of rights that the owner of an object has vis-à-vis others,[1] civil law countries with their tradition rooted in Roman law generally are still largely influenced by an understanding of 'property' as one solid right that the owner has – albeit vis-à-vis third parties – with regard to the material object that he or she 'owns'.[2] In practice, this difference may not always have a great effect, since

[1] For a detailed history and analysis of the different property foundations in the USA, see Michael Goldhammer, *Geistiges Eigentum und Eigentumstheorie* (Tübingen: Mohr Siebeck, 2012).

[2] See § 903 sentence 1 of the German Civil Code (Bürgerliches Gesetzbuch, BGB): 'The owner of a thing may ... deal with the thing at his discretion and exclude others from every influence' (translation from the website of the German government, www.gesetze-im-internet.de/englisch_bgb/index.html, last accessed 9 April 2013), indicating both the subject–object (first half-sentence) and the subject–subject (second half-sentence) relationship.

whereas, under a common law approach, the issue is which right belongs to the bundle, the decisive question from a civil law perspective is which acts are covered by the property title and which are not. However, from a theoretical point of view, in civil law countries that define 'property', as regards tangible objects, as a broad general entitlement with regard to an object, the adoption of the notion of 'property' appears to be much less appropriate in the area of exclusive rights over intangible objects, which historically have grown over time,[3] than in countries whose system is based on the common law, where any sufficiently large bundle of legal prerogatives may qualify as 'property'. Also, if the 'property' metaphor is used in civil law countries for rights granted in respect of intangible goods, this use insinuates a much greater legal power both over the intangible good and vis-à-vis third parties than is actually granted to the right-holder by statutory law. As will be shown, the effects of this different understanding of the legal concept of what constitutes 'property' in general runs like a red thread through the history of 'intellectual property' protection in most, if not all civil law states.

Secondly, not all civil law countries have encountered the same degree of difficulty in labelling the rights that in the English legal language are generally referred to as intellectual property rights as legal 'property'. Although the development of intellectual property law and theory shows rather similar characteristics in the majority of civil law states, certain differences regarding the justification and construction of intellectual property regimes in the different civil law countries persist. This renders any generalization difficult if not impossible as can be highlighted briefly by the example of France and Germany. Although in view of their common moral rights tradition in copyright, these two countries are generally cited in the same breath, in France, for example, the term 'la propriété intellectuelle' is traditionally used in opposition to 'la propriété industrielle' and thus has the main function of distinguishing artistic from industrial creations. The 'property' aspect, however, is not much disputed for industrial property rights or for authors' rights. As regards authors' rights, since French legal doctrine follows a dualistic approach that distinguishes between an author's moral and economic rights, the latter could be labelled as 'property' without much difficulty.[4] By contrast, in Germany, the authors' moral

[3] See, e.g., only for the development of the minimum rights under the Berne Convention for the Protection of Literary and Artistic Works, Sam Ricketson and Jane Ginsburg, *International Copyright and Neighbouring Rights* 2nd edn (Oxford University Press, 2005), vol. I, pp. 84ff.

[4] See André Lucas and Henri-Jacques Lucas, *Traité de la propriété littéraire et artistique* 4th edn (Paris: Lexis Nexis, 2012), Introduction, Sec. I.

and economic prerogatives are construed as a monistic right that, because of its personality rights aspect, is impossible to qualify as 'property'.[5] Hence, the equation of exclusive rights with regard to intangible objects to exclusive rights in tangible objects has for a long time been vigorously rejected in Germany, and was only embraced relatively lately. Only recently has the term 'property' ('Eigentum') been used in German legal literature for exclusive rights in intangible goods as well, in the wake of the TRIPS Agreement and increasing globalization of trade in intangible goods.

In view of these rather special legal traditions and developments, this chapter cannot be devoted to the notion of 'intellectual property' in civil law countries in general. Rather, the example of only one country – Germany – is chosen to highlight and explain some of the historic and constructive characteristics of the debate concerning the property aspect of intellectual property rights. Moreover, the focus is on the construction of copyright ('Urheberrecht'), i.e. the area of intellectual property law where the intellectual battle over the proper constriction of rights in intangible goods has mostly been fought.

1 Historical perspective

1.1 The resistance against the notion of 'Geistiges Eigentum'

Historically, beginning in the fifteenth and sixteenth centuries, the selective grant of production and/or importation privileges resulted in an early form of protection for immaterial creations and innovations. However, the need to formulate a general legal foundation for exclusive rights in intangible goods only became a pressing need in the light of the issue of the (il)legality of the reprinting of books. In Germany, unauthorized reprinting of books was a reaction to the breaking down of the system of exchanging printed sheets at book fairs, which itself was due to an increasing imbalance between the growing market demand for northern German Protestant writings and the sharply decreasing demand for southern German Catholic, largely devotional literature, which led southern German publishers increasingly to reprint northern German books.[6]

[5] See Adolf Dietz, *Das Droit Moral des Urhebers im neuen französischen und deutschen Urheberrecht* (Munich: C. H. Beck'sche Verlagsbuchhandlung, 1968).

[6] See, e.g., Ludvig Gieseke, *Vom Privileg zum Urheberrecht* (Baden-Baden: Nomos, 1995), pp. 161ff. For a bibliography, see Martin Vogel, in Gerhard Schricker, *Urheberrecht: Kommentar* 4th edn (Munich: Verlag C. H. Beck, 2010), p. 79.

The first, tentative attempts to provide for such legal foundation (Pütter, Kant, Fichte) still followed different lines of argumentation.[7] However, at the end of this early discussion, it was ascertained that the mechanical object (the book) has to be distinguished from the intellectual object (the text). In other words: the rights with regard to, on the one hand, the material object, and, on the other hand, the immaterial good (the creation, invention) embodied in the material object have to be distinguished. Secondly, in trying to provide for a legal foundation to declare the unauthorized reprinting of books illegal, these early theories were largely based on a natural rights approach. To some extent influenced also by John Locke's theory of labour, exclusive rights in intangible goods were mainly justified as resulting not from physical but from intellectual forces of the author and hence as part of the personality of the author, which had to be protected by the natural order rather than by isolated legislative grants ('Lehre vom geistigen Eigentum').[8]

However, rather than resting the legal foundation of exclusive protection for immaterial goods on a general, all-encompassing notion of 'property', the prevailing legal doctrine in Germany subsequently highlighted the analogy (Kohler) of exclusive rights in intangible goods to the exclusive rights in tangible goods ('Theorie der Immaterialgüterrechte').[9] One of the reasons was that if the notion of 'property' was not limited to tangible goods, it might lose its precise contours, since it was no longer clear which other rights might qualify as 'property' and which might not. Another reason for abandoning the 'property' theory as regards

[7] Johan Stephan Pütter, *Der Büchernachdruck nach ächten Grundsätzen des Rechts geprüft* (Göttingen: Vandenhoeck, 1774); Immanuel Kant, *Über die Unrechtmäßigkeit der Büchernachdrucke* (Berlinische Monatschrift, 1785), 1, pp. 403ff.; Johann Gottlieb Fichte, *Beweis der Unrechtmäßigkeit des Büchernachdrucks – Ein Räsonnement und eine Parabel* (Berlinische Monatschrift, 1793), 1, pp. 443ff.

[8] For detailed discussion see, e.g., Barbara Dölemeyer and Diethelm Klippel, 'Theorie des gewerblichen Rechtsschutzes und Urheberrechts' in F-K. Beier *et al.* (eds.), *Festschrift zum hundertjährigen Bestehen der Deutschen Vereinigung für gewerblichen Rechtsschutz und Urheberrecht* (Weinheim: VCH Verlagsgesellschaft, 1991), vol. I, pp. 198ff.; Ludwig Gieseke, *Die geschichtliche Entwicklung des deutschen Urheberrechts* (Göttingen: Otto Schwarz, 1957), pp. 23ff.

[9] Josef Kohler, *Urheberrecht an Schriftwerken und Verlagsrecht* (Stuttgart: Enke, 1907). In recent literature see, e.g., Volker Jänich, *Geistiges Eigentum – Eine Komplementärerscheinung zum Sacheigentum?* (Tübingen: Mohr Siebeck, 2002), pp. 90ff.; Ansgar Ohly, 'Geistiges Eigentum?' (2003) *JuristenZeitung* 545; Horst-Peter Götting, 'Der Begriff des Geistigen Eigentums' (2006) *Gewerblicher Rechtsschutz und Urheberrecht* 353; Matthias Leistner, '"Immaterialgut" als Flucht aus dem Sachbegriff' in Stefan Leible, Matthias Lehmann and Herbert Zech (eds.), *Unkörperliche Güter im Zivilrecht* (Tübingen: Mohr Siebeck, 2011), pp. 201ff.

immaterial goods was the fact that towards the end of the nineteenth century the scope of 'property' was much discussed in general civil law. In 1900, the conflict between Pandects law, which was derived from Roman law, on the one hand, and Germanic common law, on the other hand, was solved by the German Civil Code in favour of the former by limiting the notion of 'property' to physical, tangible objects. Indeed, the formulation of what was then the new § 903 of the German Federal Supreme Court left no doubt: 'The owner of a thing may, to the extent that a statute or third-party rights do not conflict with this, deal with the thing at his discretion and exclude others from every influence.'[10] The practice of not using 'property' in order to describe and qualify exclusive rights in intangible goods thus appears to have been both an intellectual reaction (to avoid a notion with too uncertain boundaries) and a defensive measure (to avoid being criticized by general civil law specialists for improperly using a precisely defined term).

As regards authors' rights, the situation was also influenced by the fact that – as already explained above – the monistic theory prevailing in Germany, which is based on the theory of personality rights (Neustetel, Bluntschli, Gareis and Gierke[11]) sees economic and moral rights of the artist not as two distinct rights but as two sets of legal prerogatives of one and the same right. Because it is not possible to 'own' one's personality, authors' rights in Germany cannot, therefore, by definition qualify as 'property' (it is only the economic use rights derived from the author's right that might qualify as 'property' at all). In addition, it proves difficult to bring patent, trade mark and authors' rights law under

[10] See above, note 2. According to § 90 of the German Civil Code, a 'thing' ('Sache') is defined as 'only corporeal objects' ('körperliche Sachen'). For discussion see, e.g., Thomas Rüfner, 'Savigny und der Sachbegriff des BGB' in Stefan Leible, Matthias Lehmann and Herbert Zech (eds.), *Unkörperliche Güter im Zivilrecht* (Tübingen: Mohr Siebeck, 2011), pp. 33ff.

[11] Leopold Joseph Neustetel, *Der Büchernachdruck nach römischem Recht betrachtet* (Heidelberg: Groos, 1824); Johann Caspar Bluntschli, *Das sogenannte Schrifteigenthum. Das Autorrecht. Kritische Ueberschau der deutschen Gesetzgebung und Rechtswissenschaft* (Munich: 1853); Carl Gareis, 'Das juristische Wesen der Autorrechte, sowie des Firmen- und Markenschutzes', *Archiv für Theorie und Praxis des Allgemeinen Deutschen Handels- und Wechselrechts* (1877), pp. 185ff.; Otto Friedrich von Gierke, *Deutsches Privatrecht* (Leipzig: Duncker und Humblot, 1895), vol. I. For an overview see Jürgen Simon, *Das allgemeine Persönlichkeitsrecht und seine gewerblichen Erscheinungsformen* (Berlin: Duncker & Humblot, 1981); Diethelm Klippel, 'Die Idee des geistigen Eigentums in Naturrecht und Rechtsphilosophie des 19. Jahrhunderts' in Elmar Wadle (ed.), *Historische Studien zum Urheberrecht in Europa* (Berlin: Duncker & Humblot, 1993), pp. 121ff.

one and the same heading, although it should be noted that the notion 'Immaterialgüterrecht' (Troller;[12] to be translated as 'immaterial goods law') was and still is favoured mainly in Switzerland. Even if the ideological impetus of these explanations has recently been deconstructed in legal literature,[13] for roughly one century the notion of 'property' continued not to be retained as the leading model for describing, justifying and grouping together what in the Anglo-American language and legal system easily fits under the notion of 'intellectual property'. It was only towards the end of the twentieth century that the notion of 'property' ('geistiges Eigentum') found its way back into the general legal discourse; this time, however, not as a legal qualifying term, but rather as shorthand for the different statutory exclusive regimes with regard to intangible goods. The way for this return may have been paved by the reformation and transformation of German trade mark law in the mid 1980s from a law that – in view of its historical ties to the names of producers – was conceptually rooted in personality rights to a property right that was freely transferable, even detached from the production site of the goods that the sign used to designate. Probably more important, however, was the growing awareness of immaterial goods and the rights attached thereto in the information society both at the level of national economics and of individual firms and the resulting emphasis on economic rights. Last but not least, ensuing globalization, TRIPS and the desire to speak in the same language as the international, English-speaking discourse, led to a revival of the term 'intellectual property' in Germany as well. Of course, in as much as the use of the term 'property' for exclusive rights granted to intangible goods both supports and strengthens neo-liberal economic theories, it also triggers critical remarks with regard to both its hidden assumptions and masked side-effects.[14]

1.2 'Geistiges Eigentum' et al. *as reflected in the name of the Munich Max Planck Institute*

In sum, although somewhat anecdotal, the history of the notion and understanding of 'intellectual property' in Germany is rather well

[12] Alois Troller, *Immaterialgüterrecht* 3rd edn, (Basel: Helbing & Lichtenhahn, 1985), vol. I, pp. 17ff.

[13] See, in particular, Stephan Meder, *Gottlieb Plancks Vorlesungen über "Immaterialgüterrecht" und das "Geistige Eigentum"* (2012) *UFITA*, pp. 171ff.

[14] See also below, section 2.

reflected in the history of the institutional self-description of the Munich Max Planck Institute, a leading institute devoted to the research of IP law. The Max Planck Institute for Foreign and International Patent, Copyright and Competition Law was founded in 1966, in continuation of an earlier university institute that was then described as being 'for patent, trade mark and copyright law'. The Max Planck Institute's initial name both highlighted the aspect of territoriality of intellectual property laws and emphasized the difference between industrial and intellectual property, which in '*droit d'auteur*' countries is mainly due to the personality rights' component of '*droit d'auteur*' and '*Urheberrecht*'.

When the institute was renamed the Institute for Intellectual Property, Competition and Tax Law in 2002, the change to 'intellectual property' may, of course, largely have been due to a need to shorten the name in view of the newly added tax law division. However, it also somehow seems to reflect the then prevailing emphasis on property rights in the wake of the neo-liberal theories of the Chicago school.

When the two departments of the Institute separated a decade later, 'intellectual property' ('Geistiges Eigentum') was dropped by the Institute's current directors and (at least in the German version of the Institute's name) was replaced by the term 'Immaterialgüterrecht' instead. This translates an important shift in perspective: when looking for the appropriate legal regime for intangible goods, 'Geistiges Eigentum' is only one possible form of regulation. Hence, to opt for 'Geistiges Eigentum' would have anticipated the result of the quest for an appropriate legal regime. Of course, in the Institute's English name, the notion of 'intellectual property' was retained. However, this only highlights the fact that while the English term for 'property' may well be the common translation of the German notion of 'Eigentum', the two legal concepts are far from being identical.[15]

2 How far does the analogy carry?

It is, of course, one thing to describe the history of notions in the sense of retracing the change in their meaning and use. It is yet another thing to point out the functional tasks for which a particular notion has been designed and which it accomplishes when it is used in legal, political and societal discourse.

[15] It should be noted that the name of the MPI will see another change in the near future, due to an expansion by the Department of Economics.

In focusing now on this second aspect, three points will be highlighted briefly in this subsection: the difference between 'property' as defined and understood in constitutional and in statutory law; the extent to which common rules can be derived from 'property' with regard to tangible and intangible goods; and, finally, the power of 'property' as a metaphor.

2.1 *Two notions of 'property': statutory and constitutional*

Article 17(2) of the Charter of Fundamental Rights of the European Union explicitly protects 'intellectual property' under the heading of the 'right to property'. Similarly, in Germany, the Constitutional Court (Bundesverfassungsgericht) has held on several occasions[16] that copyright is covered by the constitutional guarantee of property.[17] It is interesting to note that the German Constitutional Court justified this conclusion not by referring to the characteristics of authors' rights, but rather by invoking the securing and defensive role of the constitutional property clause as a guarantee for authors' freedom to act by way of exercising economic rights.

Moreover, it seems worth noting that the notion of 'property' as protected under constitutional law – and hence probably under any human rights charter as well – is not identical to 'property' as defined by statutory law. The reason is that the two legal instruments do not pursue identical objectives. This may be somewhat surprising from an Anglo-American perspective where the different institutional functions of the different bodies of law are generally less marked. In civil law countries, however, whereas the fundamental right as circumscribed in a constitutional charter guarantees 'property' as an institution against its abolition, undue restriction or taking by the state, 'property' as defined by way of a simple legal norm serves the function both of granting the property right and of defining its limits vis-à-vis private parties. Hence, within certain limits – which themselves derive from constitutional law – a constitutional definition of 'property' leaves the legislature some leeway in drawing the exact boundaries of the exclusivity granted as 'property' under statutory law. Or, in other words, if 'property' as defined in

[16] BVerfGE 31, 229 of 7 July 1971, 1 BvR 765/66 – Kirchen- und Schulgebrauch – For details and subsequent development see, e.g., Frank Fechner, *Geistiges Eigentum und Verfassung – Schöpferische Leistungen unter dem Schutz des Grundgesetzes* (Tübingen: Mohr Siebeck, 1999) and Bernd Grzeszick, *Geistiges Eigentum und Art. 14 GG* (2007) Zeitschrift für Urheber- und Medienrecht 344.

[17] Art. 14(1) of the German Grundgesetz.

a constitution and a charter were identical to 'property' as granted by statutory law, the legislature would be deprived of the ability to define the scope of 'property' in a broader or narrower way, thus preventing it from exercising its fundamental task of regulation by way of statutory definitions and rules.

From this, two practical conclusions can be drawn. Firstly, not all variations of the statutory scope of 'property' are necessarily in conflict with the constitutional guarantee of 'property'. As a matter of fact, within the limits set by the constitutional guarantee of property, the legislature is even free to cut back on existing statutory protection. Examples may be rare due to the historic tendency of intellectual property rights to enlarge and the duration of protection to increase. However, an illustrative example occurred on the occasion of the entering into force of the German Copyright Act of 1965, which awards performing artists legal status as owners of neighbouring rights. In doing so, the legislature deprived performers of some of the exclusive rights and the longer protection that they enjoyed in the case law as fictitious adaptors, prior to the entering into force of the new Act. According to the German Constitutional Court, the shortening of the term as such, and even the application of the shorter term to performances made before the entering into force of the new Act, did not violate the constitutional guarantee of 'property'. However, it was regarded as a constitutional violation that the new Act calculated the term of protection on the basis of certain acts that were of no legal relevance before it entered into force. Consequently, a new section was added to the Copyright Act in order to remove this illegal retroactive effect.[18]

Secondly, not all statutory rights with characteristics that may be described as 'property', or at least having an exclusive effect similar to 'property', are automatically protected by the constitutional guarantee of property. Here also, two German examples may be cited. The first of these concerns the right to a person's own image. Initially granted merely as a defensive right – as well as an exception to copyright – in the Artistic Copyright Act of 1907, which had made the reproduction and public display of a person's own image subject to the depicted person's consent,[19] this right was in the ensuing century developed by the

[18] BVerfGE 31, 275 of 8 July 1971, 1 BvR 766/66 – Schallplatten, and § 135a of the German Copyright Act.

[19] See § 22(1) Kunsturhebergesetz (KUG), according to which '[p]ortraits may only be distributed and publicly displayed with the consent of the person portrayed'. A similar rule was already contained in the Bavarian Copyright Act of 1865 and in the Federal

civil courts into an almost complete property right. Over time, the initial remedy of merely injunctive relief was supplemented by claims for unjust enrichment and damages, and in a more recent landmark decision, the right was even declared hereditary.[20] In addition, according to legal literature the economic rights with regard to a person's own image should be regarded as transferable during their lifetime and it should be possible to grant 'property'-like use rights.[21] However, the Constitutional Court concluded that this did not mean that the right to one's own image was 'property' within the meaning of the Constitution. As a matter of fact, the German Constitutional Court did not even address the property issue, but rather described the marketability as resulting from the notoriety of the life of the person in question, which, of course, seems a remote allusion to John Locke's labour theory.[22] The second example concerns domain names, which are often of considerable value and which can be legally transferred. However, the Constitutional Court in Germany has denied domain names protection under the 'property' guarantee of the Constitution and only considers the contractually founded use right as benefiting from constitutional protection.[23] It is true that even if, in these instances, the legal position granted by statutory law does not qualify as 'property' in the constitutional sense, the legislature is not barred from designing the statutory legal regime in a way which qualifies it as such.

2.2 *De facto 'property'*

It should also be noted in this respect that certain legal rights, although they are not 'property' in the classic sense, can in practice be exercised in a way that closely models the effects of exercising a true property right. One example that comes to mind derives from unfair competition law. While it is the case that legal norms that regulate competitive behaviour

Photography Author's Act (Gesetz betreffend den Urheberschutz an Werken der Photographie) of 1876.

20 BGHZ 143, 214 of 1 December 1999, I ZR 49/97– Marlene Dietrich.

21 For a summary of the development see Horst-Peter Götting, 'Ideeller und kommerzieller Persönlichkeitsschutz' in Horst-Peter Götting, Christian Schertz and Walter Seitz (eds.), *Beck'sches Handbuch des Persönlichkeitsrechts* (Munich: 2008), pp. 195ff.; Thomas Dreier and Louisa Specht, in Thomas Dreier and Gernot Schulze, *Urheberrecht, Kommentar*, 4th edn, (Munich: 2013), § 22 KUG para. 36.

22 BVerfGK 9, 83 of 22 August 2006, 1 BvR 1168/04 – Werbekampagne mit blauem Engel.

23 BVerfGK 4, 210 of 24 November 2004, 1 BvR 1306/02 – ad.acta.de.

are only sanctioned by way of injunctive relief, a contractual promise that is made against payment not to exercise this right vis-à-vis the contracting party, coupled with the premise to enjoin others from performing the acts in question, almost has the same effect as a 'property' right, even if the contract as such is only binding on the contracting parties and does not have direct effect on third parties. Similarly, the use of digital rights management (DRM) technology has a certain potential to create, if not property rights, at least de facto property, and it has hence been accused of constituting 'private legislation' in the sense of 'code as code', that is, a private governance system by which technology – and not the law – regulates which acts users are authorized – or, perhaps more accurately, enabled – to carry out.[24]

Finally, another issue is the extent to which mere contracts might be used in order to create de facto property. One such example is the case of recognized exclusive distributorship agreements, where the courts give legal effect to contractual prohibitions to resell original merchandise that was put onto the market by the original manufacturer to outsiders, which may, of course, still be explained by the exceptions to the doctrine of exhaustion.[25] Whether such effects can be achieved in the absence of any intellectual property right is, however, an open issue. Recently, in an *obiter dictum*, the German Federal Supreme Court, in upholding a contractual prohibition to pass on the access code necessary to access copyrighted material for which the distribution right was exhausted, seems to hint at moves in this direction. Of course, it should be noted that, up until now, in such cases some underlying copyright could still be found.[26]

2.3 *Reconciling legal rules on material and immaterial property*

Another issue regarding the question of how far the 'property' analogy may carry is to find out the extent to which the legal treatment of tangible and intangible goods can be reconciled under the umbrella of one and the same concept, and the extent to which using the same concept rather

[24] Pamela Samuelson, 'Digital Rights Management {and, or, vs.} the Law' (2003) 46 *Communications of the ACM* 41, also available at http://people.ischool.berkeley.edu/~pam/papers/acm%20on%20drm.pdf (last accessed 9 April 2013).

[25] Art. 7(2) of the Trade Mark Directive 95/2008/EC and Art. 13(2) of the Community Trade Mark Regulation (EC) 207/2009.

[26] See, in particular, BGH of 11 February 2010, I ZR 178/08, GRUR 2010, 822 – Half-Life 2; see also BGH of 29 April 2010, I ZR 39/08, GRUR 2011, 56 – Session-ID, where even non-effective technical protection measures were held to constitute a sufficient declaration of the will to prohibit linking.

masks irreconcilable underlying differences. In other words, apart from reservations that can be historically explained, are there essential differences that would speak against an indiscriminate application of the concept of 'property' to both tangible and intangible goods?

This question has many aspects that cannot be fully discussed here.[27] Of course, the non-rivalrous and ubiquitous character of intangible goods – which tangible goods do not possess – is a fundamental fact that cannot be analysed away. From this, it follows that as regards tangible goods, one of the functions of the legal exclusivity is to secure to the owner the factual possibility of using the object for him or herself (because if another person uses a rivalrous good, the owner is prevented from using it him or herself). In contrast, the holder of rights in an intangible good can use this intangible good for him or herself, even if at the same time someone else makes use of the very same intangible good (because of the non-rivalrous nature of the intangible good). What both legal rights have in common, therefore, is the aim of providing the legal basis to enable the right-holder to exclude others from using the particular good in question. Hence, the common treatment has to tie in with the character of the exclusive rights granted. In other words, if any similarity attaches, it is only at the level of the formulation of the exclusivity of rights. Indeed, as can well be demonstrated by the German legal texts, the exclusive rights with respect to intangible goods in intellectual property legislation are modelled on the corresponding language used in the general Civil Code (Bürgerliches Gesetzbuch, BGB) to express the characteristics of property in tangible goods.[28] But does this mean that the same rules apply to both types of 'property'?

Of course, numerous differences can be ascertained. Obviously, the most striking of these differences is that property protection of intangible goods is not limited in time, whereas the exclusive protection of intangible goods generally is (with the most notable exception of trade marks). Similarly, the exclusivity regarding intangible goods is subject to much greater limitations and exceptions than the exclusivity with regard to tangible objects. And, to name just a third marked difference, at the international level, contrary to property in tangible goods, which is

[27] For extensive discussion, see in particular Alexander Peukert, *Güterzuordnung als Rechtsprinzip* (Tübingen: Mohr Siebeck, 2008); Goldhammer, *Geistiges Eigentum und Eigentumstheorie*.

[28] Cf. § 15(1) and (2) of the German Copyright Act ('The author shall have the exclusive right to …') and § 903 of the German Civil Code ('The owner may … deal with the [object he owns] at his discretion and exclude others from every influence').

customarily recognized as a principle of public international law, in spite of globalization and the Internet, the trans-border protection of intangible goods is still strictly based on the principle of territoriality. Even the mutual recognition of non-registrable rights is not guaranteed, unless the principles of national treatment or reciprocity have been laid down in an international treaty to which the countries in question are parties.

However, it also seems possible to argue the contrary and point out that in view of the generally limited life span of physical goods (with the exception of land) and because of the fact that property in one physical object does not bar someone else from making productive use of another identical tangible object, there is no need to generally limit property in tangible objects in time. In addition, many property rights in tangible objects are subject to quite a number of use restrictions (you must not use your piano in the middle of the night; you are not allowed to drive your car on whatever, in your country, is the 'wrong' side of the road; you may not be allowed to build your house in the way you want or plant whatever you want to plant on your land, and so on). These use restrictions may also vary from country to country (you may not consume alcoholic beverages in an Islamic country; you must carry alcohol in a brown bag in public places in the USA; you may not import meat products into the USA, and so on) so that it would indeed be misleading to reserve the term 'property' for a legal power that is unlimited in time and scope. In sum, all of the differences previously mentioned between exclusive rights with regard to tangible objects on the one hand and intangible goods on the other, do not, as such, render it impossible to use the same notion in both instances.

However, in spite of the appeal of achieving the utmost unity of law, the question is whether, for practical purposes, it really makes sense to affix one and the same label to two rights, or set of rights, which show so many differences.[29] In order not to be misunderstood: the common label may well serve as the starting point for any exercise of looking for corresponding solutions in the other area of law and eventually transferring solutions from one area to the other. But one has to be very careful to overlook neither fundamental differences, nor differences regarding the underlying policy issues that the respective rules are designed to address. For example, any attempt to solve issues concerning the exact scope of use

[29] The same question can be asked with regard to common rules and principles underlying the different intellectual property regimes. For an attempt to formulate common principles and even statutory provisions for the whole intellectual property area in Germany, see Hans-Jürgen Ahrens and Mary-Rose McGuire *Modellgesetz für geistiges Eigentum* (Munich: Sellier, 2012).

rights with regard to physical copies of an intangible work by way of analogies to the rules pertaining to the physical object itself will invariably create insoluble difficulties.[30] Similarly, in ascertaining the payment of damages in the case of intellectual property infringement, referring to the general tort law rule of civil law, which is aimed at making the infringed party whole, misses the fundamental difference between the infringement of exclusive rights in tangible and intangible goods, because what is generally at stake once an intellectual property right has been infringed is not compensation for a loss (a value destroyed), but rather attribution of the proceeds resulting from the infringement (a value created). In Germany, the Civil Code does contain a rule that addresses the distribution of income resulting from dealing in someone else's affairs, including dealings with someone else's property.[31] In fact, the rule orders the person who deals with someone else's property to hand over the resulting profits to the person who had the right to conduct the affairs in question. This rule of general civil law is similar to the rule in intellectual property law according to which the infringed right-holder can calculate his damages as the profits made by the infringing party – as an alternative to actual damages and the licence fee that an authorized licensee would have paid. However, in civil law this only applies if the infringer acted knowingly, whereas in intellectual property cases liability is triggered by mere negligence. Assuming this difference in treatment is justified, any attempt to reconcile the two conflicting rules would appear to be counterproductive.[32]

Finally, it seems worth noting that, even in civil law, the notion of 'property' itself seems to offer few guidelines if one has to find out whether or not newly developed forms of economic exploitation of tangible goods are to be considered as falling within the scope of an existing exclusive right. In particular, a problem arises if the act in question neither violates or even interacts with the physical substance of the object, nor disturbs the owner's possession thereof. To cite yet again some German examples: regarding the material use of a tangible object, the German Courts have held that locking a ship into a harbour constitutes an infringement of the

[30] An excellent example in this respect is CJEU Case C-128/11, *UsedSoft GmbH* v. *Oracle International Corp.* [2012] ECR I-0000 (3 July 2012), in which the Court tries to bring the online transmission of a data set representing a computer program under the notion of 'sale of goods'.

[31] § 687 (2) BGB.

[32] For detailed discussion under German law see, e.g., Thomas Dreier, *Kompensation und Prävention* (Tübingen: Mohr Siebeck, 2002), pp. 216ff.

property right (since it deprives the owner of the intrinsic use value of the ship), whereas preventing a ship from unloading its cargo in a particular port does not (because the owner could still use the ship on the open seas and in other harbours).[33] Regarding the immaterial use of a tangible object by way of taking and subsequently marketing photographs, in a recent case, the German Federal Supreme Court explicitly rejected the argument that taking photographs of an object is part of the property right in the object. Nevertheless, the Court recognized the existence of an exclusive right based not on the property right in the object photographed, but on the property right of the owner of the grounds on which the photographs were taken.[34] Justified or not, these few decisions already demonstrate how vague the definition of what constitutes 'property' is even in civil law countries. Not surprisingly, any analogy between 'property' in tangible objects and 'property' in intangible objects proves to be even less prone to achieving meaningful legal results.

2.4 *'Property' as a metaphor*

In view of the differences just described, the use of the broad term 'property' for exclusive rights in intangible goods indeed seems not to refer to a precise legal concept, but rather constitutes an ideologically motivated metaphorical use in the ongoing debate on the propertization of public goods.[35] As such, the 'property' metaphor proves to be rather strong. On the one hand, the particular strength of the 'property' metaphor results

[33] BGHZ 55, 153 of 21 December 1970, II ZR 133/68.

[34] BGH of 17 December 2010, V 45/10, GRUR 2011, 323 – Preußische Gärten und Parkanlagen; for critique see, e.g., Thomas Dreier, 'Lässt sich das Spiel in der Nachspielzeit noch drehen? – Zum Zusammenwirken von "Hartplatzhelden.de" und "Preußische Gärten und Parkanlagen"' in Anke Schierholz and Ferdinand Melichar (eds.), *Kunst, Geld und Recht, Festschrift für Gerhard Pfennig zum 65. Geburtstag* (Munich: Beck, 2011), pp. 15ff., and Peukert, *Güterzuordnung als Rechtsprinzip*, pp. 137ff.

[35] A brief account of propertization tendencies is given by Hannes Siegrist (ed.), *Entgrenzung des Eigentums in modernen Gesellschaften und Rechtskulturen* Comparativ 5/6 2006 (Leipziger Universitätsverlag, 2007) (in general); and Hannes Siegrist, 'Strategien und Prozesse der "Propertisierung" kultureller Beziehungen – Die Rolle von Urheber- und geistigen Eigentumsrechten in der Institutionalisierung moderner europäischer Kulturen' in Stefan Leible, Ansgar Ohly and Herbert Zech (eds.), *Wissen – Märkte – Geistiges Eigentum* (Tübingen: Mohr Siebeck, 2010), pp. 3ff. (regarding intangible goods). For metaphorical use of the term 'property' see also William St Clair, 'Metaphors of Intellectual Property' in Ronan Deazley, Martin Kretschmer and Lionel Bently (eds.), *Privilege and Property – Essays on the History of Copyright* (Cambridge: Open Book, 2010), pp. 397ff. (including reference to the related metaphor of 'piracy').

from the fact that it is easily understood by lay persons who, in general, feel very strongly about private property. On the other hand, in countries that have adopted an understanding of 'property' as one unitary right – which hardly allows for a differentiated evaluation of the functional differences and justifications of the individual legal prerogatives that come with it – the analogy alluded to by the metaphor of 'property' points clearly towards a strong, all-encompassing set of exclusive rights at the expense of exceptions and limitations. This is in marked contrast to legal systems that have embraced the bundle theory. In such legal systems, the notion of 'property' as such does not at all prejudice the scope of the rights granted as part of the bundle. Also in such systems, both the rights granted with regard to material and immaterial goods can be subjected to the objectivizing criterion of economic efficiency, which during the last decades has become the yardstick of what should and what should not form part of the bundle. In marked contrast to this understanding, stands the 'more is better than less' approach inspired by the metaphor of all-encompassing 'property', as expressed with particular clarity in the EU Information Society Directive which states that '[a] harmonised legal framework on copyright and related rights ... while providing for a high level of protection of intellectual property, will foster substantial investment in creativity and innovation', and '[a]ny harmonisation of copyright and related rights must take as a basis a high level of protection, since such rights are crucial to intellectual creation'.[36] It is needless to point out that such an approach contradicts the economic wisdom according to which the optimum is to be found not in maximum protection, but in a form of reduced exclusivity somewhere in between no protection and high level protection[37] (assuming, of course that both no protection and too much protection may stifle creativity and innovation and that granting some form of intellectual property protection has a positive effect on creativity and innovation).[38]

[36] Directive 2001/29/EC of the European Parliament and of the Council of 22 May 2011, on the harmonisation of certain aspects of copyright and related rights in the information society, [2001]OJ L 167/10, Recitals 4 and 9.

[37] Ejan Mackaay, *Law and Economics for Civil Law Systems* (Cheltenham: Edward Elgar, 2013), Chapter 9, Part 3.B.

[38] However, it should be mentioned that this traditional assumption has recently once more been questioned on the basis of empirical evidence regarding both a comparison of the German and English book market between the Statute of Anne and the enactment of the first authors' rights laws in German States on the one hand, and the decline in the volume of newly published books in the German States after that date on the other hand. See

It therefore comes as no surprise that the 'property' metaphor is mainly used by right-holders as a rhetorical, if not ideological, tool in order to justify their demands for an increase in exclusive protection, in particular in view of the loss of control over reproduction and dissemination of copyrighted works in digital form over the Internet. At the same time, the 'property' metaphor is used in order to fend off any attempts to enlarge the breathing space for innovation and creativity opened up by exceptions and limitations, as well as to justify the superiority of the rationale of exclusion over the rationale of access.

In addition, the 'property' metaphor is particularly strong when it refers to the notion of 'property' as retained by human rights and constitutional freedoms, rather than to the statutory notion of 'property'. Although human rights and related constitutional concepts of 'property' provide – as has been explained[39] – for greater flexibility, it is the link to the guarantee of personal freedom and the absolute protection as secured by the constitutional guarantee of 'property' as an institution that is responsible for the particular strength of the metaphor. It may be added that, in a similar way, an indirect reference is made to the human rights or constitutional notion of 'property' whenever broad exclusive rights are justified on the basis of the three-step test, which defines the maximum scope of the exceptions and limitations to the exclusive rights that individual states may provide in their national intellectual property legislation.[40] This is achieved by positing that a proper interpretation of 'normal exploitation' – the second step of the three-step-test – should require that any thinkable possibility, both present and future, to exploit an immaterial good that is protected by an intellectual property right be reserved to the right-holder.

But even if the ideological mechanism of the 'property' metaphor may be understood intellectually, a psychological anchor of high, rather than low, protection is set each time the metaphor of 'property' is brought up in political discourse. Apart from intellectual property tradition and

Eckhard Höffner, *Geschichte und Wesen des Urheberrechts* (Munich: Verlag Europäische Wirtschaft 2010), vol. II, pp. 253, 308.

[39] See above, section 2.1.

[40] Art. 9 Berne Convention; Arts. 13, 26(2), 30 TRIPS; Art. 10(2) WCT and Art. 16(2) WPPT. In the form of Art. 13 TRIPS, the test is formulated for copyright as follows: 'Members shall confine limitations or exceptions to exclusive rights to certain special cases which do not conflict with a normal exploitation of the work and do not unreasonably prejudice the legitimate interests of the right holder.'

lobbying efforts, which tend to be stronger on the side of right-holders than on the side of those whose activity is based on a limitation or exception to the intellectual property protection, the anchor-effect may also serve to explain why the resulting legislative compromise ultimately agreed upon tends to favour higher over lower levels of intellectual property protection.[41]

3 The future

3.1 New criticism

As regards the current intellectual debate in German legal literature, several lines of argumentation can be discerned that are more or less critical of the 'property' association that is inherent in the rather powerful metaphor of the term 'intellectual property'. In the 1970s, the relatively small number of critics mainly focused on discrepancies between the classic concept of the individual creator and the reality of creative activities in the emerging copyright industries where most works were created by employees or as commissioned works.[42] Today, most critics share the common belief that the intellectual property system tends to be over-protective and over-complex, either with regard to innovation and creativity in general, or as regards information value-added services, the dissemination of scientific information or the freedom for artistic creation in particular. It seems worth noting in this respect that criticism of increasing 'propertization' – which is more often than not justified by the 'property' metaphor – is no longer voiced solely by IP outsiders or mere users of intellectual goods. Rather, such concerns seem to be increasingly shared by right-holders, who feel increasingly burdened by the overhead of transaction costs caused by the search for intellectual property rights that might stand in the way of their own creative and innovative activity. It seems that the metaphor of 'property' and the related metaphor of 'piracy' are slowly but continuously losing some of their grip.[43] However, in spite

[41] For the mechanism of 'anchors' see, e.g., Daniel Kahneman, *Thinking, Fast and Slow* (London: Penguin, 2011), pp. 119ff.

[42] See, in particular, Manfred Rehbinder, *Urheberrecht* 16th edn, (Munich: Beck, 2010), para. 624.

[43] See, e.g., Horst-Peter Götting and Anja Lunze (eds.), *Überprotektion durch Geistiges Eigentum?– Festschrift zum 10-jährigen Bestehen des Studiengangs "International Studies in Intellectual Property Law"* (Baden-Baden: Nomos, 2009). Likewise, it should be noted that, at their annual meetings, the German Association for the Protection of Intellectual

of their commonly shared fundamental concern, the new approaches are all but uniform both as regards their methodology and the solutions that are proposed. The new approaches thus seem to reflect a time of transition that is still in search of a new paradigm.[44] Without going into detail, one paradigm shift can be discerned. In general, the critical voices consider intellectual property legislation no longer as a regulation that exclusively or predominantly serves the purpose of protecting the interests of right-holders. Rather, the function of intellectual property legislation is seen in the accommodation of the interests of creators, producers, competitors and users alike, thus creating an appropriate legal framework for the knowledge and information society.[45] From this, it follows that the 'property' metaphor and its unilateral focus on the rights of the owner of the property are no longer regarded as the motivating and justifying force behind the system changes proposed. Apart from this, less radical approaches, which mostly aim at separating rights of individual creators and rights of producers,[46] can be discerned. These include those which take market failure and functioning competition as their starting point. From this angle, intellectual property rights are not understood as the rule that has its ramifications in any 'property' concept of natural justice and/or labour theory, but rather as an exception designed merely to cure market failures and prevent distortion of competition.[47] Once the

Property (Deutsche Vereinigung für gewerblichen Rechtsschutz und Urheberrecht, GRUR) has already twice discussed the topic of 'Hypertrophy of IP rights' (Hypertrophie der Schutzrechte, 2004) and 'IP rights – function and limits' (Schutzrechte – Funktion und Begrenzung, 2010).

44 For the paradigm change in science, which has also become a general cultural guiding concept ('Leitbegriff') see Thomas Kuhn, *The Structure of Scientific Revolutions* (Chicago University Press, 1996), pp. 43ff, available at www.f.waseda.jp/sidoli/Kuhn_Structure_of_Scientific_Revolutions.pdf (last accessed 9 April 2013).

45 See, e.g., Reto M. Hilty, *Verbotsrecht vs. Vergütungsanspruch – Suche nach den Konsequenzen der tripolaren Interessenlage im Urheberrecht, Festschrift für Gerhardt Schricker* (Munich: Beck, 2005), pp. 325ff. (Tripolar approach); Thomas Dreier, 'Regulating Competition by Way of Copyright Limitations and Exceptions' in Paul Torremans (ed.), *Copyright Law: A Handbook of Contemporary Research* (Cheltenham: Edward Elgar, 2007), pp. 232, 236ff. (Quadrupolar approach).

46 For such an approach see, e.g., Till Kreutzer, *Das Modell des deutschen Urheberrechts und Regelungsalternativen* (Baden-Baden: Nomos, 2008); Karl-Nikolaus Peifer, 'The Return of the Commons: Copyright History as a Common Source' in Ronan Deazley, Martin Kretschmer and Lionel Bently (eds.), *Privilege and Property – Essays on the History of Copyright* (Cambridge: Open Book, 2010), pp. 347ff.

47 See, e.g., Reto M. Hilty, 'Sündenbock Urheberrecht?' in Ansgar Ohly and Diethelm Klippel (eds.), *Geistiges Eigentum und Gemeinfreiheit* (Tübingen: Mohr Siebeck, 2007), pp. 107ff.

'property' metaphor has been discarded as the leading principle underlying copyright, even the shortening of the term of protection and the reintroduction of formalities are open to reconsideration in the current copyright debate.[48]

3.2 ... and the Pirate Party

Finally, towards the end of the twentieth century and the beginning of the twenty-first century, with the advent of digital and networking technologies that made copying copyrighted material such as music and film and its distribution over the Internet via peer-to-peer file sharing and similar software tools possible at low cost, the issue of 'property' with regard to copyright has even arrived at the centre of public debate. The music industry's rather aggressive attempts to enforce copyright on the Internet, mainly vis-à-vis young individuals and the resulting transmission of names and addresses of file-sharers,[49] as well as growing discontent with patenting strategies by both pharmaceutical and software companies, have all contributed in quite a number of states (amongst them Germany) to the formation and rise of the Pirate Party.

On a practical level, the more or less fundamental opposition to intellectual property most notably led to the defeat of the Anti-Counterfeit Trade Agreement by the European Parliament.[50] On a theoretical level, it is postulated that intellectual property 'does not exist'.[51] What is meant by this categorical refutation of a well-established notion is, of course, that immaterial goods are non-rivalrous, which as such is not disputed by proponents of intellectual property legislation. What this categorical refutation of the notion of 'property' – which appears to be triggered by

[48] For the Pirate Party, see www.piratenpartei.de/informations-in-english/copyright (last accessed 9 April 2013) and in general Stef van Gompel, *Formalities in Copyright Law* (Alphen aan den Rijn: Klewer, 2011).

[49] For the attempt to reconcile enforcement (property) interests and data protection policies, see CJEU cases C-275/06 *Promusicae* v. *Telefonica*, [2008] ECR I-271, Case C-557/07 *LSG-Gesellschaft zur Wahrnehmung von Leistungsschutzrechten* v. *Tele2 Telecommunication GmbH*, [2009] I-1227; Case C-70/10 *Scarlet Extended* v. *SABAM*, [2011] I-0000 and Case C-360/10 *SABAM* v. *Netlog*, [2012] ECR I-0000.

[50] 4 July 2012, available at:www.europarl.europa.eu/news/en/pressroom/content/20120217BKG38488/html/ACTA-before-the-European-Parliament (last accessed 9 April 2013).

[51] See, e.g., www.piratenpartei.de/informations-in-english/copyright; www.piraten-sachsen.de/2012/03/16/warum-es-kein-geistiges-eigentum-gibt; wiki.piratenpartei.de/Warum_Eigentum_nicht_geistig_sein_kann (all accessed 9 April 2013).

a rather romantic penchant and desire for 'freedom' in the Internet's virtual space – does not grasp, however, is that it is precisely the purpose of intellectual property legislation to create an artificial scarcity of possibilities to use intangible goods, and that this is achieved by way of granting exclusive rights to immaterial goods that are modelled after the exclusive rights with regard to material goods.

Moreover, in renouncing the very idea of intellectual 'property' altogether, this new, radical thinking fails to take into account the intellectual distinction carved out, in a rather painful and lengthy process, between the material object (the book, the data set) on the one hand and the immaterial good embodied therein (the music, the text) on the other hand. Admittedly, it may be argued that the abandonment of this distinction allows a more accurate description of a reality in which enforcing exclusive rights becomes increasingly difficult. In any event, supporters of the Pirate Party do recognize the possibility of technically exercising some form of 'possession' over digital data. Typically, they then oscillate between the damnation of digital rights management on the one hand and support for an Apple-i Tunes-type model of distributing and selling intellectual content by way of closed, proprietary business models on the other.

However, this new way of looking at immaterial goods and the legal regime by which immaterial goods are governed prompts new questions. Namely, how will the creation of innovative achievements of the mind be financed and how will creators and inventors be remunerated for their activity in the future? Even if viable alternatives have still to be formulated, intellectual 'property' certainly is not the only answer to this question.

6

Properties of copyright

Exclusion, exclusivity, non-interference and authority

HUGH BREAKEY

Introduction

This chapter analyses the nature and structure of the property rights proposed by contemporary philosophical and legal theories of property – paying particular attention to factors of exclusion and exclusivity – before exploring the implications of these theories for one part of intellectual property: copyright. It argues that two theories of property in particular give a defensible – though slightly different – account of copyright: the right to exclude others from performing an activity, and protecting a specific activity from harm. More broadly, the chapter shows how different visions of property capture different features of copyright law.

Section 1 describes four different cases where a particular individual has entitlements to particular resources. It uses the Hohfeldian framework to explain the role of exclusion and exclusivity at work in these entitlements, and pins down the slippery notion of a 'right to exclude'. In section 2, these four results are used as templates of the four major property theories in the contemporary literature. With this analysis in tow, section 3 appraises how these four different types of property ideas apply to the objects of copyright. It considers the types of entitlements that emerge from their application, assessing the closeness of fit between these results and actual copyright law.

1 Exclusion, prohibition and exclusivity: a Hohfeldian analysis

What is the essence of property? One attractive answer – and our point of departure here – is the idea that property involves a 'right to exclude'. The general thought that property may be explained by notions of exclusion and exclusivity is a perennial one, dating back to Locke and Blackstone, and finding voice in several major contemporary property theories.[1] Yet in a way this is surprising, as the idea of a 'right to exclude' is itself not entirely clear, as is the relation between the two concepts of exclusion and exclusivity. If 'exclusion' connotes having a right to exclude, and 'exclusivity' is the property of being the only person with a particular entitlement, it is not at all obvious that the former follows analytically from the latter, or vice versa (as we will see). The opacity of this 'right to exclude' allows ambiguity and equivocation to flourish. For instance, in just one article Thomas Merrill understands the right to exclude to apply in very different ways to a myriad of entities: to *resources*, to *actions*, to *interests* and even recursively to *the right itself*.[2] Not only is shifting content being applied to very different metaphysical entities, the locutions themselves are not perspicuous. It is unclear, for instance, whether *excluding* someone from interference is different from simply *prohibiting* them from interfering. But if it is not different, then many ordinary rights against interference must be categorized as property rights, which is counterintuitive.

With this in mind, this section explores the ways in which making an entitlement exclusive (making one person the *only* person who holds that entitlement) changes that entitlement into a recognizable property right, and whether, in so doing, it creates a right to exclude.

A standard definition of 'exclude' is to act so as to 'deny (someone) access to a place, group, or privilege'. Setting aside the special case of exclusion from a group, and since a privilege connotes a privilege to perform an activity, there are in the context of property two potential meanings of a duty to exclude oneself, one applying to places and another to activities. (A 'duty to exclude oneself' is admittedly a cumbersome phrase; unfortunately it is necessary. A property owner usually does not have a right to exclude in the sense of a general entitlement to remove trespassers. Rather, what she has is a right that they do not trespass; they owe her a duty to exclude themselves.)

Thanks to all the discussants at the Concepts of Property in Intellectual Property Law workshop at Sussex University in August 2011, especially Lionel Bently, Robert Burrell and Helena Howe. I am also grateful to Paul Formosa and Bas van der Vossen for helpful comments on earlier drafts of this chapter.

[1] John Locke, *Two Treatises of Government* (New York: Hafner, 1690/1947), II: 27; William Blackstone, *Commentaries on the Laws of England*, 1st edn (Oxford: Clarendon, 1765–69), Bk. 2, p. 2; James Penner, *The Idea of Property in Law* (Oxford: Clarendon, 1997); Shyamkrishna Balganesh, 'Demystifying the Right to Exclude: Of Property, Inviolability and Automatic Injunctions' (2008) 31 *Harvard Journal of Law and Public Policy* 593; Thomas Merrill, 'Property and the Right to Exclude' (1998) 77 *Nebraska Law Review* 730.

[2] Merrill, 'Property and the Right to Exclude'.

A duty to exclude oneself from a *place* carries a plain enough meaning, namely to physically 'keep off' a resource. If Bill excludes himself from Blackacre, then he accepts that he may not enter it; he may not cross its physical borders. I will term this *exclude (Trespass)* or exclude_T, keeping in mind that trespass in this context strictly connotes border-crossing, and not a broader concern with non-interference.

Applied to *activities*, the right to exclude is not entirely straightforward.[3] Because exclusion-from-a-thing is framed around exclusive liberties to use that thing, I will take it that the implied connotation when applied to activities is the exclusive liberty to perform the activity – that is, the duty of all non-owners not themselves to engage in the specific activity that the owner is entitled to perform. The constraint on others may be universally applicable ('no one *anywhere in the world*, except me, may perform the dance I created') or tied to a specific locale ('no one may hunt *in this forest* except me'). With its focus on proscribing one particular activity to all but one particular agent (and perhaps her delegates), I will call this *exclude (Monopolize)* or exclude_M.

Hence, if Annie has a right to exclude_T Bill from Blackacre, then Bill must not trespass across Blackacre's borders, while if Annie has a right to exclude_M Bill from hunting on Blackacre, then Bill may not hunt on Blackacre (though he may be allowed to enter it for other reasons).

1.1 Recapping Hohfeld

In property theory it is often supposed that we can move logically from a property-holder having an exclusive right to their having a right to exclude.[4] To the contrary, however, the fact that Annie has an exclusive entitlement need not imply that she has a right to exclude_T or exclude_M. To see this, and to investigate more generally the way exclusivity relates to exclusion, it is necessary to review Hohfeld's analysis of rights and jural relations.[5]

[3] The term might be used to connote non-interference or harm-protection. However, as section 1.3 below describes, it is possible to have harm-protection without zones of exclusion or exclusive entitlements. For this reason it is dealt with separately.

[4] An important exception is Larissa Katz, 'Exclusion and Exclusivity in Property Law' (2008) 58 *University of Toronto Law Journal* 275.

[5] Wesley Hohfeld, *Fundamental Legal Conceptions, as Applied in Judicial Reasoning*, Walter Cook (ed.) (New Haven: Yale University, 1946). One further, controversial, part of Hohfeld's project aimed to recast the *in rem* feature of property rights. That aspect is not utilized here.

Hohfeld famously distilled larger legal entitlements into their building blocks – the basic and irreducible components out of which all more complex entitlements were constructed. These 'jural relations' (as he termed them) are tightly linked with one another; the existence of one jural relation held by a person implies (by Hohfeldian *correlation*) the existence of its correlative held by another, while the lack of a jural relation in one person implies (by Hohfeldian *opposition*) that that person holds its jural opposite. This can be briefly stated as follows:

Liberty (privilege):

Person A has a *liberty* to do action X with respect to another person B when A has no duty to B not to do X. For example, in an ordinary case Annie will have a liberty (with respect to some other beach-goer Bill) to swim at a public beach if she is not under any duty to Bill not to swim at the beach. The necessary correlative of Annie's liberty is the absence of a right in Bill (a 'no-right') that Annie refrain from swimming. The opposite of a liberty is a duty; if Annie does not have a liberty to swim, then she by definition must have a duty not to swim.

Claim-right:

Person A has a claim on another person B to do X when B is under a duty to A to perform X. For instance, Annie has a claim-right that Bill not hit her – a claim that correlates with Bill's duty to Annie to refrain from hitting her. The definitional correlative of Annie's claim-right is Bill's duty. If Annie does not have a claim-right that Bill do X, then (via Hohfeldian opposition) she has no-right that he do X.

Power:

Person A has a power over person B with respect to X when A can alter B's jural relations with respect to X. For instance, when Annie alters Bill's liberties by waiving her claim-right that he not kiss her, she exercises her power to dissolve Bill's prior duty. Promising, waiving and selling are all examples of using powers because they all involve the agent altering people's duties. The correlative of Annie's power to change Bill's normative standing is Bill's 'liability' to have his jural relations changed by Annie. If Annie does not have a power over Bill with respect to X, then Hohfeldian opposition requires she has a 'disability' – the lack of power to change his normative standing with respect to X.

Immunity:

Person A has an immunity against a person B with respect to X if B cannot alter A's claims or liberties with respect to X. For instance, if Annie has an immunity against Bill with respect to her freedom of association, then Bill cannot impose new duties on her to refrain from associating (with Charles, say). By Hohfeldian correlation, if Annie has an immunity from Bill changing her jural relations with respect to X, then Bill has a disability to do so. By Hohfeldian opposition, if Annie does not have an immunity with respect to Bill, then he does have the power to change her normative standing, and she has a liability.

These relations are set out in Table 6.1.

Table 6.1 *Hohfeldian correlatives and opposites*

Jural Relation:	claim-right	liberty	power	immunity
Jural Correlatives:	duty	no-right	liability	disability
Jural Opposites:	no-right	duty	disability	liability

If Annie has one of the first set of jural relations in the top row of Table 6.1, then there necessarily must be some person or persons who have the jural correlative of that entitlement (directly below it in the table). Conversely, if Annie *does not* have a particular jural relation, then she necessarily has its opposite (in the bottom row).

The remainder of this section considers in turn four situations where a particular individual has entitlements to a particular resource. The purpose is to sharpen our understanding of exactly how exclusion is related to exclusivity. In Cases C1 and C2, exclusive entitlements lead to recognizable rights to exclude. Case C3 illustrates how proprietorial attachments may occur without requiring either a right to exclude or exclusivity. Case C4 involves exclusivity without necessitating a right to exclude. Paralleling this analysis, section 2 uses these four cases to illustrate four major theories of property.

1.2 Case C1: From exclusive liberty of use to the right to exclude$_T$

In Case C1, Annie has the right to enter and use a piece of land (Blackacre), in the sense of being *permitted* to do so. (For our purposes here and throughout, consider 'use' to connote *open-ended use*, such that while there may be some discrete limitations on her use, the uses Annie may put to Blackacre cannot be finitely enumerated. When we turn in Case C2 to consider specific, discrete activities, I will refer to Annie 'acting in' a place, rather than her 'using' it.)

In Case C1, Annie has a Hohfeldian liberty:

(C1.1) Annie has a general liberty to enter and use Blackacre (she has no duty to anyone not to enter and use the land).

And via Hohfeldian correlation:

(C1.2) All others have no-right that Annie refrain from entering and using Blackacre.

Now add that Annie has the *exclusive* liberty to enter and use Blackacre. If no other person has the liberty to enter and use Blackacre, then from Hohfeldian opposition we derive that:

(C1.3) All others have a duty (to Annie[6]) not to enter or use Blackacre.

And then by Hohfeldian correlation:

(C1.4) Annie has a claim-right against all others that they do not enter or use Blackacre.

As a result, Annie has a claim-right to exclude$_T$ Bill from Blackacre; if Bill crosses Blackacre's boundaries without Annie's permission, then he has acted in a way that is exclusively granted to Annie. From an exclusive liberty to enter and use (or to *possess* and use, if we turn from land to chattels), a claim-right to exclude$_T$ is derived. This effectively creates a zone of non-interference in which Annie can act unmolested by intrusions from others. Note, though, that the non-interference in question is not indexed to the protection of any particular activity of Annie's. It is derivative of the physical *boundary* that is created by all other people's duties not to trespass. Annie's exclusive liberty to enter and use does not of itself imply that she has (say) protections against her neighbours playing loud music late at night. The neighbours are not in so doing entering, possessing or using her resource. They may be making it difficult for Annie to use the resource to get a good night's rest, but that use was not protected from harm (for which see Case C3 in section 1.4 below).

1.3 Case C2: From exclusive liberty of action to the right to exclude$_M$

In Case C2, Annie has the right to fish in a stream (Whitewater), by which, again, we mean only that she is *permitted* to fish in Whitewater.

(C2.1) Annie has a general liberty to fish in Whitewater (she has no duty to anyone not to fish in Whitewater).

Via Hohfeldian correlation C2.1 implies:

(C2.2) All others have no-right that Annie refrain from fishing in Whitewater.

Now add that Annie's entitlement is an exclusive one (and, again, that the exclusiveness is owed to Annie).

As in Case C1, from Hohfeldian opposition we derive:

[6] The directionality of the duty ('to Annie') must be superadded here, for it is possible that Annie could be the beneficiary of the duty without it being owed *to her*.

(C2.3) All others have a duty to Annie not to fish in Whitewater.

And then by Hohfeldian correlation we can formulate Annie's entitlement:

(C2.4) Annie has a claim-right against all others that they do not fish in Whitewater.

As in Case C1, from an exclusively held Hohfeldian liberty we derive claim-rights to exclude, in this case claim-rights to exclude$_M$. Annie can exclude all others from the activity of fishing in the stream. If Bill fishes in Whitewater without Annie's permission, then he has acted in a way that is exclusively granted to Annie. However, she cannot – at least, not on the basis of the entitlements in C2.4 alone – exclude$_T$ Bill from entering or otherwise using the stream. Indeed, Annie's claim-right to exclude$_M$ does not guarantee that others cannot harm or interfere with her fishing endeavours by, say, poisoning all the fish in Whitewater. In a given situation Annie may well also have that entitlement, but it does not follow simply from the fact of her exclusive liberty.

1.4 Case C3: Claim rights against harm

In Case C3, Annie has a claim-right that others do not *interfere with or harm* her activity of fishing in the stream; all other people are duty-bound not to interfere with Annie's fishing activities, and they cannot impact on the stream in such a way as to deplete it as a fishing resource. Call this a 'property-protected activity'.[7]

(C3.1) Annie has a claim-right against interference in and harm of her fishing activities in Whitewater.
(C3.2) Others are duty-bound not to interfere with or harm Annie's fishing in Whitewater.

In some cases, harm-protection may necessitate exclusivity of the liberty to perform that action. If Whitewater were small, and intensive fishing gear were available, then other fishers on the stream would deplete its stocks, and so harm Whitewater *qua* Annie's fishing resource. If so, then harm-protection of fishing in Whitewater would have to include the exclusivity of the activity of fishing on the stream, meaning that C3.1 implied also:

(C3.2a) Others are duty-bound not to fish in the stream.

[7] Here I follow Hugh Breakey, 'Two Concepts of Property: Ownership of Things and Property in Activities' (2011) 42 *The Philosophical Forum* 239.

This would not be a surprising state of affairs. Often, a prime way to impact on the prospects of an activity on a resource is by engaging competitively in exactly that activity. As such, claim-rights to harm-protection can imply rights to exclude$_M$.[8] On the other hand, they need not. If the stream were long and fishing gear non-intensive, then a limited amount of other fishers on the stream might not impact on Annie's fishing. In this case C3.1 would not necessitate C3.2a. Both Annie and Bill would have property-protected fishing rights in Whitewater; each of their rights would be proprietorial, but not exclusive (because there are two of them holding the same entitlement).

If Annie holds the claim-rights against harm-protection *exclusively* then this will imply:

(C3.3) Others have no-right against people interfering in their fishing in Whitewater.[9]

And by Hohfeldian correlation:

(C3.4) Annie is (and people are) at liberty to interfere with others' fishing in Whitewater.

There is a sense in which the addition of exclusivity to Annie's claim-rights, as expressed in C3.3 (or even the addition of exclusivity to the liberty to perform the action, as expressed in C3.2a), does not add substantially to Annie's entitlements, at least with respect to her own actions and their prospects. With or without these explicit additions, C3.1 alone ensures that no-one can act to harm Annie's fishing exploits on the stream. If C3.1 does not necessitate Annie having the exclusivity present in C3.2a or C3.3, then the addition of exclusivity will not impact materially on the prospects of her fishing (because *ex hypothesi* those entitlements were not necessary to protect her fishing from harmful interference). Despite this, the entitlements of the exclusive liberty (C3.2a) or the exclusive claim-right (C3.3) may be extremely valuable to Annie if she has the power to sell them or license them out. Even if another ten fishers would not impact at all on her fishing activities, Annie would benefit from having the exclusive claim-rights of C3.3, for they would enable her to exclusively license

[8] It is even possible they could include rights to exclude$_T$, for instance if the stream was extremely ecologically fragile.

[9] C3.3 describes the situation where Annie's claim-right is exclusive: she is the only one whose fishing in Whitewater is protected. To complicate matters, however, what can be implied when it is asserted that Annie has an exclusive claim-right against interference in her activity is that Annie has (a) an exclusive *liberty* to perform the activity, and that she has (b) a claim-right of non-interference. This is the conjunction of C3.1 and C3.2a.

out the right to fish to those others. Even bearing this in mind, it is still worth emphasis that in C3.1 Annie can have a recognizably proprietorial entitlement to a specific resource (that is property-protection for her fishing in Whitewater) *without* that activity giving her a right to exclude_T or a right to exclude_M, and – indeed – without her holding that entitlement exclusively.

1.5 *Case C4: Powers of disposition and exclusivity*

Suppose now – Case C4 – that Annie has *disposition* over the exclusive fishing rights in Whitewater that she held in Case C2; that is, she can waive, gift, license, abandon or trade them. These entitlements are each the jural relation of *power*; waiver and license allow Annie to alter the duties regarding Whitewater that others owe to her (for instance by allowing certain others to fish in Whitewater), while gift and trade allow Annie to entirely dispose of her entitlement package (liberties, claim-rights, powers and all) by fully transferring it to others.

In Hohfeld's terms:

(C4.1) Annie has the power to dispose of her fishing rights in Whitewater.

Via Hohfeldian correlation:

(C4.2) All others have a liability such that Annie can change their normative standing with respect to fishing in Whitewater.[10]

While Annie's power of disposition in C4.1 does not explicitly include mention of exclusivity, it can seem implied. If others can unilaterally gift or transfer Annie's fishing rights, for example, then it is puzzling how their powers of disposition interact with, and leave intact, Annie's power of disposition described in C4.1. (This was not the situation in Cases C1 and C2 involving Annie's liberties. A non-exclusive liberty is quite understandable, and the addition of exclusivity implies very new, distinct entitlements, namely claim-rights to exclude.) As such, it appears that powers of disposition necessarily include exclusivity, and so by Hohfeldian opposition that:

(C4.3) All others have disabilities with respect to the disposition of Annie's fishing rights in Whitewater.

The correlative of C4.3 is:

[10] The liability is a complex one because, inter alia, recipients of gifts have a complementary power of rejecting the gift.

(C4.4) Annie has an immunity from having her entitlements to fish in Whitewater transferred without her consent.

In this case, the exclusivity of Annie's powers of disposition does not *in itself* result in a power to exclude$_M$ or to exclude$_T$. The exclusive power to dispose does not exclude others in any further way than the initial exclusive fishing right accomplished. Indeed, this exclusive power does not prohibit others from *doing* anything; it simply determines that others do not have the legal capability to accomplish a transfer of the entitlements. While C4.4 is framed in terms of Annie's exclusive disposition over her entitlements from Case C2, the situation is entirely parallel with respect to Annie's entitlements to Blackacre considered in Case C1, or her protections from harm in Case C3. Annie's exclusive disposition over those rights adds an important feature to her property rights in each case, but in itself it does not create rights to exclude.

However, there is a sense in which disposition provides a key element of the right to exclude, such that without Annie's entitlements including substantial powers of disposition we may resist characterizing Annie's entitlements in C1.4 and C2.4 as a full-fledged right to exclude. Both the notion of 'right' and the notion of 'exclude' suggest this. With respect to 'right', a common view of rights is that they serve a *gatekeeper function*; they describe a normative boundary around a person and her actions that the person can open or close at will. This position is the centrepiece of the 'Will' or 'Choice' theories of rights, associated with the work of H. L. A. Hart, whereby having a right conceptually entails the capacity to alter another person's normative standing – to have Hohfeldian powers over them.[11] If we think that – at least in the ordinary case – rights are best understood as gates that may be opened or closed at will, then a right to exclude must include exclusive powers of disposition.

This view gains further support from the thought that this right to exclude, as a *right*, is *owed to* Annie. It is intuitive to think that if the duties others have to exclude themselves from the property are owed to Annie, then such duties should not be performed against her direct expressed will. They are owed to her, after all.[12]

[11] Herbert Hart, *Essays on Bentham* (Oxford: Clarendon, 1982), pp. 183–8; Herbert Hart, 'Are There Any Natural Rights?' (1955) 64 *Philosophical Review* 175; Hillel Steiner, 'Working Rights' in Matthew Kramer, N. Simmonds and Hillel Steiner (eds.), *A Debate over Rights* (Oxford and New York: Clarendon Press, 1998), p. 247.

[12] It is of course arguable that at least some of the rights owed to Annie are not waivable (these being her 'inalienable rights'). Even in such cases, however, limitations on alienability are usually imposed *for the benefit of* the right-holder, and owed to her in that

Turning from the implications of the term 'right' to the term 'exclude', it is arguable that, as a verb describing a volitional action, 'exclude' suggests that exclusion is not automatic, but is at the discretion of the person empowered to exclude. Comparatively, 'a right that everyone else be excluded' does not carry this extra connotation of discretion. Such a right points to an entitlement to a state of affairs, not to an exercise of will. A right to perform a volitional act, however, does carry this extra connotation of wilfulness, suggesting that a right to exclude also includes a right *not* to exclude.

For these three reasons – (i) the choice factor implied in the concept of a right; (ii) the fact that rights are *owed to* the right-holder; and (iii) the nature of 'exclude' as a volitional verb – some powers of disposition appear to be a necessary but not sufficient element of a right to exclude.

1.6 Summation

The results of the foregoing analysis are as follows. Regarding liberties, there is no necessary implication from the mere presence of a liberty to its being exclusive; the addition of exclusivity adds decisively to the entitlement by creating claim-rights to exclude. The grant of exclusivity to a specific activity creates a right to exclude$_M$; the grant of exclusivity to liberties of entry, possession and use creates a right to exclude$_T$. Turning to property-protected activities, the proprietorial entitlements that protect an activity from harm can inhere even if the entitlement is not exclusive. Regarding powers, a power of disposition already implies the condition that those powers are exclusively held. While the exclusivity of the power of disposition does not in itself create rights to exclude, it is plausible to think that the reverse is true: some discretionary powers are constituent features of a right to exclude.

2 Exclusion, exclusivity, prohibition and disposition in property theory

Each of the four cases explored above represents a different theoretical position on the nature of property.

sense. This special case aside, a general presumption of Annie's discretionary waiver and control seems appropriate.

2.1 *The right to exclude$_T$: 'ownership of the thing'*

Case C1 involved Annie having exclusive liberties of possession, entry and use, and hence a right to exclude$_T$ others from possessing or entering. Such a right is widely held to be a signature feature of property. Many modern property theories – 'Exclusion Theories', as they are termed – have as their centrepiece this claim-right against physical trespass by others, of which James Penner's work is perhaps the best developed.[13] Penner's 'exclusion thesis' determines that 'the right to property is a right to exclude others from things which is grounded by the interest we have in the use of things'.[14] While interest in use grounds the right, the right itself is constituted by the duties others have to exclude$_T$ themselves from the object.[15] Thus the essence of property is held to be a claim-right that others exclude themselves from physically entering, possessing or using the object; that they 'keep off' it.

2.2 *The right to exclude$_M$: 'ownership of the activity'*

In Case C2 Annie had the right to exclude$_M$ others from performing an activity that she alone could perform. Combined with discretionary powers to license others to perform the activity, this entitlement has seemed to some the *sine qua non* of property: 'Without freedom to bar one man from a certain activity and to allow another man to engage in that activity we would have no property.'[16]

On this footing, ownership of an activity comprises:

- Others holding duties to refrain from performing ('exclude$_M$ themselves from') that activity.
- The owner having the liberty to engage in the activity.
- The owner having wide powers of waiver and alienation, allowing others to perform the activity at her discretion.

A paradigm of ownership of an activity would be a guild monopoly of the seventeenth century, such as a *letters patent* in selling salt or law books. Much older examples are known. While many aboriginal cultures routinely observed exclusive entitlements over songs, myths and magic spells,

[13] Penner, *The Idea of Property in Law*; Felix Cohen, 'Dialogue on Private Property' (1954) 9 *Rutgers Law Review* 357; Merrill, 'Property and the Right to Exclude'.

[14] Penner, *The Idea of Property in Law*, p. 71.

[15] *Ibid.*

[16] Cohen, 'Dialogue on Private Property', 321.

Lowie notes that for the Trobriand islanders: 'Dances are more definitely individual property, the original inventor having the right to perform it in his village. If another village takes a fancy to this song and dance, it has to purchase the right to perform it.'[17]

2.3 *Property-protected activities*

In Case C3 Annie's entitlement to fish in Whitewater did not necessarily involve a right to exclude (in either sense) or a right of exclusive disposition. Rather, the entitlement granted was of the protection of an activity or set of activities from harm or interference. Now momentary protection from bodily harm, or occurrent protection from interference in an activity that is actually being performed, is just an ordinary right, as distinct from a property right. However, when the protection attaches to particular resources and applies whether or not the activity is at that moment being performed, a recognizably proprietorial right emerges. On the property-protection approach, then, the question is not (or not primarily) whether physical boundary-crossing occurred, but whether harm – especially economic harm – was dealt to the property-owner as she engaged in the protected activities.

These protected activities may be very specific, as occurs with hunting, foraging or mining rights. Such rights – like Annie's fishing right in Whitewater – protect the property-holder's liberty to perform the specific activity and claim-right against interference in their performing that activity, as well as the protection of the resource against harms that would impair its capacity to function as a resource for performing that activity, and the property-holder's ownership of the fruits of that activity.[18] Alternatively, a wide cluster of activities may be protected – for instance in protecting an owner's 'quiet enjoyment' of his land.[19] Rather than making central trespass across borders, this property right shifts the focus to questions of harm, nuisance, interference and worsening with regard to activities taken on the land,[20] and neighbours are required to use their

[17] Robert H. Lowie, 'Incorporeal Property in Primitive Society' (1928) 37 *Yale Law Journal* 551 at 561.

[18] Breakey, 'Two Concepts of Property', 244–6.

[19] Eric Freyfogle, *The Land We Share* (London: Shearwater Books, 2003), pp. 16, 56. Further protected activities can include 'reasonable', 'indigenous', 'traditional', 'prior', 'natural' and 'historical' uses.

[20] See *ibid.*; Joseph Singer, *Entitlement* (London: Yale University Press, 2000), pp. 87–91; Katz, 'Exclusion and Exclusivity in Property Law'.

property according to the ancient *sic utere tuo* rule: 'Use your own so as to cause no harm.'[21] To be sure, these concepts of harm and non-interference will often overlap with trespass, but they are not coextensive. In some cases a boundary-crossing will not interfere with the property-holder's activities, and there will be 'no-harm, no-foul'. In other cases, harm can occur without border-crossing – such as when Annie pumps out groundwater to the point where Bill's land collapses, or when the dam Annie builds on her property causes Bill's land to flood.

In sum, harm-protection of activities – either specific activities or broad clusters of activities – is a distinct organizing idea for property, separate from property conceived as the right to exclude.

2.4 Exclusive disposition and authority theory

In Case C4, Annie had exclusive disposition over her entitlements, such that she could waive, license, transfer or abandon them. There are several ways that disposition can be implicated in property theories. It can be conceived as a vital ingredient added to other types of entitlements to grant them the status of property, or it can be understood as the essence of property itself.

In terms of the first mode (as a necessary addition to other elements of property), if property involves the right to exclude$_M$ or the right to exclude$_T$, then substantial powers of disposition are required in order to vindicate the volitional, discretionary aspect of excluding; powers of waiver, license and abandonment will be required, and powers of full transfer (sale) of the entire package of entitlements are at least suggested.[22] The combination of exclusive powers of disposition with the right to exclude$_T$ creates the familiar tripartite notion of property as the amalgamated rights to exclusive acquisition, use and disposal over an object.[23] Finally, at least some powers of disposition are implicated in the harm-protected activity considered in sections 1.3 and 2.3. As the common law apothegm goes, *volenti non fit injuria* – 'to he who consents, no harm is done'. After all, rights against harm need to be sensitive to the holder's waiver so they are not themselves impediments to her projects.

[21] Freyfogle, *The Land We Share*, pp. 67–83; Singer, *Entitlement*, pp. 34–9.
[22] Penner, *The Idea of Property in Law*, pp. 77–103.
[23] Adam Mossoff, 'What Is Property?' (2003) 45 *Arizona Law Review* 371 at 376.

Other theorists have taken the view that, rather than being merely one element of property, exclusive and sweeping powers of disposition constitute property's very essence. Section 1.4 described reasons why powers of disposition are implied by the idea of *rights* in general. These powers to dispose are even more intuitive in the context of property rights, where the 'gatekeeper' aspect is manifest: 'The right to property is like a gate, not a wall … [it] permits him to make a social use of his property, by selectively excluding others, which is to say by selectively allowing some to enter.'[24] There is a long-standing and popular view that a thing is property if, and only if, it can be traded in a marketplace. Avihay Dorfman takes a more theory-based tack, arguing that powers of exclusive disposition are needed to distinguish the right of property from lesser entitlements like possession: 'Being an owner involves a special normative power – that is, the power to change (in some nontrivial measure) the rights and duties that non-owners have toward the owner with respect to an object.'[25] I will call this conceptualization of property as exclusive disposition '*Authority Theory*'.

3 Copyright and property

This section takes the four property theories outlined in section 2 – right to exclude$_T$, right to exclude$_M$, property-protected activities and exclusive disposition – and appraises how they apply to the objects of copyright. It shows how the different concepts of property cast light on the subtle and distinctive types of freedom and control present within various aspects of copyright.

At the outset, however, it must be acknowledged that no single theory of property can possibly explain all the nuances of copyright law, even if we were to confine the analysis to a single jurisdiction. Copyright lies at the intersection of a wide range of human rights and social utilities. Just as real property has countless exceptions to its functioning in the abstract (for example, regulation, zoning, taxation and takings), so too does copyright. The question at issue, then, is whether a concept of property approximates the macro-level functioning of copyright closely enough to be considered its basic organizing idea.

[24] Penner, *The Idea of Property in Law*, p. 74.

[25] Avihay Dorfman, 'Private Ownership' (2010) 16 *Legal Theory* 1 at 16.

3.1 *'Ownership of the idea/expression': the right to exclude$_T$*

The most intuitive way of conceptualizing copyright as property, at first blush, is modelled directly on the right to exclude$_T$. The 'thing' in this case (the *res*) is identified as being the novel idea or the created expression.[26] Thus we arrive at 'ownership of the idea'; the creator, as owner of what she creates, has open-ended liberties to use and manage her created idea (or expression), while all others are required to exclude$_T$ themselves from using her creation or engaging with it. However, while the 'ownership of thing' approach gives an attractive account of tangible property, in application to copyright it is of limited appeal, with numerous authors recognizing that copyright does not, should not and cannot require non-owners to 'keep off' ideas or texts.

An initial challenge for this approach to copyright is to clarify exactly what the owned entity is. Is the owned thing the precise wording in the text – the *expression* of the idea? Or is it the particular *ideas* that are set out in the work? The problem is that in different contexts copyright can protect either one (and sometimes both, or neither). The classic example of copyright violation remains the verbatim copying of expression, but in a widening variety of cases direct copying of the text is not necessary. In modern copyright law:

> close approximation of the plot of a novel or play, preparation of a screenplay based on the novel, use of the characters from a movie or book to create an unauthorized sequel – all these are now understood to constitute infringements.[27]

But the central problem for this theory is simply that it advances an overly strong characterization of the rights of the copyright owner. In copyright, no one is required to exclude themselves from using or interacting with the idea (or from using or interacting with the expression in order to get at

[26] An alternative is to consider whether exclusionary property rights (right to exclude$_T$) over *tangible* objects (such as physical books) and contract can combine to create copyright-like institutions. See Hugh Breakey, 'Liberalism and Intellectual Property Rights' (2009) 8 *Politics, Philosophy and Economics* 329. This approach results in a weak copyright system, approximating only some features of copyright law. It may be, however, that such a regime has affinities with earlier literary property regimes, whose protections were applied to less abstract entities. Brad Sherman and Lionel Bently, *The Making of Modern Intellectual Property Law* (Cambridge University Press, 1999).

[27] William W. Fisher III, 'The Growth of Intellectual Property: A History of the Ownership of Ideas in the United States' in David Vaver (ed.), *Intellectual Property Rights* (London: Routledge, 2006), p. 74.

the underlying ideas). Such a right of exclusion would require unauthorized others being under a duty not to apprehend the idea or expression in the first place, or – having been unable to look away in time – being under a duty not to think about the idea and interact with it mentally or in communication.[28] Copyright requires no such duties, and never has:

> An actual right that may be close to a true right [to exclude$_T$, in my terms] to an idea is the right of the State to its official secrets, which might be regarded as a property right to certain information, since the law imposes a general duty on everyone to exclude themselves from it.[29]

To explain: copyright does not prohibit use of any of the general ideas, themes, narratives or methodologies put forward in a work. Direct and flagrant copying of such abstract ideas has always been allowed.[30] Even for more particular ideas that do have some protection in copyright, there must also be *substantial* copying in order to violate copyright; merely copying the narrative structure of one scene into a large and otherwise original work will not attract copyright action. Further, copyright protection has always been subject to important fair-use/fair-dealing exceptions, allowing its use for privileged purposes of education, history, journalism, critique, commentary and satire. For these protected activities, direct communication of both particular ideas and the exact expression are privileged. Indeed, for purposes of personal research substantial direct copying is often allowed. Finally, copyright regimes have various mechanisms for ensuring the dissemination of the works – mechanisms over which the copyright-holder has few powers of control or limitation. An important provision here is the 'first-sale' provision that allows first-buyers of books to loan, rent or sell those books, allowing for the existence of libraries.

Ultimately, the deliberate, conscious use of copyrighted ideas and expressions by non-owners is the rule, not the exception. If property necessarily implies exclusive open-ended use – and so the right to exclude$_T$ – then *copyright is not property.*

[28] Jessica Litman, *Digital Copyright* (New York: Prometheus Books, 2006), p. 13; Penner, *The Idea of Property in Law*, pp. 109, 119–20.

[29] *Ibid.*, p. 120.

[30] *Nichols* v. *Universal Pictures Corporation*, 45 F.2d 119, 121 (2d Cir. 1930) *cert. denied*, 282 US 902. On the 'copyright exceptions' discussed in this section and hereafter, see Robert Burrell and Allison Coleman, *Copyright Exceptions: The Digital Impact* (New York: Cambridge University Press, 2005); Hugh Breakey, 'Natural Intellectual Property Rights and the Public Domain' (2010) 73 *The Modern Law Review* 208 at 212–16.

3.2 *'Ownership of the activity': the right to exclude$_M$*

The 'exclusive activity' approach empowers the owner alone to perform certain activities; bound by the owner's right to exclude$_M$, all others must refrain from these activities unless they have the owner's consent. While it is rarely articulated explicitly as an 'exclusive activity' approach, this is a common way of picturing copyright.[31] In Wendy Gordon's words:

> Persons who enjoy a work in the ways reserved to the copyright owner's exclusive control – for example, reproducing the work verbatim, adapting it for use in new works, or publicly performing it – may be liable for injunctions, damages, accounting for profits, criminal penalties, and other sanction.[32]

The ownership of activity grants the copyright-holder an exclusive liberty regarding the activities of substantial verbatim reproduction, fashioning (closely) derivative works and (commercial or large-scale) public performance.

This position maps well onto copyright's functioning. The problems encountered by the 'ownership of the idea' approach are largely avoided. There is no sweeping duty to avoid general use of the idea, so apprehending and thinking about the idea pose no problems. The derivative use of broad ideas and abstract methodologies is not an annexed activity of the owner, so it is not prohibited in non-owners. Fair use usually does not require large-scale verbatim copying and so is not prohibited. (However, the larger-scale copying that is granted for the purposes of personal research is not so easily assimilated.) And first-sale doctrines allowing second-hand book stores and libraries are unproblematic: such doctrines do not involve reproduction, adaptation or public performance.[33] Thus the 'ownership of activity' approach for the most part makes room for the major copyright exceptions.

While avoiding the unhelpful absolutism of the 'ownership of idea' approach, this approach retains an important feature of this view – the *trespassory* notion of ownership and exclusion. Policing copyright need not require difficult questions such as evaluating the loss of revenue from

[31] E.g. Cohen, 'Dialogue on Private Propery', 369; Penner, *The Idea of Property in Law*, pp.109, 119–20.

[32] Wendy Gordon, 'An Inquiry into the Merits of Copyright: The Challenges of Consistency, Consent, and Encouragement Theory' (1989) 41 *Stanford Law Review* 1343 at 1366.

[33] Though modern libraries may allow electronic copying in various forms, and this may trespass across the exclusionary right.

the work's target audience. All that need be shown is that the non-owner engaged in an activity that was prohibited. 'For realty, physical intrusion triggers restitution; for copyright, violation of a specified exclusive right does the same.'[34] If trespass, rather than harm, is the central organizing idea of property, then ownership of the activity is an apt proprietorial model for copyright.

3.3 *Copyright as a property-protected activity*

This approach to property protects a particular activity or set of activities from those actions of others that would interfere with it, or harm the natural fruits of performing it. On this approach, copyright resembles other property-protected activities like Annie's fishing rights in section 1.4. The activity in question might be framed as: 'Authoring and vending one's work to those members of the work's target readership who wish to buy it (and managing such vending).' These terms require some explanation. The author, Peter, has property in the activity of selling his book to all those readers who want to buy it at Peter's asking price. 'Vending one's work to those members of the work's target readership who wish to buy it' is not the same as merely giving the agent the liberty to bring the product to market. The expanded sense of non-interference offered by property-protection precludes others from selling Peter's work to his buyers – from *usurping his target audience*, as the point is sometimes put. Others can convince third parties not to buy Peter's work, of course – they can write different and superior books, or pen devastating critiques of Peter's book. They just cannot interfere with the activity of Peter vending his book to his target audience by getting Peter's book to them before he can. Ultimately, this type of protection aims to protect the natural consequences of Peter's activity of being a professional author; namely, Peter being able to create works that potential readers wish to read and are willing to pay for, and his being unimpeded in selling his work to them. This activity is itself one instantiation of a broader action-type, namely the activity of creating a product that many people wish were available to them, and of selling it to all of those people who are willing to purchase it at the asking price.[35] (Ordinary property rights over land and chattels protect this

[34] Gordon, 'Merits of Copyright', 1379.

[35] This activity can be understood prior to and independently of its legal protection. Contrary to some property theorists' claims, in copyright there is something that 'pre-exists the legal protection'. Boudewiqn Bouckaert, 'What Is Property?' (1990) 13 *Harvard Journal of Law & Public Policy* 775 at 797.

larger productive activity in many contexts – but the creation of literary works is not one of them.)

As formulated above, Peter's property right is not necessarily to sell to every person who might want to use the book. The activity in question involves creating a product that people wish were available, and selling to those people. This class of people is the book's 'target readership' or 'natural audience' – usually those who read the book for enjoyment and edification. But not all those who will want to read the book are necessarily pleased it was created in the first place; social scientists using the book as evidence of some political change, or journalists reporting on aspects of its historical context, for example, are not target readers in this sense. Such persons would go on collecting and analysing social data irrespective of whether these books are being created – but if such books *are* created, then they will need to access them to perform their roles.

As with 'ownership of activity', this notion of property captures much of copyright's actual functioning. Authors are protected from direct 'piracy' in the sense of others copying and vending a work in any way that usurps the author's target audience, and from other activities that effectively provide the author's target audience with his work – for instance by public performance of it or by the creation of closely derivative works (such as abridgements, and perhaps sequels). Copyright owners often hold strong powers to deny access to their work to those who are clearly members of the target audience for the work and who have the capacity to pay for it. This is exactly the protection foregrounded in the harm-protection approach, where the acid test is always whether the potentially infringing activity effectively provides the work's target audience with the work in such a way as to replace sales.

Such a property-protection approach allows the key copyright exceptions. Ideas are not owned, so their apprehension and excogitation are not prohibited. Copying large-scale genres, styles and methodologies do not involve simply providing Peter's work to his readers – such derivative writings will offer something new to readers, and may well not replace the original work from being purchased in any case. Fair use (even when requiring substantial copying) is justified so long as the effect is not to simply provide target buyers with the core of the work itself. Research exemptions are unproblematic so long as the researchers are not the target readers of that type of work, but will clash with the property-protection approach when they are.

First-sale doctrines and library privileges are more problematic. In these cases it is an empirical issue whether such practices replace customers who would otherwise have purchased the work, or instead whether institutions such as libraries provide an additional potential purchaser of the work. To the extent the latter is true, these provisions could be assimilated.

3.3.1 Similarities and differences between the 'ownership of activity' approach and the 'property-protected activity' approach

While the 'ownership of activity' approach and the 'property-protected activity' approach are different theories conceptually, in application to ideational projects they have quite (though not exactly) similar results. Is this result surprising?

It should not be. Often a key way of stopping a person gathering the fruits of their activity is to do *exactly* what they are doing (usually with an eye towards gaining those fruits yourself). This is as true in non-physical projects as it is with respect to fishing a river. One can interfere with another's project by (say) broadcasting on exactly their wavelength, or using exactly the (trade) mark they use to distinguish their products. For this reason, granting ownership of an activity is often a key way of achieving the property-protection of that activity. So too for copyright, as Wendy Gordon notes: 'An exclusion right against copying greatly increases the copyright owner's ability to prevent strangers from interfering with her ability to market the work.'[36] That is, the best way of respecting an author's property in the activity of authoring and vending her work may be to grant her ownership of the activity of publishing it.

That said, there are differences between the two approaches. First, property-protection comports better with royalties and compulsory licences. The holder of a property-protected activity cannot necessarily prevent others interacting with their activity; they merely must not have their natural consequences of that activity worsened. So if appropriate economic compensation is forthcoming, such interactions need not be prohibited. On a like footing, if we think that copyright should be especially responsive to economic interests, as distinguished from other interests the author may have in controlling access and use,[37] then the property-protection approach will be apt. This approach facilitates

[36] Gordon, 'Merits of Copyright', 1390.

[37] Wendy Gordon, 'Towards a Jurisprudence of Benefits: The Norms of Copyright and the Problem of Private Censorship' (1990) 57 *University of Chicago Law Review* 1009 at 1041–2.

a narrowly defined protection of economic activity – as opposed to the ownership of activity approach, where the right to exclude$_M$ makes no distinction between exclusion for profit and exclusion for suppression. Still, the ownership of activity approach arguably aligns better with existing law on this point; copyright has been used to suppress speech for personal and ideological reasons, for instance to defend the esoteric writings of Scientology.[38]

Second, the property-protecting activities approach fits better with the dissolution of the property rights at the end of the copyright period. Property-protection of an activity naturally ceases when the property-holder ceases to be able to perform the activity – namely, at their point of death. So dissolution of the property rights after this event seems appropriate. Furthermore, as a generalization, most copyrighted works make their largest sales in the early years after their first release, and inflation, interest and the time-discounting of rational economic actors makes early returns comparatively more valuable than later ones. As such, protection of the activity of vending matters most in the early years (and decades) and comparatively less as time goes on.

3.4 *Exclusive disposition, authority theory and copyright*

Both the theories just explored carry consequences for powers of disposition. The right to exclude$_M$ carries a gatekeeper power, not only allowing the person the exclusive liberty to perform the act, but also granting them the power to authorize others to perform it. For its part, because the property-protected activity approach foregrounds protection against harm to the activity, and since *volenti non fit injuria*, the property-holder is authorized to allow others to publish and vend the work when it is beneficial, rather than harmful, to his goals.

In the context of copyright, two points about discretionary disposition are worth particular note. First, one way entitlement-holders can finely craft the types of duties they do and do not want with respect to their published work is by use of devices like the Creative Commons licences, where authors can elect via a unilateral licence to cede many of the rights that copyright vests in them, in order to better align the duties owed to them with the purposes they have for the work.[39]

[38] Ann Brill and Ashley Packard, 'Silencing Scientology's Critics on the Internet: A Mission Impossible?' (1997) 19 *Communications and the Law* 1.

[39] Lawrence Lessig, 'The Creative Commons' (2004) 65 *Montana Law Review* 1.

Second, it should not be forgotten that *abandonment*, as much as sale, is an important power of disposition. In cases where the copyright-holder perceives the copyright duties held by others to be an impediment to her purposes (perhaps altruistic goals, or a desire to increase the dissemination of her ideas), she needs to be able to dispense with them entirely and unequivocally. Contemporary copyright regimes do not deal particularly well with the case of abandonment, to the point where some theorists have argued that copyright entitlements cannot be abandoned.[40] In this respect copyright regimes are less proprietorial than property theory would imply.[41]

All these powers of exclusive disposition will be all the more significant from the standpoint of the Authority Theory, which holds that unrestrained powers of disposition are essential to property rights. Emphasizing the importance of the copyright-holder's control and authority over the duties they are owed, this approach would embrace all those mechanisms allowing copyright-holders to fully determine the normative standing of others with respect to the work, including by measures such as fine-grained licences (including Creative Commons licences), sale and abandonment. Equally though, Authority Theory conflicts with all restrictions on the owner's will in matters of disposition, such as occur in compulsory licensing, first-sale provisions, inalienable moral rights and – arguably – the dissolution of the property right at the end of the copyright period.

4 Conclusion

A Canadian government report on the revision of copyright once declared, 'ownership is ownership is ownership. The copyright owner owns the intellectual works in the same sense as the landowner owns land.'[42] This chapter has argued that such a position is doubly wrong. First, there are different and conflicting types of ownership, each shaped around different normative fundaments: exclusion, exclusivity, non-interference and authority. Second, one of the most compelling theories of property with respect to physical objects – the 'ownership of thing' approach – was

[40] See Robert Burrell and Emily Hudson's chapter in this collection.

[41] Previous regimes that required registration for copyright were therefore more property-like, as authors could abandon their property claims over a work simply by failing to register it or renew its registration.

[42] Cited in Carys J. Craig, 'Locke, Labour and Limiting the Author's Right: A Warning against a Lockean Approach to Copyright Law' (2002) 28 *Queen's Law Journal* 1 at 13.

found to be untenable with respect to copyright. However, two other recognizably proprietorial theories do offer a plausible account of copyright as property – the ownership of activities built on a right to exclude$_M$ and the property-protection of an activity protecting it from harm and interference. While giving similar results in many circumstances, the two theories nevertheless diverge on several issues, and it is possible that different appraisals of compulsory licensing or library exemptions (for example) may reflect the deeper, even tacit, undergirding vision of property that predominates in a given case.

7

Alienability and copyright law

SHYAMKRISHNA BALGANESH

Introduction

Debates about whether and to what extent copyright is a form of property abound in the literature, and remain by and large inconclusive.[1] Structured as a set of 'exclusive rights' that are vested in an author, who the law treats as the 'owner' of those rights, copyright seems to be modelled on the idea and structure of property law.[2] The rhetoric of 'literary property', which accompanied the passage of the first copyright statute, the Statute of Anne, confirms this intuition.[3]

Discussions of copyright law's nexus to property, however, invariably come to revolve around the relationship between copyright's exclusive rights framework and the 'right to exclude', taken to be central to the very idea of property.[4] Exclusion and exclusivity seem to imply an emphasis on control and unilateral decision-making, which copyright scholars routinely accept as translating well from the institution of property to that of copyright. This idea was captured rather prophetically by Justice Oliver

Many thanks to Jane Marie Russell, University of Pennsylvania Law School J.D. Class of 2014, for excellent research assistance.

[1] See, e.g., Shyamkrishna Balganesh, 'Debunking Blackstonian Copyright' (2009) 118 *Yale Law Journal* 1126; Richard A. Epstein, 'Liberty Versus Property: Cracks in the Foundations of Copyright Law' (2005) 42 *San Diego Law Review* 1; Adam Mossoff, 'Is Copyright Property' (2005) 42 *San Diego Law Review* 29.

[2] 17 USC § 106 (2002).

[3] Mark Rose, *Authors and Owners: The Invention of Copyright* (Cambridge, MA: Harvard University Press, 1993).

[4] For the general connection between property and the right to exclude: see Thomas W. Merrill, 'Property and the Right to Exclude' 77 *Nebraska Law Review* (1998) 730; Shyamkrishna Balganesh, 'Demystifying the Right to Exclude: Of Property, Inviolability, and Automatic Injunctions' (2008) 31 *Harvard Journal of Law & Public Policy* 593; Lior Jacob Strahilevitz, 'Information Asymmetries and the Right to Exclude' (2006) 104 *Michigan Law Review* (2006) 1835.

Wendell Holmes, Jr, who famously observed that '[t]he notion of property ... consists in the right to exclude others from interference with the more or less free doing with it as one wills' but that in copyright, property's notion of '[t]he right to exclude is not directed to an object in possession or owned, but is in vacuo, so to speak'.[5] Despite his concession that copyright law's conception of property operates rather differently from that of tangible property, his fundamental basis for the copyright–property analogy originated in the idea of exclusion, and in its being common to both institutions. This tradition today informs most analyses of the copyright–property interface in the United States.

The uni-dimensional focus on exclusion and its contribution to copyright's basic legal architecture has had the effect of directing attention away from other equally important analytical overlaps between copyright and property. Foremost among these is the idea of *alienability*. An essential attribute of ownership, alienability refers to the transmissibility or transferability of whatever forms the object of the property right in question (that is, of the *res*). The power of the owner, the property right-holder, to alienate the object and any rights over it is taken to be a critical component of the bundle of rights that ownership is thought to constitute. Indeed, there are even instances where the absence of such a power (or the inalienability of the right) is taken to imply that the interest in question is not a property right at all.[6] Despite this reality, the idea of alienability has received comparatively little sustained analysis among property theorists.[7] It is therefore hardly surprising that copyright scholars focusing on the copyright–property interface have also focused their attention elsewhere.

Yet alienability as a concept is hardly orthogonal to the structure of copyright and its normative edifice. Ever since its inception, there has remained little doubt that the rights granted by copyright could be assigned or traded away by their original recipients.[8] Indeed, scholars have noted how this was in some ways central to the process by which the first copyright statute came into existence. Publishers supported vesting copyright in authors only because they believed they might be able to acquire these rights in some way or form through the market in due

[5] *White Smith Music Publishing Co.* v. *Apollo Co.*, 209 US 1 at 19 (1908).

[6] Margaret Jane Radin, 'Market-Inalienability' (1987) 100 *Harvard Law Review* 1849 at 1890.

[7] Lee Anne Fennell, 'Adjusting Alienability' (2009) 122 *Harvard Law Review* 1403 at 1405.

[8] Statute of Anne 1710, 8 Anne cl. 19, §II.

course.[9] Over the course of its existence then, and right from its birth, copyright law has had to confront the question of alienability – whether of its own structure of rights or of its various manifestations – in one form or another. And as is to be expected, each of these confrontations made fairly important structural alterations to the content and functioning of the various rights constitutive of copyright.

This chapter examines the interaction between copyright and the concept of alienability to show that it holds important structural and normative lessons for our understanding of the nature of the copyright entitlement, and its limitations. My use of the word 'interaction' is deliberate here, since my focus is not just on the question of whether and how inalienability restrictions internal to copyright doctrine motivate our theoretical understanding of copyright and its allied rights (for example, moral rights), a project that others have focused on previously.[10] The chapter will instead attempt to understand how the copyright entitlement has addressed the basic common law principle (underlying the idea of property) that free alienability ought to remain a default, even if that principle originates outside the domain of copyright doctrine.

More specifically, I look at the interaction in three contexts involving the copyright entitlement, each of varying functional amplitude. The first context involves the rather straightforward manifestation of alienability in copyright's core apparatus, its exclusive rights. While the law has always allowed for alienability here, we see interesting debates about the forms in which such alienability may manifest itself. The second context involves the physical manifestation of the copyright entitlement, that is the chattel in which it is embodied, and the restrictions that copyright may (or put more precisely, may not) impose on its alienability. Much of this interaction is contained in the origins of the 'first sale' doctrine, which emanates from the law's fundamental protection of the basic alienability of the physical embodiment.[11] The third context involves a narrower dimension of the copyright entitlement, namely its conferral of the right to sue for infringement on its holder. In this manifestation, copyright bears a close resemblance to an ordinary actionable claim, which introduces a host of

[9] Rose, *Authors and Owners*, p. 42.

[10] See, e.g., Neil Netanel, 'Copyright Alienability Restrictions and the Enhancement of Author Autonomy: A Normative Evaluation' (1993) 24 *Rutgers Law Journal* 347; Neil Netanel, 'Alienability Restrictions and the Enhancement of Author Autonomy in United States and Continental Copyright Law' (1994) 12 *Cardozo Arts & Entertainment Law Journal* 1.

[11] 17 USC § 109(a) (2008).

additional considerations from debates over the alienability of actionable claims into our understanding of the copyright entitlement. Each of these interactions between copyright and the idea of alienability has played an important role in defining the scope of copyright's peripheries as a functional matter. Additionally though, by telling us what copyright is not, they hold important conceptual and normative lessons for what copyright actually is, which this chapter will attempt to unravel.

The chapter unfolds in three sections. Section one will begin with a brief overview of alienability's role in property, and the idea of market inalienability. Section two then moves to understanding the interaction between copyright and alienability at three different levels: in terms of its exclusive rights, through its possible restrictions on the physical embodiment, and in its manifestation as an actionable claim. Finally, section three tries to extract a few important analytical and normative lessons for copyright that flow from these interactions.

1 Property, alienability and inalienability

Speaking of the connection between property and alienation, Sir William Blackstone famously observed that 'property best answers the purposes of civil life, especially in commercial countries, when its transfer and circulation are totally free and unrestrained'.[12] This principle was to soon become a basic tenet of the common law of property, wherein restraints on the free alienability of both personal and real property are routinely disfavoured. Free alienability thus emerged as a bedrock idea and attribute of ownership. Property theorists routinely identify it as an essential component of the institution. Tony Honoré in his essay on ownership identifies alienability as a standard incident of ownership,[13] and Richard Epstein describes it as one of three identifying features of private property.[14]

Alienability is, however, more than just a descriptive reality of property and ownership. It is additionally believed to be normatively justifiable, especially in libertarian and utilitarian terms. The idea of free alienability comports with the owner's basic autonomy. If property is about the owner's 'despotic dominion' over an object, which in turn manifests itself in

[12] William Blackstone, *Commentaries on the Laws of England* 4 vols. (Oxford: Clarendon Press, 1765–9) vol. II, p. 287.

[13] Tony Honoré, 'Ownership' in Tony Honoré, *Making Law Bind: Essays Legal and Philosophical* (New York: Oxford University Press, 1987), pp. 161, 170–1.

[14] Richard A. Epstein, 'Why Restrain Alienation?' (1985) 85 *Columbia Law Review* 970 at 971.

the idea of exclusion, such dominion becomes operationally meaningless unless the owner has the right and the ability to disentangle himself or herself from the object.[15] Alienability is also thought to be efficiency- (and by implication, welfare-) enhancing, in the utilitarian understanding.[16] In this understanding, alienability allows resources to be put to their most efficient use through market trades, and impediments to such trades are treated as 'inefficient constraints'.[17]

The real puzzle in relation to alienability is, however, to be found in its converse, the idea of inalienability. At its simplest, inalienability refers to the phenomenon under which certain objects or rights are prohibited from being traded on the open market or exchanged freely. The prohibition may be in whole or in part, generalized or contextual.[18] The puzzle that this presents then is explaining why, despite the law's default in favour of free alienability, there are innumerable contexts wherein inalienability rules dominate. From one point of view, these situations represent an understanding that the rights that people have over these objects are not property rights *strictu sensu*, while from another they remain property rights, but weak variants of the same.[19] Scholars have over the years offered a wide variety of justifications for such inalienability restrictions. Some are intrinsic to the *res* in question, while others are extrinsic or instrumental in their character.

Beyond this, however, the alienability–inalienability debate plays an important *constitutive* role in debates about the idea of property. When an interest is rendered inalienable by a legal rule, it can either be treated as a non-proprietary interest or as a form of property, but with special attributes. Few scholars, mostly property dogmatists or essentialists, adopt the former argument. Adopting the latter as opposed to the former approach, however, requires conceding that property interests can exist in varying forms, that is with differing degrees of alienability. Margaret Radin characterizes such an approach as a 'pluralist' one.[20] Limited inalienability, in such an understanding, need not be seen as detracting from an entitlement's structure as a form of property. It derives instead from normative considerations that are integral to the entitlement, but are only ever realized indirectly. In this constitutive role then, inalienability

[15] Blackstone, *Commentaries*, p. 2; Epstein, 'Why Restraint Alienation?' 971.
[16] Epstein, 'Why Restrain Alienation?' 971–2.
[17] Susan Rose-Ackerman, 'Inalienability' (1985) 85 *Columbia Law Review* 931 at 931.
[18] Radin, 'Market-Inalienability' 1852.
[19] *Ibid.* 1890. [20] *Ibid.*

brings to the surface analytical and normative considerations underlying an institution (and its entitlement structure) that would have otherwise gone unnoticed, thereby allowing for a richer account of the entitlement and its justification. An example will help sharpen this point.

Most common law jurisdictions recognize the concept of moral rights in their copyright laws, and almost all of them disallow the transfer or alienation of these rights.[21] Yet several countries, the USA included, allow a creator to waive his or her moral rights in favour of another party, and place no restriction on such waivers being compensated, that is operating as a commercial trade.[22] Moral rights are in this sense partially inalienable as a conceptual matter, and can be contrasted with rights such as fundamental rights (for example, the right to life or free speech) that are completely inalienable in that they cannot even be waived contractually. Despite this partial inalienability, moral rights are sometimes described as property rights that are capable of being 'owned' by creators.[23] Market considerations are thus hardly anathema to their functioning. Yet the limited inalienability that they exhibit tells us something about their structure, and perhaps most importantly about the confluence of normative considerations that seem to motivate their very existence. By allowing them to be traded only when the creator is a party to the trade, the law does not just seem to be endowing these rights only with autonomy- and personality-based considerations. It can additionally be seen as promoting a more targeted utilitarian goal, where the welfare of the creator is prioritized over that of society more generally. Their limited alienability in this sense highlights the possibility that simplistic accounts of such rights as being motivated entirely by deontological considerations may indeed be incomplete.

This is precisely what a focus on copyright law's domains of alienability and inalienability can do for our understanding of its entitlement structure. Over-simplified analogies (of copyright) to real property have all too often produced expansive doctrinal changes and come at great social cost. Recognizing – through an analysis of alienability – that the idea of property is itself pluralistic[24] will go some distance to injecting a

[21] Mira Sundara Rajan, *Moral Rights: Principles, Practice and New Technology* (New York: Oxford University Press, 2011); 17 USC § 106A(e) (2012).

[22] 17 USC § 106A(e)(1) (2012).

[23] 17 USC § 106A(e)(2) (2012).

[24] For a recent account, see Hanoch Dagan, 'Inside Property' (2013) 63 *University of Toronto Law Journal* 1.

degree of nuance into any reliance on property metaphors and analogies in copyright thinking.

2 The copyright–alienability interaction

Free alienability remains an important principle of common law property, and artificial restrictions on alienability are routinely frowned upon. Yet free alienability need not imply absolute alienability. There remain numerous contexts in which the law either allows, or indeed imposes, restrictions on the domain of an entitlement's alienability. While this certainly does not imply that the entitlement somehow becomes inalienable as such, it does in the process shed light on the analytical structure of the entitlement and its normative values. So it is with copyright too. While copyright is, by default, an alienable entitlement, it does confront the idea of inalienability, and the common law's disapproval of restraints on free alienation, in its different functional manifestations.

2.1 The alienability of copyright's exclusive rights

Ever since its origins, copyright's basic structure of exclusive rights has been considered freely alienable.[25] Under US law, as it stands today, the owner of copyright in a work is free to assign it away either in whole or in part, effectively converting the assignee into the new owner.[26] Yet this was not the case prior to 1976. Under the US Copyright Act of 1909, a copyright owner could only ever alienate the set of statutory exclusive rights granted *as a whole*.[27] In other words, the owner was not free to divide them up and transfer them to others individually. This was known as the doctrine of 'indivisibility', and it originated in the English case of *Jeffreys* v. *Boosey*, where the House of Lords emphasized that copyright by principle was 'one and indivisible'.[28] The primary reason for the doctrine was the belief that allowing an owner to divide up the bundle of rights and alienate them independently could result in a defendant being subject to a multiplicity of lawsuits – from different owners – for a

[25] Rose, *Authors and Owners*, pp. 42–3; US Copyright Act of 1790, § 1, 1 Stat. 124 (1790).

[26] 17 USC §201(d) (2005).

[27] Melville B. Nimmer and David Nimmer, *Nimmer on Copyright*, 11gs. (Menands: Matthew Bender, 2012), vol. III, §10.01.

[28] *Jeffreys* v. *Boosey* [1854] 10 ER 681 at 703.

single action.[29] Indivisibility thus gave rise to a unitary conception of the copyright entitlement and its proprietary nature.

The Copyright Act of 1976 abolished the doctrine of indivisibility and effectively replaced it with a principle of infinite divisibility.[30] Not only did it permit each of copyright's enumerated rights to be individually alienated, but it also permitted idiosyncratic sub-rights to be created from the enumerated rights and alienated/assigned independently as well.[31] The idea behind this move was to give copyright owners greater bargaining power vis-à-vis intermediaries and publishers. Scholars have noted how this move contributed to the fragmentation of the copyright entitlement.[32] The assignee of each right or sub-right was treated as the 'owner' of that particular right, and given independent standing to commence a lawsuit for infringement.

Leaving aside the policy concerns motivating the change, however, the move away from a unitary conception of the copyright entitlement has arguably resulted in an important and hitherto underappreciated conceptual alteration to copyright as well. The indivisibility-motivated approach spoke of one copyright and one owner of such copyright, whose interests the system was directed at preserving and protecting. The new approach allows for multiple owners of the rights constitutive of copyright, and looks to protect each of their interests against the defendant's specific actions. It may be true, as David Nimmer points out, that the new approach does not simplistically treat each right as a new copyright in the work, there still being only one copyright in the work.[33] Yet, it modifies our understanding of copyright by converting it into what he describes as a 'label for a collection of diverse property rights'.[34] As an analytical matter, the process had copyright law move its focus from the object being protected to the precise form and context of such protection more directly. Copyright law in the process moved from performing the constitutive role of describing the contours of the author's interest to taking that interest as a pre-determined given and focusing on a framework for protecting its various manifestations – characteristic of changes seen in the move from property to tort.[35]

[29] Nimmer and Nimmer, *Nimmer on Copyright*, vol. III, §10.01[A].

[30] *Ibid.* §10.02. [31] 17 USC § 201(d)(2) (2012).

[32] Molly Shaffer Van Houweling, 'Author Autonomy and Atomism in Copyright Law' (2010) 96 *Virginia Law Review* 549 at 561.

[33] Nimmer and Nimmer, *Nimmer on Copyright*, vol. III, §10.01[A].

[34] *Ibid.* §10.01[A].

[35] Shyamkrishna Balganesh, 'Property Along the Tort Spectrum' (2006) 35 *Common Law World Review* 135; Shyamkrishna Balganesh, 'Quasi-Property: Like, But Not Quite Property' (2012) 160 *University of Pennsylvania Law Review* 1889.

A characteristic feature of property institutions and regimes is that they mediate their signal (usually an exclusionary one) through an object, the thing (or the *res*).[36] This is in contrast to tort or liability regimes that as a structural matter focus more on the actions and their effects rather than an identifiable object. Henry Smith captures this distinction well and notes that tort law takes the action as its basic unit of analysis, and that whereas 'property gives the owner a general right to repel invasions (of an open-ended variety); the more purely tort perspective scrutinizes each particular invasion (or conflicting activity) and announces which ones are impermissible and which ones are permissible'.[37] I have elsewhere described liability regimes that seek to simulate property's exclusionary core as 'quasi-property' interests.[38] Yet the basic point remains the same: tort law (or put more broadly, liability regimes) focuses on the granular actions, usually of an actual or putative defendant – even when their goals are similar to those of property regimes. Copyright's move from alienability as a whole (that is, the unitary conception) to idiosyncratic alienability seems to map onto this distinction rather well. Whereas in the former, the regime's focus was the 'work' and a single copyright in the work, in the latter it seems to be the rights held by actors, which are in turn defined in terms of the actions that they enable and disable. For instance, the exclusive right to distribute a literary work in paperback enables its owner to so distribute the work in the specified form, and simultaneously disables all others from doing so without permission from the owner of that right.

The move from owning a copyright to owning specific rights collectively constitutive of copyright is thus of some conceptual significance, and reveals a shifting emphasis in the law. Even though the law continues to speak of an 'owner' for each right, rather than just a holder, the move arguably dilutes the regime of its singular focus on the thing-ness of the copyright in question.

2.2 *The alienability of copyright's physical embodiment*

Among the different rights that copyright grants to a creator is the exclusive right to distribute the work.[39] Such distribution can, however, come

[36] James Penner, *The Idea of Property in Law* (New York: Oxford University Press, 2000), pp. 71–2.

[37] Henry Smith, 'Modularity and Morality in the Law of Torts' (2011) 4 *Journal of Tort Law* 14.

[38] Balganesh, 'Quasi-Property'.

[39] 17 USC § 106(3) (2002).

in different forms. One such form involves distributing a physical asset, that is a chattel that embodies the expressive work protected by copyright. In distributing a novel, a bookseller is thus effectively distributing the expressive content embodied in the novel. Assuming that the content was under copyright, a distribution of the novel would seem to infringe the exclusive right to distribute the work that the copyright owner was granted. If the exclusive right to distribute the work were expansively construed in this fashion, it would in effect place a restraint on what owners of a chattel could do whenever the chattel contained copyrighted expression. The owner of a book, lawfully acquired at a bookstore, would be violating the author's copyright when he/she sought to sell or give it to someone else.

On the face of things then, the plain reading of the distribution right runs up against the idea that all tangible property remains freely alienable, an idea that applies to both realty and chattels. The distribution right would not just restrict the forms or types of alienation that a chattel could be subjected to, but would effectively eviscerate such chattels (that is, those embodying copyrighted works) of all alienability. To solve this conflict, a doctrine known as the 'first sale doctrine' emerged, which exempts transfers of the chattel containing the work from infringement, if the transferor obtained the original copy (embodied in the chattel) lawfully.[40] Codified today, it thus permits 'the owner of a particular copy' that is 'lawfully made' under the statute 'to sell or otherwise dispose of the possession of that copy' without liability for infringement.[41]

Nimmer points out that the idea behind the first sale doctrine is to prevent copyright's distribution right from becoming 'a device for controlling the disposition of the tangible personal property that embodies the copyrighted work'.[42] Avoiding restraints on trade and alienation thus motivated the origins of the first sale doctrine in large measure. Without the first sale doctrine, the distribution right would operate as a legal or equitable servitude on the chattel, both of which are generally disfavoured in the common law.[43]

The principle of free alienability and the law's disfavour of restraints on alienation thus operate as external constraints on the shape of the

[40] Nimmer and Nimmer, *Nimmer on Copyright*, vol. II, §8.12.

[41] 17 USC § 109(a) (2008).

[42] Nimmer and Nimmer, *Nimmer on Copyright*, vol. II, §8.12[A].

[43] Zechariah Chafee, Jr, 'Equitable Servitudes on Chattels' (1928) 41 *Harvard Law Review* 945 at 1007.

copyright entitlement. Copyright's exclusive right to distribute the work thus appears to take a subordinate place to the right to freely alienate the physical resource that the owner of the chattel-embodiment is granted. It is important to appreciate that it is not simply that the chattel owner's property rights override copyright's exclusive rights, since there are indeed numerous contexts where copyright's set of exclusive rights is allowed to place restrictions on what the chattel owner can do. For instance, the copyright holder's exclusive right to reproduce the work, or to publicly perform it, place rather significant restrictions on what the chattel owner can do when the chattel embodies the protected work.[44] The first sale doctrine has no applicability in that context, since no 'sale' is implicated. It is only the chattel owner's right to freely alienate the chattel that the copyright entitlement is prohibited from interfering with.

On deeper examination though, the law's seeming preference for the free alienability of the chattel over the copyright owner's exclusive right to distribute and control the work remains largely superficial. The first sale doctrine is structured as an exception to infringement, rather than an affirmative entitlement as such. In other words, the law might have achieved the same functional result by implying a non-exclusive licence to distribute the work in any lawful owner of the physical embodiment; yet it chose not to. The effect of such a presumption would have been the same as the first sale doctrine, but it would have clothed the avowed preference for free alienability in a licence rather than a defence. The good faith purchaser doctrine, or the doctrine of the 'good faith purchaser for value', has long been central to the free alienability of physical chattels.[45] Under this rule, the purchaser of a chattel obtains title to it even when the seller's title is voidable, as long as the purchaser acted in good faith and without knowledge of the underlying taint.[46] The doctrine emerged in an effort to aid commercial transactions, and avoid burdening them with the costs of having to examine the legality of a chain title backwards in time during each successive alienation. It acted, in other words, as support for the principle of free alienability.

Yet the first sale doctrine contains no analogue to the good faith purchaser rule. As currently structured, a valid invocation of the first sale

[44] 17 USC § 106(4) and (5) (2002).
[45] Grant Gilmore, 'The Commercial Doctrine of Good Faith Purchase' (1954) *Yale Law Journal* 1057.
[46] *Ibid*. 1057–62.

doctrine is contingent on the first copy of the work being 'lawfully made' in compliance with the copyright statute.[47] When the first copy is tainted – for example by being unauthorized – its taint affects all subsequent owners of the copy, regardless of their good faith or lack of knowledge as to this taint. Thus, if a publishing house were to infringe an author's work, print a thousand copies of a work, and succeed in selling them to innocent buyers at bookstores, every subsequent sale by an innocent buyer would qualify as an infringement of the distribution right. In other words, every good faith purchaser risks becoming an infringer, since everything depends on the legality (that is lawfulness) of the first copy.

Indeed, the US Supreme Court reaffirmed this position in a very recent decision, where it was called upon to interpret the true scope of the phrase 'lawfully made', on which the legality of a first sale turns under the Act of 1976.[48] The Court concluded that the phrase suggested 'an effort to distinguish those copies that were made lawfully from those that were not' in order to serve copyright's objective of 'combatting piracy'.[49] By disallowing piratical copies from being sold, even when obtained in good faith or innocently, copyright law is today seen to be furthering its 'traditional' objectives,[50] even though as a historical matter early US copyright law excused sellers from liability for good faith sales of infringing copies, that is, when done unknowingly.[51]

An implied licence-based approach would have solved this problem. By having the lawfulness of distribution follow the lawfulness in the alienation of the physical embodiment – rather than the lawfulness of the original act of copying, purchasers without notice of the original illegality, and thereafter seeking to alienate the physical embodiment in good faith, would remain unaffected. Put simply, current copyright law's allowance for the free alienability of the physical chattel seems to stop if the first copy was an unauthorized one; at which point it reverts to encumbering all subsequent alienations with possible illegality – quite contrary to the common law's basic ideal as manifested in the good faith purchaser doctrine.

The conceptual lesson from this particular confrontation between copyright and the principle of alienability is somewhat indirect. On the

[47] 17 USC §109(a) (2008).

[48] *Kirtsaeng* v. *John Wiley & Sons, Inc.*, No. 11-697, 2013 U.S. LEXIS 2371 (19 March 2013).

[49] *Ibid.* 20. [50] *Ibid.*

[51] R. Anthony Reese, 'Innocent Infringement in US Copyright Law: A History' (2007) 30 *Columbia Journal of Law and the Arts* 133 at 160.

face of things, copyright law and its entitlement structure seems to show great respect for the common law's ideal of free alienability in relation to physical chattels. Yet this respect is somewhat limited, for it fails to fully internalize the scope and contours of the common law ideal. In some ways, copyright law's choice of not granting every good faith purchaser of a copy of the work an implied, non-exclusive licence to distribute the work by further sale, is perhaps an indication that copyright law is seeking to preserve the autonomy of the copyright owner to choose that such licences be obtained through the market. The copyright owner's ability to alienate the entitlement (or a part of it) is thus in practice better protected than the chattel owner's right of free alienability.

2.3 The alienability of copyright's right to sue

As an analytical matter, the copyright entitlement is structured as a grant of exclusive rights over the work (to reproduce, distribute, perform, and so on) to the author.[52] The entitlement is then rendered enforceable by empowering the holder of these rights with the power to commence an action against others for interferences with these rights – which copyright law treats as an infringement. Technically speaking, this power (or right) to sue for infringement is not a part of the enumerated bundle of rights conferred on the copyright holder; yet it is integral to copyright's very functioning, since without it the exclusivity promised by the entitlement is potentially meaningless.

Unlike tangible (that is physical) resources, the subject matter of copyright – expression – is a non-rival resource. This means that multiple, simultaneous uses of the resource are possible without interfering with one another. Now when a copyright holder is granted the 'exclusive' right to perform certain actions in relation to expression, this exclusivity – as a functional matter – depends entirely on the legal regime for its validation. In other words, the exclusivity that copyright law promises authors is one of pure *de jure* significance rather than one where a de facto reality is converted into a *de jure* reality by operation of law (as it is in relation to tangible objects).[53] This *de jure* significance in turn emanates from copyright's grant of the right to commence an action for infringement on

[52] 17 USC § 106 (2002).

[53] T. Cyprian Williams, 'Property, Things in Action, and Copyright' (1895) 11 *Law Quarterly Review* 223 at 232.

owners. The right to sue for infringement thus sustains copyright's bundle of exclusive rights, even though it is not an internal part of it.

Despite the centrality to copyright of the right to sue, it remains an open question whether it is capable of being alienated (that is assigned) in the same way as copyright's other exclusive rights. The prevailing consensus, in the USA at least, is that copyright's bare right to sue is incapable of being alienated, independent of any of the exclusive rights enumerated by the statute.[54] While the inalienability of copyright's bare right to sue is often justified by reference to the structure of the copyright statute and its purposes, at least part of the reason, one suspects, derives from the common law's historic discomfort with the alienability of actionable claims.[55]

Early in its development, and right until the nineteenth century, the common law viewed actionable claims, or 'choses in action', as incapable of being freely assigned.[56] This position was motivated in large part by the belief that litigation was an evil worthy of being avoided, and allowing third parties to acquire and continue litigation that they were not directly involved in served no social purpose whatsoever.[57] In due course, this belief came to be relaxed, with the law eventually drawing a distinction between personal and non-personal claims and allowing assignments of the latter though not of the former.[58] While a host of non-personal claims are today treated as freely alienable by the law, copyright claims remain inalienable. I have elsewhere suggested that this rule is deeply flawed and fails to capitalize on the important role that third parties can play in helping the copyright system realize its core objectives.[59] The inalienability of copyright claims, however, also sheds important conceptual light on the structure of the copyright entitlement, at least as perceived by the system.

[54] *Silvers* v. *Sony Pictures*, 402 F.3d 881 (9th Cir. 2005); *Eden Toys* v. *Marshall Field & Co.*, 675 F.2d 498 (2d Cir. 1982); *Righthaven* v. *Democratic Underground*, 791 F.Supp.2d 968 (D. Nev. 2011).

[55] Courts premise their holdings largely on the structure of the Copyright Act and Congress' objectives in enacting it. See, e.g., *Silvers*, 402 F.3d at 885–887.

[56] W. S. Holdsworth, 'The History of the Treatment of "Choses" in Action by the Common Law' (1920) 33 *Harvard Law Review* 997; James Barr Ames, 'The Disseisin of Chattels III: Inalienability of Choses in Action' (1890) 3 *Harvard Law Review* 23.

[57] Ames, 'The Disseisin of Chattels III' 339.

[58] Anthony J. Sebok, 'The Inauthentic Claim' (2011) 64 *Vanderbilt Law Review* 61 at 74.

[59] Shyamkrishna Balganesh, 'Copyright Infringement Markets' (2013) 113 *Columbia Law Review* (forthcoming).

Underlying the inalienability of copyright claims is the belief that as an analytical matter, copyright's exclusive rights over (and relating to) its *res*, original expression, are somehow different from the right to ensure such exclusivity through private enforcement. Copyright's right to sue is thus taken to be of little analytical significance when disconnected from copyright's other exclusive rights. This understanding tracks the historic distinction that scholars made to justify the inalienability of choses in action, namely between transfers of the *res* of a property right and transfers of the right to exclude that constituted the property right.[60] According to this argument, best articulated by James Barr Ames, whereas the former (that is the exclusive rights to the *res*) could be alienated, the latter (that is the right to exclude others from it) was a mere 'chose' and incapable of being transferred since it was based on a right–duty relationship that was personal, and implicated individuals.[61] Only through the consent of all the individuals involved, then, could such a transfer come about. Ames characterized this rule of inalienability as a 'principle of universal law'.[62] Yet as later Legal Realists such as Walter Wheeler Cook pointed out, Ames' argument rested on a dual understanding of the idea of a transfer.[63] By noting that only the *res* and not its surrounding relationships could be transferred, Ames was referring to the physical delivery of the *res* and no more. Yet even when the *res* of a property right is transferred, rights do indeed get transferred even though they are not physically delivered, so to speak.[64] The transfer operates by extinguishing the first set of relationships and recreating a second one in its image. If it could happen during outright transfers of the *res*, then why should it not be allowed during alienations of the right to exclude, independent of the *res*, that is as a chose? As Cook thus concluded: 'it does not seem possible to recognize that the transfer or assignment of a chose in action involved anything fundamentally different from what is involved in a transfer of a chose in possession.'[65] In due course, therefore, the rule of inalienability came to crumble, as its analytical foundations were shown to be baseless.

The distinction between the right to possess the *res* and the right to exclude others from the *res* that informed the rule of inalienability becomes ever more tenuous when we move to copyright. The exclusive

[60] Ames, 'The Disseisin of Chattels III' 339–40.

[61] *Ibid.* 339. [62] *Ibid.*

[63] Walter Wheeler Cook, 'The Alienability of Choses in Action' (1916) 29 *Harvard Law Review* 816 at 817.

[64] *Ibid.* 817–18. [65] *Ibid.* 817.

rights that copyright grants an owner are not exclusive possessory rights of the kind that real property gives owners. They are instead rights that operate by disabling others from performing certain actions.[66] Copyright's rights become exclusive, owing to the non-rivalrous nature of expression, only when they impose correlative duties on all others. Given this reality, it should mean, going by Ames' logic, that copyright's exclusive rights can never be transferred. And yet such alienability has existed ever since copyright's inception.

The alternative position that this leads us to, however, is the possibility that the copyright entitlement as a whole – even in relation to its exclusive rights – is nothing more than a chose in action, given its dependence on the right–duty relationship as an analytical and functional matter. Indeed, prominent lawyers and scholars adopted this position in their analysis of copyright towards the end of the nineteenth century. Copyright's entitlement was thus understood by some to be 'a right to a duty of forbearance' that 'merely imposes a restriction on others' freedom of action'.[67] Conveying nothing of a possessory nature, but a mere entitlement to prevent others from acting, it could only be rendered functional 'by action against infringers' and was thus taken to be analogous to a 'thing in action'.[68]

In due course, as choses in action came to be understood as freely alienable, and as being associated largely with contractual debts, scholars moved away from this position, perhaps for functional reasons. Yet the core analytical insight remains just as true now as it was then. Ironically then, copyright law's continuing reluctance to allow its right to sue to be freely alienated or assigned (in the USA, at least) reveals important analytical details about its core structure of exclusive rights, and the possibility that, strictly speaking, it remains no more than a mere actionable claim, even if alienable in its unmatured form.

3 Lessons: the myth of thing-ness in copyright

Copyright's interaction with the principle of alienability in different contexts is highly illuminative of its core architecture and functioning. Simplistic characterizations of copyright as just another property regime,

[66] Shyamkrishna Balganesh, 'The Obligatory Structure of Copyright Law: Unbundling the Wrong of Copying' (2012) 125 *Harvard Law Review* 1664 at 1669.

[67] Williams, 'Property, Things in Action, and Copyright' 232.

[68] *Ibid.*

coupled with an extensive reliance on real property metaphors and analogies to understand and operationalize its principal concepts and devices, has all too easily prevented much detailed analysis of copyright's basic analytical structure.[69] From the interactions described in the previous section, I identify a few important (and interrelated) structural lessons that may be drawn about copyright.

Copyright's rejection of the unitary conception of the entitlement bundle, its acceptance of the principle of infinite divisibility, and its reluctance to allow anything other than its core set of enumerated exclusive rights to be alienated suggest a richer account of copyright's *res* that it simulates its exclusionary regime around. The standard property analogy assumes that copyright's object, analogous to tangible property's 'thing', is manifested in the original expression that the regime is directed at protecting. In its standard setting, property operates by giving an owner a set of exclusive possessory privileges in relation to a thing, with those privileges being protected by an exclusionary right, that is the oft-referenced right to exclude.[70] Since copyright's subject matter is an intangible, that is expression, the privileges that it grants an owner are not possessory at all – yet they nonetheless are exclusive. Instead of operating in the realm of possession, the exclusivity relates to the performance of certain specified actions in relation to the expression. And as noted earlier, since expression remains non-rival, this exclusivity must of necessity come about by disabling or forbidding similar actions by others.

What this points to then is that copyright's core emphasis lies not in the identification of a thing (or *res*) along the lines of traditional property regimes, but instead in a focus on specific actions that are in turn thought to be equivalent (though not identical) to the possessory privileges granted to owners of tangible resources. Henry Smith describes this distinction as one between 'exclusion-' and 'governance-' based approaches to delineating property rights in intangibles.[71] While this is true, I think it also highlights an important move in copyright law beyond the move away from exclusion, namely the fusion of the ideas of *exclusion* and *exclusivity*. Exclusion refers to the power and/or act of excluding others from an identifiable object, whereas exclusivity focuses

[69] Neil Weinstock Netanel, *Copyright's Paradox* (New York: Oxford University Press, 2008); Balganesh, 'Debunking Blackstonian Copyright'.

[70] James W. Harris, *Property and Justice* (New York: Oxford University Press, 2002), p. 63.

[71] Henry Smith, 'Exclusion versus Governance: Two Strategies for Delineating Property Rights' (2002) 31 *Journal of Legal Studies* 453; Henry Smith, 'Intellectual Property as Property' (2007) 116 *Yale Law Journal* 1742.

on an owner's control over the resource as it affects others.[72] The two are related, but operate in different ways. Exclusion need not entail exclusivity, and conversely, exclusivity need not be protected by exclusion. In relation to standard real property rights, the two of course go together: the owner has a set of exclusive use privileges in a resource, protected by a right to exclude others from the said resource. In recent work, Larissa Katz has argued that whereas exclusion focuses on identifying and protecting the boundaries of the protected object, exclusivity refers to the agenda-setting control that the owner has over such object, analogous to 'sovereignty'.[73]

In relation to traditional tangible resources, exclusion and exclusivity operate differently in so far as the obligations that they impose on everyone other than the owner. Exclusion entails the imposition of a duty of forbearance (or a duty of inviolability) from the identified thing on others; whereas an owner's exclusivity in possession operates as a privilege that allows and enables the owner to do what he/she chooses to with the resource without others being endowed with analogous privileges (that is the so called sole agenda-setting authority).[74] The power to set the agenda for a resource is thus an affirmative enablement, unlike the simple imposition on others of an obligation to stay away from a resource. What is thus crucial to appreciate is that in relation to tangible resources, exclusion operates as a negative liberty while exclusivity operates as a positive liberty.[75]

When we move to copyright, however, as an analytical matter, both exclusion and exclusivity operate as negative liberties. Since possession is theoretically and practically impossible and the subject matter in question is non-rivalrous, the exclusivity only ever relates to a specified set of actions in relation to protected expression over which the owner is given an exclusive privilege. Yet since these privileges are perfectly capable of being exercised by multiple individuals simultaneously without interfering with one another, the exclusivity must be realized through a form of forbearance that essentially tracks the form of forbearance seen in relation to exclusion. But since there is no possessable thing that forms

[72] Larissa Katz, 'Exclusion and Exclusivity in Property Law' (2008) 58 *University of Toronto Law Journal* 275 at 290.

[73] *Ibid.*

[74] Balganesh, 'Demystifying the Right to Exclude' 611–14.

[75] See generally, Isaiah Berlin, 'Two Concepts of Liberty' in Isaiah Berlin, *Four Essays on Liberty* (Oxford University Press, 1969).

the focal point of the exclusivity, it focuses instead on the specific actions that copyright's grant of exclusivity privileges – which has the analytical effect of collapsing the ideas of forbearance from the *res* and forbearance from certain actions. Or put more directly, it collapses the distinction between exclusion and exclusivity. If property does indeed revolve around the 'right to exclude', copyright's underemphasis of exclusion for exclusivity must render it an anomaly within the world of property, or render it a non-proprietary entitlement.

The point has deep functional implications beyond just the analytical and conceptual. First, in taking copyright's basic structure as built around the idea of property, scholars have long tried to identify a thing or *res* for copyright, in an effort to move it closer to the boundary-based framework utilized by property rights centred around the right to exclude. The argument made here would suggest instead that this search is misplaced, for it mistakes the nature of copyright's exclusivity. Copyright's entitlement is hardly about a 'thing', but is instead about actions that indirectly relate to specified subject matter. Yet that should hardly, in and of itself, merit courts' reliance on real property metaphors. The law of battery renders actionable certain actions that constitute interferences with one's bodily integrity. Its focus remains those specific actions – and it thereby does not convert one's body into a thing. So it is with copyright too. Its focus is on potential liability for certain actions (mostly revolving around expressive copying) – no more, no less.

Second, given the centrality of forbearance and disablement to the copyright entitlement's functioning, enforcement – or at the least the threat of such enforcement – remains central to the system. Most discussions of copyright law, and of copyright reform, view copyright litigation as orthogonal to the system, and worthy of being minimized whenever possible. What this ignores is the reality that when shrunk down to its core, copyright operates as an actionable claim (or a 'chose'), and as a result of which its significance derives from the very *actionability* of the claim. Copyright's entitlement thus functions in the 'shadow of the law', or under the continuous threat of private enforcement.[76] Copyright reform efforts would thus do well to look at ways to streamline existing infringement litigation and make it more effective, rather than jettison it altogether.

[76] Robert H. Mnookin and Lewis Kornhauser, 'Bargaining in the Shadow of the Law: The Case of Divorce' (1979) 88 *Yale Law Journal* 950.

Third, given copyright's preference for actions over the *res*, and its willingness to scrutinize a defendant's actions *ex post* during the liability determination, courts, scholars and policy-makers ought perhaps to reconsider their ready recourse to real property metaphors and ideas in structuring the copyright system. They might instead come to recognize that concepts, ideas and structures from other liability-driven areas of private law such as the law of torts, or of unjust enrichment, provide copyright law with mechanisms that are more directly suited not just to its analytical structure, but also to its various normative goals and purposes.[77]

4 Conclusion

In thinking about property law concepts and ideas that may be used to shed light on the structure and functioning of copyright law, scholars regularly overlook alienability. In this chapter I have tried to show that thinking about copyright through the idea of alienability presents us with important and underappreciated insights into the nature of the copyright entitlement and its core architecture. The analysis reveals that existing uses of property ideas to study the institution of copyright all too often blind themselves to the somewhat unique ways in which the copyright entitlement merges the ideas of exclusion and exclusivity, while reorienting the focus away from the idea of a 'thing' and towards potential defendants' specific actions that are presumed harmful, and therefore actionable.

A larger problem highlighted by these deficiencies is that attempts to apply property concepts and ideas to copyright begin with a monolithic, uni-dimensional conception of property. This conception usually carries the features commonly described in the common law as associated with the fee simple absolute. Rarely ever do these attempts remain willing to work with a richer and normatively plural conception of property, since this complicates the picture and renders both the object and referent in the metaphor somewhat unstable. The perceived need for stability, in other words, tries to begin by fixing the idea of property, and then using it to analogize and/or explain different dimensions of copyright.

What my analysis here suggests – or at least hints at instead – is that we are perhaps much better off analytically when we recognize *both* property

[77] See, e.g., Shyamkrishna Balganesh, 'Foreseeability and Copyright Incentives' (2009) 122 *Harvard Law Review* 1569; Shyamkrishna Balganesh, 'Normativity of Copying in Copyright Law' (2012) 62 *Duke Law Journal* 203.

and copyright as being in a dialectic conversation with each other at all times, rather than simply assuming that one influences the other. The way we think about the ideas of exclusion and alienation in standard property forms sheds important light on copyright and its functioning. At the same time, copyright's operationalization of exclusivity, its reliance on forbearance and its serial underemphasis of a *res* seem to reveal not just that copyright does not follow established patterns of property thinking, but also perhaps that the very idea of property may necessitate reorientation to accommodate what copyright law and doctrine have done with its foundational devices. It is only when this inexorable tension between object and referent reaches an acceptable working equilibrium that debates about *whether* and *how* copyright is a form of property will ever come close to being resolved.

PART II

Re-shaping intellectual property rights: the role of concepts from wider property law

8

Limiting copyright through property

MICHAEL A. CARRIER

In recent years, copyright has become more like property. Copyright has expanded to take on property-like powers that are broad and last essentially forever. In addition, industry leaders, courts, and scholars discuss copyright in terms of strong property rights.

In this chapter I first show how copyright has become more like property. I next show how limits are central to property. Third, I explain why it is appropriate to limit a propertized copyright. Fourth, I offer some examples of copyright limits.

1 The propertization of copyright

One indication that copyright has become more like property can be found in statements made by leading government officials and copyright holders. Another indication is evident from the scope and duration of the rights themselves.

1.1 Statements

In recent years copyright has been discussed in increasingly absolutist terms. In continually strengthening copyright, courts have characterized it as a type of property.[1] Assertions of the piracy of copyrighted works and the 'theft' of property also have been proclaimed from the highest

Portions of this chapter are adapted from Michael A. Carrier, 'The Propertization of Copyright', in Peter K. Yu (ed.), *Intellectual Property and Information Wealth: Issues and Practices in the Digital Age* (Westport: Praeger, 2006) and Michael A. Carrier, 'Copyright and Innovation: The Untold Story' (2012) *Wisconsin Law Review* 891.

[1] See, e.g., *Chavez* v. *Arte Publico Press*, 204 F.3d 601 at 605 n.6 (5th Cir. 2000); *Lane* v. *First National Bank*, 871 F.2d 166 at 174 (1st Cir. 1989); *Roth* v. *Pritkin*, 710 F.2d 934 at 939 (2d Cir. 1983).

levels of the US government. President Barack Obama stated that '[i]t's not right when another country lets our movies, music, and software be pirated'.[2] Commerce Secretary Gary Locke highlighted the 'rampant piracy of music, and of intellectual property', and warned that '[p]iracy is flat, unadulterated theft' and 'should be dealt with accordingly'.[3]

Vice President Biden has spoken out even more strongly, announcing that 'piracy is theft, clean and simple'.[4] According to Biden, piracy is 'no different than a guy walking down … Fifth Avenue and smashing the window of Tiffany's and reaching in and grabbing what's in the window'.[5]

To similar effect, as a Senator, Biden stated that 'every day, thieves steal millions of dollars of American intellectual property from its rightful owners' and that 'it's a crime'.[6] In fact, Intellectual Property (IP) is 'an immensely valuable resource' and not protecting it is 'equivalent to letting coal be stolen from our mines, water taken from our streams and our rivers, and oil out of the ground'.[7] Biden lamented that 'we don't seem to think about it that way' or 'approach it as if it were a natural resource being stolen'.[8]

In addition, administration officials Victoria Espinel (IP Enforcement Coordinator), Aneesh Chopra (US Chief Technology Officer), and Howard Schmidt (Special Assistant to the President) explained the need for legislation to confront 'online piracy', which 'is a real problem that harms the American economy and threatens jobs for significant numbers of middle class workers'.[9] Piracy 'harms everyone from struggling artists to production crews, and from startup social media companies to large

[2] Chloe Albanesius, 'Obama Tackles Piracy, Startups in State of the Union' (24 January 2012), available at: www.pcmag.com/article2/0,2817,2399309,00.asp (last accessed 10 April 2013).

[3] Commerce Secretary Gary Locke, Remarks at Intellectual Property Enforcement, Belmont University, Nashville, Tennessee (30 August 2010), available at: www.commerce.gov/news/speech/2010/08/30/remarks-intellectual-property-enforcement-belmont-university-nashville-tennes (last accessed 10 April 2013).

[4] Greg Sandoval, 'Biden to File Sharers: "Piracy is Theft"', (22 June 2010), available at: http://news.cnet.com/8301-31001_3-20008432-261.html (last accessed 29 April 2013).

[5] *Ibid.*

[6] Statement of Sen. Biden, Evaluating International Intellectual Property Piracy: Hearing Before the Sen. Comm. on Foreign Relations, 108th Cong. 2d Sess (2004), available at: http://ftp.resource.org/gpo.gov/hearings/108s/96570.txt (last accessed 10 April 2013).

[7] *Ibid.* [8] *Ibid.*

[9] Victoria Espinel, Aneesh Chopra, and Howard Schmidt, 'Combating Online Piracy while Protecting an Open and Innovative Internet', available at: https://petitions.whitehouse.gov/response/combating-online-piracy-while-protecting-open-and-innovative-internet (last accessed 29 April 2013).

movie studios'.[10] And while the administration is 'strongly committed to the vigorous enforcement of intellectual property rights, existing tools are not strong enough to root out the worst online pirates beyond our borders'.[11]

Discussion of these issues was widespread in the debate over the PROTECT IP Act (PIPA) and Stop Online Piracy Act (SOPA).[12] Representative Lamar Smith (R-TX), the SOPA sponsor, explained that the bill does not 'threaten online freedoms' but 'does threaten the profits generated by those who wilfully steal intellectual property by trafficking in counterfeit or pirated goods'.[13] Smith stated that '[t]he problem of rogue sites is real, immediate, and widespread', with 'IP theft cost[ing] the US economy more than $100 billion annually' and 'the loss of thousands of American jobs'.[14] Similarly, Senator Sherrod Brown (D-OH) worried that 'illegal file sharing and unauthorized copying of digital material prevents musicians … from reaping the fruits of their labor' and 'has the potential to stifle artistic creativity and compromise electronic innovation'.[15]

Companies have emphasized this trend even more strongly. Leaders in the music and movie industries have sought to 'protect private property from being pillaged'[16] and to defend against having 'their property taken from them'.[17] In addition, some artists have lamented the 'piracy' of their works. While many artists have applauded the widespread distribution of their works, others have focused on theft and piracy. Britney Spears, for example, said that file-sharing was 'the same thing' as someone 'go[ing] into a CD store and steal[ing] a CD' since 'people [are] going into the computers and logging on and stealing our music'.[18] Dr Dre lamented that

[10] *Ibid.* [11] *Ibid.*

[12] Stop Online Piracy Act, H.R. 3261, 112th Cong. (2011); Preventing Real Online Threats to Economic Creativity and Theft of Intellectual Property Act of 2011, S. 968, 112th Cong. (2011).

[13] Lamar Smith, 'Defending SOPA: It would protect American businesses without infringing on freedoms' (1 December 2011), available at: www.nationalreview.com/articles/284535/defending-sopa-lamar-smith (last accessed 10 April 2013).

[14] *Ibid.*

[15] Sherrod Brown, Letter to Constituent (19 January 2012), available at: http://projects.propublica.org/sopa/B000944 (last accessed 10 April 2013).

[16] Edmund Sanders and Jube Shiver, Jr, 'Digital TV Copyright Concerns Tentatively Resolved by Group', *LA Times* (26 April 2002), at C5.

[17] Doug Bedell, 'Internet Piracy Enforcement Flounders with Rise of MP3', *Dallas Morning News* (27 July 1999), at 1F.

[18] Lisa M. Bowman, 'Superstars Blast File Swapping' (25 September 2002), available at: http://news.cnet.com/Superstars-blast-file-swapping/2100-1027_3-959537.html (last accessed 29 April 2013).

Napster was 'just a new high-tech way of bootlegging'.[19] And Paul Stanley from Kiss stated that just as someone who 'grab[s] an album and leave[s] a store' is 'put in handcuffs', file-sharing is 'like me stealing your car and telling you I'm sharing your transportation'.[20]

1.2 *Propertization*

In addition to the statements discussed in the previous section, copyright has become more like property in its expansion of the duration and scope of rights to basically unlimited dimensions. In property law, fee simple ownership of a plot of land lasts forever and grants unlimited rights such as the rights to exclude, use, and transfer.

While each of the fields that make up 'intellectual property' has expanded in the past generation, copyright has grown at least as much as any of the others. I show in this section how the duration and scope of copyright have burgeoned far beyond their historic proportions.

Of all the dimensions of copyright, duration has garnered the most attention. The US copyright term was initially fourteen years, with a potential renewal term of another fourteen years.[21] In 1831 Congress lengthened the maximum possible term from twenty-eight to forty-two years, and it extended this term to fifty-six years in 1909.[22] In the Copyright Act of 1976, Congress provided that new works would receive protection for the life of the author plus fifty years.[23] Most recently, the Sonny Bono Copyright Term Extension Act of 1998 added twenty years of protection to this term. The current copyright term thus is the life of the author plus seventy years.[24]

Accompanying these extensions of copyright duration are increasingly powerful rights granted to copyright holders. Copyright law initially protected only against copying, allowing uses such as translations,

[19] Dr Dre, 'Break Em' Off', available at: www.kronick.com/2.0/issue31/drdre.shtml (last accessed 10 April 2013).

[20] Kiss Talks About Music Piracy (7 October 2009), available at: www.devtopics.com/kiss-talks-about-music-piracy/ (last accessed 10 April 2013).

[21] Act of May 31, 1790, ch. 15, § 1, 1 Stat. 124, 124.

[22] Act of Feb. 3, 1831, ch. 16, §§ 1–2, 4 Stat. 436, 436–37 (42 years); Copyright Act of 1909, Pub. L. No. 60–349, ch. 320, § 23, 35 Stat. 1075, 1080 (56 years).

[23] Copyright Act of 1976, § 302, Pub. L. No. 94–553, 90 Stat. 2541, 2572.

[24] Pub. L. No. 105–298, § 102, 112 Stat. 2827, 2827 (codified at 17 USC § 302(a) (2000)). For corporate, anonymous, or works-for-hire authors the copyright lasts until the earlier of 95 years from publication or 120 years from creation. 17 USC § 302(c) (2000).

abridgments, and public performances.[25] The rights protected by copyright then gradually expanded, with the Copyright Act of 1870 granting the right to dramatize, the Copyright Act of 1909 providing the right to make translations, and the 1976 Act granting the exclusive right to prepare derivative works such as adaptations and transformations.[26] This expansion has greatly increased the power of copyright holders: protection for derivative works, for example, reserves for copyright holders the ability to exploit their works in secondary markets and provides no rights to those who improve copyrightable expression without the consent of copyright holders.[27]

The Digital Millennium Copyright Act (DMCA) also has strengthened the rights of copyright holders.[28] Among other things, the DMCA prevents the 'circumvent[ion of] a technological measure that effectively controls access to a [protected] work'.[29] To the extent that works are increasingly accessed in digital form, copyright holders thus have greater control over the use of their works. For example, the anti-circumvention provisions of the DMCA allow copyright holders to block access to uncopyrightable parts of works, parts that have entered the public domain, and parts for which unlicensed access would otherwise have been allowable under the fair use defence.[30]

The effects of copyright's increased duration and scope are magnified by its expanded subject matter: more and more categories of works are protectable, and the public domain is shrinking. The 1790 Copyright Act applied only to books, maps, and charts.[31] The nineteenth century saw an expansion to engravings and prints, musical compositions, dramatic works, photographs, paintings, drawings, and sculptures.[32] Growth

[25] Act of May 31, 1790, ch. 15, § 1, 1 Stat. 124, 124 (granting the exclusive right to 'print, reprint, publish, or vend the [work]'); *Lawrence* v. *Dana*, 15 F. Cas. 26 at 59 (C.C.D. Mass. 1869) (No. 8136) (abridgment is not infringement); *Stowe* v. *Thomas*, 23 F. Cas. 201 at 208 (C.C.E.D. Pa. 1853) (No. 13,514) (translation is not infringement).

[26] Act of July 8, 1870, ch. 230, § 86, 16 Stat. 198, 212; Copyright Act of 1909, Pub. L. No. 60–349, ch. 320, 35 Stat. 1075, 1075; Copyright Act of 1976, Pub. L. No. 94–553, ch. 1, § 101, 90 Stat. 2541, 2542.

[27] 17 USC § 103(a) (2000).

[28] Pub. L. No. 105–304, 112 Stat. 2860 (1998).

[29] 17 USC § 1201(a)(1)(A).

[30] E.g., David Nimmer, 'A Riff on Fair Use in the Digital Millennium Copyright Act' (2000) 148 *University of Pennsylvania Law Review* 673 at 702–40.

[31] Act of May 31, 1790, ch. 15, § 1, 1 Stat. 124, 124.

[32] Act of Apr. 29, 1802, ch. 36, § 2, 2 Stat. 171, 171 (engravings and prints); Act of Feb. 3, 1831, ch. 16, § 1, 4 Stat. 436, 436 (musical compositions); Act of Aug. 18, 1856, ch. 169, 11 Stat. 138, 139 (dramatic works); Act of Mar. 3, 1865, ch. 126, § 1, 13 Stat. 540, 540

continued in the twentieth century with the application of copyright protection to motion pictures, computer programs, sound recordings, dance, and architectural works.[33] As one commentator has synthesized: 'We have gone from a regime where a tiny part of creative content was controlled to a regime where most of the most useful and valuable creative content is controlled for every significant use.'[34]

In short, as confirmed by statements of government officials and industry representatives, the duration and scope of copyright today have expanded to the point that they are nearly absolute in nature, demonstrating the propertization of the field.

2 The limits of property

Discussion of property today tends to focus on absolute rights. In fact, numerous limits restrict property rights. Each of the three central property rights – the rights to exclude, use, and transfer – are cabined by an array of limits. In other work I have described fifty such limits.[35] In this chapter I focus on fifteen of these, describing particularly important limits on the right to exclude, the right to transfer, and the right to use.

2.1 Limits on right to exclude

The right to exclude is often considered to be the paramount right in the 'bundle of rights' composing property. Nonetheless, it is subject to numerous limits. Five I discuss in this section are easements, imminent necessity, the public trust doctrine, encroachment law, and anti-discrimination in public accommodations.

(photographs); Act of July 8, 1870, ch. 230, § 86, 16 Stat. 198, 212B (paintings, drawings, and sculptures).

[33] Act of Aug. 24, 1912, Pub. L. No. 62–303, ch. 356, 37 Stat. 488, 488 (motion pictures); Copyright Act of 1976, Pub. L. No. 94–553, ch. 1, § 102, 90 Stat. 2541, 2544–34 (computer programs); Act of Oct. 15, 1971, Pub. L. No. 92–140, 85 Stat. 391, 391 (sound recordings); Copyright Act of 1976, Pub. L. No. 94–553, ch. 1, § 101, 90 Stat. 2541, 2543 (dance); Architectural Works Copyright Protection Act, tit. 7, §§ 702–03, 104 Stat. 5133, 5133 (1990) (building design).

[34] Lawrence Lessig, *The Future of Ideas: The Fate of the Commons in a Connected World* (New York: Random House, 2001), p. 346.

[35] Michael A. Carrier, 'Cabining Intellectual Property Through a Property Paradigm' (2004) 54 *Duke Law Journal* 1.

An easement is an interest in land that allows a person to use land owned by another.[36] Easements can be express or implied. Express easements appear explicitly in written instruments such as deeds and wills.[37] Easements implied from an apparent and continuous use occur when one part of a formerly united tract of land is used for the benefit of another part; an underground sewer pipe is a typical example.[38] Easements by necessity make landlocked land available to the market and allow owners to leave their property. Each of these express and implied easements limits the ability of landowners to exclude others from their land.

Imminent necessity privileges entry onto another's land to save lives or property, or to avoid other serious harm.[39] Accepted justifications include avoiding an imminent public disaster, fleeing from an attacking animal, reclaiming or removing chattel that has entered the property, abating a private nuisance, and executing a court order.[40] The privilege also extends to a firefighter putting out a fire and a police officer in hot pursuit of a fleeing suspect or making an arrest for a criminal offence.[41] Each of these important purposes counsels limits on the owner's right to exclude.

States also exercise control over land pursuant to the public trust doctrine. This doctrine makes states trustees of navigable waters to preserve the public's right to use the waters for commerce, fishing, navigation, and recreational activities.[42] The doctrine provides rights of access over private property to reach beaches or public waters. Courts traditionally reserved for the public the area between the ocean and wet-sand areas of the beach; more recent cases have extended this area to the dry sand.[43] In addition, courts have applied the doctrine to wildlife, marshlands, historical areas, cemeteries, and archaeological sites.[44]

The law of encroachments limits the right to exclude by preventing courts from issuing an injunction when parts of buildings or other structures intrude onto other people's land. In particular, modern courts

[36] David A. Thomas and George W. Thompson (eds.), *Thompson on Real Property* (Charlottesville: Michie, 1994), para. 60.02(a), p. 391.

[37] Michael Allen Wolf (ed.), *Powell on Real Property* (New Providence: Lexis Nexis, 2000), para. 34.04[1], p. 34–24.

[38] E.g., *Van Sandt* v. *Royster*, 83 P.2d 698 (Kan. 1938).

[39] Restatement (Second) of Torts (1977) § 197.

[40] Carrier, 'Cabining Intellectual Property', 66 (citing sources).

[41] *Ibid.*, 66–7.

[42] Wolf, *Powell on Real Property*, paras. 64A.04[3][g], 64A-42.

[43] E.g., *Matthews* v. *Bay Head Improvement Ass'n.*, 471 A.2d 355, 368–69 (N.J. 1984).

[44] See Maureen Ryan, 'Cyberspace as Public Space: A Public Trust Paradigm for Copyright in a Digital World' (2000) 79 *Oregon Law Review* 647 at 698.

will not enjoin encroachments that are minimal, that would be costly to remove, and that result from innocent mistakes.[45] For example, one court refused to issue an injunction when a high-rise parking garage encroached a total of 1.3 square feet onto the plaintiff's property and reduced the property's market value by $200, but would have cost $500,000 to remove.[46]

A final limit involves anti-discrimination rules in public accommodations. Such accommodations, which are facilities that are open to the public and hold themselves out as ready to serve the public, cannot exclude people based on categories such as race, religion, or disability.[47] Public accommodations include categories such as innkeepers (including hotels and motels), common carriers (including trains, ships, and taxis), and, to a lesser extent, places of entertainment and hospitals.[48]

2.2 Limits on right to transfer

In addition to limits on landowners' rights to exclude, courts and legislatures have also recognized numerous limits on the right to transfer. Some of those limits include adverse possession, the unenforceability of restraints on alienation, eminent domain, the refusal to enforce racial covenants, and anti-discrimination statutes.

An absolute right to transfer would guarantee an owner's right not to transfer. The doctrine of adverse possession intrudes upon this right, forcing a transfer when the possessor can demonstrate certain requirements. The typical elements a plaintiff must prove are (1) possession that is (2) open and notorious, (3) hostile, (4) continuous, and (5) exclusive (6) for the statute of limitations period.[49] Adverse possession serves purposes such as clearing stale claims, quieting title, recognizing the possessor's

[45] E.g., Olivia Leigh Weeks, 'Comment, Much Ado About Mighty Little – North Carolina and the Application of the Relative Hardship Doctrine to Encroachments of Permanent Structures on the Property of Another' (1989) 12 *Campbell Law Review* 71 at 74–7.

[46] *Urban Site Venture II Ltd.* v. *Levering Assocs. Ltd.*, 665 A.2d 1062, 1063 (Md. 1995).

[47] See generally Civil Rights Act of 1964, §§ 42 USC 2000e to 2000e-17 (2000); Americans with Disabilities Act of 1990, 42 USC §§ 12,101–12,213 (2000).

[48] See *Doe* v. *Bridgeton Hosp. Ass'n.*, 366 A.2d 641, 646 (N.J. 1976) (hospital); Civil Rights Act of 1964, 42 USC § 2000a(b)(1)–(4) (inns, restaurants, gas stations, and places of entertainment); Americans with Disabilities Act, 42 USC § 12,181(7) (restaurants, theatres, retail stores, banks, barber shops, doctors' and lawyers' offices, museums, parks, educational institutions, day care centres, and other locations).

[49] E.g., Thomas and Thompson, *Thompson on Real Property*, para. 87.05, p. 111.

ties to the land, and encouraging the development of land. For any of these purposes the doctrine forces the transfer of land from its owner.

Limits also cabin the conditions of transfer. For example, courts typically strike down total restraints on alienation, which prevent the transfer of property interests. Such restraints make property unmarketable, prevent it from being used by others who would have a greater ability to develop the land, and discourage improvements to land.[50] Partial restraints on alienation prevent the transfer of an interest for a certain period of time or limit the range of potential transferees.[51] Most courts invalidate temporal restraints, which present some of the same dangers as total alienation restraints.[52]

A much-discussed limit on the right to transfer is the power of eminent domain. Pursuant to this power, landowners must transfer their interests to the government. An essential element of sovereignty, eminent domain allows states to appropriate private property to promote the general welfare of society.[53] Historically, the government employed this power only for uses such as military bases, post offices, highways, parks, and schools. More recently, however, the government has invoked eminent domain for urban renewal, land redistribution, and commercial, industrial, and housing development.[54] In 2005 the Supreme Court, in *Kelo* v. *City of New London*,[55] held that economic development constitutes a 'public use' necessary for the government's exercise of eminent domain. In the wake of Kelo, many state legislatures limited such power, but eminent domain nonetheless remains a limit on the right to transfer.

Another example of a limit on transfer involves the courts' refusal to enforce racial covenants. Such a rule advances social justice and inhibits segregation. In the seminal case of *Shelley* v. *Kraemer*,[56] the Supreme Court prohibited judicial enforcement of racial covenants, holding that such enforcement violated the Equal Protection Clause of the Fourteenth Amendment. The doctrine thus denies owners the right to refuse to transfer property for reasons relating to a person's race.

Anti-discrimination statutes provide the final, related example. The Fair Housing Act (Title VIII of the Civil Rights Act of 1968) prohibits the

[50] See *ibid.*, para. 29.03(b), pp. 707–8.
[51] See Wolf, *Powell on Real Property*, para. 77.03, pp. 77–9.
[52] *Ibid.*
[53] Thomas and Thompson, *Thompson on Real Property*, paras. 80.01(b)(1)–(2), pp. 283–4.
[54] John G. Sprankling, *Understanding Property Law* (New York: Lexis, 2000), para. 39.01 p. 640.
[55] 125 S. Ct. 2655 (2005). [56] 334 US 1 (1948).

refusal to sell or rent a dwelling on the grounds of 'race, color, religion, sex, familial status, or national origin'.[57] The Civil Rights Act of 1866 provides that all United States citizens 'shall have the same right ... as is enjoyed by white citizens ... to inherit, purchase, lease, sell, hold, and convey real and personal property'.[58] Additionally, several states have barred discrimination on the basis of marital status or sexual orientation.[59]

2.3 Limits on right to use

The final set of limits restricts landowners' rights to use. Such limits include zoning, nuisance, takings, government regulations, and lateral support.

One ubiquitous limit on use, affecting nearly all land in the United States, is zoning. Zoning ordinances typically divide land into residential, commercial, and industrial districts and allow only certain uses in each district.[60] Zoning has expanded far beyond its initial compass as an early-twentieth-century response to the '[s]moke, odors, noise, disease, filth, [and] overcrowding' of urban areas.[61] Today it serves to increase safety, promote health and welfare, conserve natural resources, maintain community purposes, and encourage the most appropriate use of land.[62]

The law of nuisance provides another limit on the use of land. A nuisance is a substantial and unreasonable interference with another's use or enjoyment of land, and often takes the form of noise, odours, or pollution.[63] Interference with another's use of land is unreasonable, according to the Restatement (Second) of Torts, if 'the gravity of the harm outweighs the utility of the actor's conduct'.[64] Protecting land against unreasonable interference – which often takes the form of unpleasantness, discomfort, and danger – ensures that landowners' investment in property will not be dissipated.[65]

[57] 42 USC § 3604(a) (2000).

[58] 42 USC § 1982 (2000).

[59] See, e.g., *Smith* v. *Fair Employment & Hous. Comm'n.*, 913 P.2d 909 at 918 (Cal. 1996) (marital status); *Poff* v. *Caro*, 549 A.2d 900 at 904 (N.J. Super. Ct. Law Div. 1987) (sexual orientation); *Braschi* v. *Stahl Assocs.*, 543 N.E.2d 49 at 55 (N.Y. 1989) (same).

[60] See Wolf, *Powell on Real Property*, para. 79C.01, 79C-7.

[61] Sprankling, *Understanding Property Law*, para. 36.03(B)(1) p. 591.

[62] Wolf, *Powell on Real Property*, paras. 79C.03[2], 79C-40 to 79C-70.

[63] *Ibid.*, paras. 64.02[2], [3], at 64–10 to 64–11.

[64] Restatement (Second) of Torts § 826(a) (1979).

[65] Joseph William Singer, *Introduction to Property* (New York: Aspen, 2005), para. 3.1, p. 102.

Landowners' rights to use their property also yield to governmental actions and regulations. This issue often arises in the area of takings jurisprudence. Takings law determines the point at which government restrictions so interfere with private owners' use of land that the land is effectively 'taken' from owners and the government must pay 'just compensation'.[66] Although takings doctrine presents one of the thorniest areas of property law, it also illustrates limits on the right to use property.

Even government regulations that do not reach the level of takings restrict owners' use of property. The range of conceivable regulations is all-encompassing, including safety, fire, health, and building codes; zoning ordinances; wetlands, shore-lands, and green belt ordinances; clean air and water acts; growth control ordinances; and historic protection zones.[67]

A final limitation on the right to use is the obligation of lateral support that neighbours owe to each other. The doctrine of lateral support grants landowners 'the right to be free from the collapse of [their] land caused by the excavations of [their] neighbors' land'.[68] Heightening this obligation is the need to provide artificial support and the application of the obligation to successive owners of excavated land.[69] In preventing the collapse of dwellings, the doctrine of lateral support demonstrates an obvious limit on the right to use land.

In short, the fifteen limits described in this section demonstrate that the rights granted by property law are far from absolute. Rather, landowners' rights to exclude, transfer, and use are subject to significant limits.

3 Applying property limits to copyright

The first two sections of this chapter have demonstrated that copyright has rapidly been assuming the characteristics of property and that limits are at the core of property. This section takes the next step, explaining why it is appropriate to apply limits to copyright. In particular, it demonstrates that (1) the traditional story justifying copyright is inaccurate in many cases, (2) the dangers of copyright are at least as significant as

[66] The Fifth Amendment provides: '[N]or shall private property be taken for public use, without just compensation.' US Constitution.

[67] William B. Stoebuck, *The Law of Property* (St Paul: West Group, 2000), para. 9.1, p. 518.

[68] Wolf, *Powell on Real Property*, para. 63.01.

[69] E.g., *Keck* v. *Longoria*, 771 S.W.2d 808, 810 (Ark. Ct. App. 1989) (artificial support); *Gorton* v. *Schofield*, 41 N.E.2d 12, 15 (Mass. 1942) (successive owners).

those accompanying property, and (3) limiting copyright is appropriate given the limits at the core of property.

First, the traditional story justifying copyright is inaccurate in many cases. The traditional story is that a right to exclude is necessary to allow creators to appropriate the rewards from their works. Creative works are 'public goods' because information is non-exclusive and non-rivalrous. Non-exclusivity prevents owners from excluding others from the possession of information. Non-rivalrousness magnifies this danger because one person's consumption does not diminish the amount of the good for others to consume – that is, multiple persons can use information without depleting it.[70]

As a result of these conditions, 'free-riders' who have not incurred the costs of creation are tempted to imitate inventions others have developed. Allowing such imitation could deter future creators. To prevent this result, the copyright laws grant creators a right to exclude. This right permits them to charge prices in excess of the marginal cost of producing their creations so they can not only recover their initial expenditures but also receive profits.[71]

As often as it is repeated, however, the traditional story is subject to question in copyright law. Although certain works, such as large-budget motion pictures, might not be created absent copyright protection, many others would. For many works, non-copyright-based incentives such as lead time, network effects, and sales in advance of entering the market are more important catalysts for creation.[72] Further questioning the need for copyright, many forms of creative expression – such as fashions, new words and slogans, jokes, magic tricks, and the food industry – have flourished in the absence of protection.[73]

At the same time, the increasing digitization of creative works and rise of the Internet have played a significant role in reducing the need for copyright to provide incentives to distribute works. Content distributors traditionally have undertaken substantial investments in manufacturing,

[70] Carrier, 'Cabining Intellectual Property', 32.

[71] E.g., Stephen Breyer, 'The Uneasy Case for Copyright: A Study of Copyright in Books, Photocopies, and Computer Programs' (1970) 84 *Harvard Law Review* 281 at 282, 294.

[72] *Ibid.*

[73] Tom G. Palmer, 'Intellectual Property: A Non-Posnerian Law and Economics Approach' (1989) 12 *Hamline Law Review* 261 at 287; Jessica Litman, *Digital Copyright* (New York: Prometheus, 2001), pp. 105–6; Kal Raustiala and Chris Sprigman, 'The Piracy Paradox: Innovation and Intellectual Property in Fashion Design' (2006) 92 *Virginia Law Review* 1687.

printing, packaging, and distribution.[74] The Internet significantly reduces these costs. The fixed costs in cyberspace are minimal, and the marginal cost of reproducing and distributing digital copies is zero.[75] In addition, the public internalizes distribution and copying costs by buying the components needed to connect to the Internet.[76] The lessened need for distribution incentives, together with the presence of non-copyright-based incentives, frequently calls into question the case for copyright, at least in its currently bloated form.

Second, expansive copyright leads to multiple dangers, which include monopoly loss and restricted cumulative development, speech, and the decentralization needed for democracy.

The first danger is monopoly loss. The right to exclude carves out for copyright holders periods in which only they can sell or license their products. Such a right may provide incentives by allowing the recovery of expenditures and profits. But to the extent that other products are imperfect substitutes for the protected invention, it also allows inventors to charge a price significantly above the marginal cost of production. Copyright holders thus could reap monopoly profits as well as bring about 'deadweight loss', as consumers who would pay more than the marginal cost but less than the monopoly price will not buy the works.[77]

The second danger is the thwarted cumulative development of creative works. Because artists often build on earlier works, they need access to unprotected works in the public domain. There are many examples of this: composers recombine sounds they have heard; novelists draw on other plots; playwrights use other literary characters; and cinematographers, actors, choreographers, architects, and sculptors transform existing works.[78] But absent access to building blocks in the public domain, many works would not be created. The expansion of the duration, subject matter, and rights of copyright have in fact kept many works out of the

[74] Raymond Shih Ray Ku, 'The Creative Destruction of Copyright: Napster and the New Economics of Digital Technology' (2002) 69 *University of Chicago Law Review* 263 at 294–6.

[75] *Ibid.*, 300. [76] *Ibid.*, 301.

[77] E.g., William W. Fisher III, 'Reconstructing the Fair Use Doctrine' (1988) 101 *Harvard Law Review* 1659 at 1700–02.

[78] Jessica Litman, 'The Public Domain' (1990) 39 *Emory Law Journal* 965 at 966–7; Lessig, *The Future of Ideas*, pp. 9, 13, 105; Siva Vaidhyanathan, *Copyrights and Copywrongs: The Rise of Intellectual Property and How it Threatens Creativity* (New York University Press, 2001), p. 117; Dennis S. Karjala, 'The Term of Copyright' in Laura N. Gasaway (ed.), *Growing Pains: Adapting Copyright for Education and Society* (Littleton: Rothman & Co., 1997), pp. 33, 46.

public domain, threatening grave consequences for multigenerational creation.

Copyright's expansion also limits speech. Copyright holders have ever greater ability to block expression commenting on copyrighted works, including political commentary, news reporting, parody, cultural critique, church dissent, and historical scholarship. Courts traditionally have reconciled the copyrightable protection of expression with the First Amendment guarantees of free speech by pointing to limits on copyright such as its limited term, the idea–expression dichotomy, and the fair use exception. But to the extent these limits are no longer effective, the First Amendment faces real dangers.[79]

Finally, expansive copyright threatens the decentralization that is essential for democracy. Decentralization allows challenges to the prevailing orthodoxy and permits smaller entities to contribute to public discourse.[80] Yet vertical and horizontal consolidation have swept through the entertainment industry in recent years, increasing the control possessed by a few companies and making it more difficult for outsiders to use copyrighted works controlled by these entities.[81]

In short, the expansion of copyright threatens monopoly loss as well as severe consequences for the public domain, speech, and the decentralization and discourse that are crucial to democracy. Moreover, these dangers appear to be more significant than those appearing in property law. Property law admittedly has its own dangers, such as the fostering of inequalities between owners and non-owners and an 'anti-commons' where underutilization of resources results from multiple owners possessing exclusionary rights. But the dangers to the market, speech, and democracy presented by an expansive copyright regime are far greater than those that appear in property: in comparison to copyright, land is a less direct input into commercial products, less often forms a building block for future generations of development, and less frequently serves as a vehicle for expression.

Third, if property, with all its varied rationales, is subject to such a multitude of limits, then certainly copyright should be. In addition to serving numerous non-utilitarian purposes such as rewarding an owner's

[79] Neil Weinstock Netanel, 'Locating Copyright Within the First Amendment Skein' (2001) 54 *Stanford Law Review* 1 at 7–30.

[80] See Yochai Benkler, 'Free as the Air to Common Use: First Amendment Constraints on Enclosure of the Public Domain' (1999) 74 *New York University Law Review* 354 at 377–81.

[81] Carrier, 'Cabining Intellectual Property', 98–100.

labour and recognizing an owner's 'personhood' interest in her land, property serves two important utilitarian goals: preventing the overuse of resources and providing incentives for development. US copyright law, in contrast, is primarily utilitarian in nature, and even then promotes only one goal. In contrast to tangible resources, information cannot be depleted; copyright thus does not seek to prevent overuse but rather only to promote development.

Not surprisingly, then, the rights granted by property, even as curbed by limits, traditionally have been more powerful than copyright's confined rights, which historically have applied to narrow subject matter for finite time periods. But the recent expansion of copyright rights and the diminution of limits have altered this relationship, erasing copyright's subordinate position. Despite its recent expansion, copyright is still justified only for the single purpose of providing incentives – with even that purpose subject to serious question in many cases – and so, a bulked-up copyright needs limits in a way that its tapered historical version did not. If property, which effectively serves more goals than copyright, can offer meaningful limits, then so can copyright.

In short, the conclusion of this section is that limits on copyright rights are appropriate given that the traditional story of copyright is often inaccurate and that copyright protection poses significant dangers. Nor can copyright escape the imposition of limits by claiming that property (which is replete with limits) is characterized by much stronger dangers.

4 Some limits on copyright

In the first three sections I have demonstrated (1) the propertization of copyright, (2) the multitude of limits in property, and (3) the propriety of applying limits to copyright. This section offers some representative limits on copyright.

One difficulty, of course, involves the determination of which limits to adopt. Before offering my approach, it is worth considering two other possible approaches. One would apply at a specific level, mapping particular property doctrines (such as adverse possession) to copyright. This is not appropriate because of the different policies and requirements underlying various doctrines in property and copyright law. Another approach would, at the broadest level, impose general 'duties' on copyright holders. But such an analysis would not specify how to determine those duties.

The approach that is most defensible is intermediate in nature, importing limits at thematic levels. As I demonstrate elsewhere, the themes of development, necessity, and equity explain the limits of property law.[82] Implementing limits consistent with these themes also is appropriate for copyright. Courts and Congress have already recognized limits that promote development, necessity, and equity in copyright law. Additionally, the scheme offers the opportunity to recognize new defences.

In this section I first discuss some of the limits that already appear in copyright doctrine. These include the fair use defence, exclusions from liability, compulsory licences, the first sale doctrine, copyright misuse, and equitable estoppel. I then articulate two additional defences that courts could recognize under a fair use analysis, which would privilege uses that increase the diversity of viewpoints making up a robust dialogue essential to democracy ('necessary fair use'), and uses that accord with widely followed societal practices ('equitable fair use').

In terms of existing defences, the fair use defence is perhaps the most fundamental limit on the copyright holder's rights. One application recognized by courts applies to uses that are 'transformative', altering the original or offering the work for a new purpose. The Supreme Court elevated the significance of this use in *Campbell* v. *Acuff-Rose Music, Inc.*,[83] explaining that transformative works further 'the goal of copyright, to promote science and the arts'.[84] Parodies, book reviews, and criticism, for example, thus will typically receive the privilege. Such uses promise to increase the types of works in the marketplace by encouraging critical works that copyright holders would naturally be reluctant to license. The uses also serve as a limit on the rights of copyright holders.

A second limit courts have recognized under the fair use defence is reverse engineering for the purpose of promoting interoperability. 'Reverse engineering' refers to 'starting with the known product and working backward to divine the process which aided in its development or manufacture'.[85] Because computer software typically is distributed in object code form, which cannot be read by humans, reverse engineering is necessary for software developers to create compatible products. But the process of working backwards from object code to human-readable source code involves decompilation or disassembly, which entails making a copy of the work – a practice that courts have found to constitute

[82] *Ibid.*, 52–81. [83] 510 US 569 at 579 (1994).

[84] *Ibid.*

[85] *Kewanee Oil Co.* v. *Bicron Corp.*, 416 US 470 at 476 (1973).

infringement.[86] Recognition of this defence encourages more software developers to introduce new products into the marketplace.

Third, copyright law carves out from infringement liability exclusions for several types of activity, including acts of libraries, certain activity in the public interest, and the making of ephemeral copies. Section 108 of Title 17 of the US Code allows public libraries and archives to reproduce and distribute copyrighted works for purposes such as preservation, the replacement of damaged or missing copies, inter-library loan requests, and the promotion of research.[87] Section 110 exempts from infringement an array of public performances that cohere under the heading 'public interest': face-to-face teaching, instructional broadcasting, religious services, certain non-profit performances, and transmissions of non-dramatic and dramatic literary works to visually disabled individuals.[88] Finally, Section 112 exempts radio broadcasters from infringement liability when they make copies of copyrighted works to facilitate the transmission of the works.[89]

Fourth, copyright law contains an array of compulsory licences, which require payment – but not permission – for certain uses. To pick three examples, such licences allow (1) public broadcasters to perform or display works during broadcast transmissions, (2) the retransmission of broadcasts by cable and satellite television companies, and (3) 'cover' licences for musical works.[90]

Fifth, the 'first sale' doctrine limits a copyright owner's right to control distribution of the copyrighted work. In particular, it allows purchasers to dispose of lawful copies in whatever fashion they wish, including by destruction, resale, donation, or lease.[91] The rationale for the doctrine is 'to prevent the copyright owner from restraining the free alienability of goods'.[92] Absent this doctrine, persons possessing copies of a copyrighted work would be required to negotiate with the copyright owner every time they wished to discard or lend their copies.[93]

Sixth, the doctrine of copyright misuse prevents copyright owners who engage in certain types of misconduct from enforcing the copyright. The

86 Julie E. Cohen and Mark A. Lemley, 'Patent Scope and Innovation in the Software Industry' (2001) 89 *California Law Review* 1 at 16 fn. 52.

87 17 USC § 108(a)–(e).

88 17 USC § 110. 89 17 USC § 112.

90 17 USC §§ 111, 115, 118. 91 17 USC § 109(a).

92 Marshall A. Leaffer, *Understanding Copyright Law* (New York: Bender & Co, 1999), para. 8.18(A)–(K), pp. 324–37.

93 *Ibid.*

doctrine grew out of the unclean hands defence and the doctrine of patent misuse.[94] The purpose of copyright misuse is to prevent copyright holders from reaching beyond the statutory bounds of their rights, such as when they force customers to avoid dealing with competitors.[95]

Seventh, equitable estoppel applies when a copyright defendant can prove that the plaintiff's actions reasonably induced the defendant to change position. When, for example, a copyright holder encourages an alleged infringer to reproduce the copyrighted work, the holder will not be able to enforce the copyright.[96]

The propertization of copyright leads not only to the recognition of currently existing defences but also to the proffering of new limits. One such limit would recognize a necessary fair use defence that would apply when the use of the copyrighted work is necessary to increase the diversity of viewpoints making up a robust dialogue essential to democracy. As the Supreme Court has recognized, 'the widest possible dissemination of information from diverse and antagonistic sources is essential to the welfare of the public.'[97]

Despite the importance of a range of viewpoints, however, information sources in society today are rapidly consolidating, with the result that fewer companies control more of the nation's dialogue and culture than ever before.[98] Vertical integration of media conglomerates in recent years has resulted in cable and broadcast networks owning much of the content that they distribute, content that typically is copyrighted.[99] Moreover, the number of outlets is shrinking due to horizontal consolidation: in the broadcast industry, for example, four national networks own nearly every major local station in the top four media markets.[100]

[94] *Alcatel USA, Inc.* v. *DGI Techs., Inc.* 166 F.3d 772 at 792 (5th Cir. 1999).

[95] *Practice Mgmt. Info. Corp.* v. *Am. Med. Ass'n.*, 121 F.3d 516 at 518–20 (9th Cir. 1997); Mark A. Lemley, 'Beyond Preemption: The Law and Policy of Intellectual Property Licensing' (1999) 87 *California Law Review* 111 at 153.

[96] Thomas F. Cotter, 'Gutenberg's Legacy: Copyright, Censorship, and Religious Pluralism' (2003) 91 California Law Review 323 at 346 n. 91.

[97] *Associated Press* v. *United States*, 326 US 1 at 20 (1945).

[98] Lawrence Lessig, *Free Culture: How Big Media Uses Technology and the Law to Lock Down Culture and Control Creativity* (New York: Hudson, 2004), pp. 162–8.

[99] Ellen P. Goodman, 'Media Policy Out of the Box: Content Abundance, Attention Scarcity, and the Failures of Digital Markets' (2004) 19 *Berkley Technology Law Journal* 1389 at 1447.

[100] Comments of The National Association of Broadcasters and Network Affiliated Stations Alliance, 2002 Biennial Regulatory Review – Review of the Commission's Broadcast Ownership Rules and Other Rules Adopted Pursuant to Section 202, at 32, MB Docket No. 02-277 (FCC filed 9 December 2002).

In addition to reducing the number of outlets for copyrighted content, concentration leads to 'bland' reporting because the networks steer clear of any controversy that might threaten their ability to sell products.[101] Relatedly, concentration excludes challenges to the status quo and fosters an 'unequal distribution of power to express ideas'.[102]

Because of the importance of a diverse array of viewpoints and because media consolidation and the expansion of copyright have reduced the number of alternative perspectives, activity that promises to counteract this trend should be privileged. In particular, activity that relies on copyrighted expression to criticize the prevailing wisdom, comment upon current events, parody popular works of culture, or develop ideas should be entitled to the defence of necessary fair use. Carving out a space in fair use jurisprudence for activity that at least modestly counteracts the consolidation of information sources and viewpoints could have beneficial effects for democracy and could constitute a new limit on copyright.

A second example of expanded fair use would encompass activity that falls within widely followed societal practices. The fact that a significant segment of society is engaging in an activity should count as a factor in deciding whether to excuse the activity. Aligning judicial treatment with common practices would reduce apparently unjust punishment and defiance of the law and would accord with notions of fairness. In *Sony Corp. of America* v. *Universal City Studios, Inc.*,[103] for example, the Court excused private, non-commercial 'time-shifting' – by which home viewers tape television programmes to watch at a later time – that was widespread and that programmers and the public considered to be ordinary and proper.[104]

Another potential application of the concept appears in the peer-to-peer file-sharing that swept the music world. Services such as Grokster, Kazaa, LimeWire, and the Pirate Bay have enabled users to share billions of files containing copyrighted sound recordings.[105] Many of the participants who upload and download copyrighted works either do not believe or do not care that their activity violates the law. In short, there is

[101] Neil Weinstock Netanel, 'Copyright and a Democratic Civil Society' (1996) 106 *Yale Law Journal* 283 at 362.

[102] See C. Edwin Baker, 'The Media That Citizens Need' (1998) 147 *University of Pennsylvania Law* Review 317 at 362; Benkler, 'Free as the Air to Common Use', 378.

[103] 464 US 417, 495 (1984).

[104] 464 US at 421; Lloyd L. Weinreb, 'Fair's Fair: A Comment on the Fair Use Doctrine' (1990) 103 *Harvard Law Review* 1137 at 1155.

[105] 'Encyclopedia: Definition of peer-to-peer network', *PCMag*, available at: www.pcmag.com/encyclopedia/term/49056/peer-to-peer-network (last accessed 29 April 2013).

a significant disconnect between societal norms, which favour the activity, and the law, which punishes it. The benefits of reconciling the two are significant enough that courts at least should consider the norms in determining whether a use is fair.

As I explain elsewhere, in each of the categories of fair use, the copyright holder could rebut the presumption of fair use by showing a substantial reduction in the quantity or quality of expressive works produced.[106] In the case of file-sharing, for example, the recording industry would have a viable, though not certain, prospect of satisfying the rebuttal by demonstrating that allowing such activity would significantly reduce the number of copyrighted works that would be created.[107] But requiring courts at least to consider widespread community practices in the analysis reintroduces a healthy dose of fairness into fair use.

5 Conclusion

In short, in its continually expanding scope and duration, copyright has come to resemble property. Property is made up of limits. It is appropriate to apply limits to copyright, and I offer a few examples of these in this chapter. But the most important point is that – despite all discussion and assumptions to the contrary – propertization provides the tools not for absolute rights but for limits on the rights provided by copyright.

[106] Carrier, 'Cabining Intellectual Property', 95–6 n. 455–457.

[107] See Alejandro Zentner, 'Measuring the Effect of Music Downloads on Music Sales', available at: http://jindal.utdallas.edu/files/effect_music_download.pdf (last accessed 29 April 2013); Felix Oberholzer and Koleman Strumpf, 'The Effect of File Sharing on Record Sales: An Empirical Analysis 3' (2004), available at: www.unc.edu/~cigar/papers/FileSharing_March2004.pdf (last accessed 10 April 2013); Tim Wu, 'When Code Isn't Law', (2003) 89(4) *Virginia Law Review* 679 at 710.

9

Property concepts in European copyright law

The case of abandonment

ROBERT BURRELL AND EMILY HUDSON

Introduction

It has long been arguable that the common law allows tangible, moveable property to be abandoned. On this view, the law allows an owner to voluntarily relinquish his or her rights, such that the thing in question becomes ownerless and returns to (or enters) the commons of unowned things. That abandonment is possible receives strong support from cases involving wrecks[1] and treasure trove,[2] and has been the preferred view amongst academic commentators for many years.[3] It is also a view that has been strengthened in the UK by the 2010 case *Robot Arenas Ltd* v. *Waterfield*.[4] In the intellectual property context, the possibility of abandonment is also well established in British Commonwealth jurisprudence in relation to the common law right to ownership of a trade mark created by the first use of a sign in the marketplace.[5] Our immediate concern in this chapter is whether it is also possible to apply a similar principle to

[1] *Arrow Shipping Co. Ltd.* v. *Tyne Improvement Commissioners (The Crystal)* [1894] AC 508; *The Tubantia* [1924] P 78.

[2] *A-G* v. *Trustees of the British Museum* [1903] 2 Ch 598; *R* v. *Hancock* [1990] 2 QB 242.

[3] See, e.g., T. Cyprian Williams, *Principles of the Law of Personal Property* 18th edn (London: Sweet & Maxwell, 1926), p. 26; R. H. Kersley, *Goodeve's Modern Law of Personal Property* 9th edn (London: Sweet & Maxwell, 1949), p. 25; Anthony Hudson, 'Abandonment' in Norman Palmer and Ewan McKendrick (eds.), *Interests in Goods* 2nd edn (London: LLP, 1998); Michael Bridge, *Personal Property Law* 3rd edn (Oxford University Press, 2002), pp. 22–3.

[4] [2010] EWHC 115. See also *Re Jigrose Pty Ltd.* [1994] 1 Qd R 382 (Supreme Court of Queensland making a finding of abandonment in a case not concerned with wrecks or treasure trove); *Wicks Estate* v. *Harnett* (2007) 48 CCLT (3d) 155 (acceptance of a general doctrine of abandonment by the Ontario Superior Court of Justice).

[5] *Mouson & Co.* v. *Boehm* (1884) 26 Ch D 398; *Weston Trade Mark* [1968] FSR 77; *North Shore Toy Company Ltd.* v. *Charles L Stevenson Ltd.* [1973] 1 NZLR 562; *Image Enterprises CC* v. *Eastman Kodak Co.* [1989] 1 FSR 353; *Marcus* v. *Sabra International Pty Ltd.* (1995)

copyright. In other words, we are keen to explore whether a copyright owner can place a work in the public domain through some overt act that manifests an intention to surrender all rights in the work. Such an act might come, for example, in the form of a dedication of the work to the public domain, through the application of a Creative Commons Zero or 'CC0' notice, or by way of some other express representation by the author that he or she gives up all claim to copyright.[6] It is firmly established in the United States that copyright can be abandoned,[7] abandonment is also possible in India[8] and we have argued elsewhere for the judicial recognition of a similar rule in Australia.[9]

In this chapter we consider the prospects for a doctrine of abandonment of copyright being accepted in the UK. We begin by setting out various justifications for allowing copyright to be abandoned. In addition to making an economic case for abandonment, we emphasise – perhaps counter-intuitively – that abandonment can be seen as *protective* of

30 IPR 261; *Lucas Finance Pty Ltd.* v. *Dig This Enterprises Pty Ltd.* [2007] ATMO 35. This somewhat unusual right only prevents the subsequent registration of a substantially identical mark, not the use of such a mark in the marketplace (although such use might constitute passing off). It has not survived the European harmonisation of trade mark law in the UK or Republic of Ireland and seems to be little remembered in those jurisdictions. It continues, however, to play an important role in some Commonwealth jurisdictions, including Australia and New Zealand.

6 See, e.g., *Oravec* v. *Sunny Isles Luxury Ventures LC*, 469 F Supp 2d 1148 (SD Fla, 2006) (discussed below).

7 *National Comics Publications Inc.* v. *Fawcett Publications Inc.* 191 F 2d 594 (2nd Cir, 1951). For a comprehensive list of US cases dealing with the abandonment of copyright see William F. Patry, *Patry on Copyright* (West Thomson Reuters, 2009), vol. II, para. 5:155.

8 See Indian Copyright Act 1957, s. 21(1) (as amended by the Copyright Amendment Act 2012): 'The author of a work may relinquish all or any of the rights comprised in the copyright in the work by giving notice in the prescribed form to the Registrar of Copyrights or by way of public notice and thereupon such rights shall, subject to the provisions of subsection (3), cease to exist from the date of the notice.'

9 Emily Hudson and Robert Burrell, 'Abandonment, Copyright and Orphaned Works: What Does it Mean to Take the Proprietary Nature of Intellectual Property Rights Seriously?' (2011) 35 *Melbourne University Law Review* 971. In *Australian Olympic Committee Inc.* v. *Big Fights Inc.* [1999] FCA 1042; (1999) 46 IPR 53, one argument pleaded by the respondents in a copyright action brought by the AOC was that the latter had abandoned both the physical embodiments of, and copyright in, various films. In oral submissions in the Federal Court, the copyright aspect was not pursued, and Lindgren J dealt only with the allegation that the physical films had been abandoned. Noting that the case law was inconsistent on the question of whether chattels could be abandoned, His Honour held that there was no abandonment on the facts in any event, as no intention to abandon (either subjective or objectively) had been proven: at paras. 378–386.

authors, because it respects their capacity to control how and whether they exploit the rights granted automatically by the law. As will be seen, we find it strange that any personality-based understanding of property would require a person to be 'tethered' to a thing against their will. Given the strong arguments that can be marshalled in favour of abandonment, we would like to see abandonment being accepted as a mechanism by which copyright can be lost in the UK. However, as discussed in the final part of this chapter, the emergence of such a doctrine anywhere in the EU faces a number of legal obstacles, in particular in light of recent Court of Justice of the European Union (CJEU) jurisprudence.

The difficulty of reconciling a doctrine of abandonment with the CJEU's current stance on copyright goes to a more general issue of considerable significance. Like many commentators, we are of the view that intellectual property rights now frequently overreach. It has been argued that one reason for this state of affairs is the weight afforded to the proprietary nature of such rights, which (it is said) supports stronger and broader rights. We are sceptical of this argument, however, as it fails to recognise that property rights are frequently more fragile and less all-encompassing than this analysis suggests. Thus, when the question of what it means to treat intellectual property as property is scrutinised in further detail, a very different narrative unfolds. Specifically, we would suggest that some of the excesses of our current intellectual property system are caused precisely by our failure to treat intellectual property like other property rights. One potentially productive line of enquiry, therefore, is to look to general property law doctrines for ways of *limiting* intellectual property rights. In the EU context, however, this is only possible to the extent that the harmonisation process is understood to have left undisturbed the surrounding national property systems into which intellectual property rights fit. As a matter of constitutional principle, this should be uncontroversial, but in practice the CJEU may well decline to accept that a limiting rule is truly 'external' to a harmonised intellectual property regime. To our minds this sheds light on an issue that is of considerable importance to the issues this volume is seeking to explore: the use and development of legal concepts that sit outwith intellectual property law to constrain intellectual property rights could very well be hampered by the judiciary prioritising transnational harmonisation of rules over considerations of efficiency, the protection of authorial interests and doctrinal consistency in national property rules.

1 Abandonment and externalities

In order to develop the case for abandonment, it is helpful to start by considering how else the law might categorise a representation to the effect that the copyright owner no longer has any interest in exploiting his or her rights. We will consider what is arguably the strongest example of abandonment: an unequivocal statement that a person desires that the work be unowned and available to all, for instance through a dedication of the work to the public domain. As noted above, abandonment has been conceived as the *voluntary* loss of rights, and so one challenge for courts has been in distinguishing between facts from which an intention to abandon can be inferred and mere forgetfulness or laziness (which is not enough).[10] This deliberation becomes particularly significant where there is no express statement by the owner, but rather a series of acts or omissions that might be consistent with abandonment.

In the case of a dedication of a work to the public domain, the only alternative under English law would be to treat the dedication as creating a general licence to copy and redistribute the work.[11] As Phillip Johnson has explored in detail, such a licence would be revocable by the copyright owner at will.[12] No consideration would have been given for the grant of the licence, and there is neither statutory nor judicial authority to support the creation of a category of irrevocable 'bare' licence.

The starting point for the economic case for abandonment has to be that copyright is given first and foremost as an incentive to invest in the creation of works. If the person whom the law is trying to incentivise chooses to renounce his or her entitlement, this should not be a matter of concern.[13] On the contrary, it has long been recognised that many types of work would be created and shared even in the absence of copyright

[10] See, e.g., *Moffatt* v. *Kazana* [1969] 2 QB 152, 156 (commenting, in passing, on the distinction between abandonment and mere forgetfulness); *Moorhouse* v. *Angus and Robertson (No. 1) Pty Ltd.* [1981] 1 NSWLR 700 (discussing the role of intention in any doctrine of abandonment); *Re Jigrose Pty Ltd.* [1994] 1 Qd R 382 at 385 (accepting that intention is the key concept that differentiates abandonment from mere loss of goods).

[11] Bearing in mind there is also authority that a licence can be expressed to be for the benefit of the world at large: see, e.g., *Mellor* v. *Australian Broadcasting Commission* [1940] AC 491.

[12] Phillip Johnson, '"Dedicating" Copyright to the Public Domain' (2008) 71 *Modern Law Review* 587.

[13] See also Robert A. Kreiss, 'Abandoning Copyrights to Try to Cut Off Termination Rights' (1993) 58 *Missouri Law Review* 85 at 99: '[T]he copyright system is an incentive system, not a coercive one ... nothing in the Constitution or the Copyright Act compels an author to accept the benefits of copyright.'

protection.[14] Allowing copyright to be abandoned provides one way of reconciling the automaticity of copyright protection with creative processes and practices that are divorced from copyright's system of rewards. However, the fact that many works would be created even without copyright protection does not tell the whole story, as attention needs to be given not just to the position of original authors, but also to those involved in acts of public dissemination and the creation of derivative works. It is therefore necessary to consider how a purported abandonment of copyright might impact on the decisions of these actors.

Consider, for instance, a hypothetical investor who wishes to distribute a work that has been dedicated to the public domain. The first issue that would need to be considered by such an investor is whether it is possible to rely on the copyright owner's attempt to surrender his or her rights in the work. In the absence of a clearly established abandonment doctrine, any well-informed investor would have to be concerned that a court would treat the purported abandonment as creating no more than a revocable licence. Admittedly, it might be possible to reassure the investor that the doctrine of estoppel might provide some further protection should the licence be withdrawn, but lack of certainty over permissible future uses might well be sufficient to make an abandoned work a commercially unattractive proposition.[15] Consequently, a refusal to recognise a doctrine of abandonment might have a chilling effect on the circulation of works that have been dedicated to the public domain. This would seem to run directly counter to the reason why a copyright owner would seek to place a work in the public domain in the first place (namely, to facilitate access and re-use), and would potentially stymie other benefits, such as enhanced reputation. The latter point is particularly important when we think about why the rational utility-maximising individual of economic theory might choose to abandon copyright. For homo economicus, the principal motivation for abandoning copyright would be to trade the benefits of copyright for the reputational advantages that might be expected

[14] See, most famously, Stephen Breyer, 'The Uneasy Case for Copyright: A Study of Copyright in Books, Photocopies, and Computer Programs' (1970) 84 *Harvard Law Review* 281.

[15] In particular, where a user had become aware that the licence to use the work had been revoked prior to commencing the impugned activity, estoppel could offer no defence. Even in cases where the user is able to demonstrate detrimental reliance, the extent of the protection that estoppel would provide as regards future uses would be highly uncertain (for example, the user might be able to continue to distribute copies of a work that had already been made but could well be prevented from producing new copies; in the case of sales of digital copies distribution might well have to be halted immediately).

to flow from wider dissemination of his work.[16] Such reputational benefits might come not merely in the form of 'psychic income' but also in the form of financial benefits through, for example, increases in consulting income, ticket sales or the asking price for original works.[17] Our normal starting point is that it is for the copyright owner to determine the terms under which a work is offered to the public, and to deny the possibility of abandonment would run counter to this free market philosophy.

It might be objected that an owner who was prepared to abandon copyright would also be prepared to enter into a binding contractual arrangement with a would-be user or distributor of his or her work. However, to insist on the parties entering into such an arrangement would be to impose avoidable transaction costs on them, a situation that is particularly undesirable given that many who seek to dedicate a work to the public domain are presumably wishing to facilitate access and re-use without the logistical constraints and costs of licensing. We therefore believe the starting presumption must be that abandonment is the more efficient mechanism.

Thus far, we have argued that abandonment is the most efficient means of ensuring that distributors have the confidence to invest in the circulation of works that have been dedicated to the public domain. However, this confidence will be irrelevant if it is offset by countervailing disadvantages, for instance if it is not possible for investors to recoup their costs of redistribution. If this is so, there will still be an underinvestment in (and hence undersupply of) abandoned works. Once we take into account the need of investors to capture positive externalities created by their investment, might it be more efficient to treat abandonment as creating only a revocable licence? Consider the following argument made by Landes and Posner in their call for copyright protection to be made perpetually renewable:

> Suppose an enterprising publisher has only a twenty per cent chance of success with obscure public-domain authors. He publishes the works of five such authors in order to have one success. In the absence of copyright protection, other publishers can wait and see which author sells and then bring out their own version of his works. Publishers who wait avoid the

[16] The choice of possessive pronoun reflects the androcentric nature of homo economicus: see, most famously, Ulla Grapard, 'Robinson Crusoe: The Quintessential Economic Man?' (1995) 1 *Feminist Economics* 33.

[17] These examples assume that the owner's name would appear on the work. This is an issue to which we return when considering the relationship between abandonment and moral rights.

> costs of failure, but their free riding on the market information developed by the first to publish reduces the incentive of any publisher to search for potentially successful public domain works.[18]

Much the same logic could be applied to abandoned works: in order to guarantee investment in creative productions, some exclusivity of rights is required; and in order to ensure that exclusivity of rights remains possible, owners must be able to revoke an act of abandonment so that copyright can be assigned to an interested investor. It might be possible, moreover, to bolster concerns about underinvestment in the distribution of abandoned works by reference to an important distinction between abandonment as it applies to chattels and abandonment as it would apply to copyright. In the case of chattels, abandonment is often a mere prelude to rights vesting in another, with abandonment serving as a vehicle whereby a person who later takes possession of a chattel becomes its owner.[19] In contrast, in the copyright context abandonment would serve to place a work in the public domain once and for all. In the absence of a mechanism by which a third party can 'take possession' of a work, it might be argued that it is preferable to treat a so-called abandonment as merely creating a licence that can be revoked in favour of a party who later manages to convince the abandoning owner to reconsider the terms under which the work is accessed and disseminated.[20] This would preserve the possibility of a third party gaining exclusive rights over the work, which on this argument would allow our hypothetical investor to better capture positive externalities and prevent free riding.

To our minds, however, this argument suffers from at least three significant flaws. First, it ignores the fact that there are categories of distributor who are likely to be much less concerned about internalising benefits. Just as there are creators who produce works without regard to copyright's incentives, there are distributors who are motivated by other considerations. This is most obviously true of cultural institutions such as libraries, museums and archives. We have made the case elsewhere that such institutions sometimes take possession of works in circumstances where

[18] William M. Landes and Richard A. Posner, 'Indefinitely Renewable Copyright' (2003) 70 *University of Chicago Law Review* 471 at 489.

[19] As occurred in *Re Jigrose Pty Ltd.* [1994] 1 Qd R 382, where the purchasers of land were able to appropriate to themselves abandoned bales of hay.

[20] For example, an author who has dedicated his or her work to the public domain might be convinced by a publisher that commercial publication will in fact lead to faster or wider dissemination of the work.

copyright ought to be deemed to have been abandoned.[21] When freed from the constraints imposed by copyright law, cultural institutions are generally keen to make works widely available through publicly funded digitisation projects. Indeed, the ability to provide public access is often a precondition for project funding, making it unsurprising that much existing digitisation work has targeted public domain material, as this has the effect of by-passing copyright considerations.[22] It is also increasingly the case that institutions are seeking to release content online with minimal restrictions on re-use, furthering both the philosophical goal of providing access to information and the pragmatic goal of reducing transaction costs.

Secondly, the above argument fails to take account of other mechanisms that allow distributors to recover their costs. Consider, for example, an investor who intends to translate an abandoned work or who wishes to arrange for an abandoned work to be turned into a film. In either case the investor will acquire copyright in the final product and will enjoy an extensive set of rights to control the reproduction, performance and further adaptation of the new work.[23] The same would also be true of a person who invested significant labour in reworking a manuscript to make it suitable for publication – such a person is highly likely to be treated as having created an original derivative work that will attract its own copyright protection.[24] Further protection against free riding is conferred by 'neighbouring rights' that provide separate protection for sound recordings, broadcasts and the typographical arrangement of published editions.[25] One justification for such rights is that they assist commercial actors to recover the costs of distributing works that do not enjoy copyright protection. The last of the aforementioned rights means, for example, that a publisher who wishes to produce a rival edition of a newly (re)published public domain book must at least go to the trouble of arranging for the work to be re-typeset, which will go some way to both limit the free-rider

[21] Hudson and Burrell, 'Abandonment, Copyright and Orphaned Works', 999–1001.

[22] See, e.g., Emily Hudson, *Copyright Exceptions: The Experiences of Cultural Institutions in the United States, Canada and Australia* (2011, Ph.D. thesis, Law, The University of Melbourne), pp. 35–8.

[23] Provided, of course, that the investor has put in place appropriate contractual arrangements with the translator, director, etc.

[24] See, e.g., *Hyperion Records Ltd* v. *Sawkins* [2005] EWCA Civ 565 (Sawkins held to have produced original works through his efforts in creating performing editions of old musical scores written for the courts of Louis XIV and Louis XV).

[25] See, e.g., Copyright, Designs and Patents Act 1988, s. 1(1).

effect and preserve the first mover's lead-time.[26] Insofar as the law fails to provide rights to persons investing in public domain works, this is sometimes because the person making the investment will have other ways of capturing the benefit of his or her outlay. For instance, a person who stages an abandoned or out-of-copyright play can secure a return by controlling access to the premises in which it is being performed. In cases where the investor's costs are extremely low, there may be sufficient levels of redistribution even in the absence of any additional copyright-related mechanism to recoup costs, in particular for some forms of online communication.[27]

This brings us to a third important point: to the extent that there is empirical evidence on the actual behaviours of those dealing with public domain works, it fails to support the claim that lack of rights leads to underinvestment. In an important study, Paul Heald has compared best-selling works of fiction produced in the period 1913–1922 with those produced in the period 1923–1932. In the United States, works in the former category are all in the public domain, whilst works in the latter are still in copyright.[28] Heald demonstrates that public domain works are more likely to be in print than those still in copyright, with the divergence between the two groups of works having increased over recent years (something that Heald tentatively links to improvements in technology that have lowered the costs of producing new editions of public domain works). It should also be borne in mind that this study was conducted in the context of a legal system that does not recognise typographical arrangement copyright. There is therefore no reason to predict that allowing literary copyright to be abandoned would lead to an undersupply of such works

[26] In a limited category of cases, the distributor would also be able to rely on the so-called 'publication right'. This right vests in a person who publishes for the first time a previously unpublished work after the expiry of copyright protection. This right lasts for 25 years and confers a level of protection that is closely akin to copyright. See, in the UK, The Copyright and Related Rights Regulations 1996, Reg. 16 and, more generally, Directive 2006/116/EC of the European Parliament and of the Council on the Term of Protection of Copyright and Certain Related Rights, [2006] OJ L 372/12, Art. 4. It should be emphasised, however, that on our analysis (explained in detail in the final section of this chapter) abandonment does not serve to curtail the duration of copyright.

[27] Consider, for example, works to which a CC0 notice has been attached. People who use such notices are likely to be firm believers in the free circulation of works and are very likely to make their works available online. Once a work is in digital form the costs of distribution are close to zero.

[28] Paul J. Heald, 'Property Rights and the Efficient Exploitation of Copyrighted Works: An Empirical Analysis of Public Domain and Copyrighted Fiction Bestsellers' (2008) 93 *Minnesota Law Review* 1031.

in the UK. Admittedly, other types of work might be more susceptible to an undersupply problem, but it is down to defenders of this position to provide robust evidence to support their case, and they must do so against the background of the suite of rights that are already provided to distributors who invest in public domain material.

Consequently, any argument for allowing abandoned works to be 're-owned' that rests on the need to provide an incentive to distributors (which would, in turn, provide support for treating a purported abandonment as creating a revocable licence) is in our view flawed. More generally, any attempt to draw parallels between tangible property and copyright as regards the need for re-ownership needs to take account of significant differences between the two forms of property. Chattels are rivalrous goods. The possession and use of a chattel by one person largely precludes its possession and use by others. Assigning property rights over rivalrous goods serves a number of important functions: it helps reduce public order and private policing costs; it encourages the optimal use of resources by allowing users of property to internalise the benefits of expenditure aimed at maintaining the property; and it facilitates voluntary, utility-maximising exchanges. Crucially, these arguments apply with as much force to things that have been abandoned as they do to things that have never been owned. There is, therefore, a strong economic case for allowing abandoned chattels to become re-owned. In contrast, because copyright works are (generally understood to be) non-rivalrous goods, the economic case for allowing re-ownership is much weaker. Copyright works can be 'possessed' and enjoyed by many people simultaneously. Refusing to permit a work to become re-owned does not, therefore, create anything like the same onerous public order and policing costs that would be associated with the adoption of such a rule in relation to chattels; there are few maintenance costs; and works can be shared, such that there is no need for a market mechanism to ensure that they are allocated to a limited class of persons who would value them most highly.

However, Landes and Posner have a further concern, one that casts doubt on the standard assumption that copyright works are non-rivalrous.[29] They argue that some works may be subject to 'congestion externalities'. The kernel of this argument is that the unrestrained use of works in the

[29] To be more precise, Landes and Posner draw on a realisation in the economic literature that 'rivalry and non-rivalry are extremes, and there are many goods that lie somewhere between the extremes': John Leach, *A Course in Public Economics* (Cambridge University Press, 2004), p. 155 (giving the example of the enjoyment of a film in a cinema being to some degree inversely correlated to the proportion of seats that are occupied).

public domain may lead to a work becoming 'overexposed', which may in turn lead to a downward shift in the demand for such a work and hence a loss of social value.[30] Landes and Posner's congestion thesis represents an ambitious attempt to cast copyright in the role of internalising negative as well as positive externalities. In so doing, they seek to bring copyright within the core of Demsetzian property theory, drawing an express analogy between the overuse of copyright works and the overgrazing of common land.[31] This argument is important in the present context because it suggests that ownership will often be more efficient than non-ownership; that abandonment may lead to a work becoming overused, whilst allowing 'reownership' (that is, permitting an 'abandonment' to be withdrawn) leaves open the possibility that rights will end up in the hands of a person who will husband the work, preserving its value over time.

Ultimately, however, Landes and Posner's argument is unconvincing. As a matter of everyday experience it is hard to identify examples of cases where our enjoyment of a work is diminished by others reading, watching or listening to the same work: it is a claim that simply fails to mesh with our everyday experience of how we consume and enjoy popular books, music, films and television programmes. On the contrary, our enjoyment is often enhanced if we have the opportunity to discuss and share experiences with those who have consumed the same cultural products; each additional consumer may therefore enhance overall utility through so-called network effects.[32] One possible example of congestion externalities at work might arise for individuals who place a high value on their unique aesthetic tastes, and who therefore bemoan that they were a fan of a song, television series, video game or the like 'before it was popular'. However, there are many types of work that are entirely immune even to this 'I liked it first' effect.[33] It is hard, for example, to see how there could be any room

[30] Landes and Posner, 'Indefinitely Renewable Copyright', 484–8.

[31] *Ibid.* and see Harold Demsetz, 'Toward a Theory of Property Rights' (1967) 57 *The American Economic Review (Papers and Proceedings)* 347. It should perhaps also be noted that although Demsetz did include a passing mention of copyright and patents in his seminal paper (at 359), the substantive discussion focuses exclusively on property rights as a mechanism for ensuring that negative externalities are internalised. The idea that property rights ought to be used to internalise positive externalities is much more controversial. See, e.g., Mark A. Lemley, 'Property, Intellectual Property and Free Riding' (2005) 83 *Texas Law Review* 1031; Brett M. Frischmann and Mark A. Lemley, 'Spillovers' (2007) 100 *Columbia Law Review* 257.

[32] See Stewart E. Sterk, 'Intellectualizing Property: The Tenuous Connections between Land and Copyright' (2005) 83 *Washington University Law Quarterly* 417 at 440.

[33] It might also be added that it is extremely difficult to see that such an effect could ever persist for so long as to be relevant in debates about the duration of protection, but this

for an application of this effect in the case of databases or other factual works.[34] Moreover, even in the case of works that are susceptible to this effect, it seems fanciful to suggest that the loss of utility suffered by such people would ever lead to a net loss of utility across society as a whole.

In our view, in the absence of compelling empirical evidence of congestion externalities at work, there is simply no reason to suppose that such externalities will produce a deadweight loss when compared with the extra utility gained by consumers through increased access to works. The most convincing examples of potential congestion externalities given by Landes and Posner concern the use of images of well-known cartoon characters and the like. But here they seem concerned, at least in no small part, with trade mark-type uses of such characters. The extent to which the termination of copyright protection ought to be accompanied by a cessation of trade mark rights is a complex and controversial question. For present purposes, it is enough to note that the assumption that once copyright has expired all uses of a character become fair game, although reasonable in the USA, does not necessarily reflect the position in other jurisdictions.[35] Moreover, other critics of Landes and Posner's congestion externalities thesis have argued that this aspect of their theory falsely equates loss of value to the owner of the character with loss of value to society as a whole.[36]

In conclusion, therefore, we are of the view that the economic case for abandonment survives Landes and Posner's congestion externality thesis (which although developed in support of perpetual copyright could be readily employed as an argument against abandonment). It is not the 'tragedy of the commons' that need concern us in the copyright context; rather it is the 'tragedy of the anticommons'.[37]

is not a point we press here given that our concern is with the application of a doctrine of abandonment.

[34] See Dennis S. Karjala, 'Congestion Externalities and Extended Copyright Protection' (2006) 94 *Georgetown Law Journal* 1065 at 1081 (making the point that even if congestion externalities exist, they cannot possibly be said to arise in relation to all types of work and using as examples digital databases, maps and factual compilations).

[35] Compare *Dastar Corp.* v. *Twentieth Century Fox Film Corp.* (2003) 539 US 23 with, e.g., *Christodoulou* v. *Disney Enterprises Inc.* (2005) 156 FCR 344 (Federal Court of Australia, where Crennan J takes a fact-specific view of when the use of the name of a public domain literary character might amount to trade mark infringement).

[36] Sterk, 'Intellectualizing Property', 441 (noting, for example, that as the value of a character such as Mickey Mouse falls, the value of other characters such as Barney and Big Bird may increase).

[37] The term 'tragedy of the anticommons' was initially coined by Michael A. Heller in 'The Tragedy of the Anticommons: Property in the Transition from Marx to Markets'

2 Abandonment and the rights of authors

Arguments for the recognition of a doctrine of abandonment grounded in concerns about economic efficiency are all very well, but for many people the values that copyright law serves and embodies are not primarily economic in nature. Consideration must therefore be given to how a doctrine of abandonment appears when judged from the perspective of someone who believes in the sanctity of authors' rights. Here we should perhaps emphasise that we are not arguing that all countries ought to acknowledge the possibility of abandonment. We believe that in many common law countries, acceptance of a doctrine of abandonment would likely produce outcomes that are favourable to authors. However, we accept that abandonment is likely to appear unattractive in some *droit d'auteur* countries because it would fit poorly with the broader copyright regime. Nevertheless we hope to demonstrate that there is no theoretical objection to abandonment from an author's rights perspective, and that any resistance to abandonment in *droit d'auteur* countries is better seen as flowing from second order concerns relating to matters such as disparity in bargaining power and ensuring conformity in matters of legal doctrine.

The desire to provide authors with strong rights is normally understood to be connected with the desire to protect the author's personality. As such it is generally thought that there is a strong conceptual connection between the author's rights tradition in Continental Europe and theories of property that connect property with personhood.[38] The question therefore becomes how a doctrine of abandonment appears when viewed from the vantage of a theoretical platform that emphasises the importance of property rights as a precondition for the constitution of the self, the achievement of autonomy and the maintenance of dignity.[39] It would seem strange, however, to suggest that a respect for these ends militates

(1998) 111 *Harvard Law Review* 621. Heller's principal concern was with the impact of overlapping rights of exclusion leading to a resource being underutilised, but the language of the anticommons has since taken on a broader usage in arguments over the scope of intellectual property protection.

[38] See, generally, Martin A. Roeder, 'The Doctrine of Moral Right: A Study in the Law of Artists, Authors and Creators' (1940) 53 *Harvard Law Review* 554; Edward J. Damich, 'The Right of Personality: A Common-Law Basis for the Protection of the Moral Rights of Authors' (1988) 23 *Georgia Law Review* 1.

[39] See, generally, Margaret Jane Radin, *Reinterpreting Property* (The University of Chicago Press, 1993).

against allowing an author to abandon his or her work. As James Penner has put it:

> One ought not to be saddled with a relationship to a thing that one does not want, and an unbreakable relation to a thing would condemn the owner to having to deal with it. It would indeed be a funny turn of events if the norms serving our interest in property in essence gave the things a person owned a power over him.[40]

Mention might also be made in this context of Hegel's view on abandonment. As a matter of abstract right, Hegel took the view that property rights are capable of abandonment:

> The reason I can alienate my property is that it is mine only in so far as I put my will into it. Hence I may abandon (derelinquere) as a res nullius anything that I have or yield it to the will of another and so into his possession, provided always that the thing in question is a thing external by nature.[41]

Admittedly, this merely begs the question of whether an authorial creation is 'a thing external by nature', but Hegel provides a surprisingly direct answer to this question:

> What is peculiarly mine in a product of my mind may, owing to the method whereby it is expressed, turn at once into something external like a 'thing' which eo ipso may then be produced by other people. The result is that by taking possession of a thing of this kind, its new owner may make his own the thoughts communicated in it.[42]

Hegelian property theory thus lends itself to the view that there is nothing in the nature of authorial creation that would suggest that copyright should be regarded as anything other than alienable by abandonment or, for that matter, assignment. That support can be drawn from Hegel for allowing copyright to be abandoned is highly significant given the status that is often accorded to Hegelian property theory in debates over the scope of copyright. In some respects, however, these observations seem to go too far. If Hegel concludes that authorial creations are to be analogised to external alienable things, then perhaps Hegelian property theory is inconsistent with the *droit d'auteur* tradition. In this vein it might

[40] James E. Penner, *The Idea of Property in Law* (Oxford: Clarendon, 1997), p. 79.

[41] Georg W. F. Hegel, *Elements of the Philosophy of Right* trans. Thomas M. Knox (Oxford: Clarendon Press, 1952), section 65. But see below for a discussion of the relationship between matters of abstract right and matters of pragmatic reasoning in Hegelian theory.

[42] *Ibid.*, s. 68.

be noted that Hegel is not comfortably categorised as a natural rights scholar.[43] Perhaps, therefore, we need to look instead to one of the other philosophers whose work is commonly said to provide a foundation for the author's rights tradition, such as Kant or Fichte. But this path might be no less fraught with difficulty. It has recently been argued, for example, that Fichte's justifications for authorial property rights provide ambiguous support at best for the shape of modern copyright law.[44]

Alternatively, we might recognise that legal systems never provide a perfect embodiment or pure reflection of a particular philosophical tradition. Legal systems must also accommodate more prosaic concerns, such as the disparity in bargaining power between authors and publishers. For Hegel the details of legal rules are the province of pragmatic reasoning, not philosophy.[45] Similarly, there is a long tradition in natural law scholarship that the precise nature and scope of all rights, including property rights, will be defined by the state, with natural law merely providing the overarching framework.[46] Thus even if respect for authors and preservation of their autonomy form the core values underlying copyright protection, a fact which on the analysis above suggests that authors ought to be able to divorce themselves from their creations in any manner they choose, it may be that other factors may arise that lead to the view that,

[43] See Jeanne L. Schroeder, 'Unnatural Rights: Hegel and Intellectual Property' (2006) 60 *University of Miami Law Review* 453 at 545 (arguing that 'Hegelian theory completely rejects any concept of natural law, let alone any natural right of property'). But compare, e.g., Thom Brooks, 'Natural Law Internalism' in Thom Brooks (ed.), *Hegel's Philosophy of Right* (Oxford: Blackwell, 2012), p. 212 (arguing that 'Hegel's conception of legal philosophy clearly sits within the natural law tradition, albeit with a twist').

[44] Mario Biagioli, 'Against Copyright: Revisiting Fichte's Proof of the Illegality of Reprinting' (2011) 86 *Notre Dame Law Review* 1847. See generally Johann Gottlieb Fichte, 'Proof of the Unlawfulness of Reprinting' (Berlin, 1793) in Lionel Bently and Martin Kretschmer (eds.), *Primary Sources on Copyright (1450–1900)*, available at: www.copyrighthistory.org (last accessed 11 April 2013).

[45] Schroeder, 'Unnatural Rights' provides a nice discussion of this issue.

[46] Thomas Aquinas, *Summa Theologica* trans. T. Gilby, (Cambridge: Blackfriars, 1966), in particular vol. XXVIII, pp. 143–55, noting, for example, that human law may be altered to reflect the 'changed conditions of life' (at p. 145). In the copyright context it is worth noting that Kant was also of the view that natural law only structures property rights; indeed, for Kant property rights can only be fully constituted by a political authority. For discussion, see Arthur Ripstein, *Force and Freedom: Kant's Legal and Political Philosophy* (Cambridge, MA: Harvard University Press, 2009), Chapter 4, and see, for example, Immanuel Kant, *The Metaphysics of Morals* (Cambridge University Press, 1996), pp. 49–50 (noting that property rights properly so-called are 'the sum of all the laws having to do with things being mine or yours').

as a practical matter, the best way of preserving authorial autonomy is to make some rights inalienable.

As noted above, one such example might be the disparity in bargaining power between creators and commercial actors, which in a system of alienable rights might result in creators being forced to give up valuable rights in order to access channels for the distribution, performance and display of their works.[47] On this view, restrictions on the alienability of rights in *droit d'auteur* countries can be seen as flowing as much from a view as to the appropriate limits of freedom of contract as they do from a particular understanding of the justifications for copyright.

Constraints on alienability imposed for practical reasons may well mean that doctrinal coherence demands that abandonment be rejected in some legal systems. It is notable, for example, that in Germany a desire to protect authors from entering into disadvantageous bargains has inspired a set of legal arrangements including the absence of a clear demarcation between moral rights and economic rights (the so-called 'monist' approach), and a prohibition on the alienability of rights. Such a system is difficult to reconcile with a doctrine of abandonment, making it unsurprising that in the *Wall Pictures Case* the Federal Supreme Court rejected the possibility of copyright being abandoned, concluding 'an abandonment of rights comparable to dereliction in the law of property is unknown to copyright law. There is no "ownerless" copyright.'[48] In the UK, on the other hand, there is a distinction between copyright (described as a property right, and capable of assignment[49]) and moral rights (incapable of assignment, but capable of being waived through an instrument using signed writing[50]).

This leads to a more general point about the interrelationship between moral rights and abandonment. In countries that separate economic rights and moral rights, abandonment of copyright should not be seen as incompatible with the continued existence of moral rights. In situations where the abandoning owner is not the author this would seem to be entirely uncontroversial. Even in cases where the author and abandoning

[47] For discussion of this and similar themes, see, generally, Neil W. Netanel, 'Copyright Alienability Restrictions and the Enhancement of Author Autonomy: A Normative Evaluation' (1993) 24 *Rutgers Law Journal* 347; Thomas F. Cotter, 'Pragmatism, Economics, and the Droit Moral' (1997) 76 *North Carolina Law Review* 1.

[48] *Wall Pictures*, Decision of the German Federal Supreme Court (Bundesgerichtsh) reported in English at (1997) 28 *International Review of Intellectual Property and Competition Law* 282 at 285.

[49] Copyright, Designs and Patents Act 1988, ss. 1(1), 90, respectively.

[50] Copyright, Designs and Patents Act 1988, ss. 94, 87(2), respectively.

owner are one and the same, there may well be many cases where the continued enforcement of moral rights would seem to be desirable as, for example, when an author wishes to be identified as the author of the work and where the abandonment of economic rights is designed to ensure that the work has the widest possible circulation.

Admittedly, more difficult questions might arise in cases where the author tries to renounce rights of all descriptions. In these cases differences in national approaches to moral rights might well lead courts to divergent conclusions on whether an abandoning act has any bearing on the subsequent enforceability of moral rights.[51] In the UK, for example, it may be that an abandonment can be relevant in a number of ways: as a general and unconditional waiver of moral rights; to the question of whether a particular treatment is 'derogatory'[52] (as an attempt to renounce all rights may bear on whether there is prejudice to the honour or reputation of the author); and to whether an author has consented to infringement of his or her moral rights.[53] The UK statute countenances a role for contract and estoppel as regards 'informal' waivers, which may give further support for the view that a general law doctrine of abandonment has some role to play in the moral rights context. In contrast, in countries within the so-called 'dualist' *droit d'auteur* tradition (that is, authors' rights countries that recognise a separation between economic and moral rights) the suggestion that a purported abandonment could have any impact on the enforceability of moral rights might be anathema. We are perfectly open to the view that the difficulties of reconciling a doctrine of abandonment with the continued operation of moral rights may be sufficiently pronounced that considerations of 'fit' demand that abandonment be rejected even in countries within the dualist tradition. The point we wish to emphasise, however, is that concerns of internal doctrinal consistency should not be conflated with the desire to protect authors per se.

That abandonment is consistent with a strong vision of authors' rights also gains support from the rights of withdrawal for changed conviction that exist in a number of *droit d'auteur* countries.[54] Such rights rest on the belief that authors ought to be able to disassociate themselves from works

[51] For a detailed discussion of the position in Australia see Hudson and Burrell, 'Abandonment, Copyright and Orphaned Works', 992–3.

[52] Copyright, Designs and Patents Act 1988, s. 80(2)(b).

[53] Copyright, Designs and Patents Act 1988, s. 87(1).

[54] See, e.g., French Intellectual Property Code 1992, Art. L.121–4; German Copyright Act 1968, Art. 42.

that no longer reflect their views or aesthetic ideals. There are, however, a number of ways in which we might try to disassociate ourselves from the things we have produced. Taking back control of our works and preventing their further circulation is one such method. This is what rights of withdrawal anticipate. But an alternative form of disassociation is to cut our products adrift, to free ourselves from the burden of thinking about them, to leave our creations to whatever fate might bring. Permitting copyright to be abandoned is the most obvious legal means of facilitating this second form of cutting ourselves off from our creations. Indeed, the latter might in some ways be said to create not merely a more immediate break from our creations, but also in some respects a more complete one.

It might be objected that there is a contradiction between insisting that abandonment can serve to sever authors from their works, whilst also insisting that abandonment can provide a mechanism whereby authors can trade short-term financial gains for longer-term reputational advantage. However, there is nothing inherently contradictory in insisting that one form of legal transaction might be used for multiple purposes. Insofar as the different motivations for abandonment may have different legal implications, these are likely to crystallise around issues connected with moral rights and the need for attribution.

Rights of withdrawal are also interesting in that they shed light on the contingent nature of assessments of whether conferral of a (Hohfeldian) power on authors is, in practice, likely to undermine their position. Many civil law countries have apparently concluded that rights of withdrawal will strengthen rather than weaken the position of authors, and under current conditions in Europe this assessment is perfectly plausible. But one only has to consider how, say, Galileo or Pashukanis might have 'chosen' to exercise a power to prevent further circulation of their work to realise that assessments of this kind are highly context-dependent.[55] We raise these examples so as to emphasise that there can be no presumption that a power to abandon copyright will in practice prove harmful to authorial interests, whereas a right of withdrawal could only ever operate in a manner that was protective of authors.

[55] For discussion of Galileo's enforced abjuration of his work see, e.g., Maurice A. Finocchiaro, *Retrying Galileo, 1633–1992* (Berkeley: University of California Press, 2005), pp. 15–16. An overview of Pashukanis' political problems and eventual disappearance and execution is provided by John Hazard in his foreword to Evgeny B. Pashukanis, *Selected Writings on Marxism and Law* (London: Academic Press, 1980). This collection also contains a translation of Pashukanis' third and final self-criticism entitled 'State and Law under Socialism'.

Perhaps the most compelling reason for refusing to recognise a doctrine of abandonment from an author's rights perspective is to protect authors from hasty or ill-considered decisions. The author who abandons his or her copyright may later come to regret this decision, particularly if it subsequently turns out to be much more valuable than had been anticipated. However, this concern is peculiar to neither copyright nor abandonment, being relevant to *any* circumstance in which rights are relinquished, whether by way of transfer to another person, placing a work in the public domain or (for *choses in possession*) returning it to the commons of unowned things. If our starting point is that respect for authors means treating them as autonomous individuals capable of discerning their own best interests, then we need to decide in what circumstances we will seek to withdraw such independence of decision-making. As noted above, disparity in bargaining power may be one such situation. It is also possible that adherence to principles such as proportionate remuneration may also tend to militate against recognising abandonment.[56] It is therefore important to reiterate that we are not advocating universal recognition of a doctrine of abandonment. Rather we are trying to demonstrate that such a doctrine is consistent with a strong vision of authors' rights. Protection of authors can manifest itself in numerous ways, and such things as proportionate remuneration and limits on authorial freedom of contract are not an inevitable consequence of adherence to personhood understandings of copyright. Beyond this our concern in this section is to try to demonstrate that in common law countries abandonment has the potential to be protective of authors.

We have already noted that a refusal to allow copyright to be abandoned might have a chilling effect on the circulation of works that have been dedicated to the public domain. This is just as undesirable from an author's rights perspective as it is from an economic perspective and would therefore suggest that abandonment ought to be possible. Abandonment might also seem attractive from an author's rights perspective in cases where an individual wishes to make a testamentary donation of a manuscript that he or she has authored to a cultural institution on the understanding that access and reuse should be entirely unrestricted. Such a donation might be intended to serve a number of significant ends – it might serve to place information into the public domain, it might shed new light on the motivations of key actors in events that are already well known and, in the case

[56] See, e.g., French Intellectual Property Code 1992, Art. L131–3 (author to receive proportional remuneration in the event that an adaptation is made of the work).

of donations made by famous authors, it might contain self-reflections on the donor's oeuvre or might consist of a work that causes us to understand the donor's previously published works differently. From the donor's perspective, abandoning copyright has the attraction of ensuring that no subsequent owner can thwart the donor's wishes by using copyright to restrict reuse of the work. Admittedly there are other steps that the donor might take to try to ensure that his or her wishes are followed (for example, copyright could be assigned to a cultural institution whose mission is such that it is highly likely to respect the grantor's wishes), but if the donor's preference is that no one should own the copyright, it is hard to see why the law should fail to provide the donor with this option.

As regards the practical implications of abandonment for authors in common law countries, consideration might also be given to the US case *Oravec* v. *Sunny Isles Luxury Ventures LC*.[57] That case concerned alleged infringement of copyright in architectural plans. The plans at issue had themselves been based on earlier plans that had been entered into an architectural competition. A term of the competition was that the author would not later assert any copyright to the entered plans, and this was held to constitute an act of abandonment. The competition organisers were presumably keen to ensure that they had an unfettered right to use the winning design, but significantly they did not see the need to secure an assignment of copyright. A clearly established abandonment doctrine thus gave the competition organisers a way of ensuring that they got the rights they needed without insisting on an assignment. In contrast, in countries where no such doctrine is recognised the organisers would have to be advised to seek a transfer of rights. This would leave authors in a significantly worse position – it is one thing to enter a competition on the basis that anyone in the world, including the author, can reuse the work; it is quite another to transfer rights in the work to those running the competition. Indeed, this can be seen in the *Oravec* case – the plaintiff had reused parts of the entered plans in later drawings, and whilst entry into the competition had restricted the elements in which he could claim copyright, there was no question of his having to seek a licence from the competition organisers. Abandonment thus allows the reworking of a work by its author (with the possibility of obtaining copyright in the new derivative work) in a way that is generally not possible where rights have been transferred.

[57] 469 F Supp 2d 1148 (SD Fla, 2006).

Admittedly the examples we have developed as to how abandonment might serve to protect the interests of authors are largely speculative. We also acknowledge that there may be other ways of achieving the same ends and these examples could no doubt be multiplied. For example, our hypothetical competition organisers could make entry subject to the grant of a non-exclusive licence (which as it would form a term of entry into the competition would not be revocable at will). We also accept that there is a role for further research to investigate, inter alia, the motivations of authors who dedicate their works to the public domain and how abandonment functions in the United States (where such a doctrine is most clearly established). Nevertheless, for the reasons we have outlined, we believe that on the currently available evidence a doctrine of abandonment has much to recommend it in the UK and other Commonwealth countries.

3 Abandonment in the European Union

The preceding analysis leads us to conclude that the UK ought to accept abandonment as a mechanism by which copyright can be lost. However, as we suggested in the introduction, we are also concerned that recognition of a doctrine of abandonment anywhere in the EU is likely to face significant obstacles in the shape of the CJEU's harmonisation agenda. Over recent years the CJEU has embarked on a programme of 'harmonization by stealth' in the copyright field.[58] This has seen the CJEU extending harmonisation beyond what has been agreed politically,[59] and could well result in the Court declaring abandonment to be incompatible with EU law. In order to explain this concern, it is first necessary to say something about where abandonment fits within copyright law.

[58] Lionel Bently, 'Harmonization By Stealth: Copyright and the ECJ', paper delivered at the 20th Annual Intellectual Property Law & Policy Conference, Fordham University School of Law, April 2012.

[59] For instance, although only databases, software and photographs are the subjects of explicit harmonization in relation to originality, the CJEU has suggested that all copyright subject-matters must be the author's 'own intellectual creation': Case C-5/08 *Infopaq International A/S* v. *Danske Dagblades Forening* [2009] ECR I-6569. Subsequent statements in Case C-393/09 *Bezpečnostní softwarová asociace – Svaz softwarové ochrany* v. *Ministry of Culture of the Czech Republic* [2011] FSR 18 have built on *Infopaq* by suggesting that this test is the sole determinant of subsistence. This may render non-compliant the UK's closed list of subject matter in s. 1 of the Copyright, Designs and Patents Act: for discussion, see, e.g., Jonathan Griffiths, '*Infopaq, BSA* and the 'Europeanisation' of UK Copyright Law' (2011) 16 *Media and Arts Law Review* 59.

A doctrine of abandonment is most naturally understood as relating to the question of *ownership* of copyright. On this view the effect of abandonment is to divest the abandoning owner of title to the work, such that copyright remains technically in existence, but is unowned and hence incapable of enforcement. The idea that copyright might 'subsist' but be 'unowned' might strike some readers as a legal fiction. But this is a situation that the law already accommodates. Consider, for example, an orphaned work that is truly ownerless in the sense that it is undoubtedly protected by copyright, but no one in the world is capable of demonstrating on the balance of probabilities that they are the copyright owner. When describing such works, we accept routinely that they remain protected by copyright, despite the absence of anyone who can claim rights. Similarly, copyright legislation sets out rules for the duration of copyright in works 'of unknown authorship',[60] implicitly accepting the fiction of the existence of copyright in works whose owner may not be capable of identification. It might, admittedly, be objected that in these cases the conclusion that copyright subsists but is unowned results from the operation of adjectival rather than substantive law; that for orphaned and anonymous works there is a mere evidentiary failure (technically there is an owner, it is just that no one can meet the burden of proof), whilst what we advance has existentialist consequences (that there is no owner at all). However, we do not see any good reason for the law to tolerate one 'legal fiction' but not the other. In short, the law already accepts the reality of 'ownerless copyright', and we therefore see no reason not to accept that abandonment operates as a rule of ownership in the copyright sphere, just as it does in relation to chattels.

The conclusion that abandonment is a rule of ownership is crucial because questions of ownership remain largely untouched by both the international conventions and the EU Copyright Directives.[61] European countries ought thus to be able to recognise abandonment if they so choose, a conclusion that ought to be fortified by the fact that EU law is

[60] Copyright, Designs and Patents Act 1988, ss. 12(3), (4).

[61] But see Directive 2009/24/EC of the European Parliament and of the Council of 23 April 2009 on the legal protection of computer programs (codified version) [2009] OJ L111/16, Art. 2(3) (computer programs created in the course of employment to be owned by the employer, unless otherwise provided by contract). Cf. Directive 96/9/EC of the European Parliament and of the Council of 11 March 1996 on the legal protection of databases [1996] OJ L77/20, recital 29 (making it clear that Member States are free to make provision to deal with employee works).

meant to operate against the background of the continued operation of national property rules.[62]

In practice, however, there are two obstacles to recognition of a doctrine of abandonment anywhere in Europe. First, rather than being classified as a rule of ownership, it might be argued that abandonment is a device that shortens the term of copyright protection. To reiterate, this is not an interpretation that we support. We say that to recognise a doctrine of abandonment is merely to apply to copyright a general legal principle that is relevant to other forms of personal property. Conceived in this way abandonment is part of a suite of rules that are simply untouched by international and regional harmonisation processes – and historically there has been no question that general legal and equitable principles can result in copyright becoming incapable of enforcement in certain circumstances[63] or can divest an owner of his or her rights.[64] But for an institution intent on broadening and deepening the harmonisation agenda there might be a strong temptation to categorise abandonment as a potential limit on the duration of protection, with the result that abandonment would fall foul of the Term Directive and hence would have to be rejected as inconsistent with European law. Although there are good reasons to prefer the rule of ownership interpretation, there is no conclusive argument against the rule of duration view. The CJEU could also find ready support in the academic literature should it wish to adopt the latter interpretation.[65]

[62] See below.

[63] For instance because of the operation of estoppel: see, e.g., *Godfrey* v. *Lees* [1995] EMLR 307 (Ch); *Baillieu* v. *Australian Electoral Commission* (1996) 63 FCR 210 (Federal Court of Australia); *Fraserside Holdings Pty Ltd* v. *Venus Adult Shops Pty Ltd.* [2005] FMCA 997 (Federal Magistrates Court of Australia). In *Fisher* v. *Brooker* [2009] 1 WLR 1764 (House of Lords) the claimant was successful in requesting declarations that he owned a share of the musical copyright in the song 'A Whiter Shade of Pale', despite have delayed for 38 years in asserting his rights. The absence of detriment to the defendants, if the claimant was now permitted to enforce his claim, was crucial to this result. However, Lord Neuberger also suggested that if the claimant tried later to seek injunctive relief against the defendants, then the Court might have regard to the claimant's delay in determining whether to exercise its discretion to grant an injunction: at paras. 74–75. For discussion, see, e.g., Hector MacQueen, 'Abandoned, Orphaned or Property For Ever? Copyright, Prescription and Personal Bar' (2010) 14 *Edinburgh Law Review* 97.

[64] For instance where an assignment that does not comply with statutory formality requirements nevertheless takes effect in equity: see, e.g., *Warner* v. *Gestetner* [1988] EIPR D 89 (Ch, unreported); *Pastefield* v. *Denham* [1999] FSR 168 (County Court).

[65] See, in particular, Johnson '"Dedicating" Copyright to the Public Domain'. For a detailed response to the specifics of Johnson's argument see Hudson and Burrell, 'Abandonment, Copyright and Orphaned Works', 987–91.

Second, even if abandonment is categorised as a rule of ownership, there is still some possibility that the CJEU would conclude that such a doctrine is incompatible with European law. This is because the Court has indicated in *Martin Luksan* v. *Petrus van der Let*[66] that a systematic interpretation of European law produces the conclusion that rules of ownership are subject to a greater degree of harmonisation than had generally been appreciated. In that case the applicant, Mr Luksan, was the scriptwriter and principal director of a documentary film entitled *Fotos von der Front* (Photos from the Front). The applicant entered into an agreement with the defendant producer, Mr van der Let. This agreement purported to create a partial assignment of copyright, with online distribution being specifically excluded from the scope of the assignment. The defendant nevertheless made the film available on the Internet and assigned the rights for this purpose to Movieeurope.com. In response to Luksan's claim for infringement, the defendant relied on a provision of Austrian law that automatically vested all exploitation rights in the producer, a provision that was not subject to contractual variation. The Court held that this provision was incompatible with European law as being 'tantamount to depriving [Luksan] of his lawfully acquired intellectual property right'.[67] The CJEU did, however, go on to say that Member States may provide for a presumption of transfer 'provided that such a presumption is not an irrebuttable one'.[68]

The facts of the *Luksan* case are far removed from any conceivable scenario in which abandonment might be at issue. However, *Luksan* may well mark merely the first step in the CJEU developing a more comprehensive set of European rules of ownership. If this occurs, it is perfectly conceivable that abandonment would be declared incompatible with EU law, particularly in a case where the abandoning owner is not the author. One can imagine, for example, the Court drawing on what was said in *Luksan* and concluding that a transfer of rights is permissible so as to allow a commercial actor to recoup its investment and subject always to the right of the author to negotiate contractually to 'retain' ownership.[69] It might therefore be concluded that where an assignee has indicated that it no longer has any interest in exploiting the copyright, rights must revest in the author, since the reason for allowing rights to be transferred in the first

[66] Case C-277/10 of 9 February 2012.
[67] At para. 70.
[68] At para. 87.
[69] At paras. 77–79.

place is no longer present. In contrast, it is much more difficult to see how the Court could find any support for a European-wide doctrine of abandonment from within the existing legislative framework. Consequently, to the extent that the Court is of the view that harmonisation impacts on abandonment, this will almost certainly only be so as to declare that abandonment is incompatible with European law.

This brings us to the broader issue flagged in the introduction. This volume seeks to explore the interrelationship between property concepts and our understanding of intellectual property rights. We have suggested on previous occasions that when rights in chattel property are mapped onto intellectual property rights, one cannot help but notice that the latter are surprisingly expansive. This provides a ready response to anyone who suggests that respecting the proprietary status of intellectual property means that we have to afford owners more expansive rights. In more concrete terms, however, it might also suggest that we should look to limiting doctrines within personal property law as a way of reining in intellectual property rights.[70] One might therefore look not merely to abandonment but also to estoppel-based arguments, the law of accession (that is, the rule of personal property law that property rights can become lost where a lesser form of property becomes attached to a greater form of property, with the effect that the lesser property right becomes subsumed)[71] or to defences in the law of conversion built around a broad principle of reasonableness.[72]

In Europe, however, the possibilities for drawing on general property law principles to constrain intellectual property rights are extremely limited. The Court might refer to Article 17 of the European Charter of Fundamental Rights, but it is difficult to see how this Article, with its general guarantee of property and its terse insistence that 'Intellectual property shall be protected'[73] could be used as a platform for developing limiting doctrines. On the contrary, it is notable that in *Luksan* Article 17

[70] See, in addition to the sources listed below, Michael A. Carrier, 'Cabining Intellectual Property through a Property Paradigm' (2004) 54 *Duke Law Journal* 1; Robert Burrell and Allison Coleman, *Copyright Exceptions: the Digital Impact* (Cambridge University Press, 2005), pp. 183–7.

[71] See further Maria Lee and Robert Burrell, 'Liability for the Escape of GM Seeds: Pursuing the "Victim"?' (2002) 65 *Modern Law Review* 517 at 525–7 (discussing the Canadian case *Monsanto Canada Inc* v. *Schmeiser* [2004] 1 SCR 902 and arguing that the Court at first instance should have taken the defendant's admixture argument much more seriously).

[72] See Emily Hudson, 'Fair Use as Reasonable Use? Lessons for Copyright from the Law of Personal Property' (forthcoming).

[73] Art. 17(2).

was cited in support of requiring Member States to maintain what the Court took to be the 'ordinary' rule of copyright ownership.[74] Similarly, to the extent that the Court is prepared to draw on Strasbourg jurisprudence dealing with Article 1 of the First Protocol to the European Convention on Human Rights,[75] this is very unlikely to provide support for the development of transnational limits on the scope of property rights – Strasbourg jurisprudence has generally focused on the extent to which limitations on property rights are permissible, not on the extent to which limitations are required. Where it has touched on the latter question, it has done so only by reference to other rights protected under the Convention[76] and hence these cases offer no support for the development of the type of doctrines we have in mind.

Moving forward, it is notable that property rights have largely been excluded from moves to create a European private law. Property rights are seen as having a different constitutional and political status that means that national decision-making needs to be afforded a greater degree of respect. This is reflected in Article 345 of the Treaty on the Functioning of the European Union (TFEU), which provides 'The Treaties shall in no way prejudice the rules in Member States governing the system of property ownership'. This provision also suggests that it would be difficult for the CJEU to develop limits on intellectual property rights based on a distinctively European notion of what it means to own property. Simultaneously, however, this provision would at least seem to provide a strong basis for the Court to respect national differences in the enforceability of intellectual property rights that are grounded in national concepts of property. As we have noted at a number of points, we are not suggesting that a Europe-wide doctrine of abandonment is necessarily desirable and Article 345 TFEU would at least seem to preserve doctrines like abandonment at the national level. However, the position is not as straightforward as Article 345 TFEU might suggest. As Daniela Caruso has noted, the EU is often keen to give the impression of 'firm competence

[74] Para. 68.

[75] See Art. 6(3) of the Treaty on European Union, which provides 'Fundamental rights, as guaranteed by the European Convention for the Protection of Human Rights and Fundamental Freedoms and as they result from the constitutional traditions common to the Member States, shall constitute general principles of the Union's law'. As to the relationship between EU law and ECHR jurisprudence see also Case C-571/10 *Kamberaj* v. *Istituto per l'Edilizia Sociale della Provincia Autonoma di Bolzano (IPES)* [2012] 2 CMLR 43.

[76] *Appleby* v. *United Kingdom* (2003) 37 EHRR 38 at para. 47 (there may be exceptional circumstances in which the right to freedom of expression would require access to land).

boundaries' and to 'reinforce the legitimacy of the Europeanising project'. But these boundaries are 'subject to continuous erosion'.[77] Placed in the context of a legal framework that calls for the 'creation of European intellectual property rights to provide uniform protection of intellectual property rights throughout the Union',[78] history suggests that the Court is very likely to favour harmonisation of rules over deference to national property concepts.[79]

This brings us back to what we regard as the single most important issue when exploring the role of property concepts in intellectual property law. We are of the view that some of the problems with the existing intellectual property regime would be ameliorated if we made a concerted attempt to create functional equivalence between intellectual property rights and other forms of property, with limiting doctrines in general property law being employed creatively to achieve this end. Unfortunately, in the European context, the prospects of this strategy being employed successfully are limited. The European judiciary, much like the Commission, is likely to remain more concerned with harmonisation than with making intellectual property law fit for purpose.

[77] See Daniela Caruso, 'Private Law and Public Stakes in European Integration: The Case of Property' (2004) 10 *European Law Journal* 751.

[78] TFEU, Art. 118.

[79] See, generally, Karen Alter, 'The European Legal System and Domestic Policy: Spillover or Backlash?' (2000) 54 *International Organization* 489 at 513: '[T]he ECJ used legal lacunae to seize new powers and delve into areas that member states considered to be their own exclusive realm.'

10

The concept of the anticommons

Useful, or ubiquitous and unnecessary?

DAVID LAMETTI

Introduction

Most contemporary property and intellectual property theorists have some familiarity with the concept of the anticommons. It is most common in current North American property theory, and while originally posited as a hypothetical construct by Frank Michelman,[1] is most closely identified with the writing of Michael Heller.[2] The construct seeks to provide remedies to situations where absolute property rights lead to nefarious results, mainly under-use. Contrary to the classical scenario posed by some efficiency-based property thinkers in which common property

For the purposes of some of the insights offered in this chapter I note that I was the Project Director between 2002 and 2007 of the McGill–Russia Civil Code Reform Project, sponsored by the Canadian International Development Agency, and continue to be consulted on Russian private law reform. A preliminary draft of this chapter was first presented at the IVAR Law & Philosophy Workshop, Krakow in 2007. I wish to thank Katrina Wyman, Larissa Katz, James Penner and Amnon Lehavi for their comments. It was later presented at the Canadian Private Law Workshop, and here I would like to thank Dennis Klimchuk, Larissa Katz (again), Stephen Smith, Lionel Smith, Evan Fox-Decent, Steven Patel and Lisa Austin. Finally, it was presented to the Progressive Property Workshop (III): thanks to Gregory Alexander, John Lovett, Hanoch Dagan, Laura Underkuffler, Eduardo Penalver and Jed Purdy. I also wish to thank research assistants Michael Bookman, Katherine Lofts, Jake Wilson and Ian Dahlman. Finally, I wish to thank Helena Howe for her suggestions and her infinite patience. Funding was provided by an F. G. Kennedy Travel Grant, the McGill Wainwright Fund and the Social Sciences and Humanities Research Council of Canada.

[1] Frank Michelman, 'Ethics, Economics and the Law of Property' in J. Rolland Pennock and John W. Chapman (eds.), *NOMOS XXIV: Ethics, Economics and the Law* (New York University Press, 1982), p. 3.

[2] See, for example, Michael A. Heller, 'The Tragedy of the Anticommons: Property in Transition from Marx to Markets' (1998) 11 *Harvard Law Review* 621. More recently he has renamed the phenomenon 'gridlock': *Gridlock Economy: How Too Much Ownership Wrecks Markets, Stops Innovation, and Costs Lives* (New York: Basic Books, 2008).

leads to the over-exploitation of a given resource – the so-called tragedy of the commons – what Heller calls the 'tragedy of the anticommons' is the scenario in which *too much* private property results in the *under-use* of resources. Such is the case especially where ownership is fragmentary and absolute. In this setting, too many right-holders failing to put their resources to use, or even one right-holder neglecting to employ the resource, can result in the resource not being used at all.

A great deal of literature has been spawned by anticommons analysis, both in identifying tragedy-of-under-use 'situations' and in proposing remedies for such situations. This research often uses the tools of economic analysis, whether these are in traditional areas of property law or of intellectual property. As stated by Stephen Munzer, it is too early to tell how enduring this phenomenon will be.[3] My question in this chapter is rather different: how necessary or useful is this concept in the first place?

The anticommons may have had its most important reapplication in the realm of intellectual property theory. Perhaps the single most compelling example of the tragedy of under-use comes from the realm of patents: the so-called 'patent thicket'. The thicket occurs where there are many patent-holders – 'owners' – who hold exclusive patent rights that are useful as part of a larger process or invention: the many patent-holders of a potential cure for a horrible disease, or a smartphone, or a sewing machine. In such complex clusters where a group of patents might be combined for a larger functional purpose, one owner of a key patent might block the whole invention from ever happening.[4] A similar idea might be developed for copyright: music sampling, for example, is precluded where a music creator using samples potentially has to clear rights for every single bit of music sampled, no matter how small. Some 'owners' may not allow sampling at all. In the end, the process is so overly complex that few songs would ever get created in this manner, resulting in a loss of many of the most creative and innovative practices in the current music industry. Samplers either have to ignore formal laws, change their choice of samples or abandon their methodology altogether. Viewed as a tragedy of under-use, each of these situations presents a net loss for society.

In my view, the thrust of anticommons scholarship is a reaction to the problems created when ownership is taken to be absolute. Given such a

[3] Stephen R. Munzer, 'The Commons and Anticommons in the Law and Theory of Property' in M. P. Golding and W. A. Edmundson (eds.), *The Blackwell Guide to the Philosophy of Law and Legal Theory* (Oxford: Blackwell, 2005), p. 148.

[4] Michael A. Heller and Rebecca S. Eisenberg, 'Can Patents Deter Innovation? The Anti-Commons in Biomedical Research' (1998) 280 *Science* 698.

degree of control, an owner can simply choose not to use his resource, acting in a completely self-regarding fashion with seriously negative consequences to society. In effect, the argument of Heller and others is a plea for limiting some of the impact of what is seen as powers falling within the traditional purview of *dominium*. It is an implicit recognition that society has legitimate expectations for the use of a resource and these may be reflected in purposes for the use of the resource that do not always conform to what the individual owner believes he can do with the resource. Some of these limiting purposes are social – for example, the wider diffusion of a base technology protected by a patent. Other limiting purposes, however, are more individualistic – the rights of another individual patent-holder whose patent requires the use of the patented technology that is not being deployed or is otherwise blocked by the base technology patent-holder. (Obviously there is a social aspect here as well.)

It is a further question for anticommons scholars as to whether a less absolutist starting point for property would affect their analysis: that is, if property or intellectual property rights were not taken to be absolute, it is conceivable that a number of tragedy-of-under-use situations might never occur. Put another way, if an obligation to put to productive use (or allow to be put to productive use) is understood to accompany the granting of a patent, a compulsory licence or outright revocation of the patent takes care of the failure to put the patent to use, all the while employing more traditional property understandings and tools, and without recourse to superfluous anticommons analysis. Certainly where objects of social wealth, as understood by society, contain a strong sense of expected uses or destination – for example what Eduardo Peñalver has called 'land's memory'[5] – such expected uses form part of the contours of property analysis. Therefore, in granting a property right in the resource to the exclusion of others, society expects the resource to be used within those contours that are explicit and implicit in the granting.

More attention must also be paid to the nature of private property relationships and to the nature of private property resources. The same is true for intellectual property rules and resources. Indeed, it may very well be that many of the problems identified as gridlock are not ownership questions at all, but rather the kind of coordination questions that any society faces in dealing with the challenge of managing complex resources and ensuing governance relationships. If this is true, then adding a construct

[5] Eduardo M. Peñalver, 'Land Virtues' (2009) 94 *Cornell Law Review* 821.

such as the anticommons to the analytic mix may be more of a hindrance than a help.

1 The idea of the anticommons

The construct is so well known in the literature that I may safely proceed from the assumption that most people now understand the basic premise of the anticommons, and its potential for tragedy. In Heller's words:

> [O]ne can understand anticommons property as the mirror image of commons property. In a commons, by definition, multiple owners are each endowed with the privilege to use a given resource, and no one has the right to exclude another. When too many owners have such privileges of use, the resource is prone to overuse – the tragedy of the commons. Canonical examples include depleted fisheries, overgrazed fields and polluted air.
>
> In the anticommons, by my definition, multiple owners are each endowed with the right to exclude others from a scarce resource, and no one has an effective privilege of use. When there are too many owners holding rights of exclusion, the resource is prone to underuse – a tragedy of the anticommons. Legal and economic scholars have mostly overlooked this tragedy, but it can appear whenever governments create new property rights.[6]

The central idea, then, is that there is an over-fragmentation of ownership rights on the same object of social wealth. Heller's initial example is that of Russia's transition economy: storefronts remained empty because too many people 'owned' rights in the storefront, allowing each owner to block or veto certain uses of the store. By contrast, sidewalk kiosks flourished in the mid 1990s because there were few impediments to setting up shop, and certainly no competing owners to block the opening and subsequent exploitation of a specific kiosk.

There is also a possibility, developed in subsequent literature especially on patents,[7] that over-fragmentation may also occur with respect to different but related objects of property. So with respect to an interrelated set of patents, one holder of a single patent necessary in a larger application, say a single medicine used as part of a cocktail of pharmaceuticals used to fight a specific illness or condition, could block other patent-holders and indeed consumers from using the whole 'invention'.

[6] Heller, 'The Tragedy of the Anticommons', 623–4.

[7] Heller and Eisenberg, 'Can Patents Deter Innovation?'

In both cases one might characterize the issue in the rhetorical terms used by Jim Harris: 'too much property?' In other words, too many ownership interests allow for one single owner to block the effective use of the resource. Given the primordial place of private property rights in Western culture, it thus stands to reason that the anticommons is not merely a simple possibility, but rather is epiphenomenal. This is certainly the conclusion that Heller reaches in the most recent summation of examples in *Gridlock Economy*: not just for Moscow storefronts and patents but also for radio frequencies, copyright law, and real estate. Everything is a potential anticommons or subject-matter for gridlock.

Let me say at the outset that the sentiment behind Heller's analysis is one that I share. Ownership interests, taken to an extreme rights-based view, can sometimes lead to nefarious consequences in terms of the (under-)use of a given resource. That being said, I am not sure that the construction of the new concept of the anticommons does any new intellectual work, and indeed might serve to obfuscate important issues in property theory. As with the metaphor of Ockham's razor, adding additional layers of complexity to an analysis does not always assist the endeavour of understanding. In my view, property theory and structures were sufficiently supple to deal with the challenges posed by under-use of the resource. (The same is also true of the challenges posed in the intellectual property example, of rights in related or neighbouring resources.)

2 Flawed points of departure

Whether in theory or in practice, I am disinclined to share a number of Heller's basic assumptions used in the construction of the anticommons model. The argument proceeds at three levels: first, at the level of the initial anecdote of Russian storefronts and what one might call the 'Russian transition economy' generally; second, at the level of existing private law and intellectual property structures and concerns; and third, at the level of property and intellectual property theory.

2.1 Russian storefronts

The Russian storefront analysis is an illustrative starting point. It is indeed true, as Heller observed, that there were many different, often conflicting, interests in certain types of property resources in transition Russia. Given some of the nuances of the Civil Code of the Russian

Federation,[8] a number of these ambiguities still exist. Nevertheless, the example may not be as convincing as one might have thought at first glance.

There is no disputing the varied interests in a single storefront immovable (using the proper civil term for land and buildings), or indeed in the other examples that Heller identified. And indeed, many of these right-holders could block the use of the immovable or at least certain uses by others. However, it is a bit of a stretch in my view to extrapolate a new theoretical construct from this aspect of Russia's transition from a centrally planned, socialist economy to a market economy. First, not all the interests in the storefront were identical and not all of them could be classified as property interests. While some of the interests were a result of hold-over interests, including state interests that existed prior to privatization, others were a result of an attempt to create new private property rights in immovables. Conflicts were mainly and simply a result of ill-defined and conflicting rights that were a result of a lack of coordination among norms in a period of fundamental change. Indeed, if it were the case that no one had an effective right of use of the storefront, this would seem to have been more a result of poorly defined rights rather than any conceptual quandary. This was (and probably still is) a transition period in which hard and soft Russian property norms were being rewritten and reconceived in light of a new reality. Kiosks arose as a simple practical solution to problems in a transition economy. That kiosks arose on Moscow streets was the result of a complex series of overlapping and inconsistent rules and interests: this was a temporary situation.

In any event, these competing rights, as described by Heller, were not all identical – lessees versus owners and other kinds of right-holders – such that the anticommons model as defined does not really hold up. Like any other more developed property system, the example illustrates that a number of different kinds of interests are possible in the same object at the same time in a private property system. These rights are part of a complex overlay of rights and obligations with sources in property and

[8] Civil Code of the Russian Federation, Peter B. Maggs and Alexei N. Zhiltsov, trans., (Moscow: HOPMA, 2003). For a general introduction to some of the issues of Russian property reform, see David Lametti, 'General Concepts of Private Law Relating to Private Property in the Civil Code of the Russian Federation and in the Civil Code of Quebec' (2005) 30 *Review of Central and East European Law* 7; 'Objects of Private Property in the Civil Code of the Russian Federation and in the Civil Code of Quebec' (2005) 30 *Review of Central and East European Law* 19; and 'Rights of Private Property in the Civil Code of the Russian Federation and in the Civil Code of Quebec' (2005) 30 *Review of Central and East European Law* 29.

contract mainly, and are functionally ordered. Indeed, as I shall discuss later, no distinction is made in Heller's analysis between property and non-property rights, or indeed between ownership and non-ownership property rights, distinctions that do serve to help us understand the way in which the fragmentation of rights is meant to be sorted. That there were problems was probably more a result of *badly done* fragmentation than fragmentation itself.

Finally, one of the central components of a functioning legal system that was lacking in Russia at the time (and still is, to a very large degree[9]) is respect for the rule of law. Many of the blockages in Heller's example were simply illegal, and with no means of redress in front of a court system not yet acquainted with rule of law standards ensuring procedural or substantive justice (and a system dealing with evolving basic norms to boot). Hence, it is in no way surprising that Russians took to the streets to sell their wares.

It may have been an error, therefore, to have focused on a transition economy from which to draw larger lessons for property theory. Indeed, other factors might better explain the initial lack of storefront merchants. For example, there was not (and still is not) an efficient and effective system of land registration in Russia (although efforts are being made). Thus if there were an 'owner' with some overarching or residual interest, he would have no way of asserting that claim. Similarly, the difficulties with the Russian justice system might have meant (and still would mean) that even if there is a clear legal hierarchy of interests in the storefront, there would be little chance of ever being able to sort out the problem logically or legally in front of a court, or even with potential recourse to a legal structure; better to resort to a strongman-protector or criminal organizations. The magnitude of the economic changes in Russia, and other factors leading to the rapid rise of kiosks and slower development of storefronts – a problem that appears to me to no longer exist in downtown Moscow or St Petersburg[10] – are less the result of an anticommons or over-fragmentation of rights than they are a result of underdevelopment of substantive and procedural norms.

[9] See the collection of essays and round-table discussions published on the rule of law and law reform in Russia: Elena V. Novikova (ed.), *Rule of Law in Russia: Issues of Implementation, Enforcement and Practice* (Moscow: Statut, 2010), and particularly the Third Roundtable Discussion on Securing Property Rights, and therein especially the intervention of Andrei G. Fedotov, pp. 341–5.

[10] I last visited Moscow in 2011 for property and IP-related consultations, and St Petersburg in 2007.

2.2 *Property governance*

Property governance, indeed all forms of governance, clearly has to tackle complex problems of competing claims, interests and goals, both individual and societal. Although the picture pointed out by Heller of a transition economy fraught with a complex mix of property interests can be partly responsible for slowing development in Russia, the challenge of having to deal with a mix of property interests is in no way unique to Russia. Common and civil law property law systems allow for the fragmentation of ownership, as well as the existence of other kinds of contractually created non-property or near-property rights in the same resource. All of this fragmentation serves to facilitate market economic interaction. Owners, lessees, shareholders, lenders, employees, state authorities and so on all have rights or enforceable interests in a going economic concern – such as a piece of real estate with a storefront – in any Western jurisdiction. While Russia's property system may have been overly complex in some unique ways – with holdovers from the previous Soviet system such as the presence of multiple state regulators and state actors as owners, for example – the fact of mixed interests is not in any way unique conceptually to Russia. The goal is effective and efficient fragmentation: in the transition economy of Russia in the mid 1990s, fragmentation was badly done. In other Western economies fragmentation is generally done better, and to the extent that fragmentation leads to problems, such mistakes generally are corrected over time.

Heller's effective claim that the anticommons is different from the formal fragmentation in legal systems is in my view unconvincing, and again revolves around the nature of ownership and other limited real rights. Here, what one might call the comparative semantics of property systems is useful: civil law and common law both allow for fragmentation, and both allow for *numerus clausus*, as both have an interest in protecting resources, efficient use or non-use, through the coherent ordering of rights. But common lawyers can get themselves into a great deal of conceptual difficulty when they use the word ownership carelessly. Although both the common law and civil law allow for an entitlement to capture the most powerful interest possible in a resource, and allow for a series of lesser entitlements in the same resource,[11] the two systems diverge in the

[11] In theory, this division of interests in the same resource can be achieved in one of two ways: either one can divide or fragment interests at the level of *ownership itself*, thus creating two or more holders or 'owners' of different 'ownership' interests or 'estates'; or one can preserve the singular ownership of property in one person while hiving off

labels that each employs. In the common law, one routinely calls *all* the entitlements 'ownership' interests. This is the case with most common law writers, and Harris provides a good example: 'What one may "own" (be entitled to) may be an ownership interest, or a lesser proprietary, or other, right. Only if the entitlement is to an ownership interest does "ownership" function as an organising idea from which concrete privileges and powers may be inferred.'[12]

That Heller and Harris (and the common law) use the term ownership so widely – often to cover all sorts of pecuniary, 'patrimonial' rights[13] – makes it impossible to understand the term without some other qualifier to give additional precision. In Becker's words, the 'varieties of ownership are not equal to full ownership'.[14] Indeed, as Heller has used the term, it covers some contractual rights as well. Thus, the multiplicity of adjectives used to qualify 'ownership' in common law thinking is the direct result of using the word 'ownership' widely and, perhaps, loosely,[15] and in Heller's case allows him to posit a situation where it appears that there are many 'owners'. Indeed, in *Gridlock Economy*, Heller often resorts to putting ownership in quotation marks.

or 'dismembering' *lesser real rights* and powers for the benefit of other persons. These dismembered rights, although when added together form the whole of the ownership package or 'bundle' of rights, are nevertheless not placed on the same conceptual level as ownership. The holder of a dismembered right merely has title to a lesser real right. Ownership of property and control thereof can thus be divorced. Of these two alternative conceptual structures, the common law takes the first view, allowing the fragmentation of 'ownership' through the doctrine of estates. The civil law opts for the latter approach, preserving ownership as a non-fragmented concept but allowing certain rights to be subtracted, even to the point where under usufruct or emphyteusis most of the real rights in the ownership bundle are part of the title of the usufructuary or emphyteutic lessee, leaving the bare owner with few of the real rights normally attributed to ownership. Thus, while fragmentation of *ownership* (ownership properly so-called) is only truly achieved in the common law, the civil law in practice can tolerate largely similar functional divisions of ownership rights.

12 James W. Harris, *Property and Justice* (Oxford University Press, 1996), p. 80.

13 The common law lacks a convenient term for patrimony – the totality of one's pecuniary assets and liabilities, including both rights *in rem* and *in personam* – though occasionally the term 'property' is used to mean this wider notion, thus adding to the confusion over the scope of ownership since in some sense we do hold or own those rights. See David Lametti, 'The Concept of Property: Relations through Objects of Social Wealth' (2003) 53 *University of Toronto Law Journal* 325 at 328.

14 Lawrence C. Becker, 'The Moral Basis of Property Rights' in J. Rolland Pennock and John W. Chapman (eds.), *NOMOS XXIV: Ethics, Economics and the Law* (New York University Press, 1982), p. 187.

15 See the discussion in Lametti, 'The Concept of Property', 356–65.

The basic point of this perhaps overly technical distinction is that property interests – call them what you will – are different in content, and none are absolute. One can think of this in terms of Honoré's incidents: the better view, implicit in Honoré's structure, is that there is some hierarchy as among the incidents. The right to control use, for example, has some pride of place. So while all the incidents help in some way to organize and define property ownership, the use of the word ownership itself for many interest-holders does not itself mean that all bundles are of equal strength, or even that the bundles conflict.

My fundamental point is that all legal systems attempt to coordinate property interests. The variety of interests in the single resource as described by Heller as ownership or proprietary interests will not be the same in terms of content, or at least should not be, in a property system with a coherent system of fragmented rights: any problems in 'blocking' are not a result of any anticommons, but rather inefficiencies and inconsistencies in the ordering of interests. It is a case of *poor* fragmentation and not the mere fact of fragmentation in and of itself. The scepticism exhibited by property systems, and especially the more formal civil law, towards the unstructured fragmentation of ownership interests – the *numerus clausus* response – is an attempt to structure and limit fragmentation.[16] The same can also be said of the attempt to classify property rights (real or *in rem*) versus personal rights (*in personam*): each generates a hierarchy that enables property interests to be ordered, providing a potential response to situations or overlapping and complex interests. Moreover, property systems will deal with the duration of fragmentation: they often provide that fragmentation, while lengthy, will ultimately be temporary. The 'owner' may be the person who has only the ultimate residual interest in the longest term, and in the end will see the fragments of the ownership bundle reunified in his hands (or will gaze upon it from the grave in the hands of his heirs). Conversely, where fragmentation might be permanent, then it is usually for one specific right with very formal barriers to creation: a real servitude, easement or *profit-à-prendre*, as well as a legal fiction removing persons from the equation and framing the fragmented property right in terms of an interest benefitting the land. That conflicting, overlapping,

[16] The *numerus clausus* problem is known to all civil lawyers, but it has surfaced in the common law, law and economics literature: see Bernard Rudden, 'Economic Theory Versus Property Law: The *Numerus Clausus* Problem' in J. Eekelaar and J. Bell (eds.), *Oxford Essays in Jurisprudence*, 3rd Series (Oxford University Press, 1987), p. 239. See also Thomas H. Merrill and Henry E. Smith, 'Optimal Standardization in the Law of Property: The *Numerus Clausus* Principle' (2000) 110 *Yale Law Journal* 1.

inefficient, ineffective and otherwise bad fragmentation and coordination of ownership and other economic rights existed in the Russian transition to private property is abundantly clear from Heller's enlightening description in his seminal article; that it is anything more than that is less convincing.

One might also consider the situation where the interests are indeed identical. Perhaps the most compelling example in *Gridlock Economy* is the situation of co-ownership, a situation often forced upon co-owners by shared inheritance. Such a situation explains the gradual disenfranchising of black farm owners over successive generations: shared inheritance over successive generations resulted in the fragmentation of equivalent co-ownership rights across too many parties. In theory, in such instances all parties are complete owners in a symmetrical fashion over the same object. While such a situation of shared ownership often works well in close-knit family contexts, where the scope of uses is in effect conditioned by the informal – but powerful – normativity of the family structure, it loses its efficacy when that closeness no longer exists.

Such a situation – negative and destructive as it often can be – does not require a new term such as anticommons. Old, indeed accurate, terminology already exists. Where there are in fact shared, identical rights in the same resource, then private law systems have identified and named the situation – joint tenancy, tenancy in common or indivision – and may have already effectively dealt with the negative aspects of such a situation:[17] that is, the shared property is either a form of common property or of private law co-ownership, a concept familiar to both the common and civil law, with common or civil law rules that have evolved or have been enacted to rectify governance problems as they arise. So even if by Heller's definition the terms anticommons or gridlock do apply to co-ownership of land, both formal private property systems and informal norms have dealt with co-ownership from perhaps their very origins as normative systems. What is more, as regards shared property, the use of the term anticommons obscures the actual situation: the simple legal terms covering the concept of co-ownership have already accurately described the nature of the unique normative challenge: *co*-ownership as

[17] The Civil Law, for example, has always had a traditional reticence towards this equal state of indivision or undivided co-ownership. It historically allowed parties to force a partition and sale at any point, often as a right that could not be waived. See, e.g., Article 815 of the French Code Civil. Recent modifications allow those in indivision to bind themselves to remaining in that state of co-ownership, though only for fixed periods: see Articles 1873ff.

among equals. So what is needed is not a new, overly wide umbrella term that seems to create some sense of inevitably or normative gravitas, but rather a reform of known, specific co-ownership institutions: where, for example, co-ownership is a structure that extends beyond family contexts, it will require specific and corrective formal norms to fill in the normative gaps heretofore dealt with by informal family norms. This will allow the institution of co-ownership to be effective, or reformed effectively where deemed wanting, without the additional intellectual baggage added by the concept of the anticommons.

It is equally important to note that property governance systems attempt to classify the objects of private property rights, unfortunately often called 'property' in English, but better expressed as *biens* in French or *beni* in Italian.[18] Thus, the categorization of realty and personalty or of immovable and movable, practical processes such as the metes and bounds description of land or bornage, the registration of charges and rights registered against parcels of land in a land register, the elaboration of essential features of an institution such as the fixation requirement in copyright or the patent description and claim, all address this fundamental impulse to describe accurately the bounds of an object of property in order to focalize the rights (i.e., set out, fragment, limit) that which may be possible with respect to the object.

With proper regard to the question of what actually is the object of property, some of the purported examples of the anticommons turn out not to pertain to the same object of property, at least as legally defined. The best example of this is that of the patent. To the extent that some would call a patent right a species of private property right – I have no truck with that – the object of property is that which is defined in the patent registration: that is, the substance of what is contained in the description and the claim. Heller's observation that the numerous drug patents necessary to create a better treatment for Alzheimer's will be subject to the veto of a single hold-out is a very real problem known as the 'patent thicket'. Strictly speaking, however, the thicket is *not* an anticommons, as each individual patent is a separate object of property. It is only by calling a grouping of all of the individual patents by the moniker of a larger object – a sewing machine, a drug cocktail, a Blackberry or an iPhone – that we get to apply the term anticommons. Admittedly this is a rather legalistic technical point, but it illustrates something much more fundamental:

[18] For better or for worse, even the officially bilingual Civil Code of Quebec falls into this practice.

the anticommons concept may not be an adequate construct to address the context or phenomenon of *adjacent* property rights, whether they be located in a series of drug patents or in a neighbourhood in Montreal. Larger collective action will be necessary to govern the case of adjacent property rights, and here as well the anticommons label may obscure the real problem, which specifically is a lack of cooperation among actors or a failure to understand the (limited) nature of their own particular property right where the rights functions as part of a larger whole.

All this points me to the conclusion – at once intuitive and technical – that legal systems and property structures have tended to deal quite well with complex and overlapping interests in the same resource. This is particularly true over time, as legal systems evolve: law reform ensures that poor fragmentation is rectified, as is the ongoing case in Russia. An additional conceptual structure does not add much and, if one is profligate with the use of the word ownership, perhaps it even tends to mischaracterize rights. In any event, such an additional construct is not necessary to understand the essence of property objects and relations, or indeed of good ordering.

2.3 Intellectual property governance

Some additional attention must be paid to intellectual property governance. Both copyright and patent are governance schemes that are specific to certain kinds of intellectual resources. I have already mentioned the point, using the example of adjacent patents and copyright fixation, that such 'resources' need to be identified (and in a way that traditional resources need not). It remains for intellectual property rights and duties, as I have argued elsewhere, to be fashioned according to the teleology of the intellectual property institution and the nature of the intellectual resource.[19] In one fundamental sense, each structure addresses the question of allocation of rights and duties over newly 'created' resources. In patents, this means the according of a strong monopoly for a period of twenty years over a narrowly defined invention. In copyright, this means

[19] See David Lametti, 'Laying Bare an Ethical Thread: From IP to Property to Private Law?' in Shyamkrishna Balganesh (ed.), *Intellectual Property and the Common Law* (Cambridge University Press, 2013); 'On Creativity, Copying and Intellectual Property' in Roberto Caso (ed.), *Plagio e Creatività: Un Dialogo tra Diritto e altri Saperi* (Università di Trento, 2011), p. 171; and 'The Virtuous P(eer): Reflections on the Ethics of File Sharing' in A. Lever (ed.), *New Frontiers in the Philosophy of Intellectual Property* (Cambridge University Press, 2011), p. 284.

the according of a more narrowly defined set of rights over a longer period of time. While the structure of each aims as a matter of practical governance to reduce the frequency of overlapping rights, neither will succeed completely. Again, however, as was the case with traditional property, the challenges of governing fragmented rights hardly necessitates the need for a new descriptive or conceptual term.

As regards patents, it has already been pointed out that what Heller and Eisenberg have called the patent anticommons had already been called the 'patent thicket'. This challenge to patent *ordering* is a long-standing problem going back to aviation and sewing machines, and is now seen in other high technology sectors such as pharmaceutical patents and in a variety of digital technology applications. The problem, which I have argued is essentially one of adjacent patents, results from the structure of patent law itself, in which rights are defined narrowly. This narrow definition, meant to restrict the scope of any given patent from according a monopoly that is too wide, turns out to be counterproductive in areas where multiple patents must interoperate in order for certain kinds of inventions to be developed and marketed. The central challenge with the patent thicket is that which is present throughout much of traditional intellectual property law: the according of a monopoly right against the backdrop of a profound scepticism against granting such monopolies.

The solution, however, lies not in a new label but rather in the formal and informal solutions that have been identified in resolving this tension. Patent pools, for example, have long been an informal normative solution whereby patent-holders coordinate among themselves in order to render more effective the challenges of both using multiple patents among the various patent owners and the task of making the technologies available to others for other applications, thereby eliminating hold-outs. Formally, the possibility of compulsory licensing, and even expropriation, remain solutions for situations in which some patent-holders do not allow their technology to be used. Finally, the complexity and cost of the current configuration of narrow patenting in pharmaceutical and technological contexts have lead some to argue for more fundamental overhauls of the patent system. Ultimately, the term anticommons is at best unhelpful, at worst misdescriptive, in helping us arrive at real conceptual and practical solutions.

As regards copyright, the use of the term anticommons is based on a conception of copyright rights that is simply too absolute. Unlike patent, copyright's 'monopoly', while much longer in terms of duration, is much less watertight in terms of powers accorded. Copyright's monopoly is thin.

It is meant to protect against copying of a substantial part of the work for economic gain, but is not meant to protect against the use of insubstantial parts of the work for any purpose (including economic purposes) or indeed more substantial parts for the purposes of fair use or fair dealing (usually non-economic). The fact that digital technology has allowed for a more rigorous control of the work by an owner while simultaneously according a power enabling new kinds of uses (such as digital sampling) that were heretofore inconceivable presents a number of formal and ethical challenges to the institution and its participants.[20] But calling such a situation an anticommons both misdescribes the nature of copyright and fails to get us any closer to a solution at a practical or ethical level. The problem lies in understanding the nature of copyright, its balances, and its ethical goals as an institution, such as knowledge curation.[21]

2.4 *Hold-outs are hold-outs*

It is often the case that owners hold out, within the legitimate scope of their demarcated property or intellectual property rights. Here I do not mean relying on an absolutist picture of copyright to resist fair use or fair dealing – such overreach is an instance of 'copyfraud', and is dealt with below – or using one's alleged patent rights as a troll would.[22] There are cases where hold-outs are legally justified. Hold-outs may not be morally justified, and may be abusive, and here I would hope to see the civil law doctrine of *abus de droit* incorporated more fully into the common law and intellectual property law in order to align the moral and the legal implications, and to ensure rights are maintained for positive reasons.[23] Whatever the case, the hold-out problem is not equal to the challenge

[20] See generally Lametti, 'The Virtuous P(eer)'.

[21] See Lametti, 'On Creativity, Copying and Intellectual Property'. See also Michael J. Madison, 'Beyond Creativity: Copyright as Knowledge Law' (2010) 12 *Vanderbilt Journal Entertainment & Technology Law* 817 (knowledge and learning as the central goals of copyright norms); 'Beyond Invention: Patent as Knowledge Law' (2011) 15 *Lewis & Clark Law Review* 71 (knowledge and learning as the central goals of patent); and 'Knowledge Curation' (2011) 86 *Notre Dame Law Review* 1957.

[22] Jason Mazzone, *Copyfraud and Other Abuses of Intellectual Property Law* (Palo Alto: Stanford University Press, 2011).

[23] See Pierre-Emmanuel Moyse, 'L'abus de droit: l'anténorme – Partie 2' (2012) 58 *McGill Law Journal* 1 (using *abus de droit* as a principle in IP governance); Kathryn Judge, 'Rethinking Copyright Misuse' (2004) 57 *Stanford Law Review* 901 (any attempt by a copyright-holder to effectively expand the purview of copyright protection to gain control over an idea or deter fair use constitutes misuse); Dan L. Burk, 'Anti-Circumvention Misuse' (2003) 50 *UCLA Law Review* 1095 (anti-circumvention measures should not

identified by the tragedy of under-use. Hold-outs can occur in cases where overlapping rights or uncoordinated fragmentation is not present: a single property owner can hold out against expropriation in a situation where no one would question the legitimacy of the property institution. At best, the term hold-out is already more than adequate to identify a situation where individual decisions, within the scope of their legal powers, can impede others – governments, other owners, etc. – from acting as they otherwise might. At worst, the term anticommons or gridlock misdescribes the situation.

3 The role of property theory

Property and intellectual property theory help us understand the institutions of private property and ownership by forcing us to pay attention to property relationships and property's resources or objects. By extension, the words or terms used to describe private property relations – rights and duties – form part of an ethical discourse that helps to illuminate the teleology of private property institutions. A similar focus helps to illuminate the study of the tragedy of under-use.

Turning first to traditional property relationships, one turns to the idea of property rights and ownership and their scope. Whatever one might say by way of critique of some of Heller's structures and constructs, it is nevertheless true that his intuition is sound: if too many unstructured rights are created in a single resource, we might create a situation where the resource is prone to under-use. The civil law's bias against indivision or undivided co-ownership (joint tenancy to common lawyers) might be seen as a response to this kind of concern. What is the basis for this intuition?

In my view, one can only truly arrive at the tragedy of the anticommons if one's point of departure is overly rights-based. That is, one must use the term and concept of ownership in an absolutist fashion in order to arrive at the tragedy of under-use phenomenon. Otherwise, with a less absolute view of property or ownership rights, the tragedy of under-use will simply not arise. This type of position – perhaps distinctly American and ironically more closely tied to current trends in the common law – would then allow for a multiplicity of 'owners' with absolute interests in the same resource. I have already argued as to why this is not the case in practice:

undermine fair use); and Lametti, 'Laying Bare an Ethical Thread' (an ethical or virtuous thread in property theory and history as a grounding for *abus de droit*).

property systems historically have tried to regulate such situations, especially with respect to important resources, and have been relatively effective in doing so. Even Russia's transition challenges, in my view, could not be attributed uniquely, perhaps if at all, to such a phenomenon.

However, the same is true in theory as well. Even a full-blooded owner in theory does not have absolute rights over a resource, as noted above. Private property rights from the fullest to the least powerful, not to mention contractual rights such as real estate leases that resemble property rights in terms of the powers and privileges in their bundle (what civil law would call a *ius in rem trans personam*), all have limitations on some or many of the so-called incidents of property, or may exclude some of the incidents altogether. The point here is that if all 'owners' are limited in terms of the scope of their powers, the very possibility of the tragedy of under-use is circumscribed. The potentially destructive veto powers of the owner may very well not be present, thus precluding the possibility of their exercise. Put another way, the range of governance options that an individual owner may have can be limited: the range of excludability that an owner may have over others in the governance of a particular resource may vary.[24]

Thus the description of the tragedy of under-use as a situation where all 'owners' of interests in the resource are in a position to block certain changes takes as its starting position a point that gives each 'owner' an interest that is more absolute than property theory generally would permit in the same object. In reality, formal or informal limitations would deal with any conflicts that might arise and before they result in the blockage of a use or resource under-use. Take the example of property held jointly in a family or business context, the true tragedy-of-under-use situation. All are owners in theory over the whole resource. However, each is limited by the rights of the others in legal terms. Moreover, a family or business hierarchy – an older sibling, a parent or a managing partner – might be the person who informally acts as the owner. The point here is that it is difficult to arrive at the conception of the anticommons without using ownership absolutely.

In *Gridlock Economy* Heller has refashioned a property spectrum, as shown in Table 10.1. It would appear that the anticommons category consists only of absolute, and fragmented, property ownership: Harris's Aunt

[24] See Larissa Katz on ownership as excludability: 'Exclusion and Exclusivity in Property Law' (2008) *University of Toronto Law Journal* 275.

Table 10.1 *Heller's property spectrum*

Commons Property	Private Property	Anticommons Property

Source: Taken from Michael A. Heller, *Gridlock Economy: How Too Much Ownership Wrecks Markets, Stops Innovation, and Costs Lives* (New York: Basic Books, 2008), pp. 18ff.

Sally of 'totality ownership'.[25] (Recall that the mere fact of fragmentation is conceptually neutral: if done properly, rights should not overlap.) At the far right of the spectrum, no pun intended, rights appear to mean one can do anything one wants with one's property objects: including blocking, vetoing and holding out. With the exception of relatively low-value resources, such absolute rights over resources simply do not exist. Ownership rights in land are always limited by a congeries of different norms at different levels, and finally are limited by the omnipresent right of the state to expropriate.[26] If this is true, the anticommons is relegated to its original Michelman state: a hypothesis about a property right posited for the sake of advancing an argument. Once context is reintroduced in any actual property situation, and limitations on property rights are properly understood, the anticommons is emptied as a practical pathology describing an exaggeration of aspects of private property or ownership. In positing the anticommons as its own point on the spectrum, Heller is perhaps guilty of reifying an extreme form of absolute property ownership before proceeding easily to demolish it. In other words, he may be inadvertently guilty of constructing the anticommons for the purposes of critiquing it: the quintessential straw man.[27]

[25] James Harris called the idea of 'totality ownership' an Aunt Sally, 'erected to be knocked down': Harris, *Property and Justice*, p. 134.

[26] I take no stance at this stage on the balance and details of expropriation regimes, other than to say that few question the power of the state to expropriate for justified reasons and using appropriate legal means: the debate is over the standards for justification as well as proper process (all of which reflects and refracts through, of course, one's view of the relationship between the individual and the state).

[27] The commons does not need the anticommons in any conceptual sense. Henry Smith's semi-commons, Heller and Dagan's Liberal commons and Lee Anne Fennell's Mixed Ownership models are all still possible: see Henry E. Smith, 'Exclusion versus Governance: Two Strategies for Delineating Property Rights' (2002) 31 *Journal of Legal Studies* 453 at 480; Michael Heller and Hanoch Dagan, 'The Liberal Commons' (2001) 110 *Yale Law Journal* 549; and Lee Anne Fennell, 'Commons, Anticommons, Semicommons'

I would add that, anecdotally, it is my experience that some American scholars and thinkers have the greatest tendency to treat property in this most absolute fashion.[28] Perhaps the result of the constitutionalization of an absolutely framed property right, or perhaps the result of a history where land scarcity was not a large problem, there is certainly a dominant discourse in American property thinking that treats property as a fundamental, natural and absolute right. It is also an attitude that has permeated lay discourse. And perhaps as a result of a pendulum-like reaction to Soviet communism, from my own anecdotal experience in Russia, Heller is certainly right when he implies that the vision of private property in Russia in the mid 1990s may have also been extremely absolutist.

American legal scholarship, much to its credit, appears to be self-correcting. A group of scholars, a number of whom are or have been associated with the Cornell Law School, are making a substantial effort to remind us not only of private property's context and its limits, but also its obligations.[29] In sharing a scepticism with Heller about the negative impact of absolute property rights, these writers, in pointing out inherent and conceptual limits to ownership, render the additional conceptual construct of the anticommons unnecessary. I would go further. I have argued elsewhere that property theory and practice needs to account for property objects as well as property relations.[30] The objects of property, in terms of their separable value, reflect the various social and contextual aspects that comprise this value. That is to say, we value land, or buildings, or patents, because of deeply held and shared views over time of how such

in Kenneth Ayotte and Henry E. Smith (eds.), *Research Handbook on the Economics of Property Law* (London: Edward Elgar, 2011). I note also that none of this critique weakens what is ultimately useful in the various commons literatures cited by Heller, such as that of Elinor Ostrom, or which came later: see e.g. Elinor Ostrom, *Governing the Commons: The Evolution of Institutions for Collective Action* (Cambridge University Press, 1990); and Charlotte Hess and Elinor Ostrom (eds.), *Understanding Knowledge as a Commons: From Theory to Practice* (Cambridge, MA: MIT, 2007).

[28] Perhaps fittingly for Heller, grounded in a Russian example, see Richard Pipes for an example of a rather absolutist conception of private property: *Property and Freedom* (New York: Vintage, 1999).

[29] See, e.g., Gregory S. Alexander, Eduardo M. Peñalver, Joseph William Singer and Laura S. Underkuffler, 'A Statement of Progressive Property', (2009) 94 *Cornell Law Review* 743; Gregory S. Alexander, 'The Social-Obligation Norm in American Property Law' (2009) 94 *Cornell Law Review* 745; Peñalver, 'Land Virtues'; Gregory S. Alexander and Eduardo M. Peñalver (eds.), *Property and Community* (New York: Oxford University Press, 2010); and Lametti, 'The Concept of Property'.

[30] Lametti, 'The Concept of Property' and David Lametti, 'The Objects of Virtue' in Gregory S. Alexander and Eduardo M. Peñalver (eds.), *Property and Community* (New York: Oxford University Press, 2010), p. 1.

objects are valuable through use over time. Relations among individuals through these objects of property – the basic definition of property relations – reflect this social aspect. Property relations are conditioned by the nature of the object in question, and thus are comprised of object-specific rights and duties. The value of a storefront property on Tverskaya Street in Moscow, or a pharmaceutical patent in Montreal, are to be understood not just in terms of the rights held by the right-holder, but also the limits and duties that social context and obligations might impose on a particular object.

The focal point of the object of property makes it much easier to understand the limitations that might be imposed on owners in these contexts. Important resources such as land will be regulated by myriad property rules, some conferring rights and others imposing limits and duties. One might frame this argument in terms of the complete control over determining the uses to which resources are put that the Heller example seems to imply: such a complete control over a resource predicated by the concept of anticommons property is only possible for objects that have very little social value. As an object becomes more valuable, it is more likely to come with strings attached, land being the prime, traditional example. This recognition of limits might in a sense be enough to deal with any instances of negative effects that Heller describes through the construct of the anticommons.

However, there may even be situations where the value of the object might require some proactive responsibilities of stewardship or even some requirement of economic use. Take the example of a valuable pharmaceutical patent. Patent protection is afforded by the state for the purposes of the betterment of society. The teleologies to the resources created by patent – an overall teleology in the institution as a whole, made explicit by the patent bargain, as well as a specific teleology for the invention articulated in the functional claim made in the patent – effectively condition the patent right and help to determine its use. The temporary monopoly protection granted by the patent right is given in exchange for bringing the useful and innovative invention to society: failure to do so justifies the granting of compulsory licences to use or even outright revocation of the right.[31] Without a putting to use or a making available (for compensation, of course), the right is potentially lost. Anticommons analysis, effectively

[31] In the Canadian Patent Act these Articles are contained in ss. 65 (abuse of patent) and 66 (conditions for compulsory licences and revocation of the patent where compulsory licences will not suffice).

positing as it does an absolute right to the ownership of patent, obscures the nature of the patent bargain and the limited nature of patent ownership. It also takes the focus away from very real problems in the patent system itself – how patent descriptions and claims are made, verified and ultimately tested for validity (and the information cost problems that would be averted), and other negative practices of patent 'trolling', 'patenting around' and 'evergreening', for example – that are the real cause of the problems with the patent system.

The concept of the anticommons, by definition, appears to view such behaviour as acceptable or normal, when it is unethical in the patent context, and correctable. The terms anticommons and gridlock put the focus in the wrong place: on the fragmentation, and not on the unethical behaviour of certain patent owners. The problem is really that it is not always morally right or ethical to rely on the letter of one's rights. Patent owners need to understand this, the general population needs to understand this, and so do government authorities, who can be notoriously reticent to use compulsory licences as a tool to control the efficacy of patents and regulate blockages.

Equally misleading conceptually is that the concept of the anticommons does not distinguish among types of objects, and hence fails to fully comprehend the entitlements or types of entitlements at play. This is an exceptionally complicated and important structural feature of both private property and intellectual property: in the institution of property we relate *through* property resources. The objects of property help to shape the possibilities of property relationships. Their characterization, and the manner in which value is ascribed to them, are exceptionally enlightening. The value of a pool of patents, each patent necessary to give value to the other to make the drug or the smartphone, is perhaps indicative that the intellectual property institution – focused as it is on single patents – has not fully captured the reality of the objects and their relations. Reform of the institution, solving the patent thicket, needs to address this interrelationship. Labelling the problem as an anticommons obscures the situation (1) by misdiagnosing the problem at the legal level as one of overlapping rights in the same resource, and (2) at the level of identifying property objects failing to ask, legally or ethically, *how* or *why* we consider the group of patents to now constitute a single resource. This latter situation may very well have evolved – from many, little, narrow, but still singly-owned patents transformed in the eyes of most into a single, larger, wider, ownable resource – thus creating a new, complex rights coordination problem. However, it is crucial that we understand the *how* and the *why*, using an inquiry that eschews simple labels.

The same is true for copyright in the sampling example cited at the outset. Here the focus is on the scope of what have been called 'user rights' by a major Supreme Court in the Anglo-American copyright tradition,[32] and what elements of copyrighted works users may legitimately use – insubstantial samples, for example – to transform and create new musical works – or indeed visual works in the form of mash-ups.[33] It is not an anticommons as such, but is the result of the understanding of the proper scope of (limited) ownership rights in individual copyrighted works.

Most of us would not go so far as to impose an analogous duty on the part of the property owner of the Moscow storefront to develop the resource as might be imposed on a patent owner. The storefront owner might simply be a speculator. Nevertheless, the fact that we might be sympathetic to the lessee or owner who is being blocked from developing tells us that even without a full-blown obligation, there is an expectation on the part of society as to how this resource will be used. Perhaps for certain other sensitive resources or valuable objects of social wealth the expectation to use might translate into a full-blown duty, such as with arable land in a context where scarcity is common. This unique resource is not fungible in the way a storefront might be. Property systems do account for such sentiments,[34] and I have contended elsewhere that the more valuable the resource, the stronger the impulse and justification to attach limits

[32] In Canada, see *CCH Canadian Ltd.* v. *Law Society of Upper Canada* [2004] 1 S.C.R. 339 (effectively importing into Canadian 'fair dealing' jurisprudence a US-like 'fair use' test, and pitching fair dealing not as a mere limitation but as a user right). The *CCH* decision on fair dealing, a 9–0 unanimous decision written by the Chief Justice of Canada, was affirmed in principle and practice in five cases rendered in July 2012 (*Alberta (Education)* v. *Canadian Copyright Licensing Agency (Access Copyright)*, 2012 SCC; *Entertainment Software Association* v. *Society of Composers, Authors and Music Publishers of Canada*, 2012 SCC; *Re:Sound* v. *Motion Picture Theatre Association of Canada*, 2012 SCC; *Society of Composers, Authors and Music Publishers of Canada, SOCAN* v. *Bell*, 2012 SCC; and *Rogers Communications Inc* v. *Society of Composers, Authors and Music Publishers of Canada*, 2012 SCC), and especially in the *Access Copyright* and *SOCAN* v. *Bell* decisions.

[33] Recent reforms brought to the Canadian Copyright Act protect users' rights to create 'mash-ups' with elements of copyrighted works: s. 29.21.

[34] See e.g. William N. R. Mitchell and Catherine Mitchell, 'Replacing Private Property: The Case for Stewardship' (1996) 55 *Cambridge Law Journal* 566; Kevin Gray, 'Equitable Property' (1996) *Current Legal Problems* 157; Lametti, 'Laying Bare an Ethical Thread'; David Lametti, 'Prescription *à la recherche du temps*: In Search of Past Time (or Recognizing Things Past)' in M.-F. Bureau and M. Dévinat (eds.), *Les livres du Code Civil du Québec* (RDUS, 2013).

and duties.[35] A better understanding of the virtue ethics of ownership will help to channel resources to better uses.

What one might call private property's social aspect is grounded in this teleology. Private property is necessarily social in part because of its underlying value and purposes – human survival, human development and flourishing, and so on – coupled with its scarcity. In short, property is social because of its ethical dimensions and implications. Add to this the relative scarcity of objects of social wealth, its distributive impact and effect on justice, as well as its inherently controversial nature, and one realizes that the concept of private property is not as thin as the tragedy of the anticommons requires. Rather, all of these factors point clearly to a concept of property that is based on more than individual rights to exclusive use. Any attempt to describe the institution, or to frame its normative structure and assess its normative weight, must take these wider interests into account.[36]

Of course, the characterization of the object is of capital importance. A Moscow storefront or apartment has a physicality that seems not only to define its parameters but also situate it in context. Individual preferences and market forces will help to determine its separable value at any given point, and provide guidance for the type of property relations that the resource will bear.

The characterization of intangible resources is more challenging, but attention to the object can render unnecessary the resort to the anticommons structure. Take the example, already noted, of a series of interrelated and complex patents. Here each patent as described is an object in and of itself, so certainly the anticommons analysis does not add anything. As noted above, if a group of interrelated patents is blocked by the holder of a single base patent, the under-use is not a result of overlapping but rather adjacent rights in the same object. In any event, the patent bargain might be sufficient in forcing a solution.[37]

This fuller understanding of private property might be sufficient in and of itself to prevent most instances of the so-called tragedy of the

[35] All of this is part of a larger Aristotelian view of property that I am developing: see Lametti, 'The Objects of Virtue'; 'Laying Bare an Ethical Thread'; and David Lametti, 'The (Virtue) Ethics of Private Property: A Framework and Implications' in Alastair Hudson (ed.), *New Perspectives on Property Law, Obligations and Restitution* (London: Cavendish Press, 2003), p. 39.

[36] Lametti, 'The Concept of Property'.

[37] I have already noted above that, in practice, informal solutions such as patent pools and technology platforms have arisen.

anticommons. Most commonly, limitations on absolute ownership rights help such rights to 'cohabit' with other right holders in the same resource. And for certain extremely valuable resources, a potential duty to use, and the subsequent loss of rights where this is not done, certainly mitigates against the possibility of under-use.

4 The potential ubiquity of the anticommons

The observations on patents and the objects of property point to a larger general concern. Given the complexity of modern economic processes and the nature of wealth-creation processes that require 'assembly', if we do not pay attention to the object of property, then we may begin to see the anticommons in every economic situation where wealth-creation is hurt by the failure of actors to cooperate. Heller hints that the banking crisis in 2008–2009 had an anticommons dimension that needed exploration. Like the bogeyman, gridlock is now everywhere. If true, as a consequence of this ubiquity the anticommons loses its conceptual usefulness or disguises what is important: the problem of this ubiquity is not an anticommons as such, but rather that property rules are miscast as absolute. Only by addressing the latter conceptualization of the problem will we get at its core.

The real challenge becomes the governance of complex economic and social institutions, and while ownership of objects of property may be part of those institutions, property governance as such – as opposed to rules about, say, banking regulations or trade regulations – may not be the solution to the problem. Attaching the anticommons label may push the analysis into the property sphere, introducing words such as ownership and property that might then skew the debate. We need to be more careful before extending a property analysis, fundamentally posited on the limited nature of ownership rights (even where these ownership rights are correctly understood as limited in nature), across a wider swathe of regulatory and governance challenges.

What is more, the term anticommons seems to imply that there is one problem, and indeed one solution, to what are in reality complex problems grounded in specific contexts. It is not simply a question of too many owners of the same object: it is about the characterization of the objects, the kinds of rights in the resource, how they are divided and how they are governed. Using a simplistic label, as we have seen, will often prevent us from identifying the specific nature of any given problem, asking the right questions and finding the appropriate solutions. The complexity of the patent thicket is not the same as the complexity of the co-ownership of land over generations. Neither is it the same as the copyright sampling issue. The problems are different – adjacent rights versus the withering of intra-family normativity versus the rights to fair transformative uses – and require different kinds of analyses. A single label makes such analyses harder from the get-go.

5 Keeping the balance

The basic point of the anticommons is that an over-fragmentation of ownership rights in the same resource could lead to under-use. A balanced view of the component aspects of private property, as well as an understanding of property structures and their purposes, in my view provides enough suppleness to account for the insights provided by the anticommons construct. Property structures do try to prevent situations of conflicting rights and minimize under-use. And they do all this without much fanfare. This renders the struggle to prevent tragedies of under-use rather commonplace. Similarly, keeping property theory balanced between rights and limits, with some attention to potential duties and property's overall teleology, further limits the situations where tragedies of under-use might arise. If all this is true, we do not really need the additional complexity of a structure such as the anticommons to describe the phenomenon.

Keeping property structures as simple as possible allows for an account of property objects and relations that focuses on rights and duties and underlying philosophies and assumptions, and allows us to track both the value of resources over time and the evolving nature of resources. If situations such as Russian storefronts and communal housing blocks of the mid 1990s seem not to fit into existing structures, perhaps they are best understood as historical idiosyncrasies and relegated precisely to that: history.

Moreover, keeping property analysis focused on property relations will allow societies to focus more directly on the governance challenges cited by Heller – the patent system in a rapidly changing technological world, the nature of creation in the world of copyright, the regulation of banks and communications, and the challenges particular to transition economies – without the problems being unnecessarily obscured by absolutist property constructs and attitudes. Not all governance challenges are property challenges; every failure to cooperate is not an anticommons.

Indeed, to state the obvious, it may be that not every instance of regulatory gridlock is an instance of anticommons property ownership.

Finally, if the goal is to understand the limits of private property or intellectual property, and the negative impact of absolute ownership, whether it be land, patents or copyright, we simply need not do it indirectly through the imposition of an additional construct. There is plenty of very good property theory – traditional and intellectual – that does it directly. In this sense, the term anticommons, as is the case with Harris's hypothetical absolute of 'totality ownership', is perhaps most useful only as the hypothetical result of absolutist ownership originally posited by Michelman. In reality, in both theory and practice we are better served in these particular governance challenges by older, more accurate property and intellectual property concepts and, where deficient, their evolution and ultimately their specific reform.

11

The commons as a reverse intellectual property – from exclusivity to inclusivity

SÉVERINE DUSOLLIER

From its early history, intellectual property has been envisioned as the leading means of organizing and enhancing creation and innovation. Its underlying premise is that intellectual creation results in public goods, either works or inventions, that by nature are non-exclusive and non-rival. First, a public good lacks exclusivity in the sense that users can access the good without paying its price and the producer of such a good has no means to impede or exclude this free benefit. Mainly due to its intangibility, creation or innovation does not provide its creator with the power to exclude unauthorized users.[1] Consequently, users are tempted to act as free-riders by not paying any remuneration to access and use the asset, and producers of the good, through lack of revenue, might not produce it at a socially optimal level.

On the other hand, non-rivalry means that a resource can be used by someone without this use depriving anyone else of a similar use, nor diminishing the value of the resource.[2] Eating an apple prevents someone else from benefitting from the same fruit, or if I share it, each of us will eat only half of it. Conversely, intellectual creation can be listened to, viewed, read, exploited into a product or used as an invention by many persons simultaneously, its value not being reduced by such a concurrent application.

This feature of public goods generates a positive externality: the author or inventor contributes to the global welfare of the society that benefits

[1] See Harold Demsetz, 'Towards a Theory of Property Rights' (1967) 57 *The American Economic Review* 347; William M. Landes and Richard A. Posner, 'An Economic Analysis of Copyright Law' 28 *Journal of Legal Studies* 326. It should be noted that the lack of exclusivity will depend on the type of public good, the technological context and capacity for exclusion.

[2] Richard Watt, *Copyright and Economic Theory – Friends or Foes?* (Cheltenham: Edward Elgar, 2000), pp. 4–5.

from her creations or inventions. Should the creator not be able to recoup her creative investment, while users can copy and enjoy works and inventions at a low cost, the resulting market failure could lead to a lack of incentive to create and innovate, and subsequently to a suboptimal level of creation.

To counter this market failure, which is likely to have dire consequences on social wealth maximization, intellectual property rights are granted to works or inventions so as to confer exclusivity and rivalry not achievable by mere material possession. The economic justification of intellectual property is thus based on both incentivization and curing the market failure of public goods. In contrast, one explanation of tangible property is the preference given to private reservation over commons. In his famous article 'The Tragedy of the Commons',[3] Hardin argues against the commons on the ground that the simultaneous use of that resource by many individuals acting independently and according to each one's self-interest, would necessarily lead to overuse and depletion. Such overuse and depletion cannot occur with intangible resources such as creation and innovation, but leaving those in the commons, so the traditional story goes, might lead to underproduction. Exclusivity is hence preferred over common use, thereby enabling creators to reap the value of what they have created, preventing free-riding at their expense.

These traditional views about property, whether tangible or intellectual, have been much contested in recent years and the right to exclude others, which is the core of private property, is now considered to be less crucial. Value, both social and economic, has been found and reaped in the exploitation of non-exclusivity and non-rivalry and 'property theory today has largely escaped from Hardin's intellectual trap'.[4] Rather than being despised and portrayed as a tragedy, the 'commons' has started to gain momentum and to be understood equally as producing some wealth.

As early as 1986, Carol Rose investigated diverse cases of inherently public property with such a happy outcome that she coined the term a 'comedy of the commons' (to reverse Hardin's prediction).[5] Such regimes of properties devoted to collective and non-commercial uses enhance

[3] Garrett Hardin, 'The Tragedy of the Commons' (1968) 162 *Science* 1243.

[4] Joshua Getzler, 'Plural Ownership, Funds, and the Aggregation of Wills' (2009) 10 *Theoretical Inquiries in Law* 241.

[5] Carol Rose, 'The Comedy of the Commons: Custom, Commerce, and Inherently Public Property' (1986) 53 *University of Chicago Law Review* 711.

sociability and even 'achieve their highest value when they are accessible to the public at large'.[6] In the economic academy, Nobel Prize winner Elinor Ostrom has equally proven that value could be extracted from a sound and generally local organization of resources held in commons (such as pastures and irrigation systems).[7] Rather than government regulation or privatization, she demonstrated that a common pool resource can be best managed by community rules that are self-determined and adapted to local conditions and that the over-exploitation of unowned or commonly owned resources could be averted by the collective action of local users.

Property itself has equally been the target of criticism when excessive exclusivity threatens to reduce, rather than maximize, the social welfare, the tragedy coming in that case from 'anti-commons'.[8] The term was coined by Heller to refer to situations when 'there are too many owners holding rights of exclusion, [so] the resource is prone to underuse'.[9]

This regained interest in the commons has spilled over into intellectual property, where scholarship and experiments have tackled the notion of commons to call into question the idea of the necessity of property in creation and innovation. Commons, referring to resources lacking exclusivity, are widespread in intellectual property. They can result from the legal delineation of the exclusivity grant in copyright and patent, such as the public domain, limitations or exceptions. Alternatively, commons have emerged from private ordering initiatives,[10] through licensing, such as in open-source software, Creative Commons or even open-source patenting. Here copyright or patent owners opt for lack of exclusivity to enable sharing and further use and dissemination of their works or inventions, thereby putting these in the commons.

Beyond such theoretical and empirical descriptions in scholarship, concrete examples of economic value yielded from commons are the

[6] *Ibid.*, 722.

[7] Elinor Ostrom, *Governing the Commons: The Evolution of Institutions for Collective Action* (Cambridge University Press, 1990).

[8] Michael A. Heller, 'The Tragedy of the Anticommons: Property in the Transition from Marx to Markets' (1989) 111 *Harvard Law Review* 621; Michael A. Heller and Rebecca S. Eisenberg, 'Can Patents Deter Innovations? The Anticommons in Biomedical Research' (1998) 280 *Science* 698.

[9] Heller and Eisenberg, 'The Tragedy of the Anticommons', 624. For discussion, see David Lametti's contribution to this collection ('The Concept of the Anticommons').

[10] Niva Elkin-Koren, 'What Contracts Cannot Do: The Limits of Private Ordering in Facilitating a Creative Commons' (2005) 74 *Fordham Law Review* 375 at 398; Séverine Dusollier, 'Sharing Access to Intellectual Property through Private Ordering' (2007) 82 *Chicago-Kent Law Review* 1391.

digitization (and monetization by advertising) by Google Books of public domain works or the development of successful business models relying on open-source software. The European digital library, EUROPEANA, which is a web portal leading to a huge collection of dozens of European public libraries, is another example of value, more social and cultural than economic, generated by public exploitation of commons.

Such developments should at least question the figure of property and exclusivity in the way intellectual property organizes the relationship to creation and innovation. Such is the aim of this chapter, which purports to look at features of non-exclusivity in intellectual property and to what extent such new models of allocating and sharing resources should matter in creation and innovation.

Section 1 will try to clarify semantics and to bridge a gap that seems to exist between the economics literature and the legal literature in their definitions of the categories lying between commons and property. Section 2 will briefly explain what different commons are envisaged here and what licensing schemes have been developed in copyright and patent to share intellectual resources. Section 3 will assess the property or non-property features in different types of commons, from public domain to open or copyleft licensing, and will underline issues elicited by their undefined status in law. In conclusion, section 4 will propose the invention of a new legal concept, the 'inclusive right' to deal with situations in (intellectual) property where non-exclusivity needs some organization and ways of enforcement.

1 Notions of commons, non-exclusivity and inclusivity

In order to cure the market failure resulting from the public goods problem associated with intangible resources, intellectual property rights create exclusivity. An exclusive right is a legal prerogative to perform an action or enjoy a resource and to deny others the same privilege. Exclusivity is the power to exclude, but it does not intrinsically lead to exclusion, as property is rather conceived as a power to decide to engage in exclusion or not.

I would employ the idea of the commons to describe situations where exclusivity is absent. Commons is not the opposite of property, as it could arise from exclusive property rights and encompass more than the mere lack of (intellectual) property to cover a broad range of intellectual resources or creation in which no exclusivity is exercised, or is exercised in a way that actually reverses such exclusivity to openness and inclusivity. In Hohfeldian terms,[11] property engenders rights and powers, whereas a commons creates privileges and immunities for the public, whether defined or undefined depending on the beneficiaries of the common use.[12]

One could also say that when a resource lacks exclusivity, the persons holding it in common enjoy inclusive entitlements. I will not at this stage elaborate as to whether these entitlements should be called rights, powers or privileges (a tricky question), but I will rather opt for the terminology of 'inclusivity' as the hallmark of commons.[13]

Inclusivity, a terminology that will lead to normative consequences discussed further at the end of this chapter, indicates the key nature of an entitlement in a good that essentially lacks any exclusivity, but has to compromise with the parallel entitlements of others. Commons are characterized by inclusivity as they are un-owned or owned in common. Anyone holding a privilege to use the resource is required to allow the same use from others. In other words, the lack of exclusivity that marks the resource held in common mirrors the inclusiveness that characterizes each separate prerogative enjoying by the commoners.

Another perception of such inclusiveness could be what Yochai Benkler has recently referred to as 'freedom-to-operate under symmetric constraints', in opposition to the asymmetric power of property.[14] One could understand this symmetry as inclusivity as it means that users enjoying such freedom have to accommodate the similar freedoms enjoyed by others and are devoid of any exclusivity, which can be defined as asymmetric power.

This symmetric freedom could serve, for Benkler, to unify the many commons analysed in economic and legal scholarship. This attempt at

[11] Wesley N. Hohfeld, 'Fundamental Legal Conceptions as Applied in Judicial Reasoning' (1913) 23 *Yale Law Journal* 16 and (1916) 26 *Yale Law Journal* 710.

[12] For an application of Hohfeld's legal terminology to commons, see Yochai Benkler, 'Between Spanish Huertas and the Open Road: A Tale of Two Commons?' (Paper presented at the 'Convening Cultural Commons' conference at New York University, 23–24 September 2011).

[13] Peter Drahos (see 'A Defence of Intellectual Commons' (1996) 16 *Consumer Policy Review* 101 at 102) has used the notion of inclusiveness in one paper to define commons in which all individuals are recognized as holding rights in common, equating inclusive commons with universal, compared to what he called an exclusive common in which the use of resources is confined to a particular group. I would depart from that categorization as the terminology of 'inclusive' refers, in my perspective, to the fact that the entitlement that one user enjoys in a resource has to count with entitlements enjoyed by other persons whom she cannot exclude.

[14] Benkler, 'Between Spanish Huertas'.

unification is not an easy task. Indeed, the two academic fields do not use the same notions of property and commons, or rather the continuum from property to commons is conceived differently from an economic or legal perspective. The notion of inclusivity developed here could pursue the same objective, as it enables us to carry out a similar analysis in the legal and economic fields as to the places and degrees of exclusivity or non-exclusivity from property to commons.

1.1 From property to commons in economy

In economy, property and commons are generally situated along a demarcating line characterized by exclusivity. Property can be defined in the economic literature as the entitlement to determine how to use a resource and who owns that resource. It is not synonymous with ownership and notions such as open-access property are used by economic literature to describe a situation where nobody owns a resource. In fact, only private property equals exclusivity and rivalry in economic understanding.

By referring to commons, on the other hand, economic research tends to designate resources held in common and shared. Property can subsist in commons and both property and commons are often mixed. Elinor Ostrom, for instance, has investigated the so-called commons property regime applying to sets of resources that are, compared to private property, non-excludable but rivalrous, and whose use, preservation and consumption are regulated by a particular social arrangement. Though apparently an oxymoron, the conjugation of commons and property serves to refer to those instances where there might be property rights in a resource, but these are held or managed in common, with the objective of sharing the use of the resource. Famous examples in economic research are fisheries,[15] irrigation systems,[16] pastures, waters and so on.[17] Under that framework, property should not be understood in a legal sense, but will encompass any regime describing the bundle of rights that persons, one or many, can enjoy in a resource.

All forms of property are thus envisaged in a continuum, ranging from open-access regimes, common-property regimes (the one favoured

[15] James M. Acheson, *The Lobster Gangs of Maine* (Hanover, NH: University Press of New England, 1988).

[16] Ostrom, *Governing the Commons*.

[17] See also for new types of commons, Charlotte Hess, 'Mapping the New Commons' (2008), available at http://ssrn.com/abstract=1356835 or http://dx.doi.org/10.2139/ssrn.1356835 (last accessed 11 April 2013).

by Ostrom's research) to private property. The difference between open-access regimes and common property is that no one has the legal right to exclude anyone from using a resource in the former, where members of a clearly defined group have the right to exclude non-members from using that resource in the latter.[18]

Exclusivity is thus gradual, from completely open commons to commons-property regimes and finally to property.

1.2 From property to non-property in law

All literature on commons in law, and particularly in intellectual property, is influenced by economics. This can be explained by two main factors. The first one comes from the emergence of the commons scholarship in economic thinking. Economists[19] have been at the forefront of tackling the notion of commons and analysing regimes, allocating resources in a collective and shared manner under the 'commons' label. The other scientific disciplines, when eventually addressing the issue of commons, have naturally followed and borrowed semantics and architecture from this first body of knowledge, even though that notion might already have some prehistory in their field (which was the case of commons in law).

The second factor is more geographic, as research on commons in law and in intellectual property started to develop in United States doctrine before spreading to other parts of the world. The extensive literature on the commons inherited from the USA cannot be strictly connected to legal or economic fields, as the boundary between both is more porous and more easily crossed by American legal scholars. This is all the more true in research about commons if one remembers that the Nobel Prize-winning work of Ostrom has veered away from traditional micro-economics to focus on institutions and their operation. No surprise then that it had some appeal in the legal academy interested in the role of institutions[20] and the way in which they organize allocation of resources and norms about such use.

18 Charlotte Hess and Elinor Ostrom, 'Ideas, Artifacts and Facilities: Information as a Common Pool Resource' (2003) 66 *Law & Contemporary Problems* 111 at 121. See also the difference proposed by Merges between wide-open commons and commons pools: Robert P. Merges, 'Property Rights Theory and the Commons: The Case of Scientific Research' (1996) 13 *Social Philosophy and Policy* 145.

19 With the notable exception of legal scholar Carol Rose in 'The Comedy of the Commons'.

20 Carol Rose, 'Ostrom and the Lawyers: the Impact of Governing the Commons on the American Legal Academy' (2011) 5 *International Journal of the Commons* 28.

From a civil law perspective, the transposition of concepts developed in law and economics around the twin notions of property and commons is more hazardous due to the gap between the legal positivism of civil law and the more open system of US jurisprudence and scholarship (which is more welcoming to law and economics methodology, for instance). For that reason, translation of concepts of commons or even property is not as straightforward as it seems to be. This is particularly true of the concept of 'property' which conveys different meanings and has more or less scope in common law and civil law traditions. Property in civil law or *droit de propriété* refers to a determined right vested in a thing (*droit réel*) and is understood as being the most complete and absolute right one can enjoy in an asset. Comparatively, property in common law is a broader concept and can encompass several situations where a person has some exclusive rights, though maybe not absolute, to use a resource.

To continue on comparative law grounds, the notion of commons exists in different forms in common law or civil law regimes. Common law recognizes different types of ownership that have been qualified as commons in the past, designating communal ownership motivated by public interest or common rights to use some land.[21]

Likewise, civil law recognizes a notion of commons surviving from Roman law:[22] the *res communes*. Defined by the French civil code as 'resources that belong to no one and whose use is common to all',[23] the *choses communes* are characterized by two features: the lack of appropriation and collective use. The scholarship that has recently rediscovered the notion[24] insists on the fact that the lack of property is not accidental but essential. The resource is not subject to appropriation, and hence cannot be qualified as a 'good'. Lack of property can indeed result from the nature of the thing, as in the case of air, sea, radio spectrum, but it is strengthened by a normative decision to exclude some things from the category of private property. One example is the public domain in intellectual property where the definition of strict conditions and a limited term for protection creates a normative impossibility of holding exclusive rights therein.

[21] See Lynda L. Butler, 'The Commons Concept: An Historical Concept With Modern Relevance' (1982) 23 *William & Mary Law Review* 835.

[22] After having been forgotten in medieval times, the notion of *res communes* suddenly reappeared when the Civil Code was drafted in 1804.

[23] Article 714 of the French civil code : 'il est des choses qui n'appartiennent à personne et dont l'usage est commun à tous' (my translation).

[24] Marie-Alice Chardeaux, *Les Choses Communes* (Paris: LGDJ, 2006).

Roman law has also transmitted to civil code the notion of *res nullius*, that is things that do not belong to anyone but, contrarily to *res communes*, are open to exclusive rights. *Res nullius* is thus a property-to-be and anyone who uses it first, by taking hold thereof will thereby gain an exclusive right of property. For that reason, a *res nullius* cannot be considered as a commons.

In comparison to the economic classification of property and commons, where both are interlaced and form a continuum of decreasing exclusivity, in law, property and commons (*choses communes*) should be considered as opposites. The *res communes* is impermeable to exclusivity and should be organized accordingly. Property is thus the domain of exclusivity, whereas commons is the domain of non-exclusivity. The separation of these concepts is less evident in common law, where commons can also include situations of property. Rules about co-ownership, intentional community and patent pools could be defined as commons-property regimes to the extent that they organize the use of things held in common but on the basis of property rights. Such things owned in common also exist in civil law, but they will be absorbed by the 'property' category, lacking the subtleties developed by economic theory on the commons.

1.3 From intellectual property to commons

Interestingly, the opposition between commons and property posited by intellectual property law occupies a middle ground between economic thinking and more general legal discourse. Research in the discipline of economics has, in particular, espoused the development of open access in intellectual property, also referred to as open innovation.[25]

The notion of the commons is nonetheless confusing in IP, for it is used without a unified terminology or regime. In scholarship, recourse to the notion serves to designate no-rights situations, such as the public domain, as well as rights-based situations, such as copyleft licensing or even patent pools (that create regimes akin to the economic notion of common-property regimes). Therefore, the concept of the commons is used to describe situations opposed to intellectual property, as in the legal opposition between property and *res communes*, and situations where property rights subsist, as in the commons-property regimes studied in

[25] See the 2012 EPIP Congress, *IP in Motion, Opening Up IP*, Leuven, 27–28 September 2012.

economics. The subpart of the commons therefore crosses both intellectual property and the public domain. In fact, the sole unifying feature could be the lack of exclusivity that will gradually increase from the public domain (no exclusivity), to open-access schemes (no exclusivity granted by exclusive rights), and in the final stage the full exclusivity of intellectual property rights exercised in a traditional and exclusionary manner.

2 The commons in intellectual property: from public domain to open licensing

Obvious candidates for commons and inclusivity can be found in intellectual property: the public domain, exceptions to exclusive rights and open-access or copyleft licensing. The public domain in intellectual property is indeed the primary contender for the category of commons. Defined as the intellectual resources that are not protected by copyright or patent, or no longer so protected (works or inventions fallen into the public domain), the public domain essentially lacks any exclusivity as no one can claim a right in the work or invention.[26]

The public domain is generally defined in the negative, as what copyright and patent law do not protect. It is composed of elements that are by themselves unprotected, whatever the circumstances of their use. The collective rights of access and use that define it are premised on the absence of an exclusive right thereto. On the face of it, it is the reverse analysis of what is protected by IP; it is what is left over once the existence of an IP right is established.

In copyright, the public domain comprises ideas, unprotected by operation of the idea–expression dichotomy, unoriginal works, excluded works (such as official texts in many countries or works lacking fixation in others) and works whose term of protection has ended. Works in which authors have decided to dedicate to the public domain could be added to this list, although the legitimacy of such relinquishment of copyright is controversial.[27]

[26] A more neutral term of 'resource' should be used here as some parts of the public domain will include resources that cannot claim copyright or patent protection as they are neither 'works' (mere ideas or facts) nor 'inventions' (discoveries, scientific rules or methods, abstract concepts).

[27] Pamela Samuelson, 'Challenges in the Mapping of the Public Domain' in Lucie Guibault and P. Bernt Hugenholtz (eds.), *The Future of the Public Domain – Identifying the Commons in Information Law* (The Hague: Kluwer Law International, 2006), p. 9; Séverine Dusollier, *Scoping Study on the Public Domain in Copyright and Related Rights* (Geneva: WIPO, 2011). This is also discussed in this collection by Robert Burrell and

In patents, abstract ideas, discoveries, inventions that do not satisfy the protection requirements by lack of novelty, of inventiveness or of industrial application, excluded subject-matter, expired inventions, (voluntarily or not) unregistered inventions, constitute the public domain.

Those elements, works or inventions, can be described as commons as they are deprived of intellectual property, hence of exclusivity. That does not mean, however, that other forms of reservation or exclusivity cannot be gained by contract, secrecy or technological restraints. Also some inventions may be excluded from intellectual property but are not deemed, as a consequence, to serve an inclusive and shared use: this is the case notably of inventions ineligible to patent on grounds of *ordre public*. Whilst theoretically in the public domain, methods of human cloning, for instance, will not create a collective right to use this invention, for the process of exclusion aims here at barring its free use or exploitation altogether.

One can also look at inclusivity not as the equivalent of non-property, but as equally embracing situations where property in a creation or invention coexists with spaces of non-exclusivity (voluntarily or not). Limitations and exceptions are indeed characterized by a lack of exclusivity: my privilege to make a private copy of a copyrighted work is not exclusive and does not prevent anyone else from benefitting from and exercising the same entitlement.[28] Accordingly, exceptions and limitations in copyright and patent can be qualified as commons as they grant privileges of use to users, either indiscriminately (e.g. parody or private copying of a work, private use of invention) or only to some defined categories (e.g. libraries for libraries' exceptions in copyright, researchers for research exception in patent). Elsewhere[29], I have argued that limitations to intellectual property rights could even be embraced by the concept of the public domain, where the latter would be split into two parts. The first one could be called the *structural public domain*, encompassing resources not protected by copyright or patent. On the other hand, from a functional perspective, exceptions to copyright or patent operate as a

Emily Hudson in their chapter, 'Property Concepts in European Copyright Law: the Case of Abandonment'.

[28] This lack of exclusivity is precisely what makes it difficult to qualify a copyright exception as a genuine right, at least in civil law terms, where a subjective right contains some dose of exclusivity. In common law, the question of qualification of an exception as a right would be differently phrased, as it would depend on the existence of a remedy of some kind.

[29] Dusollier, *Scoping Study on the Public Domain*, pp. 8–9.

public domain for they entitle anyone (or anyone in the privileged category) to use the creation or innovation. Openness here is not then linked to the resource itself but is circumstantial. This is what one could call the *functional public domain.*

The last figure in the inclusivity field of intellectual property is rather recent. It is the open innovation movement, ranging from open-source software (the origin of the concept) to creative commons and open patent. These offspring of the rampant contestation of intellectual property propose new ways of exercising intellectual property, both in ideological and legal terms.[30]

The open-source software movement initiated the development of a model of distribution insisting on the freedom to run and use a program and to copy, modify, improve and redistribute it. It also insists on the core obligation arising from such licences – the obligation to provide the source code of the software.[31] Invented by Richard Stallman as the GPL licence, which is still the archetypal open-source licence, the principle of free software has since developed into more than one hundred licences worldwide. The concept of freedom to use and share a protected work has eventually been taken over by Lawrence Lessig and his Creative Commons project which aims to develop a set of licences[32] allowing authors of copyrighted works to grant similar freedoms to use, copy, modify and distribute their works.[33]

Contagion of the open-source mechanism has even spread beyond copyright and entered the patent field.[34] Open licensing might appear as antinomic to patents as exclusive rights are what enables the recouping of the cost of an invention and its patenting; this is a very different

[30] Séverine Dusollier, 'Sharing Access to Intellectual Property through Private Ordering' (2007) 82 *Chicago-Kent Law Review* 1391.

[31] See the open source definition and its 'ten commandments'.

[32] Besides developing licences applicable outside of software, Creative Commons departs from the open-source model used in software by giving the author choices between different licences. Each licence grants diverse rights to the user. When deciding to license her work under Creative Commons, an author can choose whether she will allow the work to be modified by the user, whether she wants to limit uses of her work to non-commercial purposes and whether she wants to oblige the user to grant the same freedom of use when the latter modifies the work and publicly communicates the derivative work. Regardless of which Creative Commons licence the author chooses, a work should be attributed to its author when it is disseminated.

[33] See Lawrence Lessig, *Free Culture: How Big Media Uses Technology and the Law to Lock Down Culture and Control Creativity* (New York: Penguin, 2004), pp. 183–200.

[34] Sara Boettiger and Dan L. Burk, 'Open Source Patenting' (2004) 1 *Journal of International of Biotechnology Law* 221.

situation from copyright where the cost of acquiring the copyright is minimal (but the cost of creation can be high). Against all odds, however, open source has also been tested for patented inventions, mainly in life sciences. The most well-known working example is the Biological Open Source (BiOS) License, developed by CAMBIA, an Australian non-profit research institute from the Centre for Applications of Molecular Biology in International Agriculture. Two patents owned by this research centre are made available on conditions that resemble open source: the licence provides for a worldwide, non-exclusive, royalty-free right to make and use the technology, and includes a mechanism guaranteeing that any improvement of its technology remains free to use for all participants in the initiative. Other initiatives exist in patents.[35]

From open-source software to open patenting, all can be described as commons, as they renounce any exclusive claim in the work or invention, opting instead to grant inclusive freedoms to use and share the resource in a non-exclusive way. Those commons differ from the public domain and exceptions in many regards.

Contrary to the previous two categories,[36] such inclusivity is triggered by exclusive rights. Indeed, open-source licences generally assert a copyright or patent right in the object they govern. This was deemed to be the only strategy to ensure that no one could jeopardize openness by claiming some exclusivity, either by an intellectual property right or by a contract, on the creation or on an improved one. As Carol Rose aptly said, 'the Creative Commons idea, however, is very much a modernist kind of property'.[37]

First, the inclusivity is created by contract, through a licence,[38] and thus by the exercise of an exclusive right and by the author or patent owner

[35] See Janet Hope, 'Open Source Genetics: A Conceptual Framework' in Geertrui Van Overwalle (ed.), *Gene Patents and Collaborative Licensing Models. Patent Pools, Clearinghouses, Open Source Models and Liability Regimes* (Cambridge University Press, 2009), p. 171; Geertrui Van Overwalle, 'Of Thickets, Blocks and Gaps: Designing Tools to Resolve Obstacles in the Gene Patents Landscapes' in Geertrui Van Overwalle (ed.), *Gene Patents and Collaborative Licensing Models* (Cambridge University Press, 2009), p. 381; Arti K. Rai, 'Open and Collaborative Research: A New Model for Biomedicine' in Robert W. Hahn (ed.), *Intellectual Property Rights in Frontier Industries: Software and Biotechnology* (Washington DC: AEI Press, 2005), pp. 131, 137.

[36] In the public domain there are no exclusive rights at all, whether they are non-existent or they have lapsed, while in exceptions the exclusive rights are unenforceable or stop at that territory.

[37] Rose, 'Ostrom and the Lawyers', 24.

[38] The qualification of an open-source or Creative Commons licence as a contract is disputed, particularly under US law.

herself. This is not paradoxical if one adheres to the view that intellectual property is about exclusivity and not about exclusion – the terms not being synonymous. Exercising exclusive rights in copyright or a patent does not necessarily lead to the exclusion of others but could also include them in the use of the work or invention. In other words, in the case of open source, exclusive rights create inclusive entitlements (that are contractual rights) to the benefit of any user of the work or invention.[39]

Such recourse to contract to create freedoms has been criticized by some[40] as it relies on a private-ordering norm (the contract), which has been usually decried as disrupting the balance of IP regimes. Another effect is that such reliance on contract results in privileges only effective against the licensor or the copyright or patent owner. They are not rights against the world as property would be.

An advantage of the contractual tool is that it permits the owner to assert intellectual property rights in a work or invention and not to relinquish it in the public domain where its free use could not effectively be protected, as we will see below. Most open-access schemes intend to make any reconstitution of exclusivity impossible, hence sustaining a commons regime, and to leverage the exclusive rights of copyright or patents to guarantee and maintain the public accessibility of works and inventions and of derivative creations. In other words, commons-based initiatives 'create a self-binding commons rather than an unrestricted public domain'.[41]

The legal mechanism enabling such contagion or virality is called copyleft. The term was first used to describe all systems aiming at leaving creations open, through its opposition to 'copyright', in a play on words: opposition between the right and the left (considered as more progressive) aligns with the opposition between the exclusive *right* and the *left* referring to the waiver of copyright. The terminology also referred to the viral effect of some licences.[42]

[39] Or only to some users as the copyleft licences can discriminate between users, as it is often the case in open patenting and would be the result of opting for a Creative Commons non-commercial licence.

[40] See Niva Elkin-Koren, 'What Contracts Cannot Do: The Limits of Private Ordering in Facilitating a Creative Commons' (2005) 74 *Fordham Law Review* 375 at 398; Séverine Dusollier, 'The Master's Tools v. The Master's House: Creative Commons v. Copyright' (2006) 29 *Columbia Journal of Law & Arts* 271.

[41] Amy Kapczynski, Samantha Chaifetz, Zachary Katz and Yochai Benkler, 'Addressing Global Health Inequities: An Open Licensing Approach for University Innovations' (2005) 20 *Berkeley Technology Law Journal* 1031 at 1072.

[42] Not all open-access licences are copyleft. This is generally the case for open-source software, but there will be a copyleft effect only for Creative Commons licences opting for the Share Alike feature.

Under the copyleft clause, the freedom to improve or modify the work or invention is conditional on the obligation to distribute the modified work or invention under similar conditions of inclusiveness. This legal trick thus aims at contaminating any modified or improved work or invention first licensed under such a scheme and endeavours to attach the sharing norm to the intellectual resource itself – not only to the contractual parties.[43] The copyleft feature can lead to a particular provision or regulation applying to any user of the work or invention – almost equating the contract to a right against the world.

3 Legal organization of non-exclusivity

Though economic scholarship has addressed the topic of commons for many years, it has mostly led to a description of the management of resources held in commons and of the way in which they might, or might not, elicit social benefit. Such research sometimes integrates a normative dimension that aims to establish the best organization of and use of assets lacking any exclusivity or whose owners have decided to share in a non-exclusive manner. In law, and more particularly in intellectual property, the focus is put on property as the best way to incentivize and exploit creation and innovation. Lack of exclusivity has always been regarded as a fault that needed correction. Even the recent research on commons in intellectual property is generally confined to a description of the irruption of commons in creation and innovation or to a description (and praise) of its mechanisms. In fact, this reflection aligns itself with the reluctance of IP to enter into the field of non-exclusivity, as demonstrated by the following examples. The non-exclusivity or sharing principle we have mentioned is marked by a lack of any legal organization. This raises questions of sustainability and resilience.

3.1 The negative status of the public domain

The public domain is generally defined as encompassing intellectual elements that are not protected by copyright or patent, or whose protection has lapsed due to the expiration of the duration for protection.[44] This limitation to unprotected elements portrays the public domain as a

[43] Dusollier, 'Sharing Access to Intellectual Property', 1414–16.

[44] For the divergences between different mappings of the public domain, see Samuelson, 'Challenges in the Mapping of the Public Domain', 9.

place detached from intellectual property rights. The touchstone of the definition being the lack of copyright protection, the public domain does not create any rights or defined legal entitlements for the public. One could say that the public domain is in a 'legal limbo'.[45]

The negativity of this definition does not help to give status to the public domain, but only reinforces the perception of it as an empty territory where no protection applies, either through an intellectual property right, or by a rule of positive protection against private reservation.[46] For instance, a work that has fallen into the public domain can still be reserved through another IP right (e.g. trademark, *sui generis* right in a database in the EU) or by a contract or a technological measure. Should an author decide to relinquish her copyright, this would only precipitate her work into a public domain where anybody is free to use it or to modify it, hence benefiting from a copyright in this derivative work. In the context of patents, the decision not to register a patent in an invention would result in non-patentability only in the case of a defensive publication of the invention, but it would not reach possible improvements of the invention. This lack of a definitive status of collectiveness is precisely the reason why proponents of copyleft schemes prefer a contractually constructed commons over the public domain. This reverse-definition of intellectual property can also explain the conundrum of traditional knowledge: lacking the requirements for protection (novelty, individual authorship), traditional knowledge and folklore answer to the Western notion of the public domain and are hence open to appropriation by others through copyright or patent.[47]

A few years ago, a French court limited the exercise of the copyright of two authors who had restored a public and historical square, the Place

[45] John Cahir, 'The Public Domain: Right or Liberty?' in Charlotte Waelde and Hector MacQueen (eds.), *Intellectual Property – The Many Faces of the Public Domain* (Cheltenham: Edward Elgar, 2007), p. 39.

[46] Severine Dusollier and Valerie Laure Benabou, 'Draw Me a Public Domain' in Paul Torremans (ed.) *Copyright Law: A Handbook of Contemporary Research* (Cheltenham: Edward Elgar, 2007), p. 161.

[47] Registering a patent in traditional knowledge would require that this knowledge is not public and does not destroy the novelty of the 'invention', or that other technical features are added to the knowledge to constitute a patentable invention. Folklore will be similarly eligible to copyright protection upon the addition of an original element, which can be very minimal. See Anupam Chander and Madhavi Sunder, 'The Romance of the Public Domain' (2004) 92 *California Law Review* 1331; Johanna Gibson, 'Audiences in Tradition: Traditional Knowledge and the Public Domain' in Charlotte Waelde and Hector MacQueen (eds.), *Intellectual Property – The Many Faces of the Public Domain* (Cheltenham: Edward Elgar, 2007), p. 174.

des Terreaux in Lyon. Even though the pavement they created was considered as a work of authorship, the judge refused to enforce their copyright against a company selling postcards that reproduced the square, including their protected work, on the grounds of the public domain nature of historical buildings composing the square.[48] The postcards did not represent only or mainly the contemporary work, but the latter was so integrated in the historical square that it was impossible to copy the square without including incidentally a reproduction of the protected pavement. The key argument of the decision was that the public domain status of the buildings necessarily constrained and limited the exercise of copyright held by the authors of a derivative work to the extent required by the free reproduction of the public domain. Otherwise, copyright would indirectly be restored in the public domain work for the benefit of the authors of its restoration or modification. The decision was upheld on appeal, but on different grounds. The invocation of the public domain did not suffice in itself to confer a positive protection against such reservation by a new copyright. The Court of Appeal did state that 'the protection granted to the authors of the new design of the square should not prejudice the common enjoyment',[49] but one would search in vain in French copyright law for the legal grounds sustaining this affirmation.

All these examples demonstrate that the public domain is not inherently devoid of a sustainable rule of non-exclusivity, but is open to further commodification and a return to private reservation, through intellectual property or other means. As it is conceived in copyright and patent law, the public domain does not create in any way a separate site immune from any privatization, as the terminology of the public domain appears to signify. Few elements of the so-called public domain are completely safe from falling again into the realm of intellectual property.[50] Contrary to what the binary public/private logic suggests, the public domain often serves private property and this interdependent relationship is rooted in

[48] TGI Lyon, 4 April 2001, *Revue Internationale du Droit d'auteur*, October 2001.

[49] Lyon, 20 March 2003, *Communications – Commerce Electronique*, September 2003. The Court of Cassation has confirmed the ruling on a very different justification, not making any mention of the public domain status of the underlying work. See Cass., 15 March 2005, available at www.courdecassation.fr/jurisprudence_2/premiere_chambre_civile_568/arret_no_632.html (last accessed 11 April 2013).

[50] See more developments of that point in Séverine Dusollier, 'The Public Domain in Intellectual Property: Beyond the Metaphor of a Domain' in P. L. Jayanthi Reddy (ed.), *Intellectual Property and Public Domain* (Hyderabad: Icfai University Press, 2009), p. 31; Dusollier and Benabou, 'Draw Me a Public Domain', p. 161.

the history and economics of intellectual property.[51] The growing enclosure of the public domain does not (or rather, does not only) come from an improper expansion of intellectual property but is linked to the very functioning of a system under which the public domain is only a fallow land ill-equipped to resist encroachment by an intellectual property right, a contract or any form of reservation.

3.2 Exceptions and limitations

The status of exceptions and limitations in copyright and patents (most notably in the former) is much disputed.[52] Qualified as privileges or freedoms, they sometimes pretend to be genuine rights to use the work or invention. The effect of being considered as rights would be to grant a remedy to their beneficiaries to preserve their effective enjoyment. Exceptions such as private copying, educational use, library privileges or any other exception can indeed be limited or impeded altogether by contract or by a technological measure. This issue was fiercely discussed a few years ago when the protection of technological measures was high on the copyright agenda. Courts generally do not acknowledge that copyright exceptions are rights in the legal sense, but only defences. Besides, even when qualified as rights, they could still be overridden by contracts in many countries. Inclusivity given by exceptions to IP rights is thus fragile as it can easily be pre-empted by a contract or other form of protection.

3.3 The legal trick and the hybrid nature of the copyleft mechanism

The copyleft trick devised by the open access movement purports to counter the empty promise of the public domain. Whether in open-source software or some Creative Commons licences, the obligation to distribute modifications of the work under the same licensing regime is intended to propagate a sharing ideology along a chain of successive contracts imposing inclusiveness at each stage. The copyleft effect enables the

[51] Carol Rose, 'Romans, Roads, and Romantic Creators: Traditions of Public Property in the Information Age' (2003) 66 *Law & Contemporary Problems* 89 at 96.

[52] Lucie Guibault, *Copyright Limitations and Contracts: An Analysis of the Contractual Overridability of Limitations on Copyright* (The Hague: Kluwer Law International, 2002); Martin Kretschmer, Estelle Derclaye, Marcella Favale and Richard Watt, *The Relationship Between Copyright and Contract Law* (UK Strategic Advisory Board for Intellectual Property, 2010), available at www.ipo.gov.uk/ipresearch-relation-201007.pdf (last accessed 11 April 2013).

ideology of sharing to spill beyond of the licensing parties and contaminate subsequent creations. A similar outcome is achieved in open-source patenting through grant-back mechanisms akin to copyleft.

As Margaret Radin has explained,[53] in such viral contracts the terms of the contract accompany the work or software that is disseminated. The contract runs with the digital asset, and the licence is embedded in the object it purports to regulate. The contract even goes so far as to run with modified or improved versions of the work or software it primarily seeks to control. Therefore, copyleft transforms a mere private ordering effect – normally applicable only to the parties to the private ordering tool (i.e. the contract) – into a feature applicable to the intellectual resource itself and to any user thereof. Protection shifts from contract to something that oddly resembles a property right.

Compared to public domain or IP limitations, this form of inclusivity is the most organized and sustained. However, the extent and success of such a procedural contamination, whether by copyleft or grant-back mechanisms, requires that the chain of contracts distributing copies of the work, invention and improvements, or derivative works should not be broken at any stage. Continuity enables the open-access feature to smoothly propagate beyond the first contract, but will depend both on the scope of the virality, based on the definition of the derivative products to be contaminated, and on the legal validity of the copyleft effect.[54] Only works or inventions that are considered to be derivative or improved inventions under the conditions of the contract (or by the law where the licence only refers to the notion as defined by law) will be subject in turn to the open access norm.

Additionally, open-source licensing can propagate along a chain of successive contracts only if each contract is enforceable against its parties.[55] True, the enforceability of the licence mostly relies upon copyright or patent protection. In the absence of acceptance of the licence by the user, the copying or distribution of the software or work or use of the invention will amount to an infringement. Users should thus be encouraged to accept the licence to fully enjoy the freedoms conferred therein. However,

[53] Margaret Jane Radin, 'Humans, Computers, and Binding Commitment' (2000) 75 *Indiana Law Journal* 1125 at 1132.

[54] This point is more developed in Dusollier, 'Sharing Access to Intellectual Property', 1416–20.

[55] See Andrés Guadamuz González, 'Viral Contracts or Unenforceable Documents? Contractual Validity of Copyleft Licences' (2004) 26 *European Intellectual Property Review* 331.

the enforcement of the licence cannot solely rely on the *erga omnes* opposability of the intellectual property rights. Some obligations or rights arising from the open-access licence do not rely at all on a copyright or patent right. Rules of consent or privity will thus apply to determine whether the licence has been accepted and is enforceable.

The complexity of this contractual construction weakens the perpetuation and the sustainability of copyleft licensing (though not to a critical extent). In the final analysis, users of works enjoy inclusive rights in works or inventions only on a contractual basis.

4 Conclusion: towards a legal regime of inclusivity

The previous section described the many commons one can find in intellectual property, collecting them around a shared feature of lack of exclusivity. A commons confers inclusivity upon the individuals entitled to use a resource. Another hallmark of a commons in intellectual property is that such inclusivity has no normative consequence, or so it seems. It cannot, in most cases, lead to a remedy and is not protected against the restoration of exclusivity.

This conclusion will first summarize the findings of this chapter as to the differing characteristics of those situations of non-exclusivity in intellectual property. Then it will propose a new line of research into that inclusivity in an attempt to give it some legal flesh and blood.

4.1 Features of non-exclusivity from the public domain to property

In sum, the gradation from public domain to property could be described as follows (see also Table 11.1).

Furthest away from exclusivity is the public domain, where there is no property or exclusive right vested in the resource (or exclusive rights have lapsed). Seen from the perspective of the user, one could say that any person is entitled to use the creation, in the form of an unconditional and inclusive privilege. The public domain benefits an undefined public. On the other hand, this freedom of use is unenforceable in the sense that no individual belonging to that public has legal means or remedy to protect her privilege from encroachment (either by legal extension of copyright or patent or by private claims based on other rights or powers).

In the case of copyright or patent exceptions/limitations, no exclusive rights can be enforced against the privileged use. Property rights in the work or invention are thus unenforceable. Users, either all of them or a

Table 11.1 *Features of non-exclusivity in the different cases of commons*

	Subsisting exclusivity (to whom)	**Entitlement of the public/user**	**Conditional/ unconditional**	**Enforceability by the user**	**Nature of the norm-making**
Public domain	No exclusivity (no IP holder)	Inclusivity Privilege/ freedom	Unconditional	Unenforceable	Public ordering
Exception/limitation	No exclusive rights in that use (IP holder has no exclusive rights in that use)	Inclusivity Privilege/ freedom/ immunity	Conditional	Enforceable only through defence	Public ordering
Copyleft licensing	Exclusive rights (owned by IP holder)	Inclusivity Contractual right	Conditional	Enforceable against licensor (IP holders)	Private ordering

defined category thereof, enjoy an inclusive privilege to use the creation. Compared to the public domain, this privilege is enforceable through defence, as it can be invoked to counter a claim of copyright or patent infringement. It is thus a form of immunity that counters the exercise of others' rights.

Finally, copyleft licensing still relies on exclusive rights that subsist in the work or invention, although it creates not a privilege but genuine (contractual) rights that are enforceable as such, against the licensor. As a rule, the right is conditional as it depends on the condition that such freedoms are perpetuated (the copyleft feature) and, in open-source software, on the obligation to release the source code.

4.2 A plea for a new approach to property and non-property: the inclusive right

As Yochai Benkler warns, 'perhaps there is no grand unified theory of commons'.[56] But all commons, whether seen through the lens of economics or law, whether owned by someone or by no one, contain some feature of inclusivity. Even when commons still rely on exclusive rights to ensure their sustainability, as in open-access licensing schemes, exclusivity necessarily leads to inclusive privileges in the sense that the licensees enjoying the prerogatives to use the work or invention find themselves in a situation devoid of any exclusivity and power to exclude.

Such inclusivity should count for something. Creation and innovation are promoted both by exclusive rights and by commons. Intellectual property regimes should thus address both ways of organizing and allocating use in works or inventions. Intellectual property has for centuries organized the exclusivity in intangibles, not paying much attention to the spaces of non-exclusivity left by the delineation of subject-matter, duration and scope of rights. As Julie Cohen pleaded for copyright, it might be necessary 'to complicate [intellectual property], replacing its foundational private/public dichotomy with a more complex and fertile mix of rights and privileges'.[57]

One way of achieving this could be to look at inclusivity not only as a state to be described, but also as an organization that engenders some

[56] Benkler, 'Between Spanish Huertas'.

[57] Julie E. Cohen, 'Copyright, Commodification, and Culture: Locating the Public Domain' in Lucie Guibault and P. Bernt Hugenholtz (eds.), *The Future of the Public Domain – Identifying the Commons in Information Law* (The Hague: Kluwer Law International, 2006), p. 165.

normative consequences. Users of a work or invention, whether in the public domain, in the frame of an exception to the rights or under a copyleft licence, should have their specific entitlement acknowledged and the core feature thereof, its inclusive nature, sustained. Preserving those spaces of non-exclusivity that, as we have seen, produce social, cultural and economic value, could lead to a new legal figure that I would call 'inclusive right'. The leap from 'inclusivity' to 'right' is not an easy one and is not innocuous. Its purpose would be to add a layer of remedy and enforcement that the public domain and, to a lesser extent, exceptions have not, and that copyleft licensees have only against their licensor. The correlative of a right would also be a duty imposed on others not to interfere with the inclusivity, which will be a key outcome in intellectual property where nothing so far immunizes exceptions or public domain against reservations by other rights, contracts or technological measures.

In essence, the legal model of inclusivity to be created should, in my view, embrace some basic rules:

- An inclusive right shall never be exercised to exclude another person enjoying the same inclusive right;
- An inclusive right shall be exercised in a way that preserves the resource and its collective use;
- An inclusive right can be enforced to defeat any claim of exclusivity that could hamper the common use;[58]
- Any court decision recognizing the inclusive right against some claim of exclusivity shall automatically benefit all individuals enjoying a similar right in the work or invention;
- Any legal regime of inclusive rights would be modulated according to the particular situation concerned. The scope and effect of inclusivity would indeed vary from the public domain, where an undefined public enjoys inclusivity without condition, to commons-property regimes where exclusivity subsists against the persons that are outside of the 'club' of commoners.

The model of inclusive right proposed here is only a first sketch, whose lines and colours require more effort and work. But it is an endeavour

[58] For instance, getting a trade mark in a public domain work is normally not prohibited as the scope of the trade mark and its function would normally not hamper the free use of the public domain work for creative purposes. When it does (registering a public domain cartoon character for products such as films), the status of the public domain labelled as an inclusive right for the public could invalidate the trade mark. Likewise, a copyright exception could not be overridden by contract.

worth pursuing to unify a legal theory of commons and to inscribe in law new models of property and non-property that have proved their value in contributing to creation and innovation.

Equally, it may have some valuable effect outside intellectual property. In a world where scarcity is becoming the rule and sharing resources is a sustainability solution and a praxis in many fields, including the environment, transportation and housing, inclusive rights could potentially better organize our relationships to things held in commons. Exclusivity might soon be dethroned. It ruled in a legal kingdom marked by abundance and foolish consumption. For the sake of future generations, the world to come will require forms of ownership in tangible, natural, cultural or innovative resources that are still unknown or, at least, are not yet organized within the legal landscape.

12

Property, sustainability and patent law – could the stewardship model facilitate the promotion of green technology?

HELENA R. HOWE

Introduction

The foregoing chapters have shown that the way we approach the concept of property in intellectual property law has substantive and normative implications for the rights granted and the scope of the attendant limitations. Finding the appropriate balance between the interests of intellectual property owners and broader society is important for all aspects of intellectual property, but in some contexts it becomes critical. Climate change is one of the most pressing issues faced by the global community. The patent system has a substantial role to play in the mitigation of climate change by promoting the development and diffusion of technologies that reduce carbon emissions. However, if patent law is to play a really effective part in the promotion of so-called 'green technologies',[1] some significant adjustments need to be made to its structure and functioning. Yet progress on this front has been extremely slow, in spite of the enormity of the environmental threat and the raft of proposals showing how patent law could better support the development and dissemination of green technology. Whilst the explanation for this is complex, one factor may be the concept of property that dominates patent law. The history of environmental regulation shows that where the traditional liberal property model frames policy debates or guides judicial decision-making, the outcomes tend to reflect the central assumptions of the model: private property rights prevail over the

[1] Green technology is a general term covering environmentally sound technology (i.e. technology with a reduced environmental impact) and clean energy technology (i.e. technologies that have the potential for reducing carbon emissions).

community interest.[2] Although the impact of the dominant property concept on environmental land-use regulation is well recognised, this seems to have received less attention in the patent sphere. Alongside calling for greater consideration to be given to the nature and role of the property concept in patent law, the argument made here is that an alternative property concept – that of stewardship – would be better able to facilitate the flexible and differentiated solutions needed from patent law.

The first part of this chapter focuses on the role of the patent system in mitigating climate change. It identifies the shortcomings and potential reforms to patent law that have been proposed by a number of commentators in order to achieve optimal levels of innovation and dissemination of green technology. The aim here is not to evaluate these proposals but to use them, in the second part of the chapter, to illustrate the effect of two different proprietary models on the development of patent law. Drawing parallels with real property scholarship, it is argued that the adoption of the stewardship model would provide a more effective framework within which to pursue the patent reforms proposed.

1 Patent law and the diffusion of green technology: current shortcomings and proposed reforms

1.1 The role of patent law in the diffusion of green technology

One of the central principles governing national and international legal developments is 'sustainable development'. This requires, in essence, that we seek a level of economic and social development that is sufficient for the requirements of the present global community without compromising the ability of future generations to meet their own needs.[3] In other words, sustainable development aims to ensure that development takes place in accordance with the twin principles of inter- and intra-generational justice.[4] Sustainable development covers a variety of concerns (conservation

[2] The term 'community interest' is used in this chapter instead of 'public interest' as a fairly loose umbrella term to cover a range of concerns relating to environmental protection held by different groups of persons, global and local, present and future. For the purpose of argument, the community interest will be treated in this chapter as though it is co-extensive with the interests of potential users of green technology albeit that the position is more complex than this.

[3] World Commission on Environment and Development, *Our Common Future* (Oxford University Press, 1987) ('The Brundtland Report').

[4] Rio Declaration on Environment and Development, 1992, A/CONF.151/26 (Vol. 1).

of bio-diversity, environmental justice, pollution and waste, for example), but perhaps the most pressing is the issue of climate change. The promotion of green technology is an essential component of climate protection strategies.[5] However, this approach can only make the necessary difference to climate change if as many people as possible have access to these technologies. Whilst we need to ensure effective access to, and use of, green technology within developed countries, it is crucial that this technology is available to developing countries.[6]

The role of the patent system is to incentivise the creation and dissemination of new technology and, as such, patent law has been recognised as having a significant role to play in addressing climate change.[7] Moreover, there is a legal obligation to interpret and develop patent law consistently

[5] Kyoto Protocol to the United Nations Framework Convention on Climate Change 1997, Kyoto, 16 March 1998, in force 16 February 2005, 2303 UNTS 148; Keith E. Maskus and Ruth Okediji, *Intellectual Property Rights and Technology Transfer to Address Climate Change: Risks, Opportunities and Policy Options* (Geneva: International Centre for Trade and Sustainable Development, 2010), p. 1.

[6] David G. Ockwell, Raudiger Haum, Alexandra Mallett and Jim Watson, 'Intellectual Property Rights and Low Carbon Technology Transfer: Conflicting Discourses of Diffusion and Development' (2010) 20 *Global Environmental Change* 729 at 729; Ahmed Latif, 'The UNEP-EPO-ICTSD Study on Patents and Clean Energy' in David G. Ockwell and Alexandra Mallett (eds.), *Low-Carbon Technology Transfer* (Oxford: Earthscan, 2012), p. 95.

[7] Michael Gollin, 'Using Intellectual Property to Improve Environmental Protection' (1991) 4 *Harvard Journal of Law and Technology* 192; Natalie Derzko, 'Using Intellectual Property Law and Regulatory Processes to Foster the Innovation and Diffusion of Environmental Technologies' 20 *Harvard Environmental Law Review* 3; Matthew Rimmer, *Intellectual Property and Climate Change – Inventing Clean Technologies* (Cheltenham and Northampton, MA: Edward Elgar, 2011); Estelle Derclaye, 'Should Patent Law Help Cool the Planet? An Enquiry From the Point of View of Environmental Law: Part 1' (2009) *European Intellectual Property Review* 168; Estelle Derclaye, 'Should Patent Law Help Cool the Planet? An Enquiry From the Point of View of Environmental Law: Part 2' (2009) *European Intellectual Property Review* 227; Estelle Derclaye, 'Not only Innovation but also Collaboration, Funding, Goodwill and Commitment: which Role for Patent Laws in Post-Copenhagen Climate Change Action' (2010) 9 *The John Marshall Review of Intellectual Property Law* 657; Deborah Behles, 'The New Race – Speeding up Climate Change Innovation' (2009) 11 *North Carolina Journal of Law and Technology* 1; Robert Fair, 'Does Climate Change Justify the Compulsory Licensing of Green Technology?' (2009) 6 *Brigham Young University International Law and Management Review* 21; Keith E. Maskus, 'Intellectual Property and the Transfer of Green Technologies: an Essay on Economic Perspectives' (2009) *World Intellectual Property Journal* 133; Maskus and Okediji, *International Property Rights and Technology Transfer*; Joshua Sarnoff, 'The Patent System and Climate Change' (2011) 16 *Virginia Journal of Law and Technology* 301. Others have adopted a more sceptical position: Peter Drahos, 'Six Minutes to Midnight: Can Intellectual Property Save the World?' in Kathy Bowry, Michael Handler and Dianne Nicol (eds.), *Emerging Challenges in Intellectual Property* (Oxford University Press, 2011).

with the principle of sustainable development under EU legislation and international treaties.[8] This means that existing patent law principles and future developments should be geared towards supporting technologies that are environmentally friendly and that would make a contribution to slowing climate change. To some extent, the patent system has been able to respond to the new agenda. In the wake of the Kyoto Protocol,[9] the number of green technology patents has risen significantly.[10] There have also been a range of new initiatives and procedural changes introduced, such as the clean energy technology database established by the European Patent Office to reduce search costs for green technology and fast-tracks for green patents, as introduced by the UK Intellectual Property Office.[11] One initiative that has received significant attention is the eco-patent commons. This project enables patent owners to place patents that have an environmental value but that are not of significant economic value to the company in the 'commons' where others can use them for free.[12] Others, such as patent pools for green technology and open-patent projects, are also potentially useful tools for mitigating the effects of patent-thickets in essential technology.[13] However, whilst valuable, these initiatives are not a substitute for properly considered reform of the patent system. In some cases such initiatives may simply operate as safety valves, enabling corporations to maintain the appearance of responsibility by relinquishing control over property that is, in fact, of limited value.[14]

[8] Derclaye, 'Should Patent Law Help Cool the Planet? – Part 1', 169–70.

[9] Kyoto Protocol to the United Nations Framework Convention on Climate Change 1997, Kyoto, 16 March 1998, in force 16 February 2005, 2303 UNTS 148.

[10] Konstantinos Karachalios *et al.*, *Patents and Clean Energy: Bridging the Gap Between Evidence and Policy – Final Report*, (Munich: United Nations Environmental Programme, European Patent Office, International Centre for Trade and Sustainable Development, 2010), p. 37.

[11] *Ibid.*, pp. 88–92.

[12] World Business Council for Sustainable Development, 'Eco-patent commons', available at: www.wbcsd.org/work-program/capacity-building/eco-patent-commons.aspx (last accessed 29 April 2013).

[13] Rimmer, *Intellectual Property and Climate Change*, Chapter 8; Jamie Andrews, 'Could Open Source Technologies Help Us Solve Climate Change?' *The Ecologist*, 4 May 2010; Mariateresa Maggiolino and Maria Lilla Montagnani, 'From Open Source Software to Open Patenting – What's New in the Realm of Openness? (2011) 42 *International Review of Intellectual Property and Competition Law* 804.

[14] Mark Van Hoorebeek and William Onzivu, (2010) 'The Eco-Patent Commons and Environmental Technology Transfer: Implications for Efforts to Tackle Climate Change' (2010) 4 *Carbon and Climate Review* 13.

1.2 *The shortcomings of patent law*

A range of factors have been identified as contributing to the failure of the current system to deliver the levels of innovation and diffusion of green technology needed to make a real contribution to mitigating climate change. One issue is the technological neutrality of patent law. Patent law provides incentives for both polluting and green technology and only a weak exclusion for inventions the exploitation of which would be environmentally degrading. As a result, patent law fails to direct investment towards environmentally beneficial technology and away from that which is harmful.[15] A second criticism of the system is its tendency to give rise to patent-thickets in significant technology. In other words, rather than fostering innovation, patents may clog the individual elements of a new technology with exclusive rights, making future innovation more costly and difficult.[16] What is more, this appears more likely to happen in green technology industries than in pharmaceuticals, for example, because the markets for the former are more fragmented.[17] Particularly unappealing is the activity of so-called 'patent trolls', companies that produce nothing but that use a portfolio of patents (often on small technological advances) and threats of infringement action to obtain licence revenue.

Alongside slowing the rate of *innovation* in some sectors, it is suggested that the current system fails to support optimum levels of *dissemination* of green technology.[18] Under the present system the patent owner is granted an exclusive right to control almost all uses of the patented invention.[19] The invention may be exploited by others under licence, but for many the cost of licensing the technology will be prohibitive and it is the newest, and potentially most useful technology that will be the most expensive.[20] Evidence suggests that some developing countries are unable to gain sufficient access to green technology and one of the reasons for this is that

[15] Gollin, 'Using Intellectual Property', 195.

[16] Rimmer, *Intellectual Property and Climate Change*, Chapter 5; Maskus and Okediji, *International Property Rights and Technology Transfer*, p. 16.

[17] Sarnoff, 'The Patent System and Climate Change', 306.

[18] Behles, 'The New Race', 29; Maskus and Okediji, *International Property Rights and Technology Transfer*, p. 19.

[19] WTO Agreement on Trade Related Aspects of Intellectual Property Rights 1994 (TRIPS), Article 28.

[20] Carbon capture and storage technology, for example. See Derclaye, 'Not Only Innovation', 666.

the price of patented technology is unaffordable.[21] The cost and the terms on which patents owners seek to license their patents may also restrict the adoption of the newest and most effective green technology in *developed* countries.[22] Both public bodies and private enterprises may be unable to meet the terms on which the technology is licensed, slowing the rate at which carbon emissions are reduced.

1.3 *Proposed reforms to flexibilities, remedies and licensing*

For many commentators, therefore, patent law needs some degree of substantive remodelling or reinterpretation if the patent system is to facilitate the broadest possible diffusion of green technology. A substantial proportion of those calling for reform are proposing changes that would constrain the exclusive rights of the patent owner in order to address the issue raised above. These proposals are largely aimed at reforming the 'flexibilities' in patent law, namely the exceptions to the rights of the patent owner and the provisions relating to the compulsory licensing of the patent permitted under the Trade Related Aspects of Intellectual Property Rights Agreement 1994 (TRIPS).[23] In terms of the compulsory licensing provisions, it may be possible to make better use of the provisions that are already available. There may be the potential, for example, to interpret the concept of 'national emergency', which already exists as a ground for issuing a compulsory licence,[24] as covering climate change. Alternatively, if existing flexibilities are found to be insufficient, then some revision of the TRIPS Agreement may be necessary to enable compulsory licensing for climate change or environmental protection purposes specifically.[25]

There is also potential scope for the expansion of certain patent exceptions. Many domestic patent laws contain an exception aimed at enabling 'experimental' use of the patented invention, for example.[26] For some commentators this exception could be a highly significant tool in the promotion of green innovation, particularly for developing countries, but is at present under-used.[27] However, this type of exception would seem

[21] Sarnoff, 'The Patent System and Climate Change', 317; Maskus and Okediji, *International Property Rights and Technology Transfer*, p. 19.
[22] Rimmer, *Intellectual Property and Climate Change*, Chapter 5.
[23] TRIPS, Articles 30–31; Rimmer, *Intellectual Property and Climate Change*, pp. 92–102; Maskus and Okediji, *International Property Rights and Technology Transfer*, pp. 31–5.
[24] TRIPS, Article 31(b).
[25] Maskus and Okediji, *International Property Rights and Technology Transfer*, p. 36.
[26] For example, Patents Act 1977, s. 60(5)(b).
[27] Rimmer, *Intellectual Property and Climate Change*, pp. 92–5.

only to be really effective in promoting green technology diffusion if the concepts of 'non-commercial' and 'experimental' use can be broadly, flexibly and consistently interpreted. Drawing on earlier studies, Ockwell *et al.* have identified 'learning by doing' and adaptation of the technology for local communities as hugely significant to truly effective technology transfer.[28] In other words, it is essential to enable the people who will be using green technology that is new to a region or industry to experiment with it and adapt it to local conditions. This would suggest that patent law needs to be able to facilitate such adaptive activity, either through flexible licensing provisions, or by interpreting the experimental use exception so that some limited commercial aspect to the experimental use is permissible. Finally, there is also room for a re-evaluation of the rules governing remedies for patent infringement. It is arguable that there could be greater scope for granting damages or a reasonable royalty in lieu of an injunction to claimants where the patent relates to green technology and the community interest is adjudged to outweigh the harm caused to the patent owner.

None of this is to ignore the fact that empirical evidence is inconclusive on the precise impact of patent rights on green technology diffusion.[29] In some industries and some countries, strong patent protection will result in higher levels of innovation and dissemination of green technology and, where this is the case, circumscribing patent rights is not likely to be appropriate.[30] The point is simply that in *some* countries and *some* industries, constraints on patent rights may be highly valuable for both innovation and dissemination. This appears to be particularly true in respect of access to the most up-to-date and effective technology[31] and in the case of less developed countries.[32] It is in order to be able to respond to these situations that patent law requires reform.

28 Ockwell *et al.*, 'Intellectual Property Rights and Low Carbon Technology Transfer', 736 (citing Martin Bell and Keith Pavitt, 'Technological Accumulation and Industrial Growth: Contrasts Between Developed and Developing Countries' (1993) 2 *Industrial and Corporate Change* 157).

29 Maskus and Okediji, *International Property Rights and Technology Transfer*, pp. 6–7.

30 Frederick-Karl Beier, 'Does Compulsory Licensing Promote Technology Transfer to Developing Countries?' (1986) *European Intellectual Property Review* 363; Fair, 'Does Climate Change Justify the Compulsory Licensing of Green Technology?'; Neel Maitra, 'Alternatives to Compulsory Licensing' (2010) *Columbia Journal of Environmental Law* 35.

31 Ockwell *et al.*, 'Intellectual Property Rights and Low Carbon Technology Transfer', 734–5.

32 Maskus and Okediji, *International Property Rights and Technology Transfer*, p. 19.

Significantly, what emerges from the proposals for reform is the need for greater differentiation, improved flexibility and enhanced recognition of the obligations in patent law, at least in the context of green technology. Differential obligations are at the heart of sustainable development and action on climate change. International agreements require richer and more developed nations to shoulder a greater part of the burden of mitigation in light of their contribution to the environmental crisis and their relative economic position.[33] For technology transfer to developing countries to be successful, it is necessary to construct a system of patent law that is capable of recognising and being responsive to the different conditions under which the transfer takes place, the needs of the relevant recipients and the position of the patent owner.[34] Patent law could play a more effective role in the promotion of green technology if it were structured to take greater account of a range of factors such as these when establishing the balance between patent owners and potential users of the invention. In addition to the reforms proposed above, it is suggested that encouraging greater flexibility in licensing arrangements for green technology would be particularly valuable.[35] So, for instance, where the invention has been publicly funded – via a university or through a government grant, for example – the licence may be non-exclusive, granted at a reduced royalty rate or may enable a broader range of non-commercial uses.[36] The same claim for differentiation and flexibility can be applied to remedies and compulsory licensing. Where the patent is defensive or applied to building-block technology and/or the community need is significant, then the grant of damages or a compulsory licence, rather than an injunction, might be more appropriate.

Recognition of the community interest in the mitigation of climate change through green innovation also plays a fundamental part in these suggestions for reform. All the proposals require the patent owner to recognise and accept that ownership of a patent over green technology entails obligations to the community to exploit the rights in a manner compatible with the needs of these communities. As such, the rights of

[33] United Nations Framework Convention on Climate Change 1992, 9 May 1992, in force 21 March 1994, 1771 UNTS 107, Article 3.1; Christopher D. Stone, 'Common but Differentiated Responsibilities in International Law' (2004) 98 *American Journal of International Law* 276.

[34] David G. Ockwell and Alexandra Mallett (eds.), *Low-Carbon Technology Transfer* (Oxford: Earthscan, 2012), p. 6.

[35] Maskus and Okediji, *International Property Rights and Technology Transfer*, pp. 23–4.

[36] Rimmer, *Intellectual Property and Climate Change*, Chapter 7.

the patent owner to control the exploitation of the invention should cede to the community interest where environmental protection is judged to require it.

2 Two concepts of property and the patent system: a more fundamental reform?

2.1 The significance of the property concept in achieving patent reform

Making these changes is not proving easy. There are many reasons why achieving greater flexibility in patent law is difficult. However, one factor that has received only limited attention is the dominant property concept in patent law.[37] Yet, as in other areas of property, the model of property that shapes international patent norms will be a factor in the success – or otherwise – of reform. At a basic level, difficulties arise where the concept of property being employed is not acknowledged explicitly. According to Scott, attempts to construct responsible intellectual property laws providing appropriate levels of access and use are undermined because those negotiating the rules fail to disclose assumptions and expectations regarding the nature of intellectual property.[38] In his view, explicit recognition of these assumptions in international debate would go some way to reducing tensions over the appropriate scope of intellectual property rights.[39] It is also necessary for judges and domestic policy makers to be clear about the understanding of property that they are bringing to bear on the issue in front of them. The establishment of principled and justifiable limits to patent rights can only come through explicit discussion of

[37] The role of the dominant model of property is sometimes mentioned as a factor affecting the effective promotion of green technology. See, for example, Krishna R. Srinivas, 'Technology Transfer, Intellectual Property Rights and Climate Change' in David G. Ockwell and Alexandra Mallett (eds.), *Low-Carbon Technology Transfer* (Oxford: Earthscan, 2012), p. 109. It is also present in discussions regarding the acceptable limits of compulsory licensing. See for instance, Anthony Taubman, 'Rethinking TRIPS: "Adequate Remuneration" for Non-Voluntary Patent Licensing' 11 *Journal of International Economic Law* 927, and as a background factor in discussions on how best to achieve policy aims within the existing framework, see Maskus and Okediji, *International Property Rights and Technology Transfer*. However, it appears rarely to be the focus, as such.

[38] Geoffrey Scott, 'A Protocol for Evaluating Changing Global Attitudes Toward Innovation and Intellectual Property Regimes' (2011) 32 *University of Pennsylvania Journal of International Law* 1165.

[39] *Ibid.*

the nature and scope of the property and the claims of the community in respect of that property.[40]

In addition to being open about the model of property being used, we need to choose our model of property carefully. The way in which ownership is conceived contributes to forming the frame of reference within which decisions about property rights are made. Where there is a dispute as to whether a property owner should be able to control or use the object of property in a way that may harm the community (whether by action or omission), the concept of property adopted is likely to be a factor in shaping the perceived legitimacy of the respective claims. As Singer states:

> We approach the question of defining property rights partly by adopting conceptions of what ownership means. These conceptions are embodied in conscious or unconscious images that orient our thinking in particular directions and frame our analysis of the underlying policy question.[41]

In other words, whilst the choice of property concept will not dictate the balance between the rights of the patent owner and the community in a particular context, it will determine the framework and the language used in the determination of the appropriate balance by policy makers, legislatures and the judiciary. This in turn may affect the development of legal mechanisms, such as compulsory licensing or flexible licensing, which could balance competing interests of patent owner and community more effectively.[42]

There are a number of ways in which we can conceptualise property 'ownership'. A vast array of different approaches to the relationship between people and objects of value subsist in theory and reality, and this is as true of patent law as any other area of law.[43] This chapter focuses on two influential models of property: the traditional 'liberal' model and the 'stewardship' model. The 'liberal' model represents a 'rights-based' conception characterised by strong exclusive rights for the property owner

[40] Abdul Latif, Keith Maskus, Ruth Okediji, Jerome Reichman and Pedro Roffe, *Overcoming the Impasse on Intellectual Property and Climate Change at the UNFCCC: A Way Forward* (Geneva: International Centre for Trade and Sustainable Development, 2011).

[41] Joseph W. Singer, 'The Ownership Society and Takings of Property: Castles, Investments and Just Obligations' (2006) 30 *Harvard Environmental Law Review* 309 at 313.

[42] *Ibid.*

[43] It would be possible, for example, to trace Singer's 'investment model' in patent law (see Singer, 'The Ownership Society') or to analyse it according to the categories identified by Rotherham (see Craig Rotherham, 'Conceptions of Property in Common Law Discourse' (1998) 18 *Legal Studies* 41).

and almost no duties owed to the wider community.[44] The stewardship model presents a more community-orientated concept of property and one in which ethical concerns beyond the protection of the individual owner form an integral part of property law. Here, the owner is a steward of property in the sense that they are expected to consider community interests when dealing with the property and their rights and duties are constructed accordingly.[45]

2.2 *The liberal model*

It has been widely recognised that, where the liberal model dominates, the limitation of property rights in the community interest is more difficult, and frequently more expensive, than it might be if we were to approach the concept of 'owning' property differently.[46] The history of environmental land use regulation in the UK shows that the liberal model will undermine the development of effective property constraints in the community interest.[47] By focusing on individual rights and the protection of the property-owning individual, the model has a tendency to undervalue

[44] Anthony M. Honore, 'Ownership' in Anthony G. Guest (ed.), *Oxford Essays in Jurisprudence* (Oxford: Clarendon Press, 1961); Margaret J. Radin, 'The Liberal Conception of Property: Cross-currents in the Jurisprudence of Takings' (1988) 88 *Columbia Law Review* 1667.

[45] For example, William N. Lucy and Catherine Mitchell, 'Replacing Private Property: The Case for Stewardship' (1996) 55 *Cambridge Law Journal* 566; James P. Karp, 'A Private Property Duty of Stewardship: Our Changing Land Ethic' (1992–3) 23 *Environmental Law* 735; Murray Raff, 'Environmental Obligations and the Western Liberal Property Concept' (1998) 22 *Melbourne University Law Review* 657. The concept is also becoming increasingly influential in intellectual property law. See, for example: Roberta Kwall, 'The Author as Steward "for Limited Times"' (2008) 88 *Boston University Law Review* 685; Lior Zemer, 'Moral Rights: Limited Edition' (2011) 91 *Boston University Law Review* 1519; and Helena R. Howe, 'Copyright Limitations and the Stewardship Model of Property' (2011) *Intellectual Property Quarterly* 183.

[46] Lynton K. Caldwell, 'Rights of Ownership or Rights of Use: The Need for a New Conceptual Basis for Land Use Policy' (1974) 15 *William and Mary Law Review* 759; Raff, 'Environmental Obligations'; Gregory S. Alexander, 'Takings and the Post-Modern Dialectic of Property' (1992) 9 *Constitutional Commentary* 259; Kevin Gray, 'Equitable Property' (1994) 47 *Current Legal Problems* 157; Donald W. Large, 'This Land is Whose Land: Changing Concepts of Land as Property' (1973) *Wisconsin Law Review* 1039; Joseph L. Sax 'Takings, Private Property and Public Rights' (1971) 81 *Yale Law Journal* 149.

[47] See, for example, Patrick McAuslen, *The Ideologies of Planning Law* (Oxford: Pergamon Press, 1980); *Cooper* v. *Wandsworth Board of Works* (1863) 143 ER 414; *Newbury District Council* v. *Secretary of State for the Environment* [1981] AC 578; *R (on the application of Trailer and Marina (Leven) Ltd.* v. *Secretary of State for the Environment, Food and Rural Affairs* [2005] 1 WLR 1267.

the community interest in the property. Both potential harm done to the community through the exercise of the property rights and the community contribution to the value of the property are more easily presented as unrelated to enquiries regarding the legitimate scope of property rights.[48] The lack of recognised obligation to others means that there are very few inherent limits on the property rights.[49] Thus, where this model dominates, any form of constraint on the free exercise of the right is more likely to be perceived as an external[50] 'interference' with property requiring narrow and precisely defined construction. It also produces a base expectation that compensation should be the norm where constraints on property rights are imposed and that deviations from this norm should be closely scrutinised.[51] Moreover, the liberal model is poor at responding to changing social conditions or goals; the aim of property law from this perspective is primarily to safeguard established rights, rather than to accommodate emerging values or community needs.[52]

Both of the models discussed here are merely caricatures or 'ideas' of property that do not accurately describe the scope of ownership, whether of land or intellectual property.[53] Yet the influence of a particular understanding of property is apparent in the structure and functioning of the relevant rules governing its use and enjoyment. On that basis, it can be argued that the liberal model of property dominates much international patent law and often seems to characterise the position of developed countries on green technology diffusion. The rhetoric of strong proprietary rights, as used particularly by representatives of US and EU trade interests, has been a feature of the international negotiations on the role of patent law in the promotion of green technology.[54] Even existing TRIPS flexibilities are decried as being anti-intellectual property and technology

[48] Joseph W. Singer, 'How Property Norms Construct the Externalities of Ownership' in Gregory S. Alexander and Eduardo M. Penalver (eds.), *Property and Community* (Oxford University Press, 2010), pp. 63, 79.

[49] Honore, 'Ownership', p. 123.

[50] Frederick H. Lawson and Bernard Rudden, *The Law of Property* (Oxford: Clarendon, 2002), p. 90.

[51] See, for example: Mark Stallworthy, *Sustainability, Land Use and Environment* (London: Cavendish, 2002), p. 64; Sax, 'Takings, Private Property and Public Rights', 160. In the patent context: Davida H. Isaacs, 'Not All Property Is Created Equal – Why Modern Courts Resist Applying the Takings Clause to Patents and Why They are Right To Do So' (2007) 15 *George Mason Law Review* 1 at 20, 23; TRIPS, Article 30(h).

[52] Singer, 'The Ownership Society', 325.

[53] Laura Underkuffler, *The Idea of Property: Its Meaning and Power* (Oxford University Press, 2003), pp. 1–8, Chapter 3.

[54] Rimmer, *Intellectual Property and Climate Change*, pp. 252–3, 382.

transfer measures are often presented as undermining legitimate property interests.[55] Currently, international patent norms provide broad exclusive rights to patent owners to control the patented invention.[56] Nonetheless, in contrast to the liberal model, there is some recognition of the need to balance the rights with the public interest and an explicit acknowledgement of the obligations owed by patent owners.[57] There are also provisions to give effect to these obligations that limit the rights of the patent owner, including compulsory licensing provisions for use in cases of extreme need.[58]

However, experience of these provisions indicates that patent ownership is not really conceived as a condition of rights *and* obligations, as evidenced, for example, by the limited fulfilment of developed countries' supposed technology transfer obligations under TRIPS.[59] Whilst there is some recognition of the concept of environmental protection, for instance, as a value capable of limiting the grant of patent rights, this is only accepted as a legitimate foundation for limiting property when the environmental risk is extreme.[60] This suggests that there is a separation between the notion of property employed here and community values such as environmental protection and a tendency to allow these 'external' values to constrain property rights only in very limited circumstances. Moreover, the available exceptions and limitations to patent rights are often drafted and interpreted narrowly.[61]

Above, it was noted that a flexible experimental use exception has a potential role to play in green technology dissemination and particularly

[55] Abdul Latif, *Intellectual Property Rights and Green Technologies from Rio to Rio: An Impossible Dialogue?* (Geneva: International Centre for Trade and Sustainable Development, 2012) pp. 5–6.

[56] TRIPS, Article 28. [57] TRIPS, Article 7.

[58] TRIPS, Article 31.

[59] Karachalios *et al.*, *Patents and Clean Energy*, p. 19; Jerome de Meeus and Alain Strowel, 'Climate Change and the Debate Around Green Technology Transfer and Patent Rules: History, Prospect and Unresolved Issues' (2012) *World Intellectual Property Journal* 179 at 186.

[60] T 356/93 Plant cells/ PLANT GENETIC SYSTEMS [1995] OJ EPO 545.

[61] For example, TRIPS, Articles 13 and 36; World Trade Organization Panel Decision on *Canada: Patent Protection of Pharmaceutical Products: Complaint by the European Communities and their Member States*, 17 March 2000, WT/DS114/R at 56; *Aerotel Ltd* v. *Telco Holdings Ltd* [2006] EWCA Civ 1371, [2007] RPC 117 at para. 12, cf. G 1/07 Treatment by Surgery/MEDI-PHYSICS [2010] EPOR 25, paras. 61–66. See Lionel Bently, 'Exclusions from Patentability and Exceptions to Patentees Rights: Taking Exceptions Seriously' (2011) 64 *Current Legal Problems* 315.

in enabling developing countries to make the best use of the technology for their needs. The available exceptions in patent law are governed by Article 30 of the TRIPS Agreement. This provision permits members to 'provide limited exceptions to the exclusive rights conferred by a patent, provided such exceptions do not unreasonably conflict with the normal exploitation of the patent and do not unreasonably prejudice the legitimate interests of the patent owner, taking account of the legitimate interests of third parties'. Whilst the WTO decision in *Canada – Patent Protection*[62] accepted that an experimental use exception was compatible with TRIPS, the panel emphasised the requirement to interpret patent exceptions narrowly.[63] Moreover, the exception is limited because it does not extend to 'importing' the patented invention, which may be necessary for developing countries.[64] The influence of the liberal model means that the sort of adaptive activity that might be beneficial to a developing country user (and which may involve some limited commercial benefit) may well be perceived as interfering with the legitimate interests of the patent owner and, as such, incompatible with Article 30. An expansive approach to 'experimental' use is also at odds with the interpretation of the provision in the USA[65] and potentially in the UK. In the latter, the exception has been interpreted in such a way that any 'commercial motive' is problematic for the success of the exception.[66] This is despite the fact that the provision would appear to be drafted in fairly flexible language; it grants a defence to 'acts done for experimental purposes relating to the subject matter of the invention'.[67]

Where this model dominates, it also encourages a preference for voluntary methods of circumscribing property rights over legally imposed constraints, because the former involves no problematic 'taking' of the rights of the property owner.[68] To some extent, voluntary initiatives are valuable and are to be preferred because they can achieve flexible and differentiated licensing without compulsion. This means that owners will be more inclined to provide the know-how that accompanies the technology. The problem arises where an ideological objection to imposed constraint

[62] World Trade Organization Panel Decision on *Canada: Patent Protection of Pharmaceutical Products: Complaint by the European Communities and their Member States*, 17 March 2000, WT/DS114/R.

[63] *Ibid.* at 56. [64] *Ibid.* at 56.

[65] *Madey* v. *Duke University* 307 F.3d 1351 (2002).

[66] *Inhale Therapeutic Systems* v. *Quadrant Healthcare* [2002] RPC 419 at 463.

[67] Patents Act 1977 s. 60(5)(b).

[68] Howe, 'Copyright Limitations and the Stewardship Model', 189, 197–8.

steers policy towards voluntary measures regardless of whether or not they have the capability to provide the best outcome. The risk is that we fail to pursue the most effective course of action and instead devote energy to constructing less effective measures simply because these are more compatible with the status quo.[69] Initiatives such as the eco-patents commons provide a good illustration of a response to the climate crisis that is easy to embrace because it works within the system rather than challenging it. Whilst heralded as a significant contribution in the promotion of green technology by corporations who were forgoing financial gain for the social good, the wholly voluntary nature of the initiative means that it is likely to have only limited impact on green technology innovation and dissemination.[70]

Furthermore, the liberal model also reduces the significance of the particular subject matter of property. By focusing on the protection of individual *rights*, the particular subject matter of the property is an afterthought, rather than an integral part of any enquiry regarding the legitimate scope of ownership.[71] This failure to recognise that some property is more valuable or 'weighty'[72] than other property, combined with a tendency to undervalue the community interest, results in a failure to construct a properly differentiated system; a tendency notable in patent law.[73] The result is that factors that could give rise to flexibility over terms of licence, appropriate remedy or the level of compensation for a compulsory licence, such as public funding, for example, are not given the weight they deserve.

The reaction to compulsory licensing of patent rights by developed countries exemplifies many of the characteristic responses associated with the liberal model of property and provides a good illustration of the way in which this model serves as a barrier to effective patent reform.

[69] Carl Circo, 'Does Sustainability Require a New Theory of Property Rights?' (2009) 58 *University of Kansas Law Review* 91 at 128–9.

[70] Rimmer, *Intellectual Property and Climate Change*, pp. 323–6; Derclaye, 'Not Only Innovation', 664; see also Behles, 'The New Race', 10.

[71] David Lametti, 'The (Virtue) Ethics of Private Property' in Alastair Hudson (ed.) *New Perspectives on Property Law, Obligations and Restitution* (London: Cavendish, 2004), pp. 57–9.

[72] Alastair Hudson, 'The Unbearable Lightness of Property' in Alastair Hudson (ed.) *New Perspectives on Property Law, Obligations and Restitution* (London: Cavendish, 2004).

[73] Maskus and Okediji, *International Property Rights and Technology Transfer*, p. 23; Richard Posner, 'Do Patent and Copyright Law Restrict Competition and Creativity Excessively?', The Becker–Posner blog 30.9.12, available at: www.becker-posner-blog.com/2012/09/do-patent-and-copyright-law-restrict-competition-excessively-posner.html (recognising that overall patent law is poor on differentiation) (last accessed 12 April 2013).

Despite the existence of compulsory licence provisions in TRIPS and their long-standing role in many domestic laws, the compulsory licence is often portrayed as a draconian measure to be resisted at all costs.[74] Such non-voluntary licences may be a particularly useful tool for green technology diffusion in some developing countries, yet they are rarely used. There are many valid reasons why the compulsory licence is problematic, but, where evidence indicates that it can play a valuable role in the diffusion of green technology, the system should be equipped to facilitate this. However, the liberal model promotes a perception of the compulsory licence as a barely justifiable expropriation of the patent owner's right to exclude.[75] Where this is unacknowledged, it undermines the value of such measures by making them appear under-used and unhelpful, when really their use is not feasible due, in part, to the hurdles – both real and ideological – placed in the way of any potential user.[76] The result is that situations in which compulsory licences are capable of grant are tightly defined, which in turn makes it extremely difficult either to expand the notion of public emergency in Article 31(b), or to redraft TRIPS so as to cover environmental protection explicitly. In essence, the rhetoric of this model risks shutting off policy options and silencing discussion of challenging measures[77] such as compulsory licensing without full consideration of their role and robust questioning of supposed negative impacts.[78]

[74] De Meeus and Strowel, 'Climate Change', 192.

[75] Michael Greene, 'Three Letters Preventing the Success of International Environmental Treaties' (2009) 18 *Southeastern Environmental Law Journal* 137; Maskus and Okediji, *International Property Rights and Technology Transfer*, p. 5; Business Europe, IIPPF, and the US Chamber of Commerce, 'Joint Resolution of Business Europe, IIPPF, and the US Chamber of Commerce on Restrictions of IP Rights and Compulsory Licensing', 9 December 2008, available at: www.jetro.go.jp/theme/ip/iippf/pdf/press081222.pdf (last accessed 29 April 2013).

[76] For instance, Derclaye seems to suggest that the lack of use of the compulsory licensing provisions in the Clean Air Act (USA) indicates their lack of real value, but it could also mean that it was structurally difficult to employ them or to fulfil the conditions under which they could be granted, which she notes are difficult. Derclaye, 'Not Only Innovation', 669.

[77] See the surely unhelpful intimation that the then President of the European Patent Office, Alison Brimelow, ought not to engage with the discussion of whether patents stood in the way of green technology diffusion because it does not show the proper deference to patent property: IPKat, 'Freetards Today, Greenards Tomorrow?' 8 May 2008, The IPKat blog, available at: http://ipkitten.blogspot.co.uk/2008/05/freetards-today-greentards-tomorrow.html (last accessed 29 April 2013).

[78] Some question whether, for example, compulsory licensing has the adverse effect on innovation that is often claimed: Sarnoff, 'The Patent System', 314.

In sum, whilst there are plenty of options for constructing the flexible and differentiated patent system needed to provide optimal diffusion of green technology, the effect of this model is to undermine the proposed reforms at a structural level.

2.3 *The stewardship model*

For the effective promotion of sustainable development, we need a more community-orientated concept of property; one that can accommodate effective limits on property rights in the interests of social and environmental justice. Whilst this has been persuasively argued in the context of property in land,[79] it must also be recognised in patent law if the patent system is to make the contribution needed from it. Essentially, the stewardship model is more compatible with sustainable development objectives and provides a more sympathetic ideological framework within which to implement reforms to patent law for the mitigation of climate change. Primarily this is because, under the stewardship model, property ownership is inherently limited by obligations owed to the community that mirror the principles of inter- and intra-generational justice. The stewardship model of property, like sustainable development, involves an ethic of resource use that is imbued with obligations to take account of the needs and interests of present and future communities. In short, the property owner has rights and can expect to benefit from the property. However, property owners are stewards in the sense that they are expected to consider social and ecological values when dealing with the property and their rights and duties are constructed accordingly.[80]

The landowner under the stewardship model is commonly seen as bearing two principal duties: first, to conserve the natural resources over which they have control and, second, to accommodate the needs of the community in respect of the land, as far as is compatible with the landowner's limited rights to beneficial use of the land. It may be objected that presenting the patent owner as the steward of their invention is very different from recognising the landowner as steward of the natural world.

[79] For example, Circo, 'Does Sustainability Require a New Theory of Property Rights?'; Murray Raff, 'Toward an Ecologically Sustainable Property Concept' in Elizabeth Cooke (ed.), *Modern Studies in Property Law* (Oxford: Hart Publishing, 2005), vol. III.

[80] Raff, 'Environmental Obligations', 671; Caldwell, 'Rights of Ownership'; Lucy and Mitchell, 'Replacing Private Property'; Karp, 'A Private Property Duty of Stewardship'; Victor J. Yannacone, 'Property and Stewardship – Private Property Plus Public Interest Equals Social Property' (1978) 23 *South Dakota Law Review* 71.

However, it is questionable whether there is really so great a difference between the person who claims rights over the world's natural resources on which they have laboured and the patent owner who claims rights to control an invention that draws on a common stock of human knowledge and innovation. Moreover, regardless of any qualitative difference in creative input, inventions, like natural resources, have the potential to be of immense significance in addressing the central concerns of sustainable development. The patent owner-as-steward is not asked to 'conserve' the subject matter of his property in the same way as the landowner is required to conserve the natural world under this model, but there is no reason why they should not be expected to take environmental concerns into account in exploiting the invention. Similarly, the patent owner is unlikely to be able to alleviate need through granting access to the invention itself, but they may be expected to accept some access to the innovation at non-market rates where this is necessary to address issues of health or hunger. From this perspective, there seems to be no reason why this model cannot provide an alternative paradigm for understanding patent ownership when the same issues of environmental protection and essential needs, seen in the land context, are mediated through it.

Under this model, constraints placed on property rights in order to accommodate the community interest in reducing climate change are less likely to be perceived as an unreasonable 'interference' with extensive rights. Limits to patent rights to accommodate these concerns are, therefore, less likely to be drafted and interpreted narrowly, or their use avoided in practice.[81] Moreover, compensation is more likely to reflect the patent owner's true financial loss caused by a particular measure than a perceived need to compensate the owner for the interference with their property per se. Similarly, if limitations are inherent in patent property, there is less need to rely on less-effective, voluntary means of creating flexibility or 'constraint'. From this perspective, the reforms needed to avoid patent-thickets in green technology and to promote its global diffusion – expanding the scope of the compulsory licensing provisions or the research exception, for example – are less ideologically problematic because patent ownership is not comprised of unlimited rights. Similarly, where such licences are granted for green technology, it would follow that

[81] Caldwell, 'Rights of Ownership'; James W. Harris, *Property and Justice* (Oxford: Clarendon, 1996) p. 78; Raff, 'Environmental Obligations'; Karp, 'A Private Property Duty of Stewardship'; Kevin Gray, and Susan F. Gray, 'The Idea of Property in Land' in Susan Bright and John Dewar (eds.), *Land Law: Themes and Perspectives* (Oxford University Press, 1998); Howe, 'Copyright Limitations and the Stewardship Model', 202, 208.

levels of compensation may be reduced to reflect the obligation of the owner to accommodate access where the community need is great but ability to pay is limited and/or where, for instance, the licence would not impact severely on the owner's revenue streams.

In the same way that the rights to exploit the invention are intrinsically limited, the owner is not perceived as entitled to capture all available value from the property.[82] Where the property is of particular significance for the community, or where the value of the property has been partially contributed by the community, the rights of the owner to exploit the property for personal gain will be perceived as restricted in scope. This would suggest, for example, that through the lens of this model, publicly funded technology ought, potentially, to be treated very differently from that which has been privately funded, with the right to exclude in the former situation being seen as a more appropriate subject for limitations. Were these factors more prominent in patent law discourse, certain public sector institutions, such as universities, might be further encouraged (or even compelled) to pursue the more flexible licensing structures that evidence suggests they are potentially willing to adopt.[83] Where such patents are the subject of judicial proceedings, their publicly funded nature would be a factor in any decision. Over time such shifts in expectations and practice ought to promote a climate in which differentiated licensing becomes the commercial norm.

A more flexible and differentiated patent system should also be more easily achievable under the stewardship model because the subject matter of the property plays a more prominent role here than under the liberal model. The perception that the owner is the steward of his or her particular property brings the nature and characteristics of the subject matter of the property into focus and enables explicit consideration of the value of that property to the community.[84] Limitations to a particular type of patented property – such as green technology – become less problematic from a property perspective because the scope of ownership of that particular property is inherently limited by the community interest in environmental protection. The more the conditional nature of the property is understood and accepted, the less arbitrary limitations on those rights appear. Under this model the essential

[82] Howe, 'Copyright Limitations and the Stewardship Model', 201.
[83] Karachalios *et al.*, *Patents and Clean Energy*, p. 60.
[84] Caldwell, 'Rights of Ownership', 770; Karp, 'A Private Property Duty of Stewardship', 749, 751–3; Howe, 'Copyright Limitations and the Stewardship Model', 201.

nature of the property and/or the importance of access by a particular group can be given the weight it deserves. It might also mean that the significance of the patent to the patent owner receives more attention. So, for example, where the patent is held for defensive or blocking purposes rather than as part of the patent owner's revenue stream, this should be a significant factor when assessing levels of compensation for a compulsory licence or the nature of the remedy to be granted in a case of infringement.

Whilst they have been used largely interchangeably in this chapter, the notion of 'access' to green technology seems to suggest something different from 'diffusion'. 'Access' suggests a greater role for the community in shaping and adapting the technology. It also involves recognition that the community has a legitimate interest – even potentially a right that can be vindicated in a tribunal – to enjoy the benefits of green innovation. This raises wider issues of environmental justice and solidarity and questions about who is able to enforce these rights. Discussion of these questions is precluded here by lack of space.[85] However, the significant point in respect of this chapter is that, with the community and their interests in the property at the heart of the stewardship concept, this model is much better placed to facilitate 'access' to green technology as well as its 'diffusion'. The adoption of a stewardship model will not provide the answer to the complex question of how to balance the needs of the community in promoting the widest possible diffusion of green technology with the interests of the patent owner. However, it would go some way to supporting the development of a more flexible system in which the interests of the community are more prominent and a wider range of factors are relevant to the assessment of that balance by policy makers and the judiciary; a system in which the obligations recognised in Article 7 of TRIPS can become as significant in reality as the rights of the patent owner.

Whilst the liberal model dominates much patent law, there is some evidence of the presence of the stewardship concept. The stewardship model certainly provides a more appropriate characterisation of the position advanced by many of the developing countries in the technology transfer

[85] See, in this respect, the Convention on Access to Information, Participation in Decision-making and Access to Justice in Environmental Matters 1998, Aarhus, 25 July 1998, in force 30 October 2001, 2161 UNTS 447 and, for example, Chris Hilson, 'EU Environmental Solidarity and the Ecological Consumer: Towards a Republican Citizenship' in Malcolm Ross and Yuri Borgmann-Prebil (eds.), *Promoting Solidarity in the European Union* (Oxford University Press, 2010).

debate than the liberal model.[86] For many developing countries, the scope of the property in patent law is already conceived as inherently conditional on community need. Even the international framework of patent law does recognise that the rights of the patent owner are limited by some moral and environmental considerations.[87] At the domestic level, patent law suggests a greater ambivalence about the property concept in patent law than some of the rhetoric surrounding green technology would indicate. The UK Patents Act 1977, for example, contains a range of exceptions to the rights of the patent owner that reflect a more limited and conditional concept of property.[88] Similarly, compulsory licensing appears to be reasonably healthy in many domestic systems and is often treated as a useful tool for balancing the rights of the patent owner with the interests of the public in accessing relevant technology,[89] despite vociferous objections by developed countries to compulsory licensing at the international negotiating table. In addition, courts are frequently alive to factors that are associated with the stewardship model such as the nature of the patented invention, the significance of the patent to the parties' respective undertakings and the public interest in the exercise of the owners' rights over it.[90]

Much has been made in this regard of recent judgments in the USA and, in particular, of *eBay* v. *MercExchange*[91] in which the Supreme Court rejected the existence of a presumption in favour of the granting of an injunction in cases of infringement. Instead the Court laid down

[86] For example, AWG-LCA negotiating text, twelfth session, Tianjin, 4–9 October, 2010, FCCC/AWGLCA/2010/14, available at: http://unfccc.int/resource/docs/2010/awglca12/eng/14.pdf (last accessed 12 April 2013).

[87] TRIPS, Article 27(2).

[88] Patents Act 1977, s. 60(5)(a–h).

[89] In the UK see, for example, *Chiron Corporation* v. *Organon Teknika Limited (No. 10)* [1995] FSR 325 at 322 per Aldous LJ and the availability of licences of right under s. 46 Patents Act 1977. In the USA see, for example, *Paice LCC* v. *Toyota Motor Corporation* 504 f. 3D 1293 (2007). The appropriate remedy in *Paice* was felt to be an ongoing royalty paid by the defendants to the claimants for their continued use of the technology. Whilst the Court states that this is different from a compulsory licence (at 1313), the fundamental characteristics appear to be the same. In *Shatterproof Glass Corp.* v. *Libbey-Owens Ford Co.* 758 F. 2d 613 (1985) the same model was called a compulsory licence. In *Paice* Circuit Judge Rader states that calling it an ongoing royalty 'doesn't make it any less a compulsory licence': *Paice* v. *Toyota* 504 f. 3D 1293 (2007) at 1316; Fair, 'Does Climate Change Justify the Compulsory Licensing of Green Technology?', 27, 29.

[90] *Chiron Corporation* v. *Organon Teknika Limited (No. 10)* [1995] FSR 325 at 331–332, per Aldous J; *Rousel-Uclaf* v. *G.D. Searle & Co. Ltd.* [1977] FSR 125 at 131 per Graham J; *Illinois Tool Works Inc* v. *Autobars Co (Services) Ltd.* [1974] RPC 337.

[91] 547 US 388, 126 S Ct 1837 (2006).

four factors for consideration when exercising the discretion to grant an injunction, including the public interest.[92] *Paice LLC* v. *Toyota*[93] is notable not just because it concerns green technology – for hybrid cars – but because the Federal Circuit robustly refused to grant an injunction against Toyota and, instead, required it to pay an 'on-going royalty' to Paice to continue to use the technology.[94] The claimant company held a patent for technology in hybrid cars but, as the court points out,[95] they did not manufacture anything themselves; instead, their revenue came from licensing. The judgment implicitly recognises that patent rights should not clog innovation and thus Paice's right to exclude was trumped by the defendant who sought to make use of the technology for a beneficial purpose. These developments in the USA suggest that domestic courts might be willing to develop the flexible and differentiated approach needed for the effective promotion of green technology. However, despite some effective use being made of the courts' discretion to decide the remedy in light of the surrounding circumstances, the emphasis placed on the community interest is uneven and the tendency to protect the proprietary rights of the patent owner often prevails.[96]

It is possible that impending climate disaster and the importance of the green technology revolution will join other global crises – such as the need to prevent and treat serious disease – in providing the impetus for a shift in the concept of property in patent law. The experience in the pharmaceutical patent sector in response to the HIV epidemic could be seen as evidence of a – tentative – move to a more community-focused property concept.[97] The clear statements made in the Doha Declaration regarding the acceptability of using the compulsory licensing provisions and the expansion of the scope of these provisions for countries without a

[92] See, for example, *eBay Inc.* v. *MercExchange LLC* 547 US 388, 126 S Ct 1837 (2006); *Eli Lilley & Co.* v. *Medtronic Inc.* 496 US 661 (1990); *Zoltek Corporation* v. *United States* 442 F 3d 1345 (2006); Isaacs, 'Not All Property Is Created Equal', 35; Colleen Chien and Mark Lemley, 'Patent Holdup, the ITC and the Public Interest' (2012) 98 *Cornell Law Review* 1; Karen E. Sandrik, 'Reframing Patent Remedies' (2012) 67 *University of Miami Law Review* 95 (recognising but criticising the more flexible regime).

[93] 504 f. 3D 1293 (2007).

[94] *Ibid.* at 1313–1314. [95] *Ibid.* at 1303.

[96] See, for example, *Virgin Atlantic* v. *Premium Aircraft* [2009] EWCA Civ 1513; [2010] FSR 15 at paras. 23–27, per Jacob LJ (recognising the public interest but suggesting that the judgment in *Illinois Tool Works Inc.* v. *Autobars Co. (Services) Ltd.* [1974] RPC 337 put it too strongly).

[97] Pascal Lamy, 'Strengthening Multilateral Cooperation on IP and Public Health', 14 July 2009, available at: www.wto.org/english/news_e/sppl_e/sppl131_e.htm (last accessed 29 April 2013).

manufacturing capability perhaps indicates changing perceptions about the legitimate scope of the exclusory right in situations of serious community need.[98] This is not to suggest that we have seen a major alteration in global perceptions of patent ownership in the pharmaceutical sector, let alone across all technology sectors. However, it may indicate a shift towards a more relational understanding of patent ownership that better enables the integration of the characteristics of the invention, and the 'web of interests' that surround it,[99] into assessments regarding the appropriate scope of the rights. Meanwhile, the World Intellectual Property Organization appears to have signalled a paradigm shift in the approach to intellectual property that may contribute to a changing concept of property in patent law. One recent initiative on intellectual property and development has called for the rejection of any notion that the protection of intellectual property is an end in itself and for the re-establishment of the significance of the public policy aspects of intellectual property, whilst another study has emphasised the importance of robust exceptions and exclusions in patent law.[100] Finally, whilst many of the recent initiatives in patent law were criticised above as not going far enough to promote green technology, some may be helpful in raising awareness of alternative ownership models and showing that non- (or reduced) exclusive rights models can be commercially viable.[101]

4 Conclusion

Constructing a patent system that is capable of fulfilling its role in the mitigation of climate disaster is a task that is both essential and enormously complex. The dominant concept of property in patent law is only one factor in this complexity. Nevertheless, if the system requires further flexibilities that will constrain the rights of the patent owner in order to

[98] Declaration on the TRIPS Agreement and Public Health, 14 November 2001.

[99] Craig A. Arnold, 'The Reconstitution of Property: Property as a Web of Interests' (2002) 26 *Harvard Environmental Law* 281.

[100] World Intellectual Property Organization Development Agenda: 45 Recommendations, available at: www.wipo.int/ip-development/en/agenda/recommendations.html (last accessed 29 April 2013); Committee on Development and Intellectual Property (CDIP), Ninth Session (7–11 May 2012) – Summary by Chair, available at: www.wipo.int/ip-development/en/agenda/ (last accessed 12 April 2013); and Lionel Bently *et al.*, *Exclusions from Patentability and Exceptions and Limitations to Patentees' Rights* (Geneva: World Intellectual Property Organisation, 2010).

[101] Rimmer, *Intellectual Property and Climate Change*, Chapter 8; see also Maggiolino and Montagnani, 'From Open Source Software to Open Patenting'.

facilitate optimal diffusion of green technology, then the way in which property is framed becomes hugely significant. It is important to highlight the role played by the proprietary models in patent law in order to create a more transparent framework for dialogue. Whilst the liberal model continues to have such an influence, it undermines the creation of a patent system that is capable of contributing to sustainable development and to climate change mitigation in particular. The creation of a sustainability-compliant patent system requires a property concept better able to recognise and respond to the community interest in patented technology. To that end, any movement towards a stewardship model of property in patent law is to be supported.

INDEX

CAMBRIDGE INTELLECTUAL PROPERTY AND INFORMATION LAW

Titles in the series (formerly known as Cambridge Studies in Intellectual Property Rights)

Brad Sherman and Lionel Bently
The Making of Modern Intellectual Property Law
978 0 521 56363 5

Irini A. Stamatoudi
Copyright and Multimedia Products: A Comparative Analysis
978 0 521 80819 4

Pascal Kamina
Film Copyright in the European Union
978 0 521 77053 8

Huw Beverly-Smith
The Commercial Appropriation of Personality
978 0 521 80014 3

Mark J. Davison
The Legal Protection of Databases
978 0 521 80257 4

Robert Burrell and Allison Coleman
Copyright Exceptions: The Digital Impact
978 0 521 84726 1

Huw Beverly-Smith, Ansgar Ohly and Agnès Lucas-Schloetter
Privacy, Property and Personality: Civil Law Perspectives on Commercial Appropriation
978 0 521 82080 6

Philip Leith
Software and Patents in Europe
978 0 521 86839 6

Lionel Bently, Jennifer Davis and Jane C. Ginsburg
Trade Marks and Brands: An Interdisciplinary Critique
978 0 521 88965 0

Geertrui Van Overwalle
Gene Patents and Clearing Models
978 0 521 89673 3

Jonathan Curci
The Protection of Biodiversity and Traditional Knowledge in International Law of Intellectual Property
978 0 521 19944 5

Lionel Bently, Jennifer Davis and Jane C. Ginsburg
Copyright and Piracy: An Interdisciplinary Critique
978 0 521 19343 6

Megan Richardson and Julian Thomas
Framing Intellectual Property: Legal Constructions of Creativity and Appropriation 1840–1940
978 0 521 76756 9

Dev Gangjee
Relocating the Law of Geographical Indications
978 0 521 19202 6

Andrew Kenyon, Megan Richardson and Ng-Loy Wee-Loon
The Law of Reputation and Brands in the Asia Pacific Region
978 1 107 01772 6

Annabelle Lever
New Frontiers in the Philosophy of Intellectual Property
978 1 107 00931 8

Sigrid Sterckx and Julian Cockbain
Exclusions from Patentability: How the European Patent Office is Eroding Boundaries
978 1 107 00694 2

Sebastian Haunss
Conflicts in the Knowledge Society: The Contentious Politics of Intellectual Property
978 1 107 03642 0

Helena R. Howe and Jonathan Griffiths [Ed]
Concepts of Property in Intellectual Property Law
978 1 107 04182 0